NAMES, NATIONS,
and the
NEW TESTAMENT

*Investigating the origins of mankind
from Genesis to Acts*

MADELYN ROSE CRAIG

ROSEWOOD PUBLISHING
Canton, Ohio

Copyright © 2020 by Madelyn Rose Craig.

All rights reserved. No part of this publication may be reproduced, distributed, or transmitted in any form or by any means, including photocopying, recording, or other electronic or mechanical methods, without the prior written permission of the author, except in the case of brief quotations embodied in critical reviews and certain other noncommercial uses permitted by copyright law.

Unless noted otherwise, all Scriptural references and quotes are taken from the 1978 New International Version of the Bible.

All maps are the property of Madelyn Rose Craig.

ISBN: 978-1-7355711-0-2 (Paperback)
ISBN: 978-1-7355711-1-9 (Ebook)

Library of Congress Control Number: 2020915315

Edited by Rachel Gonzalez

Rosewood Publishing
8399 Kent Ave NE
Canton, OH, 44721

www.madelynrosecraig.com

*This book is dedicated
To my parents, who gave me a foundation in Christ;*

to the apologists who ignited my passion;

to the scholars who enlarged my learning;

to my husband, who first called me an author;

and to the next generation, that they may hear the Gospel.

TABLE OF CONTENTS

Preface: Letter from the Author XI

NAMES
1: The Beginning 1

NATIONS
2: Japheth 15
3: Gomer 21
4: The Sons of Gomer 29
5: Magog 39
6: Madai 45
7: Javan 49
8: The Sons of Javan 53
9: Tubal 61
10: Meshech 65
11: Tiras 69
12: Ham 73
13: Cush 77
14: The Sons of Cush 81
15: Nimrod 87
16: Mizraim 95
17: The Sons of Mizraim 103
18: Put 109
19: Canaan 113
20: The Sons of Canaan 119
21: Shem 145
22: Elam 149
23: Asshur 155
24: Arphaxad 165
25: The Descendants of Arphaxad 171
26: Lud 203
27: Aram 207
28: The Sons of Aram 217
29: Words and Wanderings 223

THE NEW TESTAMENT
30: To All Nations 243

Source Notes and Further Reading 251
Acknowledgments 253
About the Author 255
Chapter Notes 257
Index 301

*Save us, O Lord our God,
and gather us from the nations,
that we may give thanks to your holy name
and glory in your praise.*

~ Psalm 106:47 ~

Preface: Letter from the Author

Dear reader,

From the time I was young, I had a passion for apologetics. I would read just about every book on the subject that I could get my hands on. I studied writings from geology to biology, paleontology to astronomy, history to current events, and so much more. Yet in all of that reading, I rarely found information or research on the people after Babel, and especially on Noah's immediate descendants. If I did find such a book, it was often incomplete, outdated, or lacking substance.

In 2015, I was reading through the book of Ezekiel when I came across the names Gog and Magog, among others, and noticed they looked familiar. So, I went back to Genesis and the Table of Nations, read through the list, and noticed it was similar to the account in Acts about the day of Pentecost. Though many have made the connection before, Pentecost is a sort of reversal of what happened at Babel. Where the nations were divided by language at the Tower because of mankind's rebellion, all people were united in Christ through His obedience and forgiveness and the coming of the Holy Spirit at Pentecost. After reading these passages, I began to wonder about their application in history, and I faced some significant questions. What happened at Babel? How did the Table of Nations become the nations of the world? Does God's plan of Salvation for all people connect to these things? What does that mean for us? Thus, I began writing this book.

I wrote this book not solely for the sake of knowing where these nations went, but so that others who want to know how to defend their faith can have such a resource. This is more than a commentary on Genesis chapter 10. This is an apologetics handbook of where mankind came from, where they went, and what that means for us. A lot of preparation went into this. I read chronicles, annals, chronologies, histories, summaries, whole books, original texts, those long sections of Scripture we often skip over...you get the picture. Basically, I read all the boring stuff so you did not have to. Whole books have been written on some of these places, people, nations, and even some cities and their names! To include everything would be to compile a history of the world that – though an incredible book – would be a nearly impossible task.

Seeing the need to examine history, the world, and mankind's true origins within Scripture and why those origins matter, I condensed what I perceived to be the most useful information into this book. My goal was for this book to be a helpful reference or a guide for your daily study, your thirst for knowledge, your need to answer tough questions, or your desire to know more about yourself and where everyone came from, including you.

You may wonder why I refer to Israel so often in this book. The short answer is that I used Scripture as my basis, as any good endeavor should. However, many of the nations found in Scripture have Israel as a focal point for location, time, and religious reasons. But most of all, Israel is a focal point because it was chosen to be the nation which the Savior came from, and He is the most significant reason for me to write this book. If Christ did not come to save sinners, if mankind is not of one blood, if mankind never actually rebelled against God, if God did not make Adam and Eve in His image, why does salvation matter? Yet salvation does matter, God does want all men to be saved, and we are all descendants of those first two flawed people. That is why Genesis matters.

The answers people seek about our ancestors exist and they need to be brought to light. This is not merely for knowledge's sake, but for the purpose of showing unity in mankind and Christ. This book was written to know better the people in this wonderful world God created. This book is to help you defend your faith and to disabuse you and anyone else of incorrect notions on mankind's origins (Gen. 1:1-12:3, 1 Pet 3:15-16, 1 Tim. 2:15, 3:16-17, 4:1-5). Hopefully, someone someday will add to the research found here. After all, there are always more amazing discoveries to be made!

So thank you for taking the time to pick up this book and read it. I hope my work will be a help to you.

Blessings to you and yours,
~Madelyn Rose Craig

Part 1

—————•—————

NAMES

1: The Beginning

To begin, let us start at the beginning. In this case, we set out with the origins of mankind at Creation in Genesis. Many people have taken upon themselves the mission to seek out and document the origins of mankind. Some hold to Scripture, but others attempt to malign the Word of God and present ideas stating mankind was decidedly not human. Regardless of what has been taught, most people know little about man's beginnings and travels. Perhaps some do not care, but more often, it appears most people simply do not know. Thankfully, we can find answers in the first few chapters of Genesis. Unsurprisingly, we can find those same answers in archeology and anthropology, among the other sciences. But before we get to the sciences, let us start with the Bible and what it says about mankind's origins.

What does Scripture say on Creation?

As the name suggests, we begin our journey in Genesis. Scripture is clear on mankind's origins: God created man. We learn that the Lord made the universe and everything therein. He did not just tell us that He created but also how. He spoke everything into being in six days and

> Then God said, "Let us make mankind in our image, in our likeness, so that they may rule over the fish in the sea and the birds in the sky, over the livestock and all the wild animals, and over all the creatures that move along the ground." So God created mankind in his own image, in the image of God he created them; male and female he created them.
>
> ~ Genesis 1:26-27 ~

then rested on the seventh. The pinnacle of His creation was man and woman, collectively referred to as mankind from here on out. God makes a point to devote a whole chapter on the special creation of mankind. He not only spoke them into being but formed them out of earth and flesh, breathing into them spirit. Mankind, being made in His image, was unique and separate from the rest of God's creation. These first two people, Adam and Eve, were the progenitors of everyone. We then learn about who these people are and who they came from in Scriptural genealogies (Gen. 3-10, 1Chr. 1). We start with Genesis because that is the foundation, but this truth is reflected throughout Scripture.

The Psalms are full of praise for God's creation (Psa. 8:3-6, 19:1-4, 33:6, 102:25-28). The book of Job contains numerous passages of adoration for God's magnificent creatures and His power (Job 12:9-10, 38-41). Christ and the Gospel writers refer to Genesis, and the book of Hebrews highlights our faith in that the world was formed at God's word (Mat. 19:4-5, Mar. 10:6-7, 13:19, Luk. 3:34-38, Jhn. 1:1-5, Heb. 1:10, 11:1-3). Much of the New Testament frequently connects to passages from Genesis, more than will be listed here (Rom. 1:19-20, 1Cor. 11:7-8, 15:38-47, 2Cor. 4:6, Gal. 3:16, Eph. 3:9). Paul's speech at Athens, not to mention other passages from Acts, taught that God not only made the world but He created us as His children, desiring fellowship with us (Acts 14:15, 17:24-31). These are the descendants of Adam and Eve, our ancestors, who were separated at Babel. Furthermore, representatives of the world's nations were present in Jerusalem at Pentecost, where they heard the Gospel (Acts 2:1-12). These nations were the same that came from Adam and Eve via Noah's sons. What a fantastic story found from Genesis to Acts! So now we know we can trace our ancestry to our first parents, and we will discuss these genealogies throughout this book. But first, what were these early people like?

Who Was Early Man?

What do you think of when you hear the phrase "early man"? The first image that might come to mind may be an apish brute with a hunched back, too much hair, and crude clothing. Perhaps he looks more beast than beauty. A fact hanging over that image may say that these early "men" can neither speak nor plant, and if they can do either, they are not skilled at such tasks. This image may show a cave that looks like a hole in the ground with no items that bear even the slightest resemblance to a tool, let alone a useful one. If this is the image that comes to mind, let me be the first to tell you that it is incorrect and could hardly be further from the truth.

Early mankind was not apish or brutish. They did not look more animal than human. Instead, they were just as human as we are. They wore clothing, played music, built buildings. Early mankind buried their dead and went to war. They planted crops, harvested food, and celebrated the seasons. They married and had children. They were intelligent, with knowledge of how the world and heavens worked and having the capacity to reason, speak, and write. Furthermore, they were made by God as unique beings from the rest of His creation. They were human. But how do we know this, and why does it matter?

Scripture gives a clear picture of what mankind was like. As mentioned before, God made mankind in His image (Gen. 1:27). Mankind was given a spirit, separate from the animals (Gen. 2:7-8). This is truly what makes us distinct from the other creatures God made. Regardless of what gifts and abilities we do or do not have, we are human because we are made in the image of God and given a spirit. However, these other descriptors illustrate how most secular depictions of early man are incorrect. The Lord gave mankind the command to be fruitful and the authority to rule over everything He created (Gen. 1:28-30). Mankind was fully human, and there was only man and woman, each for the other (Gen. 2:1-23). Here we learn that companionship is a crucial part of mankind (Gen. 2:20). Not only did mankind have authority, but the earth and all therein was given as a gift to be cared for. Mankind ate only plants originally, and this did not change until after the Flood (Gen. 1:30, 9:3-4). We learn in the second chapter of Genesis, which delves further into day six of creation, that mankind could speak and had reason from the beginning (Gen. 2:19-20).

Mankind also had many other gifts and abilities in addition to language and reason. Mankind had the ability to farm and care for animals (Gen. 2:15, 4:2, 9:20-21). They had the ability to build tents, homes, and cities (Gen. 4:16-20). In fact, Cain leaves for a land called Nod and builds a city, naming it after his son, Enoch (Gen. 4:16-17). This knowledge was retained after the Flood, for Noah's descendants built the Tower and a city, but much information was lost with the division of nations, which will be discussed later. These first people also made musical instruments, such as the flute and harp, and forged both iron and bronze before the Flood! (Gen. 4:21-22) Mankind had tools and the ability to cut and shape trees; they also had the means and knowledge to put them together and seal the gaps (Gen. 6:14). Obviously, shipbuilding was also possible (Gen. 6:14-16). The Ark was a large boat with rooms, decks, a roof, and a door. Furthermore, these people knew how to store food for long periods (Gen. 6:21). They also worshiped God (Gen. 8:20). Mankind could do all this after Creation.

Evidence from archeology and anthropology demonstrates that mankind is fully human. There are neither precursors to mankind nor proto-human ancestors. There are simply humans and animals. Though some remains buried during and after the Flood have been used to support the idea that mankind was once "less evolved," these examples and interpretations are false. Those that are frauds include Piltdown man and Java man.[1] Others are animal, like *Australopithecus Afarensis*, or "Lucy."[1] Finally, there are those that are fully human: Neanderthal man, Ötzi the Iceman, Denisovans, and Cro-Magnon.

These human remains are primarily found in the north, though not entirely. For a time, these people roamed across the earth and often lived in caves, especially during the harsh winter months. For example, scientists state that though Cro-Magnon "survived in a primitive setting," they were "not primitive in mind or body."[2] They were simply early settlers who happened to live in caves.

> "Cro-Magnon does not really refer to a particular archaeological culture or a species other than Homo sapiens.... Though Cro-Magnons' head sizes were sometimes larger than our current average, if alive today they would fit into any international crowd. Their anatomy did not differ from ours—it fits well within modern human variance. The only significant difference is when they lived. These first modern-looking humans to inhabit Europe lived in cold, hard times. Many of them lived among limestone outcrops in southern France during the Ice Age."[2]

Like their forefathers, Cro-Magnon had culture and technology.[3] These people were artisans, musicians, builders, pavers, bakers, farmers, metalworkers, tool-makers, sewers, jewelers, and so much more.[3] They had ceremonies, buried their dead, practiced religion, and made art for mere pleasure and appreciation, as we do today.[3]

Much the same can be said for Neanderthal. Unlike how they are often portrayed, these people were people, not ape-like brutes.[4,5,6,7] If one were to give these portrayals of Neanderthal a shower, shave, hairbrush, and modern clothing, he would be indistinguishable from anyone else in a crowd. They made tools, fire, homes, and instruments.[8] These people also buried their dead, practiced religion, spoke, and formed intentional social and cultural bonds with one another, just as we do today.[8] They were also nomadic, and their remains are found across multiple continents.[9]

A group called Denisovans were found in eastern Europe and Asia. It has been shown that they are genetically related to those in Siberia and the Pacific Islands.[10,11,12] A different fellow, who was found in the Alps on a glacier, has come to be known as Ötzi. He died, or was killed, not too long after the Flood and probably during the Ice Age.[13] His clothing, tools, and other items found on him were neither primitive nor crude but were comparable to what would be found in any area inhabited by Europeans as few as 800-1000 years ago, or even on many people around the world today.[13]

Despite attempts to prove otherwise, every discovery points to a common ancestor of Noah rather than a proto-ape-man ancestor; there are no intermediate creatures. All these discoveries in archaeology, anthropology, and genetics show more and more the wonderful design by God and the descent through Noah and His sons, and their common descent through Adam and Eve, created by God. These facts and more can be found in detail in the articles included in the endnotes for this chapter. All this information and more shows that we were created in the image of God. Now, however, we must discuss the occasion that brought about the division of language, people, and nations.

How Did the Various Nations Arise?

Every person on earth is a descendant of the first two people: Adam and Eve. Though these creations in God's image were made in a perfect world, they rebelled, and mankind increased in wickedness to the point that God decided to destroy the whole earth, saving only Noah and his sons. After the Flood, the sons of Noah and their wives had many children. The initial descendants, or heads of the tribes and nations, are found between the account of the Flood and the account of the Tower (Gen. 10). Some people may skip over this chapter because it seems like just another boring series of sons and fathers. But it is not, and it has enormous implications on what we believe about mankind's origins. All people on earth are descended from the families found in this genealogy. After the Flood, Noah's descendants settled in the plain of Shinar (Gen. 11:2). At this point, all people still spoke only one language that God created them with (Gen. 11:1). Neither the mechanisms to speak nor speech itself with all its grammars evolved over a gradual process.

Even though the Lord commanded them to "be fruitful and fill the earth," mankind stayed in Shinar and built a city and tower lest they scatter "over the face of the whole earth" (Gen. 9:1, 11:4). What this city and tower looked like is unclear, though we know it was made of baked brick and tar (Gen. 11:2-4). The land known as Shinar encompassed a great area and probably included much of the fertile crescent. Considering that many mound, pyramid, and ziggurat structures around the world resemble each other, the Tower probably looked like these structures. As they were building, the Lord came down and saw their disobedience.

> *"The Lord said, 'If as one people speaking the same language they have begun to do this, then nothing they plan to do will be impossible for them. Come, let us go down and confuse their language so they will not be able to understand each other.'"* (Gen. 11:6-7)

The word translated here as "confuse" is in Hebrew בָּלַל, or *balal*.[14] This word literally means "to pour over" or "pour together, confound."[14] Language was poured over and confused so that there were many languages to spread across the earth. The word *Babel*, or בָּבֶל, also means confusion and was sometimes used in reference to the area of Babylon, though they are not exclusively the same location.[15,16]

Thus, language was confused as a consequence of their disobedience. With the division of tongues, so too did the nations divide and pour out across the earth. These nations came from the families in the Table of Nations (Gen. 10). This is not to say that these were the only *individuals* alive at this point; the names provided in the Table of Nations are likely heads of families, tribes, and clans with any number of people within them. There could have been even smaller divisions within each family when the languages and nations divided.

With the division of tongues, so too did technology, knowledge, abilities, and appearances separate and change. People began to look and speak differently and more distinctly than their ancestors as time went on. Information divided, and mankind slowed in technological advances. Some researchers believe it was for this reason that it was not until years after the Flood that the Egyptians jumped up to par in technology with the Babylonians, and that was likely due to Abraham.[17,18] Various nations are recognized for the unique talents and knowledge they have. It is unsurprising why places like Asia, Egypt, the Middle East, and Europe had different ways to record information. Some had paper, and others papyrus; some stone, and others vellum. Certain areas, like the Middle East, were renowned for their knowledge of astronomy. The Egyptians are recognized for preservation, Europeans and coastal people for shipbuilding, and the Steppe nations for horse-taming.

Another point to address is how the nations got where they did. In short, after the Flood and during the Ice Age, there would have been more land and ice bridges to help people travel to various places, though boats were obviously another available option. These land and ice bridges are how many northern tribes made their way to the Americas and other isles and how many southern tribes made it to the islands and Australia.

Names Dividing Nations

A crucial part of discovering who these descendants of Noah were, where they went, and what people they became is knowing names. We only know their original names given in Scripture. Then we only know their later locations once they began to settle, either leaving names behind or being given names as they established themselves. This book is not an exhaustive list of nations. Instead, it will provide some specific, identifiable peoples along with general locations. Some of the individual tribes have been lost, or they inter-married with others. Many more settled long after Babel, perhaps as the Ice Age subsided.

Though we do it less often today, people of every tribe and tongue name things, places, and people with historical, cultural, or familial significance. As time went on and the dispersed peoples became distinct groups, clan names were adopted, typically from the name of a near relative or distinctive trait (or both as could be the case). Many places would have been named after the grandsons of Noah. Still, people are often referred to by a family name. For example, a family is often referred to as the "Mr. so and so first name, middle name, last name's family" not by the individual members. Such has been the case with most reigns, nations, and, more importantly, these families of the world coming from Noah. Some familiar examples might be Caesarea, England, Petersburg, Williamsburg, Pennsylvania, Constantinople, and Alexandria. This list could continue for many books.

Names are important because they carry history with them. In the case of Noah's sons, names mark lands and people. One shining example is Israel, whose name comes from Israel, or Jacob, the father of the Israelites. Even so, many modern countries' names say little regarding their founders. Even America is named after a cartographer, not a founder or father of the nation. Still, places carry the names of their past. The Ebro river in Spain is named after a close relative of

Noah. Egypt still harkens back to its origins when words like *"msr"* appear. Some still refer to Ethiopia by the name it has carried for thousands of years: Cush. China appears to bear a name that came from a son of Canaan. These and more will be discussed within the pages of this book.

Keep in mind that names change as language changes. For example, the Old Testament was originally written in Hebrew and Aramaic, but most read a translation, which changes the ways words appear. Thus, finding each of these sons can prove difficult, especially with the passage of time, change in location, and conquests. With each of these events, the name will change in spelling, language, or in entirety. Despite all this, they can and will be traced, especially with cross-referencing. Additionally, although specific groups can be named and are named in this work, this should not be taken to mean that these are the *only* people who came from that specific son. Names changed, records were lost, and certain groups wiped out. These chapters will be merely a guide to find the general paths the descendants took.

Now, although these names help distinguish different tribes of people, in all honesty, the nations and peoples can hardly be divided. Though one goal of this book is to discover the lineage from the past to the present, the other goal is to demonstrate that Scripture speaks the truth: We are one blood, not different races. The word 'race' has been twisted to mean something degrading and even evil. Every person on earth can trace their lineage back to nations, and these nations to a few groups of people, and those groups to the sons of Noah, and Noah to Adam. In the middle of this search, I found it difficult to separate groups. When did Gomer's sons become this nation? How often did Mizraim's and Cush's descendants intermarry, and when did they become separate again? How distinct is this tribe or nation from another one? I found that most of the time, trying to divide people based on race is an effort in futility. The Assyrians are a mix of Nimrod, Arameans, Arphaxadites, and Canaanites. Babylon contains people from Nimrod, Arphaxad, Elam, and Madai. And this does not even get into the diverse ancestry of Europe. Trying to divde people into different "races" as if some developed after or before another is both pointless and harmful.

My goal is to demonstrate the accuracy and truthfulness of God's Word by following the genealogies in Scripture and the world. People have been separated in many ways, specifically racially, over the years, but this book was not made to encourage such ideas. Instead, this book is to show that we are all of one blood. This is why names are important and why our origins matter even today. We are all descendants of Adam and Eve through Noah and his sons. All are called to be saved and brought to the knowledge of the Truth.

Why Does This Matter?

As mentioned before, Genesis 10 is a chapter that many likely skip over. Readers often ignore those long lists of sons and fathers because they seem boring or unimportant. But these lists, and especially those found in the first 12 chapters of Genesis, are crucial to what we believe as Christians and what mankind believes about origins. That portion of Scripture tells us where we came from and why. The Tower of Babel tells us where we went and the reason mankind was separated. This book will explain to you why this part of Scripture is so important and how it applies to you. This book matters to you because it will help you understand where people came from – including you.

Besides providing knowledge, I hope that this book will aid you in defending your faith. The crucial point of this chapter was to introduce the fact that we are all of one blood. Mankind did not evolve, and the descendants of Noah are not separate races. We are all created with equal value in the eyes of God and formed in His image. This point cannot be stressed enough. But this world will teach everything contrary to truth. For you to better defend your faith, you must know what you believe and why you believe it. Scripture reminds us that the Lord is with us wherever we go, and go we must. We are to go into the world and make disciples of all nations.

> But in your hearts set apart Christ as Lord. Always be prepared to give an answer for the hope that you have. But do this with gentleness and respect, keeping a clear conscience, so that those who speak maliciously against your good behavior in Christ may be ashamed of their slander.
>
> ~ 1 Pet. 3:15-16 ~

To defend our faith, we must recognize it as being more than a statement we accept. To stand firm against all attacks, we must keep God's Word in our hearts and know what it is that we believe (Psa. 119:11). Many will seek out to destroy the faith with fine-sounding arguments (Col. 2:4, 1 Tim. 4:1-2, 2 Tim. 4:2-4). Therefore, we must put Christ first as Lord in our hearts and study His Word (2 Tim. 3:16-17). Then, we are to give our defense, but with gentleness (1 Pet. 3:15-16). Finally, we are to stand (Eph. 6:10-18). In doing this, we may be a witness so that others may know that they were created in the image of God and saved by His Son.

Part 2

NATIONS

2: Japheth

Expansion

Japheth is the first son of Noah discussed in the Table of Nations (Gen. 10:1-2). While Scripture does not state it plainly, Japheth was probably the first or second born, as there are references to Ham being the youngest brother (Gen. 10:21, 9:24). Whatever the case, Japheth is typically listed third when the brothers are mentioned together, possibly due to him and his descendants moving the farthest away; he appears almost a dozen times in Scripture (Gen. 5:32, 6:10, 7:13, 9:18-27, 10:1-2, 10:21; 1 Chr. 1:4-5). The name Japheth, יֶפֶת in Hebrew, means "expansion," implying the nomadic nature of his people and the way they spread out, both in number and location.[1] While there are many variations of his name, most bear a resemblance to the original, like Josephus' spelling, Japhet.[2]

The Table of Nations

In Genesis, the Table of Nations lists all the sons, and consequently the peoples, that came from each of Noah's sons. The order could be due to birth order, knowledge of a group, or proximity. In some sources, the order of these names seems to be irrelevant. Japheth's sons were Gomer, Magog, Madai, Javan, Tubal, Meshech, and Tiras (Gen. 10:2).

A handful of other works also include the family of Japheth. The *Book of Jubilees* includes Japheth's wife, Adataneses (though she is unnamed in Scripture), whom he named a mountain after out of jealousy of his brother Ham.[3] In the *Antiquities of the Jews*, Tubal is called Thobel and Meshech spelled Mosoch.[4] These same sons are in the books of *Jubilees* and *Jasher*.[5,6] Scripture implies that Japheth's sons went north, and there is extra-biblical evidence to support this location. Josephus' *Antiquities* provides insight into the Greek names for Japheth's sons. These names, or variants thereof, can be found in many nations' histories and genealogies, most of which were northern.

These are the sons of Japheth along with their sons. Gomer had three sons: Ashkenaz, Riphath, and Togarmah (Gen. 10:3). Josephus names them Aschanax, Riphah, and Thrugamma.[7] The Bible says that from Javan came, "Elishah, Tarshish, the Kittim and the Rodanim" (Gen. 10:4). The last two, the Kittim and the Rodanim, are of a nation fathered by that son, understood by the 'im' at the end of the name, though Javan's sons likely had a similar name to their nation or people name. Tarshish should already look familiar as a place name. Josephus gives Javan's sons the names Elisa, Tharsus, and Cethimus.[8] In the books of *Jubilees* and *Jasher*, the names of Japheth's grandsons are either spelled differently or excluded entirely.

These sons became the forefathers of people in Europe, the Americas, and other specific areas in the world. One should remember that these sons and their peoples were the ones alive at the time of the Tower of Babel. Japheth and his sons likely had other children afterward, but they would not be recorded because of the Dispersion and would have been unable to communicate with their relatives.

Where Was His Land?

The Table of Nations provides little specific information on where precisely the sons of Japheth went besides the ending verse, "From these the maritime peoples spread out into their territories by their clans within their nations, each with its own language," making clear that this dispersion happened post-Babel (Gen. 10:5). The *Jubilees* states Japheth divided "the land of his inheritance amongst his sons."[9]

There is no known record of a land bearing the name Japheth. Instead, his sons named lands after themselves.

There are, however, references in Scripture that allude to the general regions where his descendants dwelled. For instance, Scripture provides references of the maritime people and the people who live on the islands or "across the sea," and other similar statements that appear to be talking about Japheth's people (Gen. 10:5, Isa. 42:10, Jer. 25:22-26). In Genesis, the coastland or maritime people appear to be the descendants of Japheth that spread out over the sea on boats after the Babel event, and it is likely these other references refer to those same people. There are also other mentions of Japheth's sons in the books of the Prophets, stating that Japheth's sons went to the North. These shall be discussed in detail with each son. When those sons left for new lands, each place gained a language and name for itself after its predecessor.

According to the *Book of Jubilees*, the world was divided between the three sons of Noah.[10] The sons of Japheth all seemed to have taken or received the land of the North, specifically north of what is the Middle East, which primarily belonged to Shem.[11] According to the *Jubilees*, "they divided the earth into three parts."[12] For Japheth, "all that is towards the north is" his.[13] The *Jubilees* writes in detail of the land possessed by the brothers:

> *"This is the land which came forth for Japheth and his sons as the portion of his inheritance which he should possess for himself and his sons, for their generations for ever; five great islands, and a great land in the north. But it is cold, and the land of Ham is hot, and the land of Shem is neither hot nor cold...."*[14]

It can be assumed even from this description that the territory of Japheth was initially Europe, a cold, vast expanse of land north of Shem and Ham. In the *Book of Jubilees,* Japheth's land was to be, relative to Gomer, "the north side of the river Tina," which in an earlier passage states it poured "into the sea of Me'at."[9,13] Assuming that this river marks the divide of Asia from Europe, some have suggested Tina is the river Don, making the Me'at the modern sea of Azov.[15] Japheth is also included in various other texts. Besides appearing in some Greek myths, which will be discussed in the following, Japheth also appears in German genealogies, such as the *Royal Genealogies*, in Camden's *Britannia*, and in Spain's histories.[16, 17, 18] This places Japheth in the heart of Europe.

Notable Mentions

The Greeks, much like the Romans, had a god for nearly everything and, like most man-made religions, named their gods after something, like an event, trait, or forefather. In the case of the Greeks, their god Iapetus is derived from Japheth, their forefather. Homer mentions Iapetus in book VIII of *The Iliad*.[19] While the names might not look that similar, they are related. English, Latin, and Greek share some similarities. Where in English there would be a letter 'j', Greek or Latin might put an 'i'. Thus, one might translate Iapetus as Japetus.

Author Robert Graves in his book *The Greek Myths* compares this god with the man: "...Iapetus – the Japhet of Genesis, whom the Hebrews called Noah's son...."[20] The *Sibylline Oracles* calls Japheth "Iapetus," son of "Gaia and Uranus," ruling with Titan and Cronos.[21] This Iapetus appears to be based on Japheth, with him and his brothers a corruption of those found in Genesis. The story also retells the account of the Tower. In Assyria, they built the tower, spoke one tongue, and were stopped by God, who blew down the tower, confused language, and scattered mankind.[21]

> *"Now when the tower fell and the tongues of men*
> *Turned to all sorts of sounds, straightway all earth*
> *Was filled with men and kingdoms were divided;*
> *And then the generation tenth appeared*
> *Of mortal men, from the time when the flood*
> *Came upon earlier men."*[21]

Isidore of Seville wrote extensively on the history of peoples in his *Etymologies*, including Japheth and his relation to the Greeks through Javan.[22] Similarly, Josephus writes that Javan, the son of Japhet, became the father of the Greeks.[8] Javan is probably the root of Ionia. It should be no wonder that Noah is remembered as Uranus and his wife Gaia as they would have been the progenitors of all people after the Flood. Indeed, one might even compare some names of their other gods to Noah and other descendants, but that is a discussion for another time, remembering that these texts are not sacred like Scripture and are more like historical fiction. Still, the fact that Japheth is mentioned alongside a Babel account should show the magnitude and reality of these events.

Finally, it was accepted, at least by the 1500's, that the port at Joppa, remembered best for Jonah's attempted escape, was originally built by Japheth and called Jaffa or Yafa.[23,24,25] While Scripture does not state that Japheth built Joppa, it could be that either he or one of his descendants built it in his honor. While these are simply a handful of direct mentions of Japheth, they are not insignificant. Each shows the validity of the Bible, which states that all people came from Adam, through Noah's sons. These texts and those that will follow show not only Scripture's validity but also the trail left behind by our ancestors.

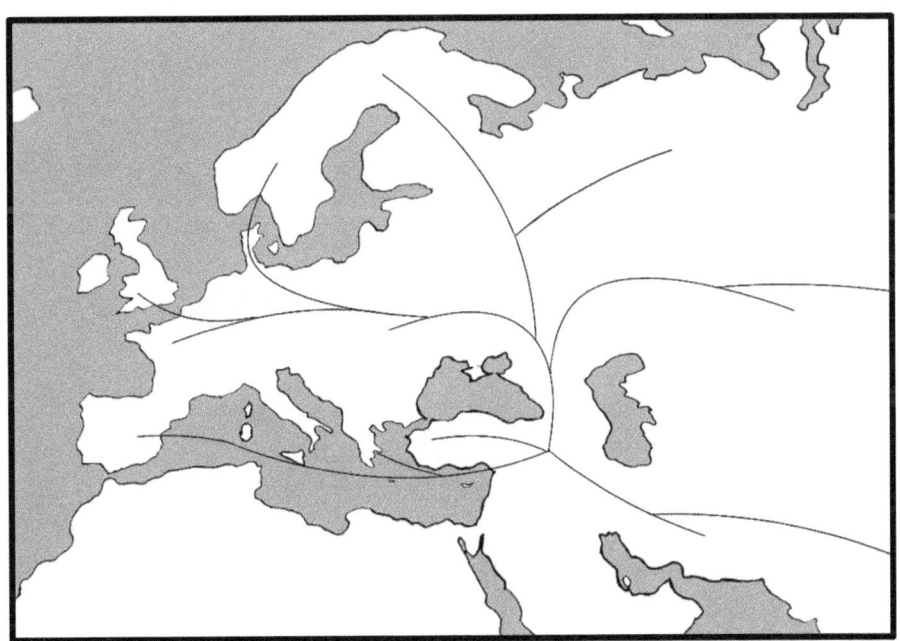

Names, Nations, and the New Testament

3: Gomer

Completion

Gomer is the first listed of Japheth's sons (Gen 10:2, 1 Chr. 1:5).[1,2,3] Perhaps this means he was the oldest, but it could also be that his descendants left first or they traveled farthest. His name is גֹּמֶר in Hebrew and means "completion."[4] Besides the chronologies, he is mentioned only once more in a prophecy concerning multiple grandsons of Noah (Ezk. 38:6). Gomer had three known sons: Ashkenaz, Riphath, and Togarmah (Gen. 10:3). His people were known by many names, each changing with time and distance, but they trace back to Gomer.

Where is This Name Found?

Gomer is a tricky name to trace. Not because he is unmentioned, but because of how often his name was altered or left behind. Texts from various nations show how his name traveled and changed over the centuries among Gomer's descendants. But this is how the legacy of the people in the Table of Nations was recorded: through the names of nations. The *Book of Jubilees* states that Gomer received from his father, who received the land of the North from Noah, the "first portion" of land, which began northeast of the river Tina.[5] His people spread far across the western parts of Europe, and even eventually to some islands and new worlds, as indicated in Genesis (Gen. 10:5). Camden wrote in his Britannia, "...the nations and families which came from Japheth first inhabited the Iles of Europe."[6] Gomer's people were nomadic, living up to Japheth's name as they traversed Europe after Babel.

Josephus recorded what the Greeks knew of Gomer during his day, "For Gomer founded those whom the Greeks called Galatians [Gauls], but were often called Gomerites."[1] This description is useful because it provides various names that Gomer's descendants were known by, which aids in tracing their paths. So, where did they go? The answer is complex. On the one hand, it is understood that part of modern-day Turkey contained Galatia, a place Paul wrote to and visited (Acts 16:6, 18:23).[7] However, the name *Galatia* was given to this area long after the Babel Dispersion. Very likely, this name came with the invading Celts, or Kelts and Gauls as they were also known. Pausanias writes of such an event when the Grecians,

> "...led the Athenians to Thermopylae to stop the incursion of the Gauls into Greece. These Gauls inhabit the most remote portion of Europe, near a great sea that is not navigable to its extremities.... It was late before the name "Gauls" came in vogue; for anciently they were called Celts both among themselves and by others."[8]

Hopefully, the word "Celt" looks familiar from studies on the British Isles. But this is not where the Celts first dwelled. The Gomeric or Celtic clans did not stay in one area. The Celts covered a large swath of Europe, some of which were later known as the Hallstatt and the La Tene cultures.[9,10] These names came from two areas in Europe where a greater concentration of Celtic evidence is found. In general, the distribution shows progress from east to west across Europe. These people would have come from Babel in the Middle East, traveled to the North, and expanded from there. As time went on and the Gomeric clans grew and split, they would call themselves and be called by different names.

The people who made up France preserved Gomer's name best. But before France was called France, it was known as Gaul.[11,12] One author describes Gaul in the following:

> "GALLIA was bounded on the N. and W. by the Ocean, on the S. by the Pyrenees and the Mediterranean, and on the E. by the Alps... It was called Gallia Transalpina or Ultior, Gallia Comata, Galatia by the Greeks, and Celtica by the natives. ... The Celtae inhabited the middle of the country."[13]

Strabo writes in his *Geography* that, "The length of Britain itself is nearly as long as that of Keltica," that is, France.[14] The Romans, specifically Julius Caesar, gave the name *Gallia Celtica* to the area and people, though he overlooked various clans that technically differed from Gomer's direct line, notably those more closely related to Gomer's brother Tubal, such as the Iberians and Aquitani.[14,15] Other tribes in the area also related to Gomer via the Celts were the Gallaecians (not to be confused with the Galatians) in northern Iberia.

Isidore of Seville described the Celts and their relatives, the Celtiberians, as those who "descended from the Celtic Gauls."[16] The Celtiberians were of two sons of Japheth. Japheth's grandson gave his name to Iberia.[17] Julius Caesar writes that "All Gaul is divided into three parts, ...the Belgae, ...the Aquitani," and "those who in their own language are called Celts, in ours Gauls."[15] The Gauls were not separate from the Celts, but there were distinctions among them. Strabo noted that "they do not all speak the same language...neither is their polity and mode of life exactly the same."[18] This language difference could indicate that some of the tribes were from a different son of Japheth or simple dialect variation. Some Gaulish clans joined with other tribes, typically Germanic, to eventually become places like France and Belgium.[19] The Aquitani became a province near Spain.

Gomer is said to be in Germany's lineage, though the veracity of this claim is uncertain. Ashkenazi, sometimes used to describe German Jews, is vaguely derived from Gomer's son Ashkenaz, who will be discussed in the next chapter. Like many names in Europe, "Germani" was given by the Romans and later adopted by the Germans.[15,20] In the *Royal Genealogies*, there is a table explaining the descent from Gomer to the Germans via the Scythians.[21] Like other extra-biblical texts, some names change, and there are additional people whose existence has yet to be corroborated, however intriguing the text may be.[21]

Another portion of the same record claims the following are among the vast relations of Gomer: Scythians, Germans, Sarmatians, Geats, Alemanni, Franks, Teutons, and of course, the Celts, Gauls, and Galatians.[21] Some of these connections may be accurate, but others may have been included because many of the Caesars divided the land in a way that did not always group people with their actual ethnic lineage and gave them new names.[18] But as we can see, it is here that the old Gomerites were known still as Gauls, Celts, and so forth.[21]

> "ASKENAZ has a Brother call'd Scytha (fay the Germans) the Father of the Scythians; for which the Germans have been of old call'd Scythians too, (Very juftly, becaufe They came moftly from old Scythia) and Germany had feveral ancient Names."[21]

The *Royal Genealogies* includes Gomer with a people called the Cimbri, likely related to the Cimbrians of northern Europe:

> "GOMER, from whom came thofe Germans call'd Combri, or Cimbri... GOMER from whom are descended the Cimbrians or Cimerians, the Phrygians, and other Nations of Leffer Afia; who fent their Colonies afterwards into the North and Weft, from whom the Gauls, decende; for They were of various sorts."[21, 22]

This list includes the Phrygians residing in Galatia, some of whom would later be present at Pentecost (Acts 2:10). As mentioned before, the name Galatia was from a later invasion of Celts, or Gauls, into Anatolia. These records may also be including other Gomeric nations residing outside modern-day Turkey, such as Georgia and the Caucasus Mountains. In these places, Gomer is called "Gamer."[23]

The British Isles collectively call Gomer's descendants Gomerians. One small group was known better in the northern part of Britain, and they were the Pictones, later known as the Picts.[24] Camden provides a list of Gomer's descendants and explains where the sons of Japheth and Gomer went, writing,

> "But Gomer his eldest sonne, in these farthest and remotest borders of Europe, gave both beginning and name to the Gomerians, which were after called Cimbrians and Cimerians."[5]

These were also in "Germanie" and "in Gaule spred exceeding."[5] From here, he notes some key name variations such as: "Gomer, Gomari, Gomaraei and Gomeritae. From these Gomarians or Gomeraeans of Gaule."[5] Camden hints these were among the origins of the Celts, Scots, and Welsh,

> *For even they call themselves ordinarily Kumero, Cymro, and Kumeri, like as a British woman Kumeraes, and the tongue itself Kumeraaeg. Neither acknowledge they any other names ... who from hence have coined in the former age these words, Cambri and Cambria."*[5]

All this shows the long journey from the original spelling of Gomer to this point. Camden adds,

> *"Why should not we then confesse that our Britans or Cumerians are the very Posteritie of Gomer, and of Gomer tooke their denomination? For the name accordeth passing well, and granted it is that they planted themselves in the utmost borders of Europe...."*[5]

Gomer and his descendants were those who "extended" themselves to the outermost portions of Europe, as even the work titled *The Cambrian Journal* states, "all Europe must be traversed before men could reach our Islands," the British Isles, and "the Britons, who dwelt at the extremity of Europe, might claim, with the name, the patrimony of Gomer."[25] Moreover, the author defends the claim that these Gomerites were those of "Galatae" who were the Gauls or Celts and "were first called Gomarai."[25]

Now there is a certain part of Britain, known in the past as Breton, once called *cornu*.[26] It was then known that the place had also been called "Cornue-Galliae," which became Cornwall.[26] The Gomeric group that moved here are the ancestors of the Gaelic groups in the Iles, including the Scots and Welsh, a relation their Gaelic language also implies. In the Welsh Book *Drych y Prif Oesoedd*, there are multiple references to Gomer as the ancestor of the Welsh people.[27] This text even uses the old word *Gymraeg* for the Welsh, nowadays known as the Cymru. These words, derived from *comborgi* and related to Cambria, are derived from other Celtic words that point back to Gomer himself.[28,29] The Irish trace their lineage to Gomer, but they just as often link to his brother Magog. This is due to multiple invasions of the British Isles, resulting in a mixed lineage. Even so, they too spoke a Gaelic language, connecting them to their fellow islanders and Gomer.

These Gomerites or Celts traveled through much of Europe, from the east to Gaul in the west, stretching down to the Mediterranean in Galatia. Of all the descendants of Gomer, and perhaps even Japheth, the Gomerites, Gomerians, Cimmerians, Kelts, or Celtic people, whatever they are named at a given time, are mentioned in dozens of historical texts from all over Europe and the Mediterranean. They were a fierce, nomadic people. While they can be traced directly to a couple of specific locations, one should remember that, like most early people, they were nomadic, leaving settlements, intermingling with other clans, and expanding across Europe to become the ancestors of the people who dwell there today. Those listed here are only a handful of the names Gomer's family has held over the centuries, but they all point to him as the common ancestor.

Notable Mentions

When it comes to Gomer, his name is the most memorable as it was preserved even when the languages his descendants spoke changed as they multiplied. But later, Gomer's descendants also had names given to them that had interesting meanings. The Gauls were named so because of their pale completion: Gaul literally means "milk-skinned."[30] The Gomerians were known for their fierce nature, and people such as Isidore suggested their names derived from their nature.[31] For example, the Franks were called so for because they were brutal, and the Britons as well.[31] The Belgae, a Gaulish tribe, were thus named because of their apparent tendency to swell with anger and their readiness for battle.[15,32] Another group in the British Isles, the Feni, meant something like "hunter" or "warrior."[33] In general, the people of Gomer were known for their fierceness and anger in battle.

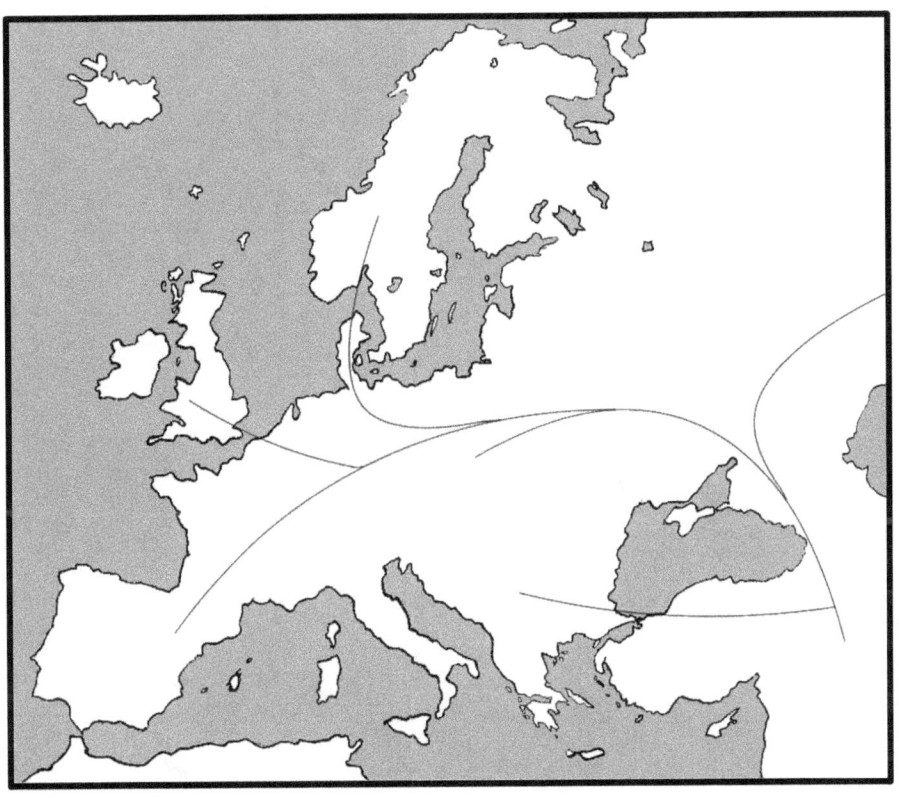

4: The Sons of Gomer

As explained in the previous chapter, many people are related to Gomer, and his descendants traveled far after the Babel Dispersion. But we can also follow the sons of Gomer that we know of across Europe and Asia, which this chapter will address.

Ashkenaz

Ashkenaz was the first son of Gomer; his name is אַשְׁכְּנַז in Hebrew (Gen 10:3).[1] The *Book of Jasher* calls him Askinaz, and Josephus writes, "Ashanax founded the Aschanaxians, who are now called by the Greeks Rheginians."[2,3] These names provide a starting point to find other names and places relating to this son. Jeremiah recorded two historical kingdoms alongside Ashkenaz: Ararat and Minni (Jer. 51:27). The Ark rested on the mountains of Ararat after the Flood (Gen. 8:4). Josephus also states, "the ark rested on the top of a certain mountain in Armenia."[4] These mountains in Armenia have the same name as the ancient kingdom of Ararat, previously called the Kingdom of Urartu.[5] Two other kingdoms of this area are found in an Assyrian text, called the Manneans and Cimmerians, or Gimirraya in their language, and were descendants of Ashkenaz.[6] The Manneans or Mannayu are the same Minni mentioned in Jeremiah.

The Cimmerians were related to the Scyths and the Gimarai or Gamirra, located "north of the kingdom of Ararat."[7,8] The Assyrians did not speak highly of the Cimmerians, for they had a reputation for being untrustworthy and war-loving. Herodotus places the Scyths, related to the Gimarai, in "upper Asia" above the Medes.[9] The Greeks placed the Scythians in southern Russia, called by the Assyrians the A/Ishkuza; the Scythians also included the Sarmatians, Saka, and Alani, among others.[10,11,12] Pliny mentioned the Alani, also Aorsi, as dwelling north of the Caucasus, possibly placing them in the Steppes.[13] The *Hou Hanshu* mentions the Alans as being part of the "Kingdom of Yancai," meaning "Vast Steppe," and was later known as the "kingdom of Alanliao."[14,15] In a history by Marcellinus, the Alani were neighbors of the Huns – well into Asia – dwelling near the Khazars and known for their horses.[16] Many of these accounts include that these people traveled into Europe. Thus, one should place Ashkenaz around and above the Black Sea and Armenia and in Eurasia.

The Black Sea itself is connected to Ashkenaz. The sea was once called the Pontic Sea, the Auxine Sea, and the Axenus.[17] This older name comes from Ashkenaz.[18,19] Strabo comments on this sea, stating it was called "Pontus Axenus" because of strong storms "to which it was subject, as well as the savage disposition of the nations who inhabited its shores, but more especially of the Scythian hordes."[20] The *Royal Genealogies* recorded Ashkenaz as the father of the those around the Black Sea, then called Euxim,

> "ASKENAZ The Father of the Askanians, of firft Inhabitants of Pontus and Bythnia twords the Euxim Sea...The Euxim is by fome call'd Axim, from Askenaz."[21]

Some of Ashkenaz's descendants dwelt around Pontus, once called Bithynia and now Turkey. A nearby lake and the land around it was once called Ascanius, though later it was held by a different brother.[22,23] Though there were more than just the handful of tribes and locations mentioned here that descended from and were inhabited by Ashkenaz's people, these are the best recognized.[24] The people of Ashkenaz appear to have split around the Black Sea and spread out across northern

Turkey, Armenia, Georgia, the lower parts of Europe, and beyond. These same people would later be present on the day of Pentecost to hear the message of the Gospel (Acts 2:9).

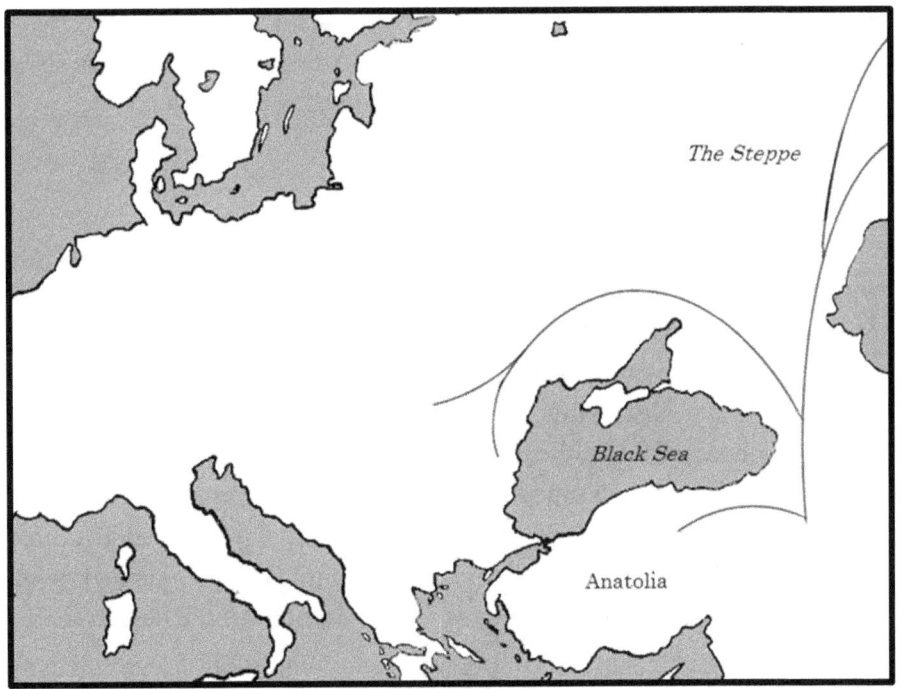

Riphath

The second listed son of Gomer is Riphath, whose name is רִיפַת in Hebrew (Gen. 10:3).[25] "Rephath" is also second in *The Book of Jasher*, which places his people in "Bartonia" by a "Ledah" river and "Gihon" sea, but this is an unknown location.[2,26] Josephus claims that "Riphath found the Ripheans, now called Paphlagonians," a claim echoed in the *Royal Genealogies*.[3,21] Finally, the *Jubilees* implies Riphath's location in the Rafa mountain range.[25]

Regarding the Paphlagonians, assuming they are related, there is a river that was once named Parthinius, and before that called Riphathenius, Rhebas, and Rhebus.[17,28,29] To the north, there was a tribe, known as both the Riphaei and the Arimphaei, who dwelt in the mountain range known to antiquity as the Ripheans.[30,31,32] The *Jubilees* mentions this range. Some scholars suggest this range might be north of the Black Sea, or perhaps the Alps, or the Caucasus, and others believe them to be the Urals of Russia; a common element, no matter the location, is that they contain the river Tanais.[33,34] Though their precise location is uncertain, Riphath's descendants clearly went into Europe like the other sons of Gomer. Perhaps he fathered one of these nations in the aforementioned mountains; perhaps he fathered them all. Of course, his people may have been engulfed altogether.

Togarmah

The third and last son of Gomer listed in Scripture is Togarmah, תּוֹגַרְמָה in Hebrew.[35] Ezekiel mentions him a couple of times within a prophecy against Gog: "Gomer with all its troops and Beth Togarmah from the far north with all its troops – the many nations with you" (Ezk. 38:6). Like other Gomerites, Togarmah is included with people of the North. The book of Ezekiel says Tyre traded with his people, and "men of Beth Togarmah exchanged workhorses, war horses, and mules for your merchandise" (Ezk. 27:14). Josephus called him Thrugramma, ancestor of the Thrugrammeans, whom the Greeks decided were "Phrygians."[3] The *Book of Jasher* says Togarmah had ten children.[36]

Josephus and Scripture imply that the people of Togarmah may have been in Anatolia. Sennacherib, a ruler of Assyria, also provided evidence that some of Togarmah's people may have lived in southern to mid-Turkey.[37] In his annals, Sennacherib mentions a city called "Tilgarimmu."[38] This city was situated near "the Border of Tabalu," which in other portions of the text is called "Tabal."[39] Tabal, possibly related to Tubal, was also in southern Turkey, as another Assyrian text by Sargon, a text specifically discussing this area's destruction, notes "...what can all the kings of Tabal do henceforth? You will press them ...and the Phrygian..."[40] Phrygia was in the middle of Anatolia, Assyria was to the south, and Til-Garimmu was between them. Another text by Sargon describes his attack on Kammanu, which is Til-Garimmu, modern Gürün.[41] As mentioned previously, these people were present to hear the Gospel on Pentecost (Acts 2:10).

The Hittites knew Togarmah as Tegarma. Suppiluliumas, "the great king, the king of the Hatti Land," recorded his attack on the peoples across the Euphrates in Anatolia, during which he "vanquished" many peoples including "half of the country of

Tegarmah."[42] This is the same "Beth Togarma," meaning house of Togarmah, that Ezekiel speaks of from the far north (Ezk. 38:6).[43,44] This Tegarmah, according to scholars, is the location of modern-day Gürün in Turkey.[45] Thus, it appears there were some peoples in what is now Turkey that belonged to the peoples of Togarmah. The nation ended after Assyria took over and scattered it.

But how should this be compared with Josephus' claim that the Togarmites are the Greek's Phrygians? It is quite possible that the Togarmites and the Phrygians split off and joined back together, or they combined with the existing Phrygians, or they joined with a different group entirely and became the Phrygians. Still, there is no external evidence saying the Phrygians were direct descendants of Togarmah. Whatever the case, the first people of Turkey were largely a mixture of Japheth's descendants.

The *Concise History of the Georgians* holds that the ancestor of the Georgian-Armenian peoples was someone called "T'orgom son of T'iras, son of Gamer, son of Japheth, son of Noah."[46] While this lineage is incorrect, for Tiras was Gomer's brother, one can see the connection. Concerning post-Babel events, the text states, "T'orgom... settled between the Masis and Aragate mountains... they spread out and enlarged their boundaries: from the Pontic Sea," the Black Sea, "...and by the mountains of the Caucasus."[46] Despite differences, the text has the names down, connecting their history to Babel.[46] Likely, Togarmah's descendants also traveled north above the Black Sea like other tribes of Gomer.

Continuing with the idea that Togarmah's people traveled northward, the following will discuss some descendants of Togarmah that are contested as it is unclear whether these lists and chronicles are accurate. Perhaps these sons did exist, but their true names were lost with the passage of time and language change. Perhaps they were not sons of Togarmah at all but sons of Hayk, who will be addressed further on. But for the sake of interest, I have provided a history for each proposed son. It could very well be that the lists are inaccurate, but if the list is close, this research may be a starting point for something in the future.

The *Concise History of the Georgians* contains a list of Togarmah's sons: Hayk, K'art'los, Bardos, Movkan, Lekan, Heros, Kovas, and Ergres.[46] Hayk, according to the Georgians and Armenians, was the first king as he "inherited half of the patrimony," most likely meaning that his father gave him half of the land among the brothers.[46] Perhaps Hayk was the only real son of Togarmah and all the other proposed descendants are his sons.

After him comes K'art'los, who gained the "Tsmak land of the north," probably north of his brother Hayk but still near to the Black Sea. Bardos "built the city of Partaw" which, looking near Armenia, is now Barda, once known as Partav and before that Partaw.[47] The text says that Bardos "built the city...in his own name."[46] To his son Movkan, according to the account, T'orgom gave the land "from the Kur river...to the head of the Alanzi river as far as the great sea."[46]

Heros received land that began at the head of the river Alazani to a lake of an obscure location. However, the *Chronicles of Jerahmeel* mention that it is called Gaghagha, a name similar to the Gargarenses mentioned by Strabo.[48,49] The nearby river Arax links to Heros.[50] T'orgrom gave the land close to the Caucasus to his son Ergres, who built a city after himself, today called Bedia.[46] The last two sons, Lekan and Kovas, are hardly mentioned, yet their names seem to have lasted best of all. These two received the "lands extending from mount Caucasus to the great Ghume river."[48] Lekas has remained as the people called Leks, also known as the "mountain peoples of Daghestan" in Russia, and Kovas is remembered in the name of the Caucasus Mountains.[51]

Jasher lists ten tribes after Togarmah: "Buzar, Parzunac, Balgar, Elicanum, Ragbib, Tarki, Bid, Zebuc, Ongal, Tilmaz."[36] Like the *Jasher* text, *The Chronicles of Jerahmeel* says,

> "Togarmah branched into ten families, who are the Cuzar, Paṣinaq, Alan, Bulgar, Kanbina, Turq, Buz, Zakhukh, Ugar, and Tulmeṣ. All of these dwell in the North, and the names of their lands are taken from their own names, and they live by the river Hetel; but Ugar, Bulgar, and Paṣinaq live by the great river called Danube."[48]

The first two names in each text are Buzar and Cuzar. The closest tribal names in the area are the Khazars of the Eurasian Steppes, which move from Europe to Asia.[52,53] This group has been linked to the peoples of Iran by language and the descendants of Madai.[54] The name Khazar could be related to the Turkic word for a leader – *khaghan* or *Khan* – a name often used for leaders of Turkish tribes, best preserved in Kazakhstan.[52,54] The Khazars were not the only tribes in the area, but one of many. Some of these were referred to in later times as the Ogurk people, and they included the following: the Saragurs, Orgurs, Onogurs, Bulgars.[52] Bulgar should look somewhat familiar as it appears on both lists. At a later point in history, the Bulgars settled Bulgaria.[56] There are also other accounts of Turkic tribes, one consisting of ten, the Onogur.[57]

The Bulgar and Ogar spoke "West Old Turkic" along with the Uygurs, perhaps of the supposed son, Ugar.[58] Ugar and Ongal seem to be closely related to the origin of the name Onogur; the name meant something like "kinship" in old Turkish, which is unsurprising if these tribes were made up of brothers.[59] They lived in the Turks' homeland in the Eurasian Steppe.[59] These nomadic tribes seem to have stayed together. They were not, however, recorded until long after Togarmah.

The Alan and Elicanum seem to be related to the Alans. Though the names are similar, these are among the suggested sons of Togarmah that most make me pause. Unlike their brothers, the Alans are linguistically related to the Scythians. Could the tribes have joined and come to be known by the Alans? This is possible, but not enough is known to be sure. The tribes of Kanbina, Tulmez, and Zakhkh of the *Jerahmeel* or Ragbib, Tilmaz, and Zubuc of *Jasher* are lost to history.[36,48] Considering the paths of the other tribes and their link to a common ancestor, assuming they were Togarmah's sons, they too probably fathered tribes that simply melded with other ancient peoples.

Parzunac of *Jasher* and Pasinaq of *Jerhameel* are also found in other texts, most notably in an old Chinese text, showing the vast expanse these early Japhetites traveled.[60] Old translations of this name appear as Pecenak and possibly mean something like "in-law clan/tribe."[59] In one Chinese text, they are called the "Pei-ju," and they seem to have been in close relation with the Steppe Turks.[60] This appears to be one of the groups documented to have spread through eastern Europe and Asia.[61] One of the closest links to the other Togarmic tribes, and by extension Turkish, is through language. Indeed, the Turkic language has been linked through the Altaic languages to Hunnic and Mongolian as well as others.[61,62,63] This would make sense if these tribes were of the original groups traveling from northern Anatolia and Armenia through the Eurasian Steppes to northeastern Eurasia, settling at various points to become the nations we know of today. Though separated now, all have a link to these Turkish tribes.[64] A few modern nations of Europe, besides Turkey, connect to these tribes because of their later return to Europe.[64]

The last of the Turkic peoples called Buz and Turq in the *Chronicles of Jerhameel* and Bib and Tarki in the *Book of Jasher*. Both could be related to the Oghuz Turks, who dwelled in the Eurasian Steppes and near Mongolia.[65] An old Turkish inscription written in a Runic script, much like other descendants of Gomer, includes their names.[66] Turq and Tarki, however, are connected to the Turkish people more clearly than some. They were known as the Kok Turks, translating something like "blue" Turk, and later as the Gokturks.[59] There are references to them in many records, and they dwelt in the Steppes.[59]

The most significant connection of all these people is through their language and culture. Their language, all forms of Turkish, connected back to the Ogurks, who spoke a Turkish tongue.[52] The Turks are closely connected to the other tribes previously mentioned though their language, which was once known as the Orkhon Script found in Mongolia.[63,67] They have been shown to have similar styles of tribal arrangement, as with the Khagan tribe leader and collections of tribes. These groups were later known as the Tiele.[52] Corresponding with Ezekiel's account and Assyrian records, the people of northern Anatolia were known for their horses.[45,68,69] All these various tribes also based their worship around one god, a sky god, which may have contributed to the exonym Blue Turks.[70,71]

Perhaps these were actual sons of Togarmah, residing in eastern Turkey, parts of Armenia, and spreading across the Eurasian Steppes. Their presence in Armenia and Georgia, however, seems not to be as strong as other tribes, like the Tabal and their neighbors. It is difficult to say with certainty the total places these nomads moved. As mentioned before, this is not an exhaustive list. It is merely a guide. But their language, names, and presence at Gürün point to Togarmah as an ancestor of people in Anatolia and Eurasia.

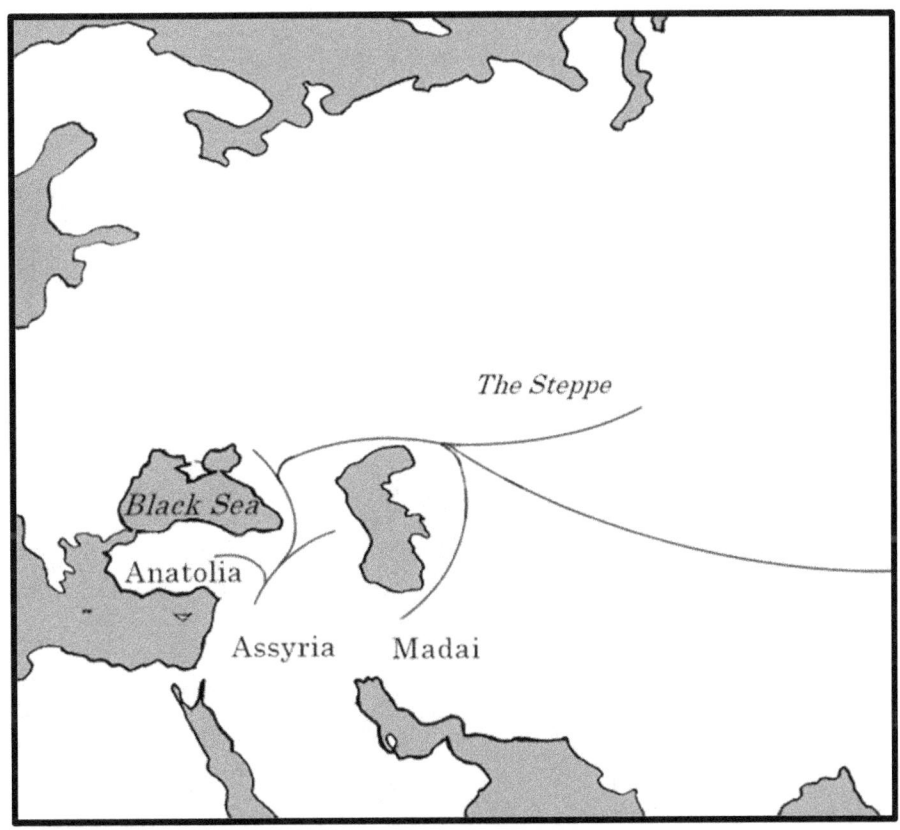

Names, Nations, and the New Testament

5: Magog

Land of Gog

Magog is the second listed of Japheth's sons, possibly because of his proximity to Gomer in addition to birth order (Gen. 10:2). In Hebrew, his name appears as מָגוֹג; in the Greek, it is Μαγώγ.[1,2] Magog's name is somewhat unique among Japheth's sons: his name means "the land of Gog." Perhaps this son's name was Gog and his *land* was called Magog. In a prophecy, Ezekiel writes against "Gog, of the land of Magog" in the North, who also ruled Meshech and Tubal (Ezk. 38-39). The book of Revelation implies his land is distant (Rev. 20:8). Still, the location of the land of Magog is challenging to pinpoint. He was a son of Japheth, which places him in the North, essentially Europe. With this in mind, there are a handful of peoples that may be from Magog.

Where is This Name Found?

There are many possible Magogite nations. His people appear to have moved from Babel via the bridge between the Caspian and Black seas toward the northernmost parts of Europe. The *Book of Jasher* only makes scant references to Magog, though the text mentions two sons.[3] In the *Book of Jubilees*, Magog receives land in "all the inner portions of the north until it reaches to the sea of Me'at."[4] According to Isidore, the Goths are distantly related to Magog and were previously called "Getae rather than Goths," and the "Dacians" were from these people, though this conclusion may be due to their proximity to the Goths and Scythians.[5] Jerome calls the Getae "ruddy and yellow-haired."[6] The Getae may have been related to the Goths of Magog. Still, the records of their people are so distant that it would be difficult to prove conclusively. Besides, the Getae are likely related to a different brother.

The most plausible nations that descended from Magog are the Scythians and Goths, or rather, the Teutonic or Germanic people of Europe.[7] These are both very large though different nations, but they are related. First, the Scythians are clearly related to Magog and Ashkenaz. Though the name is from Ashkenaz, we cannot ignore Magog's influence. Additionally, there is textual, linguistic, and cultural evidence that the Scythians were related to the Germanic tribes of Europe.[8]

According to Josephus, Magog was the progenitor of the Magogites, whom he says the "Greeks called Scythians."[9] They were also known as the Saka, the Sarmatians (not to be confused with Samaritans). Tribes of Ashkenites and some tribes of the Magogites joined together to become the great hordes of Scythians. Together, the nomadic Scythians moved across Europe and Asia where the land was "wintery," as many ancient authors described, notably Herodotus, who devoted whole swaths of his writing to the Scythians.[10,11] These people were experts in archery and animal husbandry, especially horses. The Scythians left evidence of their presence and were the ancestors of the people from southeastern Europe to the Altai Mountains in Siberia, Mongolia, and East Asia, to the Urals.[12,13,14]

There are also the Germanic people, their collective name, that are related to the Scythians of Magog. Johannes Magnus and James Anderson connect Magog to the Scandinavians as well as to the Scythians and Goths, another name for some later Germanic tribes.[15,16] Jordanes called their land area *Gothiscandza*, named so either as a later attribution or because of the link between the peoples.[17] He also claimed the Geate – that would be the Geats, not the Getae – are of the same descent as the Goths.[18] In addition, the historian Magnus includes Magog's sons: Suenno, Gethar, Thor, German, and Ubbo.[15] We should consider these proposed sons tentatively as we did the sons of Togarmah. While they may be contemporary projections on the past, that does not mean the sons did not exist, or even that these were not their names. Many sagas of the past contain the founder's names for their people, and these tales should not be overlooked. We should think of these sagas like we do some historical fiction.

Gethar's descendants likely became known as the Goths and founded Gotland or Gothland, part of Scandinavia. Gotlanders consider Guti, a man of three brothers, to be their founder, a story which perhaps came from Magog.[19] This account is in Gutnish of the Gutes, a Germanic tongue and tribe.[20] The Cimbri knew the Gutes and Jutland as Chersonese, their people settling in Norway and other parts of Scandinavia.[21] The *Royal Genealogies* says Gether may not have reigned in Gothland but Russia.[22]

Suenno is most likely the ancestor of those who became the Swedes. The oldest mention of them is by Tacitus.[23] Anderson mentions a "Suevus, or Sweno," first among his brothers.[22] However, another group that could claim ancestry to Suenno is the Suomi, also known as both the Sami and Laps, who live in Finland.[24] However, the Finns connect their ancestry to Russia and other neighboring peoples, such as the Swedes, Norse, Estonians, and even the Sami and some southern Slavic people that may be related to the Dacians.[25] In general, though, within the limits placed on knowledge of our genetic code, the Finns seem to be somewhat genetically isolated from other Europeans, though the differences are relatively small.

The Romans, namely Tacitus, made some early connections while trying to understand the northern people of Europe, such as the Finns and Sami.[23] Russia's name stems from the Rus, who descended from nomadic Swedes.[26] Additionally, the Finns use an Old Norse word for the Swedes.[26] The Sami people speak languages of the Finno-Ugric group, or Uralic, which may be part of the language group Magog was responsible for, possibly even connecting other Slavic languages.[27] Estonia also finds roots in this familial language and even shows a genetic relation.[28] The fact that now some consider Estonians as "one of the oldest European nations" for being in "the same area for over 5,000 years" is ironic considering such a time frame would have them settling in the proximity of time after Babel.[29]

Language is the best link between Magog's people. The Scythians are related to certain Germanic peoples via language and culture.[7,8,30] The Norse and Swedes are linked genetically and linguistically to the mainland Germanic tribes.[31,32] The Germanic people and languages, however, are more than Scandinavia. The Geats, Götalanders, Angles, Danes, Germans, Goths, Icelanders, and many others owe their ancestry to Magog.[33] England owes much to the Angles, Saxons, and Scandinavians.[34] Likely, these languages were separated by the distance between sons and tribes. Once certain tribes left to lands that became nations like Denmark, Norway, and Sweden, language would change. But in general, their personal histories and genealogies reflect each other– including names relating to the Saxons, Swedes, Norse, and Geats – going back to a son of Noah.[35,36,37]

Notable Mentions

The person and name of Magog have been contested due to the lore surrounding him. He is most often mentioned in Scripture within prophecies rather than the lists of names and places, although "Magog" is a place name.[38] Some people consider him to be one of the early kings of Lydia, although this has yet to be proven.[38] Other places seem to be named after him though they have nothing to do with the man himself.

In the history written by Geoffrey of Monmouth, a giant named Goemagot dwelled in the land of the Britons, amongst others.[39] The place where this giant fell is known today as Gogmagog hill.[39,40] While the current name of this hill highly resembles that of the Biblical character, and was no doubt garnered from Scripture, it seems to be a "corruption of *Gawr Madoc*," an old name of that very hill.[41] The *Lebor Gabála Érenn* says Magog was an ancestor of the Irish, but this appears to be a confusion of ancestry as the Georgians confused Tiras as Gomer's son.[42] The British stories of Magog have little to do with his presence there unless there was a confusion in the Scandinavian invasions, which is doubtful, but rather misconstruing similar names.

The name Magog means "the land of Gog."[1] Within areas possibly inhabited by Magog's people, there are names related to the word "land." The Estonians, likely of the Magogites, once called themselves Maarahvas, meaning "earth" or "land people."[43] The nearby Sami also have etymological origins meaning "land."[44] Two national epics – of the Finnish called *Kalevala* and the Estonians *Kalevipoeg* – speak of the land of Kalevala and the son of Kalev, respectively, and both deal with their lands' founding.[45,46] The names remain today in a few locations. In Finland near Russia, there is Karelia; Kaleva, meaning "land of Kaleva," or specifically "hero...place"; and another is in Estonia.[47,48] The name Kaleva is still used; it means "the land of Kalevi," relating to the old epics.[48,49] Perhaps these stories are just that, but whatever the case, it is intriguing that many of them have names as the "land of" such and such ancestor, which in this case I believe to be Magog.

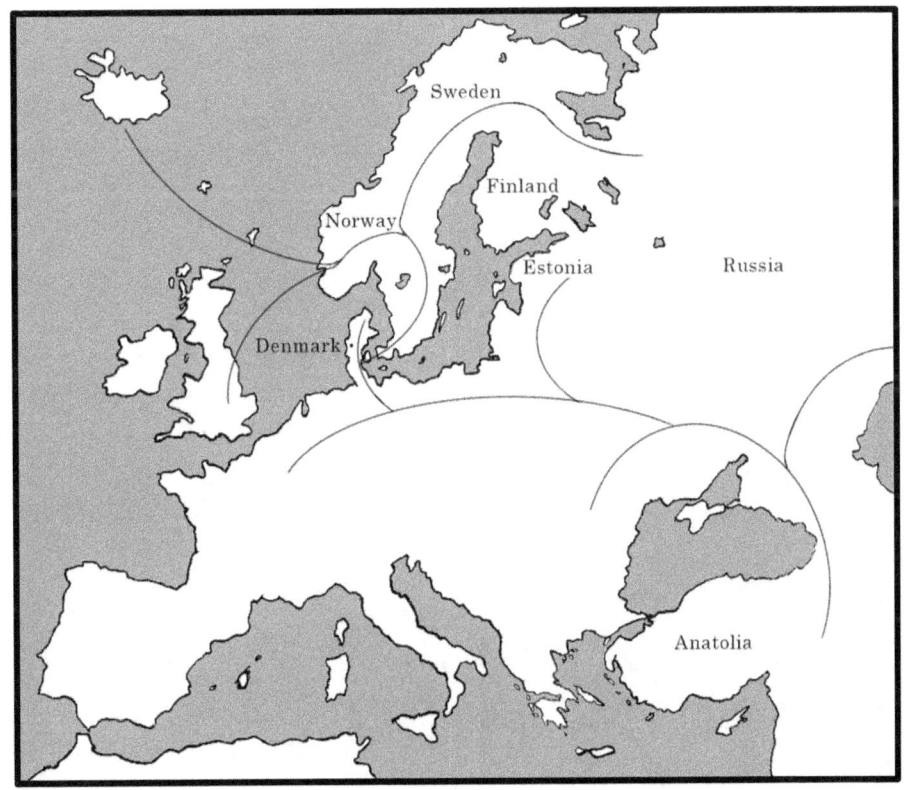

6: *Madai*

Middle Land

Madai was the third son of Gomer and one whose name was well-preserved in history. His people were used for judgment and had judgment pronounced upon them in Scripture. A descendant of his would return the Jews to Israel. Others were in the book of Acts. Even so, his name is only specifically translated thus twice in Scripture (Gen. 10:2; 1Ch. 1:5). But his people are found thirteen times in the Old Testament (Dan. 5:28-31, 6:8-15, 9:1, 11:1; 2Ki. 17:6, 18:11; Isa. 13:17; Jer. 51:11-28; Acts 2:9). Additionally, the territory of Media is defined in the books written before, during, and after the Exile (Ezr. 6:2; Est. 1:3-19, 10:2; Isa 21:2; Jer. 25:25; Dan 8:20).

There is only one word in Hebrew, מָדַי, used for Madai, Mede, Medes, and the place Media.[1] In Greek, Mede appears as Μῆδος.[2] Within Scripture, the Medes are often coupled with the peoples of Persia, Elam, and those related to or neighboring them. These people are also included in the account of the day of Pentecost when people from these regions visited Jerusalem and heard the Gospel (Acts 2:9).

Where is This Name Found?

Though he was a son of Japheth, he did not reside in Europe with the rest of his brothers. Instead, Madai dwelled in the land of Shem. We know from the Scripture referenced above that Madai dwelt in what became known as Medo-Persia, now called Iran. The *Book of Jubilees* mentions Madai as the third son of Japheth, and Josephus includes him in the *Antiquities*.[3,4] The Medes were children of Madai while the Persians came from Shem's son Elam.[5,6] In his *Antiquities*, Josephus writes that "from Madai came the Madeans" who the Greeks called Medes.[4] The *Jubilees* says Madai had a daughter named Melka who married a descendant of Shem, her mother's people.[7] Madai asked Elam, Asshur, and Ham for land "near to his wife's brother."[8] While it says he did not like "the land of the sea" allotted to him by his father, perhaps he truly wanted to stay near his wife's family.[8,9] Thus, Madai and his people remained in the "middle land" away from his brothers.

Media is included many times in Scripture, most notably around the time of the Babylonian conquest of the Middle East and that empire's subsequent fall to the Medes and Persians. Shortly after Babel, as the texts above say, Madai and Elam dwelled near each other southeast of the plain of Shinar and eventually became Medo-Persia.[10] Before this, the people of Madai appear to have split into multiple tribes, likely through numerous sons, though they all dwelled in and around modern Iran.[11] According to Herodotus and Sanskrit texts, those who resided in the land now called India came from the same people, called Aryans.[12,13] Unsurprisingly, this familial connection would explain the similarities between the Indo-European languages. Eventually, many of the western tribes joined back together in the first millennia B.C. and became a great nation. Even so, for some time, the entire area was called "*Madai*" by the Assyrians.[11]

After the fall of Israel and Judah to Assyria and then Babylon, the Medo-Persian empire took over the Babylonian empire. At that time, Daniel, one of the young men brought to Babylon, was still residing in the capital (Dan. 1:3-7, 5:11-13). Before the takeover, Daniel was brought before the Babylonian king to read a judgment stating that his kingdom was to fall "that very night...and Darius the Mede took over the kingdom" (Dan. 5:3, Isa. 13, Jer. 51). Daniel continued under the reigns of Darius and Cyrus, though these names might be for one person, originally Darius the Mede, rather than two (Dan. 6:28). The rest of the book of Daniel is quite fascinating as it foretells the rise and fall nations, including Babylon, Media, Persia, Greece, and others.

Cyrus the Great of the Medo-Persian empire sent some of the Jews back to their homeland to rebuild the temple (2Chr. 36:22-23; Ezra 1:1-4). During this time, the Jews faced opposition during the reign of Cyrus until the reign of Darius I (Ezra 4:4-5).[14] Ezra writes that this opposition continued under the reigns of Xerxes and Artaxerxes (Ezra 4:6-7). Nehemiah presumably served under this king, known as Artaxerxes I (Neh. 1:11-2:1).[14] The reign of Darius II of Persia saw the continuation of the rebuilding of Jerusalem and the temple (Ezra 4:24, 6).[14] Thus, God used the people of Madai as the means to return His people to their homeland.

The Parthians were a nearby nation to the Medes and Persians. Scripture includes them in the second chapter of Acts along with the Elamites and Medes (Acts 2:9). They once lived north of the Persian Empire in what is today Turkmenia, an area later controlled by the Turks.[15] The Parthians were taken over by the Persian empire under Darius, an event recorded in an inscription by Darius. Among the many countries that were "subject" to him, four are Persia, Elam, Babylonia, and Parthia.[16]

The Medes and the Persians became collectively known over time as the Aryans.[17] Coming from Sanskrit, it meant something like "compatriot" or "good family."[17] These names seem to be self-given as both kings Darius and Xerxes call their people Aryan and their "language and their script Aryan."[18] This name developed from Aryan to Eran and, eventually, Iran.[19] Though there is now a nation of Iran, this name once included the people in the surrounding areas.

Notable Mentions

There are other mentions of people related to Madai, however distant their relationship may be. As usual, these accounts pertain to the religion of the people. They deified their ancestors, a practice probably originating in an attempt to preserve the memory of their ancestors for future generations. While some seem hardly related at all, it shows how people preserved these names over the generations.

For instance, the Kurds consider themselves direct descendants of Noah after the Flood, most probably through Madai since they are of Iranian ancestry.[20] The Greeks kept some names, but incorporated them, albeit somewhat obscurely, into their history and mythology. They say there was a woman named Medea, sometimes referred to as Medeia, who was the wife of Jason.[21,22] She is said to have had a son named Medus, or Medeius, whom the Greeks decided was the ancestor of the Medes.[23,24] Perhaps Javan took stories to his lands and, as with Japheth, his brother also got a spot in Greek mythology though some facts were lost.

The Kachin people of Burma claim ties to Madai. They hold that there was a creation and presumably a judgment.[25] They recount the origin of a couple they refer to as the "great Nats," begat by Janun with one named La'n Koi Madai.[25] This La'n Koi Madai appears to be their ancestor and was worshiped by them.[25] Another account comes from some distant relatives, the Gaikho, who claim that they descend from Adam, or Ai-ra-bai, and Eve, Mo-ra-mu; a similar record comes from the Sgaus and Red Karens.[26] The chapter "Words and Wanderings" tells this story in more detail. Whether or not these people specifically came from Madai, they held onto their past enough to keep the early days of mankind in their histories.

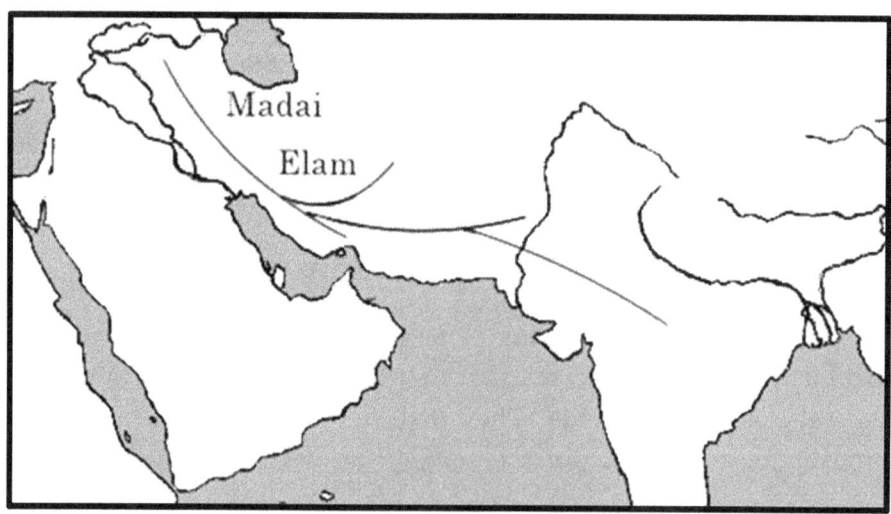

7: Javan

Ionia

Javan was the fourth son of Japheth. His people are best depicted in this verse from Genesis: "From these the maritime people spread out into their territories" (Gen. 10:5). Javan had four sons: Elishah, Tarshish, and two others called "the Kittim and the Rodanim," the last son sometimes spelled Dodanim (Gen. 10:4). Within the rest of Scripture, Javan is specifically mentioned several times. Like with Madai and others, his name denotes a specific nation or area. The Hebrew word for Javan, translated thus only twice, is יָוָן, the same word as Ionia or Greece (Isa. 66:19, Ezk. 27:13-19, Dan. 8:21, 10:20, 11:2; Zec. 9:13).[1] Once, the word יְוָנִי is translated as Grecian or Ionian (Joe. 3:6).[2]

Among the various prophecies in the books of the Major Prophets, there is a series of passages about a coming conqueror of the Medo-Persian empire. This person would bring with them a nation that engulfed all the rest until it also would one day be engulfed. Daniel writes the most on the subject, and the verses provided above contain more of the story. This famous descendant of Javan is none other than Alexander the Great, "king of Greece." The Greeks were also quite important to the New Testament world, mainly because of the language that became the lingua franca, made thus by Alexander's conquests.

The New Testament was originally written in Greek. This common language, with the help of Roman roads, brought the Gospel to the nations.

Where is This Name Found?

Unsurprisingly, Josephus recounts that Javan was from whom "Ionia and all the Grecians are derived."[3,4] Ionia was on the coast of ancient Anatolia, which is modern-day Turkey. Three of his four sons, whom Josephus names Elisa, Tharsus, and Cethimus, were said to have brought forth the Eliseans, Tharsians, and Cethim, respectively. The Eliseans, Josephus says, were then called the Aeolians; the Tharsians Cilicia and Tarsus; and the Cethim became islands like Cyprus. Similarly, the *Book of Jubilees* states that "for Javan came forth the fourth portion every island and the islands which are toward the border of Lud."[5] In the *Book of Jasher*, Javan is listed fourth among his brothers and then as the father of "Elisha, Tarshish, Chittim, and Dudonim."[6] This book later states that Javan is the father of the "Javanim who dwell in the land of Makedonia," that is, Macedonia.[7] These accounts fit with Scripture, which describes his people as dwellers of the sea.

Anderson's *Royal Genealogies* states that Javan's people were sailors "towards the coast of the Mediterranean and the Grecian Islands."[8] He also notes that the Hebrews call the people on the Isthmus of Peloponnesus "Ionians" or simply Javan, and that the Chaldees call the area "Javan Macedonia" and "The Athenians are also called Iones."[8] The Assyrians knew the Cyprians, Tarshians, and Ionians as "*mat Iadanana*," "*mat Tarsisi*," and "*mat Iaman*."[9,10] The Assyrian texts speaking of "Iamani" and "Iamaneans," noting that they had to be drawn "from the sea" or are in "the midst of the sea" like fish.[11] Thus, Javan's descendants are of the sea, especially the Mediterranean Sea, including Ionians, Anatolians, and others.

Notable Mentions

In the chapter on Japheth, I mentioned a Greek God by the name of Iapetus that may have been based on that same son of Noah. Not only is there an Iapetus in Greek Mythology, but also an Ion, a name most probably from Javan, the forefather of the Ionians.[12] One contention is, though, that their lineage is spread out further than father and son.[12] However, as neither Javan nor Japheth were actually gods, and they became deified long after their deaths, it would not be difficult to assume that the Ionians forgot the exact lineage. We should consider myths like historical fiction rather than an accurate record of history. Other Greek works mention the river Iaon, connected to Ion and the Ionians.[13] It is also possible that one faction of the Sea Peoples were descendants of Javan.[14] As shall be seen in the following chapter, the frequent sea travels of Javan's descendants may connect them to this fabled people.

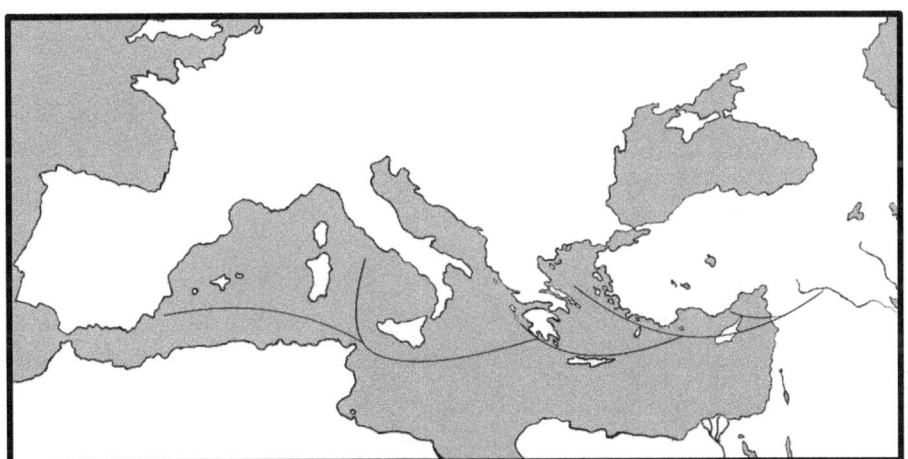

8: The Sons of Javan

The sons of Javan are best characterized by their description in Scripture: they were peoples of the sea (Gen. 10:4-5). What did this mean? While this could have included more than the Mediterranean, most likely, the initial settlements were within this Sea, including the coastland and islands found within it. These nomads of the sea were proficient sailors, had sturdy boats, and were known for their battles and trade. Because of their travels, they often joined with the people they encountered, including descendants of Shem and Ham.

Elishah

Elishah is the first listed son of Javan, and his name is אֱלִישָׁה in Hebrew (Gen. 10:4).[1] Ezekiel mentions that Tyre had "blue and purple from the coasts of Elishah," indicating that these were people of the sea (Ezk. 27:7). Josephus wrote that the people of Elishah, whom he refers to as Elisa, became the Aeolians.[2] Aeolis was a land north of Ionia in Anatolia. According to Strabo, the Aeolians were associated with the Pelasgi and Thessaly, who dwelt around the area of Aeolia and perhaps were once part of Aeolia.[3] Anderson writes in the *Royal Genealogies* that Elishah was also the father of the Peloponnesians.[4] Here, there was a city called Elis.[5] Another place perhaps named after him was the mystical Elysium, the paradise of heroes.[6] Homer's *Iliad*, however, makes this place seem like a geographical location.[7]

The Amarna tablets imply Elishah may have first settled on the island of Cyprus, leaving behind the area known then as Alashiya.[8] A distant source says that Elishah moved to Portugal with Tubal, his father's brother, and founded a people there.[9] Lusus or Lysias, who founded the Lusitanians, the early Portuguese, best fits this theory.[10,11] Now, the modern Portuguese clearly have been influenced by the Iberians, Celts, and Romans, but it appears that they also may have some ancestry from Javan. So, the people of Elishah, or perhaps Elishah himself, lived true to his name and traveled along the Isles of the Mediterranean Sea, starting at Cyprus, settling people in Ionia, and perhaps ending up in modern-day Portugal.

Tarshish

Tarshish, or Tharsus of Josephus' works, was the second son of Javan.[2] His name is תַּרְשִׁישׁ in Hebrew.[12] According to Josephus, his people came to be known as the Tharsians and dwelled in Cilicia.[2] Josephus decides upon this location mainly because the city Tarsus was in that ancient land (Acts 9:11, 21:39). Scripture mentions Tarshish over twenty times. There are references to Tarshish as a trader of gold and silver to both Israel and Tyre and the holder of goods such as ivory and tin (1Ki. 10:22; Isa. 23, 60:9; Jer. 10:9; Ezk. 27:12). Along with other nations of the world, and especially those of Greece and Anatolia, Tarshish is included as one to whom the glory of God will be proclaimed (Isa. 66:19). Most notable, though, is the account of Jonah, who, attempting to flee the Lord, gets a boat at Joppa to sail for Tarshish (Jon.1:3).

Josephus considered Cilicia in Anatolia to be the land of Tarshish. While it could be that Tarshish or his people initially settled at Tarsus, it is unlikely that they remained there. An inscription by Esarhaddon, a king of Assyria, wrote of people "in the midst of the sea" who are from "Iadanana [Cyprus], the country of Iaman [Javan] to the country of Tarsisi," whom he overcame.[13] This, seemingly, would put Tarshish somewhere near Assyria since an Assyrian king overtook it.[13] But then why place it last? Where Cyprus is closest to Assyria, then Iaman, which might be Ionia, is next in distance, that would place this Tarsisi as being farther yet. Another translation puts the latter part, "as far as Tarshish," implying that Tarshish is far away.[14] Yet many other Near Eastern texts refer to this same place. These include "*uru TAR-ZI*" and "*kur TAR-SI-SI*" in Assyrian, "*trz*" in Aramaic, "*tarsha*" from Hittite, and similar words from Greek.[15] If this region in Anatolia is the (possibly original) settlement of Tarshish, it would help explain the connection to Tyre, the Kittim, Egypt, and other regular traders. However, this need not be the sole place Tarshish settled.

A Phoenician inscription found on Sardinia, often called the Nora Stone, bears the name "*t-r-s-s*," or Tarshish.[15,16] A translation of the Nora Stone inscription reads, "From Tarshish he was driven; in Sardinia he found refuge."[16] One group of people linked to the Sardinians are the "*Sherden*" or "*sherdana*."[17] I would link these people to those of Javan, as they too are considered one of the Peoples of the Sea, some of whom attacked Egypt.[18] This area is quite far from Tarsus and could place some of Tarshish's people in the western part of the Mediterranean.

The last place to look for Tarshish's settlements is in Spain. I write about this place only because scholars often consider it, though it is contested. Herodotus writes of a place called Tartessus, located on the southern tip of Spain.[19] In his *Description of Greece*, Pausanias writes that Tartessus was a river in Iberia.[20] Metals came from here, mostly bronze, but this part of Spain is known to have gold as well.[21,22] Strabo recorded that the Tartessians lived in the south by the "silver-bedded river Tartessus," later called the Guadalquiver, and called the area Tartessis, though the Turduli came to inhabit the area.[23] Like most places, different people at various times inhabited this settlement in southern Spain. For instance, it was said above that Elishah also went to Iberia's western face. Gomer's descendants controlled the North – Gaul and Celti-Iberia – and the Phoenicians even traveled as far as Iberia.[24] But besides the Nora Stone, there is little reason to think that Tarshish certainly settled here, though his nomadic sea-people settled about the Mediterranean.

Kittim

Kittim is the third son of the Javan, whose name appears as כִּתִּים in Scripture.[25] The spelling, however, goes back and forth between Kittim and Chittim, a factor also playing into translations as well. It should be noted that Kittim is really *the* Kittim, as it is a plural word, sometimes appearing as "the Kittites," and refers to a people group rather than a singular person (Gen. 10:4).[25] Another translation would be "Cypriote," possibly one from Cyprus or other peoples of the Mediterranean.[25] Outside of chronologies, the Kittim or Chittim are mentioned in the book of Numbers as a group who would attack Asshur and Eber on the coast of the Sea (Num. 24:24). Most often, though, Chittim or Kittim is translated as Cyprus, and any time they are outside of a chronology, the word used in English is Cyprus (Num 24:24; Isa. 23:1, 12; Jer. 2:10; Ezk. 27:6). In these Old Testament passages, we find that Cyprus was an island, one seemingly connected with the above sons of Javan and Tyre.

The first mention of Cyprus in the New Testament is about Barnabas, a leader in the early Church (Acts 4:36). There are two Greek words for Cyprus in the New Testament: Κύπριος and Κύπρος. The former word is the same as the Kittim in Hebrew, translating most often as Cypriote or Cyprus in English (Acts 4:36, 11:20, 21:16).[26] The latter also appears in English as Cyprus and refers specifically to the Mediterranean island (Acts 11:19, 13:4, 15:39, 21:3, 27:4).[27] Thus, these words refer to the same peoples in Greek and Hebrew. The Kittim, then, are those who, at least in part, lived on the island of Cyprus. Even now there is a city in Cyprus, bearing a new name, that was derived from its founder: Citium, or Kition.[28]

The Kittim were not just those on Cyprus, however, and their name also referred to others on the Grecian mainland. As mentioned before, one of the most famous Grecians was Alexander the Great. Specifically, Alexander was from Macedonia, as he was the son of King Philip the Macedon.[29] In the book of Maccabees, this is called the land of the Kittim.[29] Some have theorized that the name Macedonia came from "Ma-Kittim," which meant the land of the Kittim, similar to how "beth" means house in Hebrew.[30,31,32]

Cyprus and Macedonia were not the only places referred to as Kittim. The last reference in Scripture is to the Romans. As Italy is part of the Mediterranean and an isle of the sea, there is little wonder that those of Javan settled there. Now, I do not believe that the sole ancestry of the Romans comes from Javan through the Kittim. In fact, I think they mainly come from another brother. However, Scripture says,

> "At the appointed time he will invade the South again, but this time the outcome will be different from what it was before. Ships of the western coastlands will oppose him, and he will lose heart...."[33]

The phrase translated here as "of the western coastlands" is Kittim in Hebrew.[34] This prophecy appears to be about a man named Popilius Laenas, who fought with the Seleucid and Polemic Empires, parts of the fragmented Alexandrian Empire.[34,35] The Kittim are also found in the *Dead Sea Scrolls,* whom scholars consider to be Romans.[36,37,38,39,40] The Romans are mentioned many times in the New Testament, not to mention having an entire book written to them! But besides general references in the Gospels, they first hear the Gospel on the day of Pentecost, though "visitors from Rome" might have been a broader representation than the city itself (Luk. 2:1, Jhn. 11:48, 18:28, Acts 2:10). But why are the Kittim known by such different names? The simplest and best answer is that they developed new names with time and distance, though originating from the same people.

Rodanim

Rodanim is the last of the descendants of Javan recorded in Scripture, and his name is דְדָנִים in Hebrew.[41] Like the Kittim, this son is better translated as *the* Rodanim as it was a group and not a singular person.[41] The spelling for this son goes back and forth between Rodanim and Dodanim, as the Hebrew letters for 'R' and 'D' are quite similar (Gen. 10:4, 1Ch. 1:7).[41]

There are a handful of locations associated with this son. We will begin in the New Testament. The name Rhodes, or Ῥόδος in the Greek, is a place that Paul and his companions visited (Acts 21:1).[42] Rhodes is an island among those known as the Dodecanese, which includes Patmos, where John lived in exile (Rev. 1:9).[43] Both of these names, used for centuries, probably derived from R/Dodanim, as these are among the isles of the Mediterranean, a domain of Javan's people.

One possible location for R/Dodanim is Dodana in Epirus, an ancient region in Greece.[44] If for nothing else, the name highly resembles the scriptural name. Here, the people worshiped Jupiter, or Zeus Naios, which may imply a Noahic origin.[45,46] In addition, this city of Dodana was founded, according to Plutarch, after the flood.[45] Is he referring to the Great Deluge of Genesis? Possibly, considering that many nations carry flood accounts and this city holds a name similar to a descendant of Noah.

The Egyptians encountered a people they referred to as "*drdny*," or "Dardany."[47,48] These people were recorded in a poem about the battle of Qadesh.[47] Their city and region were referred to as Dardanus – who also happens to be a Greek god and is considered the city's founder – as well as Dardania and Dardanium, located on Anatolia's Ionic coast.[49,50,51] As with Javan and Ion, Dardanus was likely derived from R/Dodanim through the practice of ancestor worship. Additionally, Dardania was near to the Trojans.[50] While these two nations are considered to have been merely allies, I believe that these two people were related. And as the Rhodians most likely derive their name from R/Dodanim, a river in this area bears the name of Rhodius.[49] These facts are further supported by other translations of the Pentateuch that name a son of Javan and his province Dordonia, which is preceded by Italia.[52]

Thus, the Dardani were around Dardania in northern Ionia, where Troy is located. Virgil's *Aeneid* calls Aeneas the Dardan on two occasions and refers to his people likewise.[53] I do not consider this a confusion of history, though perhaps not fully understood. While it is impossible to be sure that Aeneas was indeed the one who brought the Trojans to Italy, someone did.[54] In fact, scholars have speculated that some of the precursors to the Romans and early peoples of Italia were originally from Anatolia.[55]

There are some vague and partially exaggerated accounts on these people's origins, stating they are from Dardania in modern-day Turkey. According to Virgil, Aeneas of Troy was destined for the "Laurentine Tiber" in Latium.[56] This location partially overlaps with the territory of the Etruscans, which seems more than coincidental.[57] Again, this is not to say that Virgil's epic is wholly accurate. While there may have been an Aeneas, was he the one that brought the Trojans to Italy? Was there another? Perhaps he founded the early Latins. Whatever the case, it appears that Virgil had some basis for the information in his epic as some of the Italian people were partly related to the Trojans, evidenced in sources outside of Grecian history as well, who came from Javan's son R/Dodanim so many centuries ago.[58]

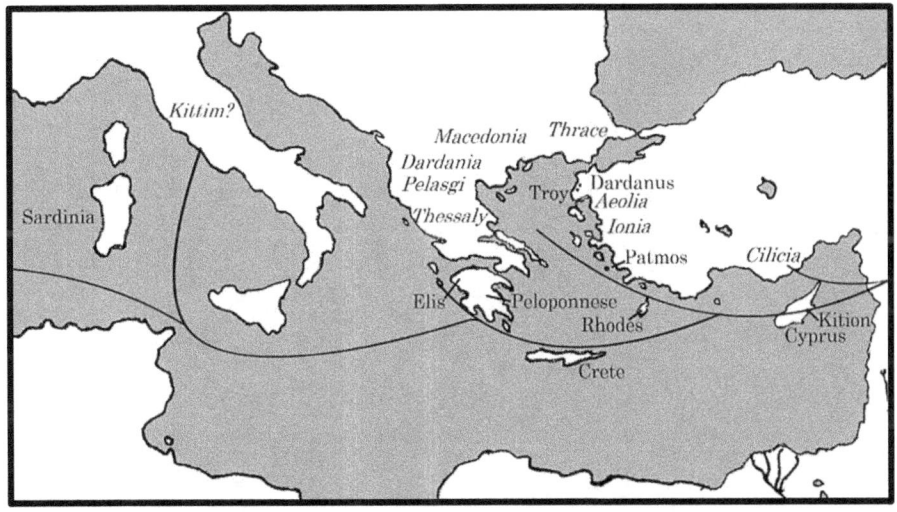

9: Tubal

Thou Shall be Brought

Tubal is the fifth son of Japheth listed in Scripture, and his name is תֻּבָל in Hebrew (Gen. 10:2, 1Ch. 1:5).[1] Besides the genealogies, his name also appears within the prophecies of both Isaiah and Ezekiel (Isa. 66:19, Ezk. 27:13, 32:26, 38:2-3, 39:1). There, Tubal is among other peoples of the earth who will hear of the Lord and glorify Him,

> "I will set a sign among them, and I will send some of those who survive to the nations – to Tarshish, to the Libyans and Lydians (famous as archers), to Tubal and Greece, and to the distant islands that have not heard of my fame or seen my glory. They will proclaim my glory among the nations." (Isa. 66:19)

Where is This Name Found?

In the book of Ezekiel, Tubal is mentioned along with Javan and Meshech as some of those who "exchanged slaves and articles of bronze" for the wares of Tyre (Ezk. 27:13). Later in Ezekiel, Tubal and Meshech are in a prophecy about Egypt, saying that they are "with all their hordes around their graves. ...because they spread their terror in the land of the living" (Ezk. 32:26). They are found together again with Gog of Magog, who appears to be the chief prince of these three peoples (Ezk. 38-39). When this happens or what these prophecies mean is unclear, but Scripture often connects these three nations.

The *Book of Jubilees* provides little information on Tubal other than that his location was near three "tongues," which could mean languages, rivers, or something else.[2] A reference in the *Book of Jasher* states that the "children of Tubal are those that dwell in the land of Tuskanah by the river Pashiah," but these names are enigmatic.[3] Though there is a resemblance to the name Tuscany in Italy, the etymology of that name is debatable. Perhaps instead of Tuscany, they were the Umbri, who Pliny considers to possibly be the oldest inhabitants of Italy, named so because they "survived the rains," or deluge, but these people likely came from a different son of Japheth and the above rivers and places have probably been lost to history.[4]

But Tubal, his land, and his people are not lost. Tubal's name comes in many forms. One is Tabal. Assyrian texts from Sennacherib's reign mention a place in southern Turkey called Tabalu or Tabal, that the Assyrians attacked along with the Til-garimmu.[5,6] Tiglath-Pileser, another Assyrian ruler, mentions the "land of Tabali," a people near to the Mushki and perhaps were the Thobelites of Josephus' works.[7,8] Some of Tubal's tribes possibly moved north, as did Meshech, and founded the city in Tobolsk in modern-day Siberia. Peoples such as the Scythians of Ashkenaz, the Togarmites, Meshech's people, and descendants of Ham, such as the Hittites also inhabited this area.[9,10]

Agreeing with the Assyrian sources, the *Royal Genealogies* say that the people of Meshech and Tubal lived near the "Euxine sea" and were "called Iberi, Tibareni, and Mofchi."[11] In a later part of the *Genealogies*, Tubal's son appears to be the namesake to the Ebro river, once called Iberus.[12] A *Brief History of Spain* again claims the same origin of Iberia, calling Tubal's son Iberus which gave rise to Iberi and Ebro.[13] The *Royal Genealogies* says Tubal himself also came to rule Iberia.[12] Similarly, the *Historia Brittonum* records that from Tubal "arose the Hebrei, Hispani, and Itali," two of which, if accurate, are clearly identifiable as the Hispani of Spain and the Itali of Italy.[14]

In a separate chronicle from Spain, the Iberians are said to have first been called the Cetubales, descended from Tubal.[15] According to a king of Spain, this name came from joining their word for tribe, "cetus," and their post-Flood forefather's name.[16] Over time, they changed from being called after Tubal to his son Iberus, who is sometimes called Ebro, and they came to be called Iberians.[16] Though they were collectively known as Iberians, the sons of Tubal split into multiple tribes, and their language would split and change with the tribes. Their language has been identified as Iberian, a mystery for most linguists. The Iberians prove a puzzle for many who have researched the Iberian Peninsula for this reason: They do not know from where they came.[17] They do not know because most researchers begin with the presupposition that the people had to originate in-situ or nearby, not by ship via Noah's sons.

Many of these tribes have been identified throughout the Iberian Peninsula. Some of the known tribes are the Bastetani, Bastuli, Carpetani, Ilergetes, and Oretani.[18] As mentioned in the chapter on Gomer, Tubal's descendants intermarried with the Celts, forming the Celtiberians of northern Spain, though they spoke a much different language than what is known today. Their language was adopted by new tribes that settled on the peninsula, changed by introduced languages, and replaced by others altogether. Spanish is considered a Romance language because of Rome's Latin influence.[19] Thus, the original Iberian language is now nonexistent.

Notable Mentions

The specific people known as Iberians do not necessarily need to be the only descendants of Tubal in Iberia. There are other people, such as the Vascones, who became the Basques, that seemed to have arisen out of nowhere; they may be of Tubal. Also, Arabic and Spanish legends tell of the division of Tubal's land among his three sons, Tarraho, Sem Tofail, and Iber.[20] The possibility that multiple sons of Tubal went to Iberia and Anatolia with Meshech's and Magog's people, not to mention elsewhere, is quite high. His sons may have taken the route through the Caucasians into Europe before settling in Iberia or taken ships like Javan's sons to get to the Peninsula. What is sure, though, is that the people of Iberia trace their lineage back to Noah and Adam.

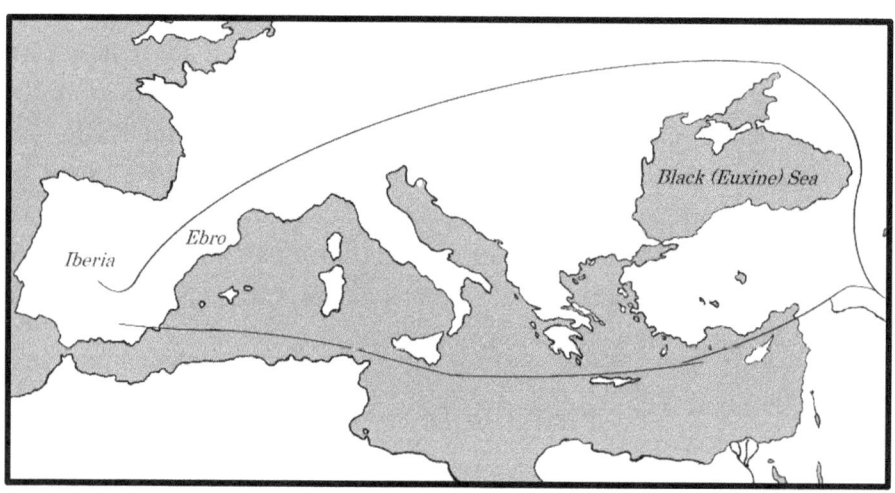

10: Meshech

Drawing Out

Scripture says Japheth's sixth son is Meshech, מֶשֶׁךְ in Hebrew.[1] Outside of the genealogies, the Old Testament mentions Meshech only a couple of times (Gen. 10:2, 1Ch. 1:5). The Psalmist writes of his people, "Woe to me that I dwell in Meshech, that I live among the tents of Kedar! Too long have I lived among those who hate peace" (Psa. 120:5-6). Meshech is found alongside his brothers Javan and Tubal in the lament against Tyre in the book of Ezekiel, as Meshech traded with that great Phoenician city (Ezk. 27:13). Meshech and Tubal are described with "hordes" and spreading terror, reaffirming the character of Meshech's people (Ezk 32:26).

Chapters 38-39 of the book of Ezekiel deal with nations mentioned before and some that will be discussed later: Magog, Tubal, Togarmah, Meshech, and Persia. Meshech is mentioned with Tubal three times in these two chapters (Ezk. 38:2-39:1). These two appear to have been near each other, and some of their tribes even combined. Gog of Magog is called the "chief prince of Meshech and Tubal" (Ezk. 38:2-3). Where does that put Meshech? Magog went to the far north in Europe, and Tubal had tribes in the east and west (Ezk. 38:15). Thus, Meshech appears to have settled in the North by his brothers.

Where is This Name Found?

The *Book of Jubilees* vaguely writes that Meshech received the "the sixth portion, all the region beyond the third tongue until it approaches the east of Gadir," possibly placing them just north and east of the Black Sea.[2] Josephus gives slightly more information about Meshech and his people. In his *Antiquities of the Jews*, Josephus writes that the "Mosocheni were founded by Mosoch; now they are the Cappadocians."[3] This information would place them in Anatolia and near the Tabali. Additionally, Josephus writes that there is still a "city call Mazaca" in that same area, claiming that it was named after the people of Meshech.[3] This city was known by many names, including Caesarea, the modern Kayseri.[4,5] Isidore's *Etymologies* says Meshech's location was in Cappadocia and the city of Mazaca.[6] Cappadocians were present on Pentecost to hear God's Word in their language (Acts 2:9).

Before they were the Cappadocians, they were known as the *Musku* by the Assyrians.[7] In the early days of Tiglath-Pileser I's reign, the *Mushkians* and "their five kings...came down" from the north "and seized the land of Kutmuhi."[8] This puts the *Mushki* north of Armenia as the *Kutmuhi* were the Commagene of Armenia; both were north of Assyria.[8] They were neighbors to the kingdom of Urartu, and they fought Assyria during Sargon's reign.[7] Herodotus and Pliny record the tribes of Meshech and Tubal as the Moschi and Tibareni as well as the Macrones and Mossynoeci.[9,10] In his *Anabasis*, Xenophon describes the Mossynoecians, near to the Moschi, as "white, the men and the women alike," worthy of note for the Grecian.[11] Strabo called them the Moschi and wrote that they lived near the Caucasus, having their own range called the Moschic near Armenia and Caucasus Iberia.[12]

The descendants of Meshech, unsurprisingly, traveled farther into the North. The *Royal Genealogies* recorded that they not only became the "Mofchi" near the Iberi and Tibareni, but they also became the "Mofcovites" of the North as well as "many other Northern Nations."[13] This would mean that some of the people of Meshech traveled into parts of Europe and Russia. Slavic histories imply that Meshech is the basis for the names of people and places like Muscovy and Moscow.[14] Others call the old name for Russia "*Moscovie*" and their chief city "*Mosco*."[15] The name given to Meshech in these histories is "*Mosokh*."[16] The

Synopsis says the name Moscow, which in Russian is "*Moskva,*" comes from "*Mosokh,*" son of "*Afet.*"[17,18] There is also the name of the Moskva River, flowing to Moscow, called "*Moscua.*"[15] Thus, Meshech's people spread from Babel to the far north, becoming some of the mid-northern nations in addition to a handful of settlements in Anatolia.

Notable Mentions

Research on the people of the Americas shows that the "natives" here are not native to these continents. Instead of arising suddenly, the Americas were settled by nomadic groups from Europe and Asia by land or sea. Consider how people might have crossed by land over the Bering Strait or by boat from Oceana to the Americas. Some of the people came from Scandinavia by traveling through northern Russia. Similarly, people of Togarmah and Ashkenaz spread across the middle of Asia from Armenia to Mongolia. The tribes of Meshech and Tubal moved into Europe and Eurasia. Each group went across the wasteland of Eurasia to the coast on the opposite side. In response to climatic changes caused by the Flood, the snow and ice of the Ice Age covered large swaths of the Northern Hemisphere.[19] This would have made previously unnavigable places traversable by foot.

These travels are documented in texts and genetic mapping. Genetic studies have shown the relationship between the people of the Americas with those of northern Asia and Europe.[20-25] You can essentially follow a genetic path from the area of the Babel event through the Eurasian Steppes to the Americas via land bridges and ocean travel. Though the dating methods are off, these genetic studies are useful in comparing the North American people to those in Europe and Asia, and largely to the line of Japheth.[26] While I do not think the people of Eurasia were the only people to travel to the Americas, I do believe that they made up most of the population in the North.

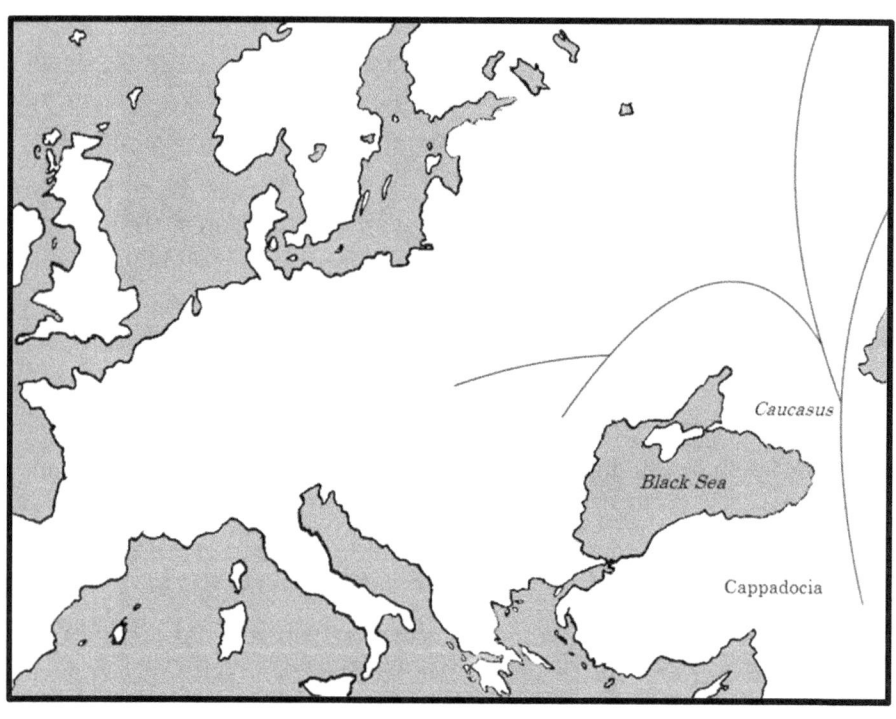

11: Tiras

Desire

Tiras is the seventh and final son of Japheth listed in Scripture (Gen. 10:2; 1Ch. 1:5). His name is תִּירָס in Hebrew and only appears twice in the entire Old Testament.[1] Thus, there is little known of his people from Scripture. The *Book of Jubilees* recorded Tiras as the seventh son of Japheth and states his land was "four great islands in the midst of the sea" and near a descendant of Shem.[2] Josephus' *Antiquities of the Jews*, however, provides a more definite location. He calls Tiras "Thiras" and his people the "Thirasians" whom the Greeks called the Thracians.[3] Likely, their name initially resembled something more like Tyrasia as Tyr lingered in their names for some time. Though Tiras' people were not always in Thrace, we will begin our search there.

Where is This Name Found?

The Thracians lived north of the Greeks and Macedonians, placing him near Javan's descendants.[4] It is unclear whether they sailed or traveled across land to get there from Babel. Isidore, like Josephus, considered the Thracians to be descendants of Tiras, "as if it were Tiracians."[5] Within their territory located in the southern part of Ukraine, there is a river once called Tyras, now the Dniester, with a port city by the same name.[6,7,8] While the tribes of Gomer and Magog inhabited this area, the name Tyras links this place to Tiras and his people.[7,9] Perhaps there is even a connection to the Alpine Tyrol. Tiras, as the father of the Thracians, also made an appearance in the Greek Pantheon, but that will be discussed at the end.[10,11,12]

The Thracians gave rise to many tribes that spread out across Europe. They also assimilated into other tribes. Consequently, their individual culture and language deteriorated, or simply changed, from the original. Some of the larger tribes and nations that sprouted up and out from the homeland were the Dacians, the Tyragetae, the Getae, the Odrysae, Romania, Ukraine, Serbia, Bulgaria, Hungary, and many more people and places.[8,13,14,15,18] The people of Tiras likely influenced the later Slavic languages and people.

Two additional groups are under much debate and mystery regarding their origins. While I maintain that more research is needed, I will offer some options. The first option is the Pelasgi, also known as the Tyrrhenian. Herodotus says these are the neighbors above the Thracians and whom Thucydides calls the *Tyrrheno-Pelasgians*, who settled in Lemnos.[16,17] Perhaps they were separate nations, but more likely, they were once one and then separated.[18] After some time, these Pelasgians moved into Italy along the Tiber.[19,20] Their neighbors were the Latini, Ombrici, and Sabini.[20]

This, of course, leads to the second contested group in Italia: the Etruscans. Their origins are perhaps more mysterious than the Pelasgi, and the following will explain the connection between these groups. As mentioned before, one city that the Pelasgi inhabited was Lemnos. This city is considered by some to have been inhabited by the Tyrsenoi, similar to the Tyrrhenians and Tiras.[21] Their name was the root of the Tyrrhenian Sea along Italy.[22] Yet this sea has another more familiar name: Tuscan.[23] This name, of course, is the same as Tuscany, Italy, which likely is derived from the name Etruscan. Etruscan was not the name of these people originally, as Strabo said they were first called the Tyrrheni, but were called the Tusci and Etrusci by the Romans.[20] Now, while the Pelasgi are likely one of the ancestors of the Etruscans, as explained above, other relatives were the Rhaeti, or Rasena, who lived in the mountains above Italia.[18,24,25,26] These people have been linked by language and location to Lemnos, likely via Tiras' Thracians.[27,28]

Two different pathways would have brought these people from the Illyrian peninsula to the Italian. The first is by land, going north from Thrace into what became the land of the Pelasgi. From there, they would pass through land primarily inhabited by Gomeric tribes and the Alpine regions of northern Italy. After that, there is nowhere to go except south into Italy, where the Etruscans are known to have lived. Another scenario is that they sailed from their northern domain around the boot of Italy to Tuscany, where the Etruscans are known to have dwelled. While this is likely, I prefer the former scenario, though the Thracians were known for seafaring. A group within the collective Sea Peoples known to the Egyptians were the *Teresh* or *Tursha*, who perhaps originated in Thrace with the Tyrrhenians, though such origins are up for debate.[29,30] The main point is that by traveling through the North, they would have mixed with many other tribes of Japheth, such as the Celts, the Germanic tribes, and even the Scythians dwelling in southern Europe. Though we need more research concerning these nations, many authors consider Tiras to be related to the mysterious Etruscans via the Thracians.[31,32,33]

Notable Mentions

Most nations recorded different gods within their genealogies and histories. Often, these gods came from ancestors who were key in a nation's founding or distant ancestry. Some nations took gods from other nations, and some kept "ancestors" that had little to do with ancestry. Such was the case with many Germanic and Scandinavian tribes of the North as well as Greece. They appear to have taken a couple of their gods from other nations, specifically Thrace.

Among the Greek pantheon, there was a god named Thrax who was considered the ancestor of the Thracians, though known later in history under the name Ares; another story says Tereus son of Mars was king of Thrace.[8,10] Many people made gods out of their ancestors, so Tiras was the reasonable basis for these gods.[11] About people's way of forming gods like themselves, one author wrote, "Thracians that theirs [gods] are blue-eyed and red-haired."[12]

The Thracians were known as a war-loving people alongside the Celts, Scythians, and other "warlike nations."[34] A couple of Germanic and Scandinavian gods had to do with war and fierceness, and these have names like Tyr and Thor. Tyr, clearly, resembles the Scriptural Tiras. Possibly deriving from the warlike Thracians, Tyr was a god of war.[35,36] Sometimes, as in the *Prose Edda*, Tyr is called a son of Odin, perhaps based on Noah, which often makes him brother to Thor.[36] It could be that they were originally one person, but with time and repeated storytelling, one man became two: Thor and Tyr. From Tyr, we get our Tuesday spelling, once *tiwesdaeg* in Old English, which came from *Tiwaz* or *Tiu*, the Germanic peoples' god of war.[37]

Thor may also have roots in Tiras. The *Prose Edda* by Sturluson gives a most intriguing history of his origins. The tale begins in "earth's centre" where the "goodliest of homes and haunts" held the city of Troy, across from Thrace.[36] Sturluson noted that Menon married Troan, Priam of Troy's daughter, and "they had a child called Tror," known to the writer and readers as Thor.[36] The legend describes him with hair "fairer than gold."[36] In other texts, he is red-bearded, like the Thracians.[38] The *Prose Edda*'s writer considered Asia to be the origin of Asgard.[36] Thrace, however, which Thor controlled, was called Thrudheim.[36] Like Tyr, Thor also got a weekday: Thursday.[39] Perhaps these two were derived from Tiras, or perhaps they were of another source altogether. Either way, these are probable connections between northern origin stories and Scripture.

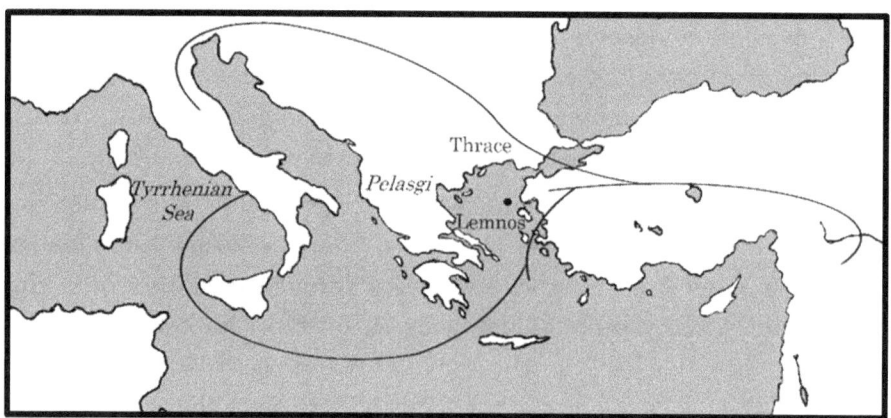

12: Ham

Hot

Ham is the second listed son of Noah, probably because of proximity to Shem, and is most likely the youngest of the brothers (Gen. 5:32, 6:10, 7:13, 9:18-24, 10:1-21, 1Ch. 1:4). According to the *Book of Jubilees*, Ham had a wife named Ne'elatama'uk and he built a city after her.[1] Ham's name has two different forms – חָם and חַם – in Scripture.[2,3] The latter is pronounced Ham, appearing only once, and means hot.[3] The other is nearly identical, Cham, and it is always translated into English as Ham or Hamite.[2] Many other historical texts prefer to use this spelling, and it is used most often in Scripture.[4] This name means hot and is often associated with Mizraim.

The Table of Nations

The Table of Nations describes the sons and descendants of Ham in greater detail than Japheth's, though not as much as Shem's. The detail found in Ham's records is because many of his people lived near to and frequently interacted with Shem's people. Ham's sons were Cush, Mizraim, Put, and Canaan (Gen. 10:6). Ham's grandsons through Cush are Seba, Havilah, Sabtah, Raamah, and Sabteca (Gen. 10:7). The name Havilah, a name also given to a son of Joktan, was likely derived from a pre-Flood location (Gen. 2:11, 10:7-29). Included also are the grandsons of Cush: Sheba and Dedan (Gen. 10:7). Finally, there is a sixth son of Cush: Nimrod, the "mighty hunter before the Lord" (Gen. 10:8-9). Scripture records that his kingdom dominated most of Mesopotamia (Gen. 10:10-12). This land, however, would later be primarily inhabited by Shem's descendants, namely Asshur. While the description is vague, "residents of Mesopotamia" were among those present on Pentecost (Acts 2:9).

Scripture also provides detailed lists of Mizraim and Canaan's descendants. Mizraim's sons were recorded as groups rather than specific sons as they are called "the Ludites, Anamites, Lehabites, Naphtuhites, Pathrusites, Casluhites (from whom the Philistines came) and Caphtorites" (Gen. 10:12-14). Canaan's descendants are Sidon, the Hittites, Jebusites, Amorites, Girgashites, Hivites, Arkites, Sinites, Arvadites, Semarites, and Hamathites (Gen. 10:15-18). Scripture says these clans "scattered" and their general border reached from Gaza in the south, to Sidon in the north, and a little past the Jordan on the east (Gen. 10:18-19).

Where Was His Land?

Just as Canaan's people scattered, so too did the people of Ham become distant to each other. Though Ham's descendants had their own land, some settled in the area settled by Shem and Japheth. In general, the territory of the Hamites was in Shinar, Canaan, and Africa. However, it appears that some of his people, along with some Japhetites, went to the far east and the Pacific.[5]

Early in Genesis, we learn that descendants of Ham from Shinar and of Shem from Elam went to war against their kin in Mesopotamia and Canaan, who are specifically said to be living in the land of Ham (Gen. 14). After their captivity, the Israelites returned from Egypt to their promised land, Canaan, where Hamites once dwelled (1Ch. 4:40-41). Three Psalms speak of the land of Ham relative to Mizraim. The first is on the tenth plague and the death of the firstborn or "first fruits" of Ham (Psa. 78:51). Later, the Psalmist writes, "Then Israel entered Egypt; Jacob lived as an alien in the land of Ham. ...they performed miraculous signs among them, his wonders in the land of Ham" (Psa.

105:23-27). In another, "They [Israel] forgot the God who saved them, who had done great things in Egypt, miracles in the land of Ham and awesome deeds by the Red Sea" (Psa. 106:22). These Psalms sing of Israel's history, God's faithfulness, and Africa's ancestry in Ham.

Ham's descendants are the same in the *Book of Jasher* except for a different spelling of Mizraim and additional sons of Phut.[6] The record notes that the cities his descendants built were named after their "fathers," and the *Book of Jubilees* implies this was after Noah's people "began to divide the earth" (Gen. 10:25).[7,8] The land of Ham is said to be hot, agreeing with the meaning of his name.[9]

> *"And for Ham came forth the second portion, beyond the Gihon towards the south ... it extends towards the west to the sea of 'Atel and ... till it reaches the sea of Ma'uk... it goes forth towards the north to the limits of Gadir and it goes forth to the coast of the waters of the sea to the waters of the great sea till it draws to the river Gihon ... and this is the land which came forth for Ham as the portion which he was to occupy for himself and his sons unto their generations for ever."*[10]

In his *Antiquities of the Jews*, Josephus names the places Ham's descendants once settled. He found it important to point out that some of the names "utterly vanished," and others were "changed" and "another sound given them, are hardly to be discovered."[11] There is, however, still hope since there are "a few ...which have kept their denominations entire."[11] Thus, some places Ham and his descendants traveled to can be found via etymology and history. Josephus says that "Chus" became Ethiopia.[11] To Mizraim, he gave the name "Mesarites," which is Egypt, called by Judeans "Mestre" and by "the Egyptians Mestreans."[11] Phut he says founded Libya and the Phutites.[11] He notes that part of this area is now called Lybyos and is near one of Mizraim's sons.[11] Canaan, the last and youngest, is known for inhabiting Judea, known previously as the land of Canaan.[11] Though most of the sons went to Africa, a few stayed in Shem's land.

Notable Mentions

In Scripture, Ham is closely associated with Egypt, and he possibly became an Egyptian god. Egyptian kingship and ancestry are as confusing as their mythology. At times, two relatives once distantly related become siblings. Such is the case of the Egyptian gods Horus and Set, also called Seth. In some sources, these two are brothers.[12] In the texts where they are brothers, Horus was to be "Lord of the Black Land," and Seth is the "Lord of the Red Land, the desert."[13] This could relate to Ham as the ruler of Africa and Shem of the Middle East.

Another fascinating association with Ham is in a place called Hamazi, mentioned in the Sumerian text *Enmerkar and the Lord of Aratta*. In this text, the land of "Subur and Hamazi" is called "many-tongued" and near Sumer, which is Shinar.[14] In this location, the Sumerian god Enki changed "the speech in their mouths."[15] Perhaps *Hamazi* was the land of Ham, becoming "many-tongued" after the god "Enki" multiplied their speech.

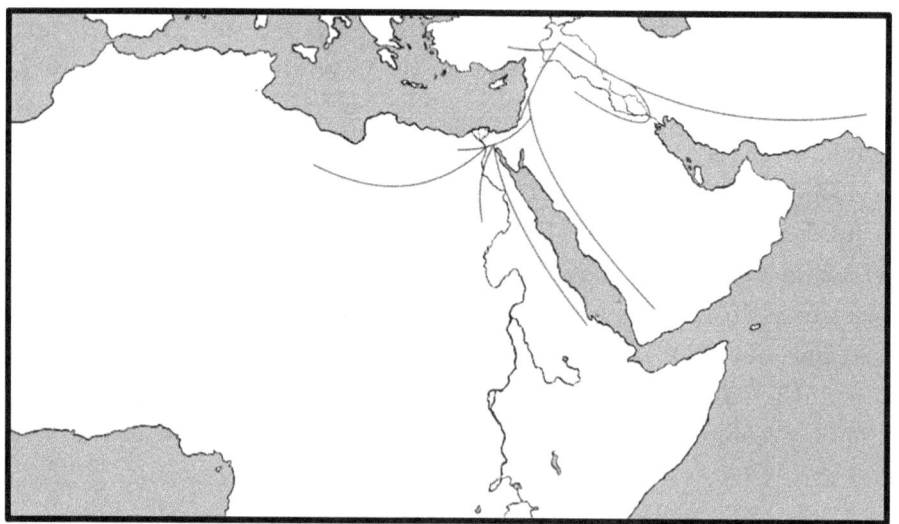

13: Cush

Black

Cush is the first son of Ham recorded in Scripture (Gen. 10:6). He had six sons: Seba, Havilah, Sabtah, Raamah, Sabteca, and, listed separately from his brothers, Nimrod (Gen. 10:6-7). In addition, Scripture includes two grandsons: Sheba and Dedan (Gen. 10:7). According to the *Book of Jubilees*, Cush, along with his father and brother Mizraim, tried to warn Canaan from settling in the land of Shem rather than his own inheritance.[1] The descendants of Cush are mentioned frequently in Scripture. In fact, there are five different words used relating to Cush and his descendants and fifty-one references to either Cush or his people in Scripture. But to better understand what his name means, we will have to look also at where his name is found.

Where is This Name Found?

The first word used for the people of Cush is כּוּשׁ, translated as Ethiopia, Cush, "black," or Ethiopians (Gen. 10:6-8, 1Ch. 1:8-10).[2] Cush was also a pre-Flood land, where his name likely derived (Gen. 2:13). Cush's land is described as a place to find precious jewels, such as topaz (Job 28:19). During the time of Israel's kings, Scripture mentions King Tirhakah of Ethiopia, who had control of Upper Egypt (2Ki. 19:9). The

Medo-Persian Empire later controlled this land (Est. 1-9). Scripture says Cush's people would know the glory of God (Psa. 68:31, 87:4). In the remaining passages, Ethiopia is part of many prophecies alongside Egypt, Lydia, Libya, and Put, some of which are brothers of Cush.[3]

Another word for the descendants of Cush is כּוּשִׁי, which is Ethiopian or Cushi in English, meaning "their blackness."[4] A Cushite brings the news of Absalom's death to King David (2Sa. 18:21-23, 31-32). When Rehoboam becomes king, Egypt, under King Shishak, attacks Israel with the aid of Libyan, Sukite, and Cushite troops (2Ch. 12:3). A Cushite army attacks Israel again during the reign of King Asa of Judah (2Ch. 14:9-13, 16:8). Some Philistines and Arabs, who were against Jehoram of Judah, lived near the Cushites (2Ch. 21:16). Jeremiah mentions the Cushites twice; one passage is about an official named Ebed-Melech who, seeing the evil done to Jeremiah, saved him from a cistern (Jer. 13:23, 38:7-12). Later, Ebed-Melech was saved from destruction in the fall of Judah (Jer. 39:16). The book of Daniel mentioned the Nubians but used the same word for Ethiopians, which implies they were once one and the same people (Dan. 11:43). Two final prophecies speak on Cush's destruction (Amo. 9:7; Zep. 2:12).

The word כּוּשִׁית is used in Numbers to describe Moses' wife (Num. 12).[5] This word specifically translates to mean a Cushite or Ethiopian woman. Moses' wife, Zipporah, was a Midianite (Exo. 2:15-21). Midian may have partial ancestry in Cush, as even Habakkuk writes, "I saw the tents of Cushan in distress, the dwellings of Midian in anguish" (Hab. 3:7). Midian was northeast of Egypt and Cush.[6] This would place some of the Cushites in the southwestern part of modern-day Saudi Arabia where some of the sons of Cush dwelled. While a different Hebrew word is used here for Cush, כּוּשָׁן, it is likely that these people are of Cushan and Abrahamic descent (Gen. 25:1-2).[7]

In Sumer, there was a city called Kish.[8] According to the *Sumerian King List*, Kish, or Kis, was the first place where there were kings.[9] Furthermore, the *Sumerian King List* recorded a flood that swept over and "kingship was lowered from heaven."[9] This tale would have been derived from the Deluge and Babel. Kish, a prominent city in early Sumer, was possibly founded by either Cush or Nimrod.[8,10,11]

The land of Cush was larger than what modern-day Ethiopia encompasses. At one point, it was the kingdom of Kush and ruled by King Tirhakah, who took over part of Egypt.[12] In his annals, Assurbanipal recorded that Tirhakah was king of "Ku-u-si," which is Ethiopia or Kush.[12] In Egyptian records, there are multiple references to Kush after Egypt regained their nation.[13,14] But in these texts, this nation is often referred to as the "wretched Kush," perhaps because of their history.[15] This same king of Kush later met defeat at the hand of King Esarhaddon, who made himself king of Kush.[16] The land is referred to in the *Tell El-Armana Letters* as the land of Kashi.[17] This area, of course, was greater than the Ethiopia known today and included Nubia as well as Sudan.[18,19] Most intriguingly, the Beja people are to have come from Kush and traveled "to the Sudan after the Flood."[20]

Notable Mentions

This large land of Cush that the ancient sources and Scripture speak of is the same place. Of course, Cush's sons also had their own tribes and nations, and not all were in Africa. Like many in Mesopotamia, the people of the western coast of Saudi Arabia near the Red Sea were of both Ham and Shem. They all would have been among the peoples represented on the day of Pentecost (Acts 2:9-11). But as Josephus writes, "time has not hurt the name of Chus; for the Ethiopians... are even at this day, both by themselves and all men in Asia, called Chusites."[21] While the name appears in different forms, it is relatively unchanged from the Cush of Scripture. The last place Scripture mentions them uses the Greek word for Ethiopia, which is Αἰθίοψ.[22] The passage is about the ministry of Philip when he followed the Spirit and was brought to an Ethiopian eunuch, "an important official in charge of all the treasury of Candace (which means "queen of the Ethiopians")" (Acts 8:27). Philip ministered the Gospel to this man and baptized him, bringing the faith to the people of Ham.

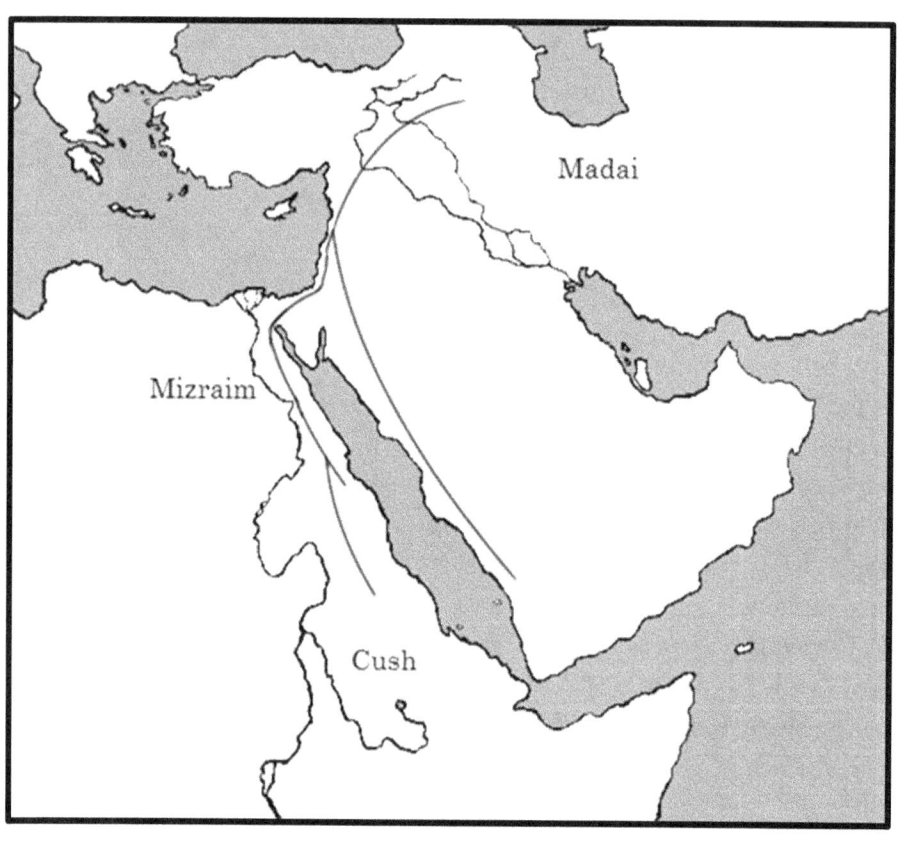

14: The Sons of Cush

Unlike the sons of Japheth, Ham's sons are found frequently in Scripture. Perhaps this is because they stayed closer to the descendants of Shem. As it is Shem's people through Abraham that we received the Scriptures, and that is the basis for this book, staying in proximity to the main figures of Scripture would result in more detail about those other people. They also, like most Middle Easterners, share some history and genealogy with Shem. Parts of their land were later ruled by or with some of Shem's descendants. In general, their land covered the area given to Ham, south of his brothers, where the land is hot. Here we will discuss each of Cush's sons. Nimrod, however, will be given his own section as he is surrounded in mystery, legend, and infamy. While none of them are mentioned specifically, because of where they lived, their descendants should be included among the representatives of the nations present at Pentecost (Acts 2:11).

Seba

The first son of Cush is Seba (Gen. 10:7). Though the name Seba, סְבָא in Hebrew, only appears four times in Scripture, there is a strong connection between his people and those of his nephew, Sheba, son of Raamah (Gen.10:7, 1Ch.1:9, Psa. 72:10, Isa. 43:3).[1] Sometimes these two relatives' names are translated identically. They likely merged, becoming one nation in the southern part of the Arabian Peninsula. According to Josephus, Seba is called Sabas and was the "founder of the Sabeans," the same as Sabas, son of Ragmus, another ancestor of the Sabeans.[2] Most other sources confirm that the people of Seba joined with his nephew Sheba's people to become the Sabeans.[3,4]

Havilah

Havilah is the second son of Cush recorded in Scripture (Gen. 10:7). Like his father, Havilah was named after an antediluvian location (Gen. 2:11). He had a common name like Seba, Sheba, and Dedan as it was also the name of a son of Joktan, brother to Peleg (Gen. 10:29). These latter people were probably named after the land the sons of Cush settled in. Havilah in Hebrew is חֲוִילָה and means circle.[5] Josephus refers to Havilah as Evilas, founder of the Evileans.[2] The descendants of Ishmael settled in the area "from Havilah to Shur, near the border of Egypt" (Gen. 25:16-18). When fighting the Amalekites, Saul attacked "from Havilah to Shur, to the east of Egypt" (1Sm. 15:7). Shur, the desert Moses led the Israelites through, was opposite Egypt on the Red Sea (Ex. 15:22). These people are said to have lived there since "ancient times" (1Sa. 27:8).

Sabtah

The third son of Cush, Sabtah, is only mentioned twice in Scripture and only in the genealogies, though his name is missing the 'h' in the second list (Gen. 10:7, 1Ch. 1:9). His name is סַבְתָּא in Hebrew.[6] Josephus calls him Sabathes and the founder of the Sabathens, who were called "by the Greeks, Astaborans."[2] Their name was preserved in the river running opposite the land of Sheba in the land of Cush. The Sembritae, possibly Josephus' Astaborans, inhabited the area around the Astaboras river.[7] Some of them may have also dwelled on the other side of the Red Sea near the other sons of Cush and founded a city called Saptah or Saptha.[8]

Raamah

Raamah is the fourth son of Cush recorded in Scripture (Gen. 10:7). He also has two sons listed along with him: Sheba and Dedan (Gen 10:7). Raamah, רַעְמָה in Hebrew, comes from a word meaning the "mane of a horse," though used only in Job when God speaks (Job 39:19).[9,10] This word comes from רַעַם or *ra'am*, meaning thunder.[11] The King James translates this passage from Job beautifully: "Have you clothed his neck with thunder?"[12] Besides the genealogies, Raamah is only mentioned again with his son Sheba, both merchants of spices, precious stones, and gold and who traded with Tyre (Ezk. 27:22).

Near the land of Sheba, there was once a nation called the Rhammaniae.[7] Strabo mentions that their town Marsiaba, which the Romans attacked, was near the "aromatic region," or the place where there were spices.[7] This city is in modern-day Yemen.[13] Another ancient city in this vicinity was Ragmat, now known as Najran.[14] This city took part in a battle against the Assyrians who took treasures but not the city.[15] These places may have been named after Ramaah.

As mentioned before, Sheba appears to be connected to Seba. Together, they became the kingdom of Sheba or the Sabeans. The name Sheba seems to have been rather popular. The Hebrew word for the Cushite Sheba is שְׁבָא, but another very similar word denotes some Israelites, appearing as שֶׁבַע ten times in Scripture.[16,17,18] Besides this, there are six other names derived from the name Sheba, including places like Beersheba and the woman Bathsheba.[19] The name appears twice in the genealogy of Shem, once as a son of Joktan and again as a grandson of Abraham (Gen. 10:28, 25:3, 1Ch. 1:22-32). The name means seven or oath.[20]

Now the people of Seba and Sheba most likely became the one country of Sheba, whose people are the Sabeans. The Sabeans themselves are mentioned only a handful of times in Scripture. The earliest record is likely from the book of Job when the Sabeans attacked Job's land and took his livestock (Job 1:14-15). For words etymologically derived from Seba, Isaiah places them alongside the Ethiopians, noting that they are tall men; Ezekiel notes they live in the desert (Isa. 45:14,

Ezk. 23:42).[21] Joel simply says the Sabeans, etymologically linked to Sheba, are "far away" (Joe. 3:8).[22]

The best-known account is of the queen of Sheba's visit to Solomon, bringing with her gifts of "gold, large quantities of spices, and precious stones" (1Ki. 10:1-13, 2Ch. 9:1-12). Job mentions the merchants of Sheba and the Psalms speak on their kings and wealth (Job 6:19, Psa. 72:10-15). Sheba is most often mentioned in relation to its merchants and wealth in gold and spices (Isa. 60:6, Jer. 6:20, Ezk 27:22-23, 38:13). In one verse, Sheba is included alongside other merchants: Raamah, Dedan, and Tarshish (Ezk. 27:22, 38:13).

The land of the Sabeans was in the lower part of the Arabian Peninsula that is now Yemen.[23,24,25] This area was known to be good for trade in "precious metals and spices," as Scripture indicates.[26] Strabo recorded these people as well, stating that a notable city of theirs is Sabata, possibly named after Seba or Sabtah, as well as a port called Saba.[7] He recorded that the Sabeans were traders of perfumes, spices, precious stones, and metals, some of which were "brought from Ethiopia," becoming quite rich from it.[7] Pliny calls them the Sabaei who were "the best known of all the tribes of Arabia, on account of their frankincense."[27] Their territory extended from "sea to sea," notably the Red Sea between them and Cush.[27]

Dedan is the second son of Ramaah (Gen. 10:7, 1Ch. 1:9). Jokshan, a son of Abraham, also had a son named Dedan, who fathered nations in the northern part of the Arabian Peninsula (Gen. 25:3, 1Ch. 1:32). Dedan and the Dedanim, דְדָן and דְדָנִי, respectively, are mentioned several times in Scripture.[28,29] There is, however, little distinction between the Semite and Cushite Dedan. All their people lived within the Arabian Peninsula and are associated with the desert. The Dedan mentioned in Jeremiah is associated with Edom, Tema, and Buz (Jer. 25:23, 49:8). In the Arabian Peninsula, there is a city now called Al-'Ula, once called Dedan, near Tayma, the Tema of Jeremiah.[30] Teman and Dedan are mentioned together also in a prophecy against Edom (Ezk. 25:13). Ezekiel places Dedan near Sheba, and Isaiah puts Dedan near Tema (Ezk. 27:13-20, Isa. 21:13).

Lastly, Ezekiel describes Sheba and Dedan as merchants (Ezk. 38:13). These people seem different in some ways, but they were definitely related and interacted with each other. Scripture places them between the Cushites and Semites, and the similar names imply a similar location. One scenario is that the Dedan of Cush settled near his brother Sheba. Later, Jokshan named his son Dedan after the land where he lived. This may be why there is no distinction between these two peoples in Scripture. Some scholars would like to place Dedan on the Persian Gulf, but I have yet to see evidence for this.[31]

Sabteca

Like Sabtah, Sabteca is only mentioned twice in Scripture, both within genealogies (Gen. 10:7, 1Ch. 1:9). He was the fifth son of Cush recorded in Scripture. His name is סַבְתְּכָא in Hebrew.[32] Josephus refers to him as Sabactus and claims he fathered the Sabactens.[2] Some writers think he joined with his brother Sabtah, hence why we know so little about this son.[3,4] Outside of Josephus, I have found no mention of the Sabactens in history, and it is reasonable to assume that he remained with his brothers, possibly in Yemen.

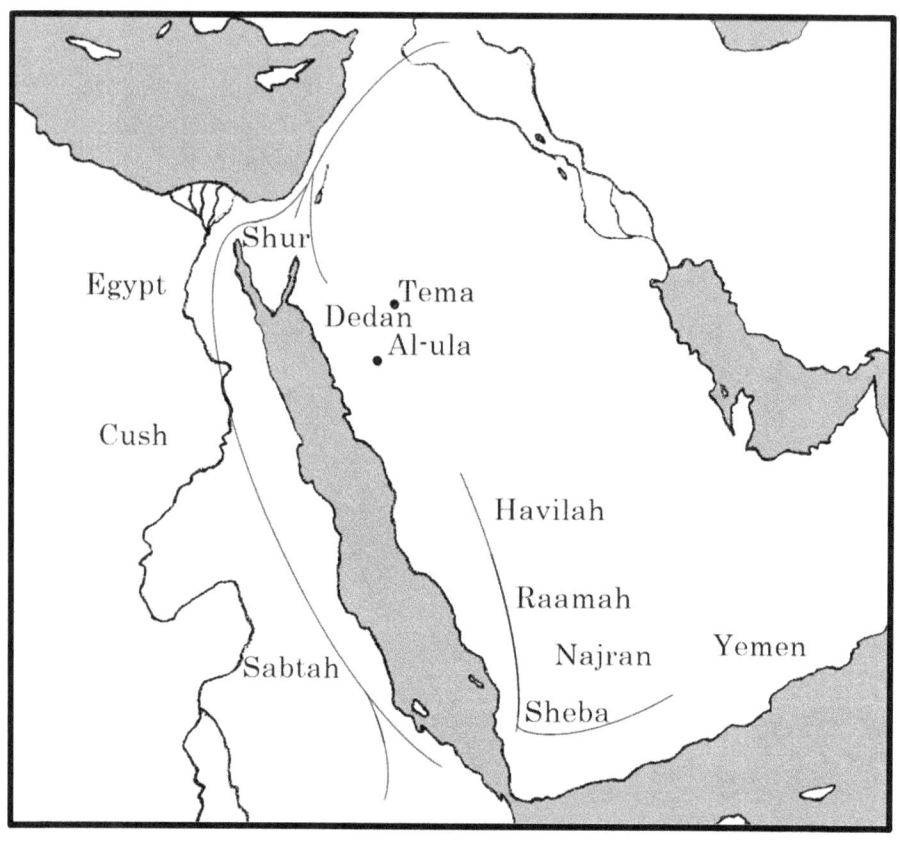

15: Nimrod

Rebellion

Nimrod is one of the most curious characters in Scripture, though he is in only four verses, two of which are in this passage from Genesis: "Cush was the father of Nimrod, who grew to be a mighty warrior on the earth. He was a mighty hunter before the Lord; that is why it is said, 'Like Nimrod, a mighty hunter before the Lord'" (Gen. 10:8-9). A similar statement is found elsewhere, "Cush was the father of Nimrod, who grew to be a mighty warrior on earth" (1Ch. 1:10). His name is נִמְרֹד in Hebrew, and he often is associated with rebellion.[1] But many questions remain on who Nimrod was. Why was he called a mighty hunter? Why is he singled out from Cush's other sons? Was it because he was the youngest or that he was ambitious in founding cities and a kingdom? There are many more questions than these, but I will answer what I can in the following.

One text states Nimrod was the son of Cush's "old age" and of a different wife than his other sons.[2] All else that we know of him is what Scripture says of his cities: Babylon, Erech, Akkad, Calneh, Nineveh, Rehoboth Ir, Calah, and Resen (Gen. 10:10-12). These cities, the focus of the history concerning Nimrod, are unlikely to be all the cities he founded. Rather, they appear to have been his greatest, for they are called the "first centers of his kingdom," and his land grew from them. This land and its surroundings are generally referred to as Mesopotamia, and it was from this area that people traveled to Jerusalem and heard the Gospel at Pentecost (Acts 2:9).

Nimrod's Great Cities

Nimrod's first city recorded in Scripture is Babel, though frequently translated as Babylon. Babylon was a great city and empire recorded so often in Scripture – nearly three hundred times – that it would be difficult to review every single occurrence here.[3] The same word used in the description of Nimrod's kingdom is found right after the Table of Nations in Genesis in the account of the Tower of Babel (Gen. 10:10, 11:1-9). Mankind was divided by language because they disobeyed God by not filling the earth after the Flood and for turning to false gods. While Scripture does not say who instigated the building, other ancient records claim that it was Nimrod who incited the sons of Ham, Shem, and Japheth to build the Tower.[4,5] In these accounts, he is considered the king of Babel, among other locations.

The word for Babel and Babylon is often translated the same. Both Babylon and Babel were on the plain of Shinar. However, Scripture does not state that the Tower was in the city of Babylon or that these are necessarily the same place.[6] This does not mean that Nimrod could not have founded both places separately, however. Furthermore, Babel may have been located at a more northern location than where the city of Babylon is.[60] In Hebrew, Babel, or בָּבֶל, means confusion, and this is what occurred at that event.[7] This word, though only translated as *Babel* twice, is essentially the same used throughout Scripture for Babylon, whether city or empire.[3,7,8] But the name Babylon as the modern reader knows it comes from the Greeks, who got the name from an Akkadian transliteration *Bab-il* or *Babilan(i)*.[9] The Sumerian name was *Ka-dingirra*.[9,10] *Babil* meant "gate of god" or "gate of the gods," which may trace its etymology to the Tower, but the Hebrew *Babel* means confusion, so the connection is strained.[9,11,12]

Regardless of location, Babylon was clearly an important city. Despite the important role Babylon plays in history, it appears the city fell into obscurity for many centuries while Akkad, Assyria, and other nearby nations took prominence in the region.[12,13] Their people also became intertwined with the Chaldeans, who will be discussed in the chapter on Arphaxad. Many kings of Babylon came from the Akkadians, Assyrians, Amorites, Kassites, and Chaldeans.[12] Babylon was recognized as an important city, especially regarding the god Marduk.[13] This center of idol worship may have also originated with Nimrod. Today, we find Babylon in modern-day Iraq.[12]

A handful of Babylon's kings are included in Scripture. Josephus says, "Nimrod, the son of Chus, stayed and tyrannized Babylon..." and he was likely Babylon's first king.[14] The first king found in Scripture is a man of Chaldean heritage named Merodach-Baladan II, son of Baladan (2Ki. 20:12, Isa. 39:1).[15] He sends King Hezekiah a gift and letter after King Hezekiah recovers from his illness. This king is known by many additional names: Marduk-apla-iddina II, Marduk-Baladan, and Berodach-Baladan.[15,16] His reign is well known from Babylonian chronicles, and just like Hezekiah, he reigned during the time of Sargon in Assyria.[15,16] Nebuchadnezzar, son of Nabopolassar the Chaldean, is a well-known figure from Scripture as he conquered Judah and led the Israelites into captivity, most notably Daniel and his friends (2Ki. 24:1-20, 25:1-8, Ezr. 5:12, Dan. 1:1-4:37).[17,18] Nabopolassar was technically king during the beginning part of the reign of Nebuchadnezzar, but he was so ill he was unable to rule and instead dwelled in a desert city while his son established the kingdom.[17,18,19]

Amel-Marduk, son of Nebuchadnezzar, in his first year as king of Babylon freed Jehoiachin 37 years after the king of Judah was taken into captivity (2Ki. 25:27, Jer. 52:31).[19] Though Babylonian records do mention this king, he is found infrequently, and it appears his rule was short-lived.[20] He appears to have possibly been murdered by his brother-in-law Neriglissar (Jer. 39:3-13).[21] The last ruler of Babylon included in Scripture is Belshazzar, son of Nabonidus and descendant of Nebuchadnezzar, possibly his grandson (Dan. 5:1-31).[22] During his reign, the kingdom of Babylon fell to the Medes and Persians. Belshazzar was not exactly a king but rather ruled in his father's stead while Nabonidus fought in Arabia, making Belshazzar second in the kingdom but "de facto king of Babylon."[22,23] This is why Belshazzar makes Daniel the third highest ruler in the kingdom during that night when Babylon fell to the Medes and the Persians.[23,24]

A place near to Babylon was a city called Kish. It is possible that while this was not a center of his kingdom, Kish may have been named after Nimrod's father, Cush. In a list of Sumerian Kings, the first king of Kish ruled "after the flood had swept" over.[25] These are the kings of the *Sumerian King List*: Al-lulim, Alalgar, En-men-lu-Anna, Wn-men-gal-Anna, Dumu-zi, En-sipa-zi-Anna, En-men-dur-Anna, Ubar-Tutu, and then the flood "swept over," after which "Ga[...]ur" ruled Kish.[26] This list is not perfect. Still, it was likely based on the pre-Flood patriarchs. This first post-flood king was not likely Nimrod, but the city could have been named after Cush. The most intriguing fact is that the account mentions a flood that divides the list of kings. Furthermore, the reigns of the kings shorten dramatically after the flood.[25] The Kassites, likely related to Madai, later settled in this city.[27,28]

Erech is the second city of Nimrod's kingdom, listed after Babel. Though not as famous as others, the city lasted a while after its founding. According to the *Sumerian King List*, Enmerkar founded the city, called Uruk in Sumerian, but his father, Mesh-ki-ang-gasher, first ruled there.[25] This king could perhaps be Cush if Enmerkar were Nimrod. Enmerkar was the same person who dealt with the lord of Aratta in the epic that includes an account on the confusion of tongues by the god Enki.[29] This same god was the one who saved mankind from the flood by means of a man named Utnapishtim in the Gilgamesh epic.[30] Atrahasis, another name for Utnapishtim, has his own account, strikingly similar to Genesis. This story recounts when their god Enki directly warned him of the coming flood.[31] Atrahasis is the one whom Enki chose to spare, who also, according to their legends, was the god who led to the creation of man.[31] The Babylonians retold the creation account, noting that man resembled a god.[31] In the *Epic of Gilgamesh*, Gilgamesh built up the walls of Uruk, though Enmerkar founded the city.[32] These people could have been based on their biblical counterparts, or perhaps these are the Sumerian names of the people themselves!

Akkad is the third city founded by Nimrod in Scripture (Gen. 10:10). The Babylonians called themselves *MAT Akkadi*, showing the relation between the peoples and cities founded by Nimrod and perhaps implying a more northern origin for Babel.[12] The area surrounding these cities was known as "the Land of Sumer and Akkad" in some cuneiform texts.[6] The city was known as *a-ga-dè*[KI].[33,34] Despite being a great city and frequently recorded, the exact location of Akkad is still uncertain. However, it was probably along the same path of cities founded by Nimrod in the plain of Shinar between the two great rivers. Though many scholars are puzzled by the location and founding of Akkad, they know it was ancient, that it became the center for the Akkadians and the Akkadian language – known in Assyria, Egypt, Babylon, and Medo-Persia – and that the name is of external, ancient origin.[33,34]

Calneh is the fourth city of Nimrod (Gen. 10:10). The Hebrew word is כַּלְנֵה, appearing three times in Scripture, discussed in the following, but with two spellings: Calneh and Calno (Gen. 10:10).[35] In His judgment against Assyria, God said, "Has not Calno fared like Carchemish? Is not Hamath like Arpad, and Samaria like Damascus?" pointing out that God punished their idolatry, and Assyria would not escape either (Isa. 10:9). Similarly, Calneh is mentioned alongside Hamath in a warning against complacency (Amo. 6:1-2). Twice Carchemish is said to have been alongside the Euphrates, so Calneh was either nearby or in the Assyrian Empire (2 Chr. 35:20, Jer. 46:2).

Genesis states Nimrod's kingdom was in the plain of Shinar: "The centers of his kingdom were...in Shinar" (Gen. 10:10). The Hebrew word for Shinar, שִׁנְעָר, appears eight times in Scripture, and its plain was the general location chosen to build the Tower (Gen. 10:10, 11:2, 14:1-9, Jos. 7:21, Isa. 11:11, Dan. 1:2, Zec. 5:11).[36] While many place this location in the south near the city of Babylon, new geological research is showing that this may have been impossible so soon after the Flood and so long before the Ice Age.[60] A new location is in the north in an area still known as Sinjar.[6] Evidence from archaeology, linguistics, and geology is showing this northern area to be the best location of the city and tower of Babel.[60]

Genesis records a war with Shinar's King Amraphel (Gen. 14:1-9). Here, these kings of Mesopotamia joined forces to rebel against Kedorlaomer (Gen. 14:1-12). Daniel recorded Israel going into the land of Shinar, and Isaiah tells of God calling them out (Dan. 1:2, Isa. 11:11). While Shinar is often translated as Babylon, this land within Mesopotamia known as Sumer was not simply the Babylonian kingdom.[6] Sumer is considered the birthplace of civilization. Though the dates are often unbiblical, scholars recognize that from Sumer come the oldest written documents and archaeological sites.[37] Sumer was known in many places around the ancient Near East. Egypt referred to the land as *Sngr*[4] or *Saenkara*, and as *Sanhar* or *Sanhara* by the Hittites.[6] The Sumerians called their language *Emegir* and their homeland *Ki-en-gi(r)*, which seems to mean "land (of) Sumerian tongue."[38,39,60] And as mentioned above, Sinjar is the modern name.[60] Elsewhere in Scripture, the land of Nimrod is said to be Assyria, further inferring a northern location for Babel, and this follows what Genesis says – that Nimrod founded Assyrian cities called Nineveh, Rehoboth Ir, Calah, and Resen (Mic. 5:6, Gen. 10:11-12). Later, however, this land was ruled and named by Shem's son Asshur (Gen. 10:22).

Nineveh is in Assyria and is best known from the account of Jonah. In fact, the book of Jonah contains the most references to the great city (Jon. 1:2, 3:2-7, 4:11). In these passages, Nineveh is described as a "very important city – a visit required three days" (Jon. 3:3). Jonah was sent to the Ninevites to warn them of God's wrath, and they repented of their sins, an event retold by Christ (Mat. 12:41, Luk 11:30). Nineveh was known as *Ninua* and *Ninuwa* in Sumerian and as *URU.NINA.KI-a* or *Ninua* in Akkadian.[40,41]

Nineveh is the city to which Sennacherib of Assyria departed after the destruction of his army by the hand of God (2Ki. 19:36, Isa. 37:37). Sennacherib referred to Nineveh as his "royal city," that is, his capital of Assyria.[42] But the city would not stay great forever, and Scripture prophesied her destruction. While Zephaniah records only a small passage of her end, Nahum is entirely devoted to the prophecy of destruction against the great city and nation (Nah., Zep. 2:13). The fall of Nineveh was recorded later, even mocked, as Phoclides noted "Nineveh in its folly" is not as strong as a "city settled upon a rock."[43,44] Now, the city lies in ruins.

The city of Calah, called *Kalhu* by Assyria, was the royal city of Sargon II and Esarhaddon before the capital was moved to Nineveh.[45]

Assuretililani was the one who made the city great, even after his ancestor Assurbanipal built a palace there.[46] In later times, the city was called Nimrud, its present name, located south of Mosul and just outside of Nineveh's ruins.[47] Here, there were two gods of some importance to the discussion of Nimrod: Ninurta and Nabu. To begin, Nabu is fascinating because he was considered the son of both Marduk and of Asher, the chief gods of Babylon and Assyria, and his temple was in Calah.[48,49,50] This god was worshiped under the names Nabu and Nabum across Mesopotamia and is considered the god of writing.[49,51] He had a ziggurat temple at Borsippa, within Calah, called Birs-Nimrud and another at Nineveh.[25,49,50,52] Ninurta was a god of the "rebel lands" in some tales, a warrior in others, and a great hero involved with the flood.[53,54] Perhaps either of these two gods, along with others, were derived from the stories about Nimrod.

The name Rehoboth Ir is mentioned a handful of times in Scripture, but only once concerning Nimrod (Gen. 10:11, 26:22). A "Shaul of Rehoboth on the river" was one of the successive kings of Edom (Gen. 36:37, 1Ch. 1:48). This river is likely one of those which flowed through Shinar, where Nimrod founded his kingdom. Though the actual location has yet to be discovered, it may be that the city became inconsequential or was part of the area surrounding Nineveh.

Resen should be in the general area between Nineveh and Calah, but no specific site has yet been found (Gen. 10:12). There are multiple ancient cities in the vicinity of Nineveh and Calah, but with it being so difficult to do research in the area, not much is known of them. For example, some nearby and particularly interesting research sites are Tell Al-Rimah and Karemlash.[55] Still, neither site shows much more signs of being Resen than any number of others in the area. This city may be another on a list of those lost to history.

Notable Mentions of a Mighty Man

Thus, Nimrod was a man of renown in Shinar and beyond, a man who built much and divided even more. His seat was in Mesopotamia around the known cities (Gen. 10:11). The *Book of Jasher* mentions that Nimrod's son, Mardon, "was worse than his father" and continued to lead the people away from God.[56] It could be that either Mardon – if that was Nimrod's son – or Nimrod himself was the inspiration for Marduk, the chief god of the Babylonians. While he may have been "split" into multiple gods, the nature and history of Marduk fit rather well with the story of Nimrod, and it is no wonder why tales of Marduk claim he was a son of Ea, the high god.[57] He is considered a hero, an avenger, and the wisest god.[57] An account about the building of Babylon calls the city "the sanctuary."[58]

There are, however, other great accounts of mighty men in the texts from Sumer, Babylon, and Mesopotamia. One story is the *Enuma Elish*, a poem containing the tale of a man named Nudimmud who abounded "in all wisdom" and "was exceedingly strong... He had no rival."[59] Some Jewish texts equate Nimrod with Amraphel of Shinar.[6,56] As mentioned before, he could always be King Enmerkar of Uruk, who struggled with the lord of Aratta, a story that mentions a Babel-like account.[29] Moreover, the actual man Nimrod and his kingship may have been forgotten, erased, or morphed by deification. Truly, while the people of Mesopotamia kept decent records, their storytelling and creativity were profound. Perhaps all these legendary people resembled their forefather, or perhaps all we will ever know of Nimrod is that he was a mighty hunter before the Lord.

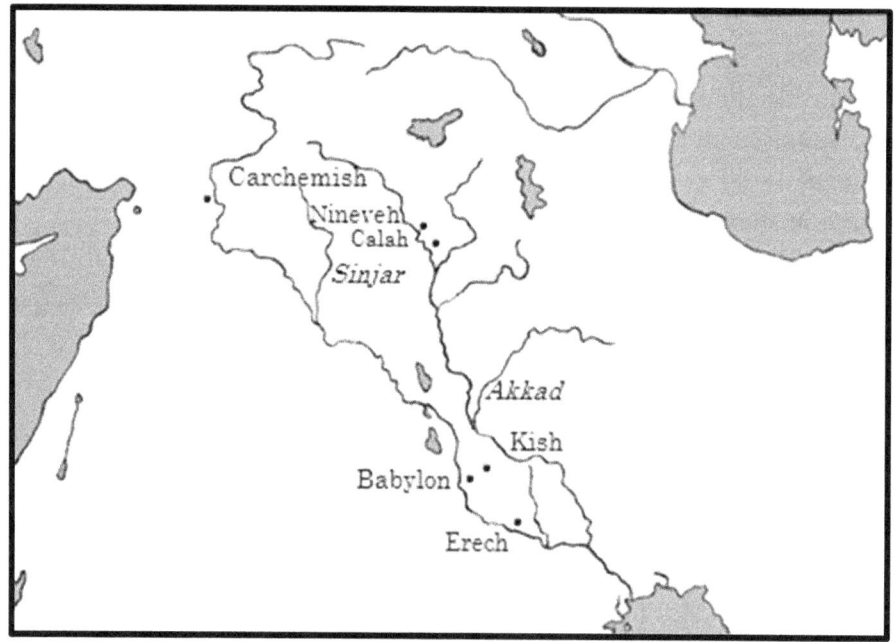

16: Mizraim

Land of the Copts; Egypt

Mizraim is the second son of Ham recorded in Scripture (Gen. 10:6, 1Ch. 1:8). His sons, listed as people groups rather than individuals, were "the Ludites, Anamites, Lehabites, Naphtuhites, Pathrusites, Casluhites (from whom the Philistines came) and Caphtorites" (Gen. 10:13-14). As a son of Ham, he inherited land within Ham's territory and north of his brother Cush.[1] His descendants "possessed the country from Gaza to Egypt."[2] Josephus explains, "all we who inhabit Judea call Egypt Mestre, and the Egyptians Mestreans."[2] Undoubtedly, Mizraim is Egypt, מִצְרַיִם in Hebrew.[3] His descendants were among those present to hear the Gospel on the day of Pentecost (Acts 2:10).

Regarding the frequency of references to his name within Scripture, Mizraim outshines Cush in every way. Outside of the genealogies, every other use of the word Mizraim in Scripture is translated as the country of Egypt. A very similar word, מִצְרִי, often translates as Egyptian.[4] This word is used less frequently than the first – only 30 times between Genesis 12 and Ezra.[5] We often know the names of these Egyptians, like Ishmael's mother Hagar, and Potiphar, who bought Joseph from Ishmaelites (Gen. 16:1, 39:1). Others are known for their offices, such as the pharaoh who ordered the deaths of the Hebrew babies, and his daughter who adopted Moses (Ex. 1:19, 2:11). Two other Egyptians are mentioned explicitly in Scripture: one for his great height – over seven feet tall – and a servant named Jarha (2Sa. 23:21, 1Ch. 2:34).

The word for Mizraim, however, is used over 680 times in 27 books of the Old Testament between Genesis and Zechariah.[6] To discuss each verse would go beyond the scope of this book, but the study would be intriguing. Suffice it to say that the Israelites encountered the Egyptians on many occasions: in their travels, enslavement, marriages, and various battles (Gen. 12:10, 41:29-30, 46-47, Ex. 1:8-13, 1Ki. 3:1, 2Ch. 12:2). Among those pharaohs were Shishak, who fought against Rehoboam; So, who ruled during the time of Hoshea of Israel and Shalmaneser of Assyria; Neco, who removed Jehoahaz from Judah; and Hophra, mentioned in prophecy (2Ch. 12:2, 36:3-4, 2Ki.17:1-4, Jer. 44:30). Also, Scripture includes Queen Taphenes of Egypt alongside her sister, who married Hadad, an Edomite (1Ki. 11:14-22).

Where is This Name Found?

Clearly, Mizraim possessed the land now called Egypt. Egypt is also called the land of Ham (Psa. 105:23, 27, 106:22). But in general, it is Mizraim that Egypt is known by in texts throughout the ancient world. The name "*Misri*" is found in the Amarna tablets, and Assyria called Lower Egypt "*Musur*" alongside the "*Kusi*," or Cush.[7,8,9] Ugaritic inscriptions referred to Egypt as *msrm*, while the Akkadians called the country "*Misru*" and "*Misri*."[10] In fact, Egyptians, to this day, refer to the land as "*Misr*."[11] Thus, the name of Mizraim was remembered long after its founder died. The name Egypt, however, was adopted much later by the Greeks, who called it "*Aigyptos*."[12,13]

Notable Mentions

With Mizraim's location established, it would be worthwhile to discuss the harmony between the Egyptian pharaohs, the Old Testament, and the rest of history. Some have already been mentioned before in the discussion on Cush, as Ethiopia controlled Egypt for a time, but the following will discuss the strictly "Egyptian" pharaohs.

But first, a side note. Egyptian chronology is sketchy and confusing at best, and I use those words intentionally. Even after years of research by Egyptologists, the timeline of the entirety of Egyptian history is something of a mystery. Starting with the great pyramids, researchers know that there was a great advancement in knowledge, something that I will hopefully shed some light on. But what happened before and after? Which of the pharaohs were actual people, which are a myth? Which names refer to the same person? Were some coregents, or ruling in different places at the same time? Were some added by proud Egyptians to make their great nation seem more ancient? Truly, the fault of Egyptian chronology lies only somewhat on those trying to piece it together. There are so many lists, so many errors, so many duplicated or incoherent rulers that it is difficult to make sense of Egyptian records. But for those who trust in God's Word, we know that the starting point for this great nation had to be from after the Babel event. This is where we will begin, though tentatively, and progress through the pharaohs of Egypt recorded in Scripture.

The first possible ruler of Egypt would, of course, be Mizraim. After all, he is Egypt in name and ancestor. But what can be known of Mizraim's rule besides this? There is one pharaoh who may fit this description: Menes, or Narmer. This pharaoh is somewhat confusing because of his name and his somewhat "legendary" fame.[14] Are these two separate people or one and the same? If different, which founded Egypt? Or was he a later descendant from the actual founder?

Perhaps Mizraim and Menes/Narmer are the same people, making this great first king of Egypt a unifier of the lands of Mizraim, or perhaps Menes/Narmer was a descendant.[14,15,16] While this would make a lot of sense if this legendary king were Mizraim, Egyptian chronologies are still being deciphered. Some researchers consider him a later descendant of Mizraim rather than the son of Ham himself, though Mizraim still would have founded Egypt.[11] Furthermore, Mizraim has two sons that might better fit this king and may answer why the name (which may be neither Menes nor Narmer) is unclear.

Naphtuhim or Pathrusim, the settlers of Middle and Upper Egypt, are the two sons that could be the hero and "founder" of Egypt.[14] Even so, the Menes/Narmer debate will probably continue until scholars can decide upon hieroglyphs with accuracy, for this legendary king could be another descendant altogether unrecorded in Scripture. After all, the period before the unification was hardly well documented. As there were multiple nations from Mizraim, this should be of little surprise. But could have Mizraim, a son, or another been the one to unify these tribes? Yes, but more research needs to be done as the number of years between Babel and the foundation and unification of Egypt is presently unclear.

Thankfully, the other pharaohs of the Old Testament are relatively easier to name. Abraham is the first to encounter a pharaoh in Scripture, doing so soon after God calls him from Ur (Gen. 11:31-12:10). According to Josephus, Abraham brought advancements in math, astronomy, and other "parts of learning" that "came from the Chaldeans," which may explain Egypt's great technological advancements.[17] Khufu is one proposed Egyptian pharaoh who may have been the ruler during Abraham's visit, a decision made because of the Pyramid at Giza, an incredible architectural feat.[18,19,20] Abraham may have aided in the technological jump Egypt made during this time.

Though Joseph's brothers first sell him to Midianites, he ends up with Ishmaelites and Potiphar before eventually serving the pharaoh, who put him "in charge of all of Egypt" and "only with respect to the throne" was the pharaoh greater (Gen. 37:20-36, 41:39-43). Who was this pharaoh? And could Joseph have been recorded as well? Some have connected Pharaoh Sesostris I with the pharaoh of Joseph's day, mainly because of a recorded famine and a particular advisor named Mentuhotep.[20,21] This Mentuhotep, though not a pharaoh, was held in high esteem among all the people, and even "great personages bowed down before him."[20,21,22] In addition, he "portioned the duties" and "kept order in the whole land.[22] Another governor "who loved his city" and lived during the reign of Sesostris I was Ameni who, because he "tilled the fields," "prolonged the life of its inhabitants" during a great famine in the land.[20,23] This account may be about Joseph's "rule" under the pharaoh.

The land given to the Israelites in Egypt was called Goshen, a land mentioned around a dozen times between the books of Genesis and Exodus (Gen. 45:10, 46:28-34, 47:1-27, 50:8, Ex. 8:22, 9:26). Goshen was in the "district of Rameses," and it was good land (Gen. 47:11). In the Psalms, the region is called Zoan (Psa. 78:12-43). This area was in the east side of the Nile Delta region, an area known at various times as Kesem and Pi-Rameses, near to other old cities such as Tanis, Qantir, and Tell El-Dab'a.[24,25,26]

Unsurprisingly, the book of the Exodus includes much information regarding Egypt and its rulers. To begin, there are likely three different pharaohs who ruled during the book's recordings. The first would be the one who came after the death of Joseph, as he "did not know about Joseph" (Ex. 1:8). This pharaoh oppressed the Israelites in Egypt, who likely spread out beyond Goshen (Gen. 47:27, Ex. 1:6-11). This pharaoh ordered that the Hebrew baby boys should be killed when they were born, even throwing them into the Nile (Ex. 1:15-22).

Scholars have found evidence of a Semitic (those related to Shem) presence and slavery in Egypt, specifically in the area of Kahun, presumed to be around the time of Pharaoh Sesostris III, what some call the Twelfth Dynasty.[27,28,29] Besides the presence of slaves, babies were found buried "in wooden boxes underneath the floors of many of the houses" in Kahun.[30] This location may have been where some of the Hebrews dwelled during their enslavement, and these babies may have been those killed, or perhaps those who died during the last plague. Though one cannot know for certain, Sesostris III is an excellent candidate for the pharaoh who enslaved the Hebrews. Whatever the case may be, the presence of Semitic peoples enslaved to the Egyptians corresponds to Scripture's account.

But after this initial enslavement, whomever it may have been started by, it continued for some time, as Scripture states, and here is where Moses comes into the picture. Clearly, the practice of killing Hebrew children was still in place to keep the Israelites' numbers low. Thus Moses' mother had to hide him both at home and in the Nile (Ex. 2:1-4). When the pharaoh's daughter goes out to the Nile, possibly to pray for a child, she sees and adopts the baby, naming him Moses (Ex. 2:5-10). While Scripture does not say for sure, this pharaoh is likely different from the one who initially enslaved the Hebrews. Thus, some scholars have linked this second pharaoh to one without a male heir, and their best choice is Amenemhet III, who left his throne to his daughter Sobekneferu.[28,31,32]

As mentioned before, the chronology of Egyptian rulers is quite scattered, and it becomes difficult to decide who may have been the ruler at the time of the Exodus. Some scholars suggest Neferhotep I as the third pharaoh.[33,34] Their reasoning for this is that his grave has never been found, none of his sons ruled, and one small coffin, perhaps of his firstborn, was found containing who was presumably his son; there is also the evidence of a sudden departure of Semitics and the location of a mass grave from that era.[33,35-39] Scripture states that all the firstborn of Egypt, from Pharaoh to livestock, died, and none of the Egyptians survived their pursuit in the Red Sea (Ex. 11:5, 14:28). There is also a poem, perhaps exaggerated and written post-Exodus, that speaks of plague in Egypt during a time of turmoil.[40] But this poem could have been speaking of the Hyksos invasion, which probably occurred after the Israelites plundered the Egyptians (Ex. 12:35-36).[41] Even so, the evidence of all these events occurring around the same time seems to point towards the Exodus of Scripture.

The next pharaoh is the one with whom Solomon made a treaty and whose daughter he married (1Ki. 3:1). Later, Scripture includes the destruction of Gezer by this same pharaoh, who gives this city to his daughter, Solomon's wife (1Ki. 9:16). A few scholars consider this to be Pharaoh Thutmosis I, mainly due to a daughter of his: Neferbity.[42,43,44] Their reasoning is that Neferbity simply "drops out" of Egyptian history; she is only really known because of her sister Hatshepsut's mortuary temple in Egypt.[42,43,45] Perhaps she disappeared because she married outside of Egypt. During this same period is Solomon's encounter with Hadad the Edomite, who flees to Egypt and marries the pharaoh's queen's sister (1Ki. 11:14-22). The Egyptian queen mentioned is named Taphenes. While there is no identifiable queen Taphenes in Egypt, perhaps this is Thutmose I's queen Ahmose whose sister was given to Hadad.[46]

The grandson of Thutmose I is Thutmose III, and he may be the Shishak of Scripture. He is mentioned first as the king ruling at the time of Rehoboam and Jeroboam, the latter of which fled to Egypt (1Ki. 11:40). Roughly five years later, this same pharaoh attacks Rehoboam and Judah, carrying off treasure from the temple and royal palace (1Ki. 14:22-26, 2Ch. 12:2-9). Similar events are recorded in the "Annals of Thutmose" at Karnak.[47] Thutmose III recorded his plundering of Megiddo and Kadesh, taking many spoils with him to Egypt.[47] Because of these similar events and the relation to the previous pharaoh who ruled during Solomon's reign, many scholars consider Thutmose III a likely candidate for the attack against Judah in Rehoboam's day.[43,48]

Prior to the fall of the Northern Kingdom of Israel, King Hoshea of Israel sought help from King So of Egypt in rebellion to King Shalmaneser of Assyria (2Ki. 17:1-4). In response, Shalmaneser put Hoshea in prison and besieged Samaria, deporting the Israelites to Halah, Gozen, and Media (2 Ki. 17:4-6). This fall, or at least the aftermath of Israel's destruction, was recorded in the stele of Merneptah, son of Ramesses II, which states, "Israel is laid waste."[49,50] Likely, either Merneptah or his father is the So of Scripture.

King Josiah of Judah also encountered an Egyptian pharaoh, though seemingly against God's command, and died because of it (2Ki. 23:29-30, 2Ch. 35:20-24). Neco, the king of Egypt, "went up to fight at Carchemish on the Euphrates," and for some reason, Josiah went out to do battle with him though Neco asks him not to as they were not fighting each other (2Ch. 35:21). After Josiah died and Neco finished fighting along with Assyria against Nebuchadnezzar, Neco returned to deal with Judah (2K. 23:33, 2Ch. 36:3, Jer. 46:2). He removed Josiah's son from the throne and took him to Egypt, placing Josiah's brother, renamed Jehoiakim, on the throne and levying taxes (2Ki. 25:30-35, 2Ch. 36:1-4). The prophet Jeremiah also wrote on the coming destruction of Egypt by the Babylonians after Neco lost to them at Carchemish (Jer. 46).

While Scripture does not say which of the two pharaohs named Neco fought Josiah, most scholars consider him to be Necho II.[51,52,53] Herodotus also recorded a battle of Necho II near Cadytis, which may be Carchemish in Assyria.[54] Josephus recorded this same account from Scripture but added that Necho II was defeated by Nebuchadnezzar, who later went down and conquered Egypt.[55] This account is well known, and Necho II is, with little doubt, the pharaoh of this time.

The last definite pharaoh recorded in Scripture is Hophra. Jeremiah said that the Lord would "hand Pharaoh Hophra king of Egypt over to his enemies who seek his life" (Jer. 44:30). It is possible that the pharaoh of Jeremiah's imprisonment and the pharaoh who ruled when Babylon besieged Jerusalem are the same (Jer. 37:4-5). He was known as Apries in Greek sources and was killed by his enemies – Egyptians who became angry with him – just as God said.[56] But before that time, he came to the aid of Judah when Nebuchadnezzar was besieging Jerusalem, though the army helped little. Eventually, both nations fell to Babylon.[57,58]

Though Egypt continued as a people, the empire and nation diminished in influence with the rise of Babylon and subsequent empires. Even so, Egypt is not entirely without notice. It was to Egypt that Mary and Joseph fled with Jesus during Herod's murder of the innocent, and there were people from Egypt present on Pentecost (Hos. 11:1, Mat. 2:13-19, Acts 2:10). From Genesis to the Gospel, Mizraim is part of God's plan of salvation for all people.

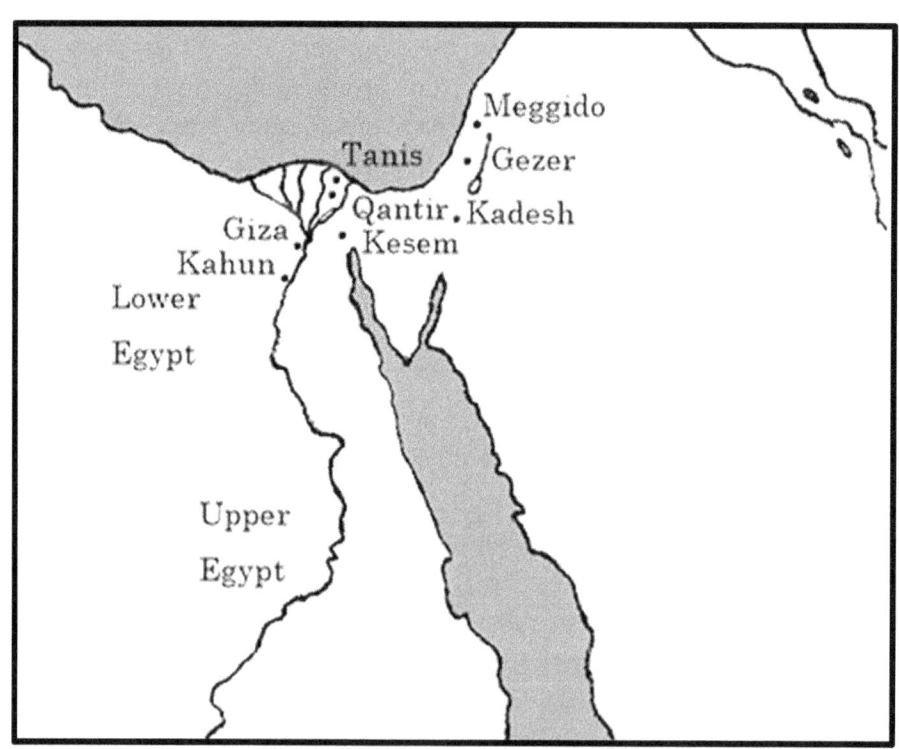

17: The Sons of Mizraim

The sons of Mizraim dwelled, initially, in the land of Mizraim, which is Egypt. Some of them spread out farther and established recognizable lands for themselves, as will be shown with the first grouping of sons. Many of these descendants merged, resulting in one son becoming the "named" person of the nation made up of a collective. Thus, they have been placed together as their histories are so intertwined, separating them would be pointless, if possible. Another matter is that while each name is a people group or tribe, they will be referred to as a singular person for simplicity's sake.

Ludim, Anamim, and Lehabim

Ludim is referenced most frequently in Scripture between the brothers, but he is also frequently confused with another person: Lud, son of Shem. Lud, however, is above the Mediterranean, while Ludim appears to be in northern Africa near his father. Within Scripture, Ludim, לוּדִיי in Hebrew, appears three times, twice in genealogies and once in Jeremiah along with Cush and Put (Gen 10:13, 1Ch. 1:11, Jer. 46:9).[1] The other word associated with Ludim's people is לֻבִי, that is, Lubim or Libyan.[2] This word is found along with the Cushites near

Egypt, Arabia, and Put (2Ch. 12:3, 16:8, Ezk. 30:5, Dan. 11:43, Nah. 3:9). And it is his relation to three of these countries – Egypt, Cush, and Put – that narrows his location.

As understood by the above etymology, Ludim dwelled in the land that came to be known as Libya. These people were among the many who heard the Gospel on Pentecost (Acts 2:10). This land, however, was first settled by his uncle Put, or Phut – who, as Josephus writes, "was the founder of Libya and called the inhabitants Phutites, from himself."[3] Later, though, the land and people of Put were joined with Lubim's, calling themselves Lybyos, as "Ludicim...called the country from himself."[4] In Greek, his country is Λιβύη and is included among the nations present on Pentecost in Acts (Acts 2:10). His brothers Anamim and Lehabim, whom Josephus calls Enemim and Labim, perhaps settled with Ludim. Lehabim, לְהָבִים in Hebrew, appears only in the genealogies along with Anamim, עֲנָמִים in Hebrew (Gen. 10:13, 1Ch. 1:11).[2,5] Their territory extended beyond the modern border of Libya to Egypt and far to the west and south.

Pliny implies in his writings to have visited Libya and noted the natives of the country call one river Fut, or Phuth, derived from their forefather Put, or Phut.[6] After listing various peoples who were currently living and had once lived in the area, which stretched a great distance at that time, he notes a river Laud, whose name has long since changed but at that time, still reflected the country's predecessor.[6] Josephus claimed these brothers stayed together. These were likely the progenitors of the tribes mentioned in Pliny's and other's works.

One of these tribes was known as the *Libu* to the Egyptians, though not described in the nicest terms as they were oft warring neighbors.[7,8] In a description regarding one chieftain, Egyptian texts recorded that the people of this tribe typically wore feathers on their heads.[9] These people likely gave rise to the modern Berbers, first shown in the tomb of Seti I, along with other inhabitants of Africa.[10] Like the written description, this relief includes feathers in the hair of the Libyans, or Berbers as they were known later. Another of these Libyan tribes were known to the Greeks as the Psylli.[11,12] Assyrian sources recorded a group from this area called the Anami, likely derived from Anamim.[13] While their names may not have been well-preserved, the presence of distinct tribes that stayed together in the land of Put and northern Africa agrees with Scripture and the writings of Josephus.

Naphtuhim

Naphtuhim is only mentioned twice in Scripture, as נַפְתֻּחִים in Hebrew (Gen. 10:13, 1Ch. 1:11).[14] There is a possibility that he remained near his father in the heart of Egypt and ruled after him. His brother Pathrusim likely dwelled near him (Jer. 44:1). Assurbanipal comments on two cities of Lower Egypt – Memphis and Nathu – whose kings confront him after he seizes some cities.[15] It is in this vicinity, specifically in Memphis, that Naphtuhim's location may be found.[16] In Scripture, Memphis is called Noph, נֹף, or מֹף, Moph.[17,18] The city is mentioned several times in Scripture and was known for its idolatry (Isa. 19:13, Jer. 2:16, 44:1, 46:14-19, Ezk 30:13-16, Hos. 9:6).

Here, there was a temple to the god Ptah, with "walls of the sovereign," who was said to have been a creator.[19] The city itself was called "*mn-nfr/men-nefer*" and may have originated with Naphtuhim, whose people may have later worshiped him in the form of the god Ptah.[20] His people would have become those who dwelled in the Lower and middle parts of Egypt and followed in his father's footsteps as ruler. His people were called "*nf pth*."[21] As mentioned in the previous chapter, Naphtuhim may be the source of Narmer, who founded Memphis.[22] But this could also be his brother Pathrusim.

Pathrusim

Like his brother before him, Pathrusim is only directly mentioned in Scripture's genealogies (Gen. 10:14, 1Ch. 1:12). His name is פַּתְרֻסִי in Hebrew.[23] This name is related to the city of Pathros, or פַּתְרוֹס, and found in Upper Egypt, which is likely where Pathrusim's descendants settled.[24] This city appears a handful of times in Scripture; most often, this second word is translated as Upper Egypt, which indicates where some of his people were located (Isa. 11:11, Jer. 44:1-15, Ezk. 29:14, 30:14). According to the *Book of Jasher*, Pathrusim joined with his brother Casloch and five new groups came from them.[25] The issue with this, however, is that Casloch is supposed to be Casluhim, or the

Philistines (Gen. 10:14). Perhaps they stayed together, but these people still left the land of Mizraim. Assyria named his land *pa-tu-ri-si*, though translated as Upper Egypt like *mu-sur* and *ku-u-si* are Egypt and Ethiopia instead of Misr and Cush.[26,27,28] Esarhaddon names himself "king of the kings of Egypt, Paturisi and Kush."[28,29] The Egyptians called the land *p-t-rsy* and preserved the name of their founder.[30]

Casluhim and Caphtorim

The history of Casluhim and Caphtorim has been somewhat puzzling to historians because of the people who came from them, namely the Philistines. Scripture is quite clear in the Table of Nations when it says that the Philistines came from Casluhim (Gen. 10:14, 1Ch 1:12). The Hebrew word for Casluhim is כַּסְלֻחִים, and it only appears in those two verses.[31] His brother Caphtorim, כַּפְתֹּרִי in Hebrew, is only mentioned once more outside of the genealogies (Deut. 2:23).[32] In this verse, the Caphtorites came from Caphtor and settled in a part of Gaza, which was part of the land of the Philistines, originally part of Canaan (Jos. 13:3). Caphtor itself, כַּפְתּוֹר in Hebrew, is referenced multiple other times.[33] Here, the Philistines are said to have come from Caphtor: "The Lord is about to destroy the Philistines, the remnant from the coasts of Caphtor" and again, "Did I not bring Israel up from Egypt, the Philistines from Caphtor...?" (Jer. 47:4, Amo. 9:7). The Caphtorites may have settled after the Casluhites and joined them. Josephus wrote on these sons, stating that their cities were destroyed in the Ethiopian war, moving them to the land of Philista.[4]

The Casluhites became the Philistines, a group frequently encountered by the Israelites. The first couple of meetings are rather friendly, as Abraham bought land from Abimelech, though later both Abraham and Isaac had trouble when the Philistines stopped up their wells (Gen. 21:32-34, 26:1-18). The Philistines, however, become hostile by the time of the Exodus (Ex. 13:17, 23:31). Their land was called Philistia, פְּלֶשֶׁת in Hebrew, and this word appears most often in Psalms or prophecy (Ex. 15:14, Psa. 60:8, 83:7, 87:4, 108:9, Isa. 14:29-31, Joe. 3:4).[34] The word for Philistine is פְּלִשְׁתִּי and appears over 280 times in Scripture.[35]

Scripture provides a relatively clear Philistine territory. Their major cities – named after tribes and their leaders – were: Gaza, Ashdod, Ashkelon, Gath, Ekron, and Avvim (Jos. 13:3). Ashkelon is one of the cities mentioned on the Merneptah Stele as falling with the rest of Canaan.[36] In Egypt, a probable origin for the Philistines was the city Pelusium. While the city is most often called as Sin or the Desert of Sin, this is the same city as Pelusium, סין in Hebrew (Ex. 16:1, 17:1, Num. 33:11).[37] In a prophecy against Egypt, Pelusium is one of the cities that will receive God's wrath (Ezk. 30:15-16).

Most verses about the Philistines are on the multiple battles between them and Israel. The encounters between the nations are many, from the time of Joshua to Samson, ending once they were defeated by Hezekiah.[38] The last few references to these great people are prophecy, and most of it negative. The Philistines, having been influenced by the Canaanites, adopted many Canaanite gods and, in turn, corrupted Israel. Because of their idolatry and hatred of Israel, God foretold their coming destruction, stating their land would be made desolate until the return of Israel.[39]

Many other nations also knew the Philistines. In the records of Rameses III, the Egyptians were possibly referring to their former brothers and neighbors as the Peleset, sometimes considered to be one of the Sea Peoples, though likely they only joined with them as the Philistines were mainly a "land faring" people.[19,40,41] Sennacherib recorded Hezekiah's defeat of the Philistines, whom the Assyrians called *Pilistaya*.[42] Sargon refers to them as the *Piliste*.[43] Other names were *Palastu, Pilista,* and *Pilistu*.[44]

Various ancient records mention the descendants of Caphtorim. Egypt called the descendants of Caphtorim, or Caphtor, *kpt3r* or *Keftiu*.[45] Some Ugaritic tablets recorded the land as Kaphtor or *kptr*, which is quite similar to Egyptian inscriptions that translate as either Kaptara or Caphtor.[46,47] The Mari Tablets also contain inscriptions of trading with the *Kap-ta-ra-i-im*.[48] A version of Casluhim is *Kasluhet* from an inscription on a tomb at Kom Ombos.[49,50] Some Caphtorites appear to have settled in or near southeastern Anatolia, but a portion, if not all of them, moved to Philistia after Casluhites. This is why Scripture says that the Philistines are descendants of both brothers.

Some scholars say Caphtor settled in or near Anatolia, and "Crete" is the translation in many referenced sources, even in the footnotes of some Bibles.⁴⁷ This location explains why the Philistines proposed the contest that led to the fight between David and Goliath, for it was popular among the Greeks.⁵¹ While Crete is not a certain location, it appears that some, or the first, people of Caphtor settled near or in southeastern Anatolia.⁵² For example, the Sidonians were not relegated to Sidon and Tyre but settled in various places about the Mediterranean. But the Philistines clearly came from these two sons, though settling in the land at different times. Perhaps the Caphtorites first settled in Crete, but it would have likely been after the sons of Japheth settled there. If so, his people were represented on the day of Pentecost (Acts 2:11).

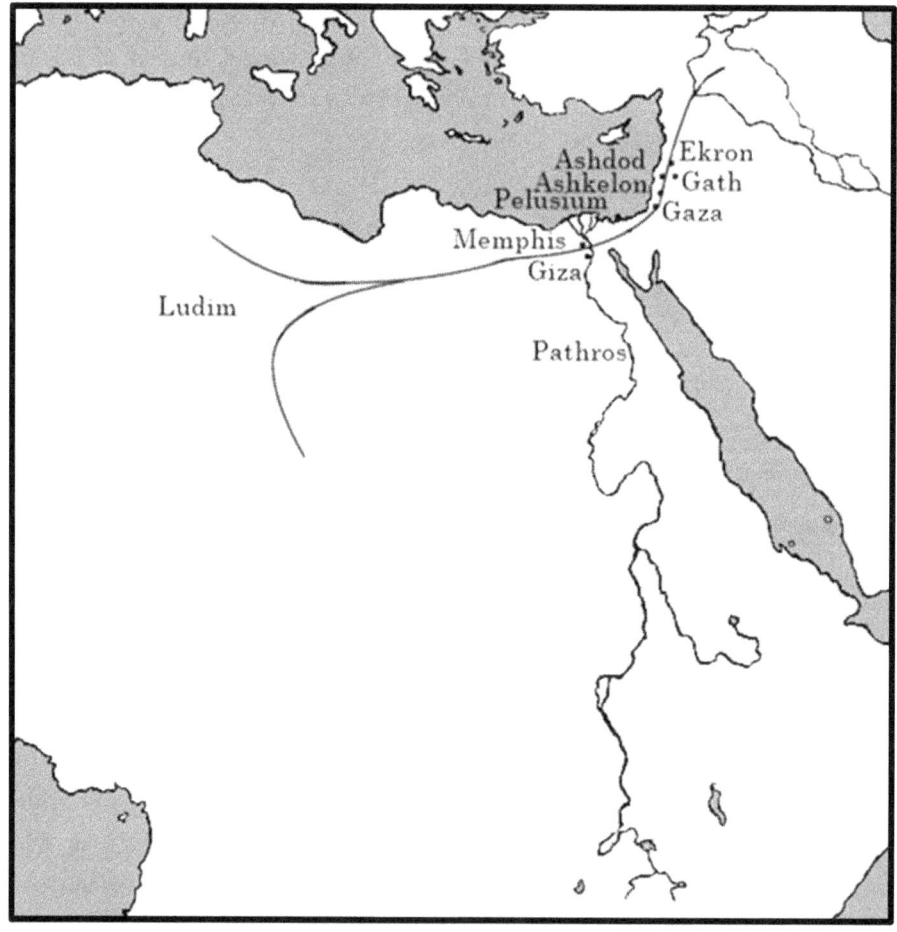

18: Put

A Bow

Put, or Phut as he is also called, is the third son of Ham (Gen. 10:6, 1Ch. 1:8). His name is פוט in Hebrew.¹ While he is not mentioned as frequently, he is often included with Mizraim or his other brother Cush. After the chronologies, Isaiah includes him next. Along with Japheth's descendants, Scripture lists Put along with his nephew Ludim and the Lydians of Shem as those who will hear and proclaim the glory of God (Isa. 66:19). In Jeremiah, Put is mentioned with his brother Cush and nephew Ludim, who were bowmen, while Put's people were shield bearers (Jer. 46:9). The book of Ezekiel says the sons of Put "hung their shields and helmets" on the walls of Egypt for aiding Egypt in battle (Ezk. 27:10, 30:5). In later prophecy, Put allies with the kingdoms of the North – Gog, Magog, and their fellows – and they will fight and fall with these other nations (Ezk. 38:3-9). Lastly, Nahum says Put and Ludim were allied with Nineveh in Assyria along with the other brothers of Put (Nah. 3:9).

Where is This Name Found?

Like his brothers, Put was given land within Ham's inheritance that was said to be west of his brother Mizraim.² Josephus recorded that

Phut received the territory now called Libya and named his people the Phutites, but later his nephew called the land Libya.[3] And this makes sense, for Libya is west of Mizraim. Further, as mentioned in the chapter on Mizraim's sons, Pliny and Ptolemy recorded a river in northern Africa, which later gained a name influenced by the Mauri but called by the natives Fut or Phuth, as well as a city named Putea, both of which are likely named after their forefather.[4,5,6]

Of course, their land stretched farther than just modern Libya, and one of the groups from Put and his nephews are known as the Berber. These people did not only dwell in Libya. Their many tribes resided in the northern part of Africa, some of which were closely connected to the Carthaginians.[4,7,8] Like with the sons of Mizraim and the modern Berbers, there were many Libyan tribes, for the "Libyans" were simply the group of tribes to the west of Egypt, encompassing more than the Libya of today.[9,10,11] Sometimes, they were called something close to their modern name; other times, they were *Tehenu*, *Tjemehu*, or *R-b*.[10,12] These various tribes include the Moors, Algerians, and possibly those along the outer coast and deeper into Africa, who joined with Mizraim's and Cush's descendants.

Notable Mentions

The Egyptians knew of and kept records on their brothers, the Libyans. Old accounts refer to them as "Pwn.t," akin to other translations of Put's name.[13] While at some point Egypt and Libya probably interacted on friendly terms, most later inscriptions in Egypt recorded them as the enemy.[14,15] A text from Babylon, however, implies the land of Phut and Mizraim were not always at odds. Nebuchadnezzar encountered and defeated a group that aided the Egyptians whom he calls the "Putu Yavan," that is, Javan Phut.[16,17] Another Babylonian name for this land is Puta.[18] While this land may be different from modern Libya, the name infers that these "troops" came from somewhere in Put's land to aid their brothers against the Babylonians. This name references both Put and Javan, son of Japheth, so there must have been a city that had been partly settled by Ionians. Neighbor to the Babylonians were the Persians, who recorded this early nation and related tribes, calling them "Putiya."[13,18,19] Finally, these people were among the many who heard the Gospel on Pentecost (Acts 2:10). Thus, the land of Put was remembered among the nations.

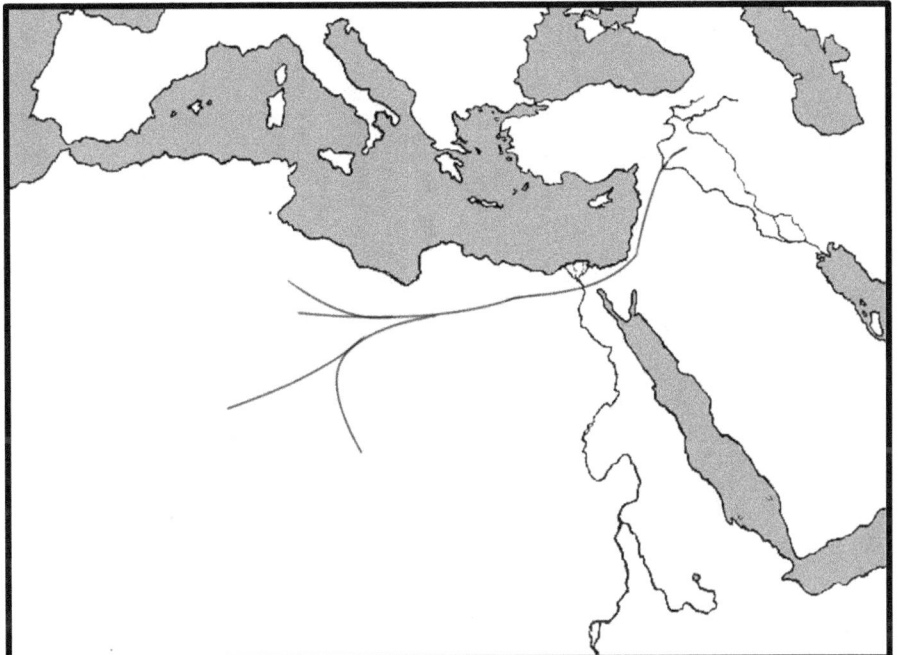

19: Canaan

Lowland; Merchant

Canaan was the fourth son of Ham, כְּנַעַן in Hebrew and transliterated *k'na'an* (Gen. 10:6, 1Ch. 1:8).[1] Even considering all the information found on his brothers, Canaan, his land, and his people may be the best known in and outside of Scripture. To this day, the land his descendants originally settled is the focus of the world's attention. While not all references to Canaan's people are not positive, his people became great on both the land and sea. Scripture recorded the following as his sons: Sidon, Heth, and the Jebusites, Amorites, Girgashites, Hivites, Arkites, Sinites, Arvadites, Zemarites, and Hamathites (Gen. 10:15-16, 1Ch. 1:13). The first son should be familiar, as his name became that of a city that joined with Tyre, both of which were ports of the Phoenicians. The second son is also familiar, for Heth became the Hittites, who until recently were only known from Scripture.[2] Besides one other son, the rest are known collectively as Canaanites.

Despite the fact he was listed last in the Table of Nations, as he was probably the youngest of the brothers, he is first referenced in the chapter before the Table. When Noah's family leaves the Ark, Ham is singled out as the father of Canaan (Gen. 9:18-22). Because of Ham's dishonorable act, Noah curses his grandson instead of his son (Gen.

9:25-27). Josephus speculates Noah did this because of near kinship and that God had blessed Ham.[3] In a way, Canaan was made famous for the curse inflicted on him, and this cannot be ignored. While many have used this curse as the excuse to commit horrendous acts against people, specifically on the sons of Ham, there is no basis for this terrible claim. If Canaan's descendants were to be punished, it was done in response to their idolatry. God already used Israel as a means to conquer the land of Canaan. But those actions may not have even been the result of the curse. The curse may have simply been to speak the consequences of Ham's actions, as God cursed the serpent and the ground after the Rebellion, or how death is the result of sin (Gen. 3:14-17, Jam. 1:15). Whatever the case, the curse did not and does not justify the evil actions of people towards Ham's descendants.

Furthermore, though many have tried to malign Scripture and falsely claim otherwise, the curse never said they would be dark-skinned. Indeed, some of Japheth's descendants were light and dark – compare people of the northern Iles to those of Persia or Asia – and some of Ham's were the same – like those from the heart of Africa to the Egyptians, Yemen, or even Asia. There is no biblical foundation for this argument. After all, God states that men are of one blood. There are none deemed worth less or more on account of skin (Gen. 1:26-28, Acts 17:26). We are all of one blood! Instead, it was a man-made lie to further the idea held by society that some nations of men were somehow less human than others. This lie will hopefully be torn down in this book, reminding the reader that every person is fully human, and everyone descends from Adam and Eve through Noah's family.

Where is This Name Found?

As we will discuss, Josephus states that what is "now called Judea" was originally the land of Canaan, corresponding to Scripture's outline.[4] The land of Canaan is often called the promised land, as it was the land given to Abraham and his descendants. According to the *Book of Jubilees*, the whole land was originally given to Shem, but Canaan took part of it for himself, despite the warning from his family.[5] Supposedly, Canaan was to inherit the land west of Put, placing him to the far reaches of Africa below Spain.[6] Perhaps he did this in spite of the curse placed on him, but this cannot be known for sure. Whatever the reason, his people dominated the area until Israel claimed their promised land, though some of his people remained there for a time afterwards.

The land that he and his descendants dwelled in reached quite far. Genesis says that the land of Canaan stretched from Sidon to Gaza and included "Sodom, Gomorrah, Admah and Seboiim, as far as Lasha" (Gen. 10:19). In addition, Scripture notes that the clans scattered, which may explain their far reaches across the earth (Gen. 10:18). The *Book of Jasher* gives a similar scattering and building account, including the cities "Sodom, Gomorrah, Admah and Zeboyim," named after the "men from the family of Ham" who built them.[7] His sons' territory extended from well into modern-day Turkey down into Egypt. Some of his nations, however, appear to have traveled much farther.

Scripture uses two different words to name Canaan and his descendants. Besides the aforementioned, כְּנַעֲנִי is also used, and only slightly less often.[8] Both translate as either Canaan or Canaanites, yet there is a slight difference in usage. In general, the first word names those in the northern land of Canaan while the second is for those in the lower part of the land.[9,10] One should remember, though, the distinction between the groups is not significant, and sometimes either word is used to describe the people in the land.

After the Table of Nations, most references to Canaan, his land, and his descendants are in respect to Abraham and Israel. God calls Abram out of Ur, and they progressively move towards the land of Canaan (Gen.10:15,11:31,12:5-6,13:7-12). Scripture specifically mentions various tribes of Canaanites then living in the land (Gen. 15:18-21). Here, God specifically promises Abram land, and many events involving Abraham occur (Gen. 16:3, 17:8, 23:2-19). Abraham even bought land from Ephron, a Hittite, to bury Sarah (Gen. 23:1-20). He sends his servant to his homeland to find a wife for his son to avoid intermarrying with the Canaanites (Gen. 24:3-37). Isaac does similarly with his son, Jacob, for Esau had married Canaanite and Ishmaelite women (Gen. 28:1-9, 36:2-6).

Jacob and his people lived and moved within the land of Canaan (Gen. 31:18, 33:18, 34:30, 35:6, 37:1). Judah and Simeon had sons by Canaanite women (Gen. 38, 46:10-12, 1Ch. 2:3). Because of the famine in Canaan, Joseph's brothers went to Egypt (Gen. 42:5-32, 44:8, 45:17-47:15, 48:3-7, 49:30). After Jacob died, he was embalmed, mourned by the Egyptians, and brought back to Canaan to be buried (Gen. 50:5-13). When the Israelites leave Egypt, they return to the land of Canaan to reclaim their inheritance.[11] Much of the conflict in the books of Joshua and Judges involved the Canaanites.[12] But at first, the people of Israel were afraid to go into Canaan because of the people living with the Canaanites (Num. 13:26-33).

During his day, David and his men attacked the remaining Canaanites, and a pharaoh captured one of their cities (2Sa. 24:7, 1Ki. 9:16). David, however, had something of a friendship with the Hittites. One of his trusted men was a Hittite named Uriah, a man who honored God and His people (2Sa. 11:11). This same man was sent to his death by David because David had committed adultery with his wife, and David was punished for it (2Sa. 11:16-17, 12:13-24,1Ch. 3:5).

Much of Scripture speaks against the Canaanites. Unfortunately, they were on a whole an idolatrous people who neither repented nor turned from their gods. When the Israelites married their people, Israel adopted their abhorrent gods (Ezr. 9:1, Ezk. 16:3, Zec 14:21). Some of the gods they served were Baal, Ashtaroth, and Molech, worshipping them in appalling ways (Jdg. 2:13, 1Ki. 11:7). For these reasons and more, the Canaanites were wiped from the land (Neh. 9:8-24, Psa. 106:38).

The Canaanites, however, were regarded as merchants throughout Mesopotamia, and their northern land was known better as Phoenicia (Job 41:6, Pro 31:24, Isa 19:18, 23:8-11, Ezk. 16:29, 17:4, Hos. 12:7, Zep 1:11, 2:5). While the various tribes of Canaan are mentioned frequently, especially in the early texts, the Phoenicians are likely the best known, though better in extra-biblical records. Due to their expanse and trade, the Canaanites were well-known to the nations surrounding them. The Amarna letters, written from Canaan to Egypt in an Akkadian-like script, contain many references to the land of Canaan and the various people who sprouted from the original people.[13,14] They referred to Canaan as "*Ki-na-ah-na*" and "*Ki-na-ah-ni*."[15] They also recorded the people north of them who came from Canaan known as the Hatti, or Hittites, whom they called the "*Ha-at-ti*," and the people of Sidon, called

"Zi-du-na."[13,15] The man who wrote the letter "guarded" Tyre.[16] The Egyptians knew the Canaanites as "p3-kn'n."[17]

Inscriptions were found in Nuzu, Mesopotamia, where there are records of cloth with a "*kinahhu*" color, translated as red-purple.[18] This name came from the Akkadian version of the name for Canaan and Phoenicia.[19,20] This is understandable, for the Canaanites were known to be merchants, and the best traders of their nation were the Phoenicians, known for their famous purple cloth.[18,21] In addition, inscriptions of Phoenician origin call the land of Canaan "*kn'n*."[21] While others called them Phoenicians, they called themselves Canaanites, clinging to their roots.[21] The Ebla Tablets contain an inscription about a Canaanite god named Dagon, "*ga-na-na*," who is called "Lord of Canaan" (Jos. 15:41, 19:27, Jdg. 16:23, 1Sa. 5:2-7, 1Ch. 10:10).[22] A Ugarit text, likely of Canaan, contains a reference to "*kn'ny*" or "the Canaanite."[23,24] But it is to the Greeks that we owe the name Phoenicia, for it came from their word "*phoenix*," describing that which was "crimson and dark purple."[24] Many nations applied this word to the Phoenicians, Canaanites of Sidon, and their purple-cloth trade.[24]

Notable Mentions

Some of their people, known as both Phoenicians and Canaanites, resided in Tyre and Sidon during Jesus' time on earth. A woman from that region came to Jesus, pleading that He would heal her daughter, and He did, praising her faith (Mat. 15:21-28). Once again, God's Word shows that He desires all people to be saved and that He cares for all people. In fact, Canaan's people can be included as being among those represented on the Day of Pentecost, where they heard the Gospel of Christ (Acts 2:9).

As a final note, I will mention that many different kingdoms came from Canaan. Each of the sons of Canaan became their own "nations" and, though Canaan is typically referred to as a homogenous group, the tribes grew more distinct with time. They also were not strong on their own, and even though they lasted a long time, they were frequently conquered and only handfuls of their people survived. The name Canaan was, for all practical purposes, demoted when the Israelites came during the conquest and they, with time, became known more and more by the separate tribal names of Canaan's sons. However, they frequently referred to themselves as Canaanites. The histories of these individual nations will be discussed in detail in the following chapter.

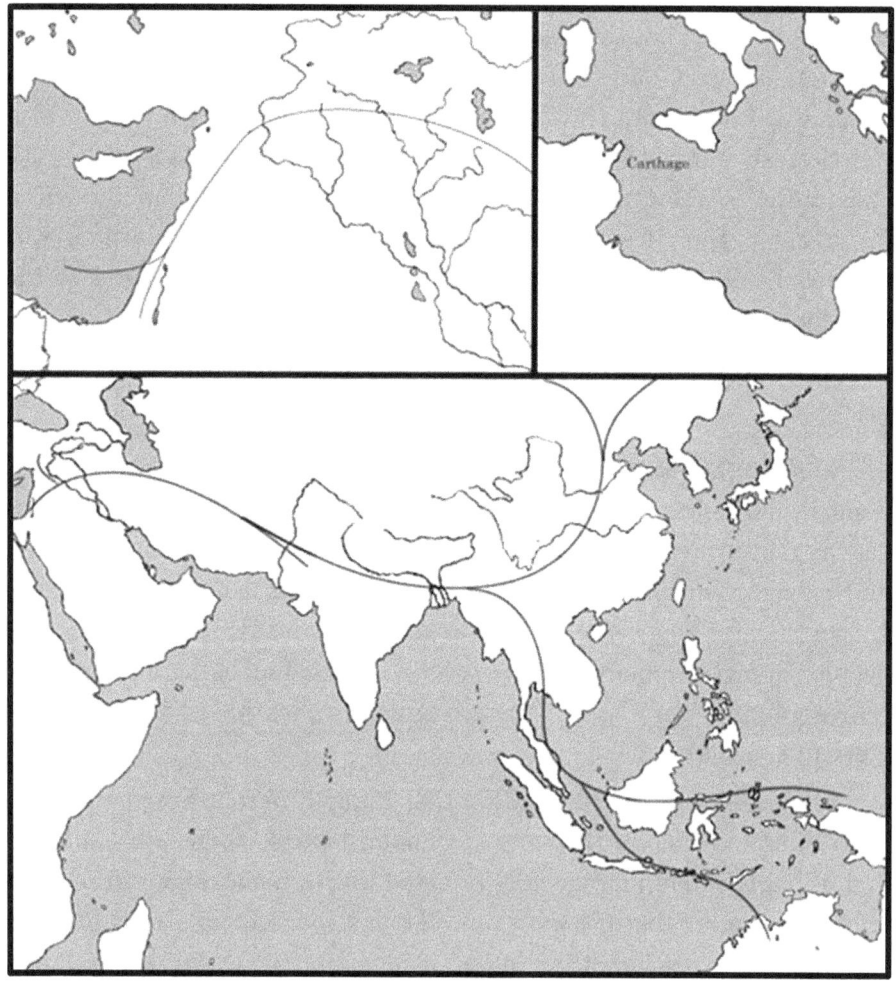

20: The Sons of Canaan

The sons of Canaan were great in number and lasting in history. Scripture provides a general boundary for the land of Canaan: "Sidon toward Gerar as far as Gaza, and then toward Sodom, Gomorrah, Admah and Zeboiim, as far as Lasha" (Gen. 10:19). At the end of that passage, the reader learns that the Canaanite tribes scattered (Gen. 10:18). Considering this information, it leads to reason that some tribes did not remain in Canaan, even if most did. Though this land was known as Canaan's land, the *Book of Jubilees* claims the land was intended for Shem.[1] Most of the Canaanites became the peoples found in the northwestern portions of the Middle East.

Sidon

Canaan's first-born is Sidon, though his name is known best by the city named after him (Gen. 10:15-19, 1Ch. 1:13). This city, along with Tyre, were the two greatest cities of the Canaanites and became centers for the Phoenicians (Jdg. 18:28, 2Sa. 24:6-7). Jacob said Zebulun's land would "extend toward Sidon" by the seashore (Gen. 49:1, 13). Much later, the book of Jeremiah notes Tyre, Sidon, and their kings are of "the coastlands across the sea," for their people were seafaring (Jer. 25:22, Hos. 9:13, Num. 13:29). This nautical nature was embraced by their descendants, the Phoenicians. There should be no surprise to learn that the Israelites did not or were unable to completely drive the Canaanites out as they became the well-known Phoenicians (Jos. 11:8, 13:4-6, 19:10-28, Jdg. 1:27-31, Neh. 13:16-17). These Canaanite cities were a stumbling block to Israel, and the Israelites were influenced by them, and they even worshipped Canaanite gods (Jdg. 10:6, 1Ki. 11:1-33, 2Ki. 23:13). And the infamous Jezebel, wife of Ahab, was a daughter of Ethbaal, king of the Sidonians (1Ki. 16:31).[2]

There was, however, sometimes a decent relationship between Israel and Tyre, the sister city of Sidon. When David ruled Israel, King Hiram I of Tyre sent cedarwood, carpenters, and stonemasons to Israel to build David's palace (2Sa. 5:11, 1Ch. 14:1).[3] Indeed, King Hiram continued this relationship with David's son Solomon, and he may have known the God of Israel (1Ki. 5:1-9, 2Ch. 2:3, 11-14). Later, Solomon gave Hiram towns in Galilee and, though Hiram was not pleased with them, called Solomon "my brother" (1Ki. 9:10-13). While building the temple, Solomon sent for a bronze craftsman named Huram, whose parentage was of Tyre and Naphtali (1Ki. 7:13-14, 2Ch. 2:13). During a famine in Israel, Elijah was sent to stay in Sidon's Zarephath with a widow (1Ki. 17:9-24, Luk 4:26). When Israel returned from exile, they gave wares to Sidon and Tyre in exchange for cedarwood (Ezr. 3:7).

Many other prophetic passages of Scripture deal with Sidon, Tyre, and the Phoenicians (Psa. 45:12, 83:7, 87:4). Jeremiah mentions Tyre and Sidon as one kingdom who would fall alongside nearby nations, such as Moab, Amon, Philistia, and Edom (Jer. 25:22, 27:3, 47:4). Isaiah devotes a chapter to Tyre, the main seaport for Sidon. As the people of Tyre and Sidon were seafaring people, much of the prophecy reflects that, mentioning harbors, seafarers, the sea itself, even settling far off lands (Isa. 23). Tyre's fame was as a merchant, and the city was from old. Ezekiel devotes three chapters to Tyre and a portion to Sidon, dealing with their trade with the world as well as their future destruction (Ezk. 26:1-29:18, 32:30). The books of Amos and Joel give the background to this destruction: the nation disregarded "a treaty of brotherhood" and sold their brothers as slaves (Joe. 3:4, Amo. 1:9-10). Zechariah says Tyre was skilled, fortified, and wealthy, yet destruction would come, a fact which will be discussed hereafter (Zec. 9:2-4).

Tyre and Sidon are in the New Testament as well. When Jesus denounced certain cities for their unrepentance, He stated that if the same miracles had been performed in Phoenician cities, they "would have repented long ago" (Mat. 11:20-22, Luk. 10:13-14). Jesus visited the area of Tyre and Sidon and healed the demon-possessed daughter of a Canaanite woman (Mat. 15:22-28, Mar. 7:24-31). While Jesus was on earth, people from all over Judea, including Tyre and Sidon, came to Him (Mar. 3:8, Luk. 6:17). In the time before his death, Herod had been "quarreling with the people of Tyre and Sidon" (Acts 12:20). Early Christians traveled through Phoenicia, including Paul and Barnabas (Acts 11:19, 15:3, 21:2-7). Thus, they were a well-recognized nation and were among the early people reached by the Gospel.

Sidon and Tyre, two great cities and seaports, were the original home and trade centers of the Phoenicians.[4,5,6] Strabo calls Tyre greater than Sidon, though the latter is mentioned more frequently because it was older.[6] In Scripture, Sidon and its inhabitants are צִידוֹן and צִידֹנִי, meaning "fisher."[7,8] The names for the Sidonians and their city in Greek are Σιδώνιος and Σιδών.[9,10] Tyre is צֹר in Hebrew, meaning rock, and her inhabitants and city in Greek are Τύριος and Τύρος.[11,12,13] However, the name of their territory became Φοινίκη or Phoenicia.[14] Though nations referred to this region by various names, many continued calling them Canaanites.

Josephus refers to this son as Sidonius and the founder of Sidon.[15] Ugaritic tablets record that there was a shrine to Asherah in Tyre and Sidon.[16] Tiglath-Pileser received tribute from Canaanite cities, including Sidon, called *Si-du-ni*.[17] During Sennacherib's reign, he removed King Luli of Sidon and gave it to Ethba'al (or Tuba'lu).[2,18] Sennacherib received tribute from Tuba'lu the Sidonite.[19] When Esarhaddon conquers Sidon, he notes that part of the city was in the sea and Tyre was on an island.[20] Tyre had connections to Egypt during the reign of Pharaoh Merneptah, and the Amarna letters call Sidon *Zi-du-na* or *Zi-tu-na*.[21,22] Tiglath-Pileser III recorded various Phoenician cities, such as Arqa and Byblos, as well as two called Zimarra and Simirra, or Sumri.[23,24] Byblos is the Greek name for the Gebal of Scripture, known as *GBL* in Ugarit and Phoenician and as *Kbn* in Egyptian.[25,26,27]

In later times, their entire people were referred to as the Phoenicians, a name that means something like red or purple, which was partly given to them by the Greeks.[28] As mentioned before, the people of *kn'n* were people who made a *kinahhu* or red-purple cloth, a color that came from certain shellfish.[6,28,29] These names came from Canaan's name first, and the color interpretation was applied later. The Phoenicians and Punics, of a settlement on the African coast, called their great city *SDN* and the people *HSDNYM*, that is, "Sidon and the Sidonians."[30] Their name for their land was "*sdn 'rs ym*" or "Sidon-Land-by-the-Sea"; even their coins knew them as seafaring people.[31]

In truth, these were people of the sea, their exploits taking them around the Mediterranean, settling in coastal places, leaving behind people such as the Punics in Carthage.[32] They still considered themselves to be Canaanite, despite the new name.[28,33,34,35] Of course, the most famous Carthaginian is Hannibal from his campaign in Italy; the second is Dido, their founder and relative of Jezebel.[36] Strabo lays out Phoenicia in his *Geography*, informing the reader it is from "Libanus and Antilibanus, …from Orthosia as far as Pelusium, and is called Phoenicia, a narrow strip of land along the sea."[37]

Finally, as prophesied in the books of the prophets and discussed above, Tyre was destroyed. The Assyrians and Babylonians, among others, controlled and besieged Tyre at various times. Josephus says the Persians held the cities before the Greeks.[38] Strabo documented that Alexander the Great razed the city after besieging it, though later it would somewhat recover.[6,38,39] The people of Sidon and Canaan were known to many nations during and after their time of prosperity. There are numerous other histories and records containing this renowned people, but they are too many to include here. Though known better by their Greek name, these were a people of Canaan.

Heth

The Hittites, or חתי in Hebrew, are descended from the second son of Canaan, known as Heth or חֵת (Gen. 10:15, 1Ch. 1:13).[40,41,42] Both names are related to the Hebrew word for terror.[43] Heth and his descendants were well-known to the Israelites. In fact, the Hittites were considered a fabrication of Scripture until recently when extra-biblical evidence of their existence was brought to light, and Scripture was shown to hold an accurate record of history once again. Though not all the encounters between these people were during war, and some Hittites were key players in the accounts of Scripture, few of the meetings between these two peoples resulted in peace. Their land was to be inherited by the descendants of Abraham, and they were to be driven out by the Lord through the Israelites.[44] Many of their people relocated and became a great nation.

Abraham is the first to have a notable encounter with the Hittites in Scripture when he encounters a Hittite named Ephron, son of Zohar, who sells land to Abraham for Sarah's grave (Gen. 23). Later, Abraham, Isaac, and Jacob would be buried in the same place (Gen. 25:7-10, 35:27-29, 49:29-33, 50:13). Isaac and Rebecca's son Esau married two Hittite women, Judith and Basemath, who were a "source of grief" to his parents (Gen 26:34-35, 27:46, 36:2).

Scripture recorded some Hittites as living near Mamre in Hebron, called Kiriath Arba by those living there (Gen. 23:2-19, Jos. 14:15). This city was founded by Arba, the forefather of the Anakites, (Num. 13:21-22, Jos. 15:13). According to these accounts, these men were giants, which may explain the stories about massive people recorded by Naram-Sin and other Mesopotamians (Gen. 6:4, Num. 13:33).[45] This land was on the West Bank of Israel, and the city remains to this day. This area is also referred to as the hill country in the same general area of the Jebusites and Amorites (Num. 13:29). God says that Israel was to inherit all the Hittite land, reaching the Euphrates at the center of the Hittite Kingdom, but Israel failed to do so (Jos. 1:4, 24:11). During the conquest of Canaan, the Hittites and their brothers fought Israel many times, and Israel captured Hebron's king (Jos. 9:1, 11:3, 12:8-10).

Not all the Hittites were completely destroyed, such as one spared from Bethel who left, took his family "to the land of the Hittites, and built a city and called it Luz," the former name of Bethel (Jdg. 1:22-26). The Hittite empire continued after the conquest of Canaan, and trade continued between Israel and the Hittites (Jdg. 3:5-6, 1Ki. 10:29, 2Ch. 1:17). Solomon also married Hittite women, though the Lord forbade it, a practice continuing even after the exile (1Ki. 11:1, Ezr. 9:1, Eze. 16:3-45). Some Hittites who remained in the land would eventually help build the temple (1Ki. 9:20, 2Ch. 8:7-8). A few Hittites were close companions to and served many leading Israelites. Two were Ahimelech and Uriah, the second a close friend of David (1Sa. 26:6, 2Sa. 23:39, 1Ch. 11:41). But David sinned against him and his wife, had Uriah killed, and paid for his actions dearly (2Sa. 11:1-12:23, 1Ki. 15:5). The Hittites are mentioned again later during a war with Aram, who flee in fear of an Egyptian and Hittite army (2Ki. 7:5-7).

The Hittites occupied land in the north that was never claimed by Israel, and their territory stretched to Anatolia. For a time, the Hittite empire grew into a great kingdom that dominated others, lasting until the Assyrians finally conquered and assimilated them into some tribes of Japheth.[46,47] Two of their greatest cities were in central Anatolia: Luwiya and Hattusa.[47] Parts of modern-day Turkey and Syria contain the greatest extent of Hittite territory outside of Canaan, including that which was recorded in Scripture. Most of the texts of the Hatti, however, refer to kings of a much later time and not much remains of their period after Babel, unless one considers them relatives of the Hattians. Possibly the oldest reference to the Hittite kingdom outside of Scripture comes from a record of Naram-Sin, king of Akkad.[45,48,49] This record mentions two kings of Hatti land: Zipani and Pamba.[48,49] The first was only king of Kanesh, but the second was king of all the Hittites.[45,48,49] He may have been an early descendant of Heth.

Egypt dealt with the Hatti as well, and they were not on friendly terms. During the reign of Seti I, a "great slaughter" was made of the "wretched Hittites."[50] The Amarna letters also discuss the land of the Hatti, most often concerning wars fought between the writer's people and the Hatti, a people they feared.[51] Thutmose III received tribute from the chief the *Kheta* or *H-t* !.[52] It was not until the reign of Rameses II that peace was made with the Hatti, whose king was Hattusilis, a peace which included a marriage.[53,54] Other texts of the Hittites contain treaties made with other nations, such as the Amurru, while Mursilis son of Suppiluliumas was king.[54] Thus, these people remained a notable nation even to the latter days of the Egyptians.

The Assyrians kept decent records of nearby nations, especially from war. The Hittites were known as *ha-at-ti* and their land as "the land of Hatti" or the "Hittite-land."[46,49,55] Though Ashurnasirpal II and

Shalmaneser III received tribute from the Hittites, there were still minor kings who oversaw the region, such as King Sangara.[56] In one account by Sargon, there is an "evil Hittite" called Ia'u-bi'di who made a claim for the throne of Hamath.[57,58] Accounting only for the records of Egypt and Assyria, the Hatti were not well-liked, often referred to as wicked, mischievous, and schemers. Despite their later dissolution as an empire, they were a real people to those of Mesopotamia and beyond, even outside of the texts mentioned, though forgotten until recently. These people were of Hamitic and not Japhetic descent, despite claims to the contrary. While the people mixed because of conquests and settled in lands inhabited by descendants of Japheth and Shem, the Hittites were of Canaan.

Jebusites

Jebus was the third son of Canaan, and his people were the Jebusites (Gen. 10:16, 1Ch. 1:14). His people are יְבוּסִי in Hebrew and his name is יְבוּס, which will be discussed below.[59,60] He and his brothers were among those who were to be driven out of the land for Abraham's descendants (Gen. 15:18-21, Ex. 3:8-17, 13:5, 23:23, 33:2, 34:11, Neh. 9:5-8). When the Israelites explored the land of Canaan, they noted its abundance, but also the great people and cities there, including the Jebusites who lived in the hill country (Num. 13:26-29). God commanded Israel to totally destroy or give over the people of the land to the Lord, including the Jebusites, for they would lead the people astray with their false gods (Deut. 7:1-6, 20:16-18, Jos. 3:10, 24:11).

After the kings of the Jebusites and their brothers in the hill country heard that the Israelites conquered Jericho and Ai, they began to war with Israel (Jos. 9:1-3). The Gibeonites deceived Israel and were spared, so King Adonizedek of Jerusalem, then called Jebus, joined with four other kings to attack the Gibeonites, but the Israelites saved them (Jos. 10:1-15). Here, they are called Amorites, but this is probably due to the Jebusites and Amorites living near each other and holding governance together. The kings of the north, south, and hill country joined to fight Israel, but they all lost to Israel (Jos. 11:1-4,12).

The portion of the land once occupied by the Jebusites and others of the hill country was given to the tribe of Judah, including an important city, here called the "Jebusite city (that is, Jerusalem)" (Jos. 15:1-8). Jerusalem was called Jebus before David renamed it (Jdg. 19:10-11). Benjamin's land reached to the "southern slope of the Jebusite city," which was built on a hill (Jos. 18:16-28). Judah and Benjamin were not able to completely expel the Jebusites, leading Israel to intermarry with them, serve their gods, and do evil in the Lord's eyes (Jos. 15:63, Jdg. 1:21, 3:5-7, Ezr. 9:1-10:3).

It was not until David became king that the high time of the Jebusites came to an end. Until that time, the Jebusites dwelled in their city Jebus, which David renamed and rebuilt (2Sa. 5:6-9, 24:16, 1Ch. 11:4-8). David built an altar to the Lord "on the threshing floor of Araunah the Jebusite" (2Sa. 24:18, 1Ch. 21:15, 18). Araunah and his sons offered his land, oxen, wood, and grain for the altar and offering to the Lord (1Ch. 21:20-23). David insisted that he pay for the land, buying it for "six hundred shekels of gold" and built an altar (1Ch. 21:28). Solomon built the Temple on this threshing floor, and some of its builders were Jebusites (1Ki. 9:20-23, 1Ch. 8:7, 2Ch. 3:1). In the book of Zechariah, God speaks against Israel's enemies, saying that the Philistine city Ekron will be like the Jebusites, but everyone left in the land will "belong to our God" (Zec. 9:7).

Outside of Scripture, some have claimed that an Assyrian and Babylonian contract tablet contains the original name for Jerusalem, Jebus, called here *Yabusu*.[61] The Akkadian-written Amarna tablets, written long after David renamed the city, included a man named Abd-hiba who writes to Egypt from Jerusalem, called *U-ru-sa-lim*.[62] The Mari tablets contain a *Yabusi'um*, considered to be Jerusalem.[63] Some of the names found in Scripture and elsewhere point scholars to assume that the Jebusites were those called Hurrian.[64,65] As will be explained, the Hurrians may have been a tribe related to the Canaanites via another son of Canaan, though such distinctions are often pointless. The Canaanites possibly were related to the Hurrians, or rather, the Hurrians to Canaan. While the Jebusites were well known in their day, they seem to have been inconsequential to most outside records.

Amorites

The Amorites are descended from the fourth son of Canaan, called אֱמֹרִי in Hebrew (Gen. 10:16, 1Ch. 1:14).[66] The Amorites were known as Emor, Amori, and Amorreus by various religious writers.[15,42,67] Shortly after Abraham is called out of Ur, Scripture records an attack by eastern Mesopotamian kings against those in the west, including the Amorites (Gen. 14:1-7). Their land is said to be in Hazezon Tamar, but they do not appear to be a great nation at this time (Gen. 14:7). Abraham allied with some Amorites: Mamre, Eschol, and Aner (Gen. 13:18, 14:13). Mamre was in what became known as Hebron. It is assumed that the place Abraham stayed is located at or near the modern sites of Ramat el-Khalil or Khirbet es-Sibte just south of Jerusalem (Gen.23:19).[68]

Unfortunately, the Amorites were steeped in the same idolatry as the rest of the Canaanites, and thus God said that Israel, specifically Joseph, would receive their land when "the sin of the Amorites" had "reached its full measure" (Gen. 15:16-21, 48:22). God frequently reminds the Israelites that He is bringing them into the land of the Canaanites, which includes the Amorites, warning His people to not practice the ways of the Canaanites, but to destroy them and to obey His commands.[69] But as should be understood by now, they were not destroyed and, besides fearing them initially, the Israelites allowed Amorites to live in the land, or could not drive them out, marrying them and adopting their practices.[70]

Another Scriptural indicator of their land is found in the book of Numbers,

> "They set out from there (that is, the Zered Valley near Moab) and camped alongside the Arnon, which is in the desert extending into Amorite territory. The Arnon is the border of Moab, between Moab and the Amorites."
> (Num. 21:13)

This would place the Amorites on the edge of Canaan, east of the Jordan, and north of Moab. Sihon, king of the Amorites, encountered Israel during this time, refused Israel's request for passage, and marched his army against them (Num. 21:21-23). Israel killed Sihon, and Reuben's tribe took his land, though they had to stop at the border of Ammon (Num. 21:24-31, Deut. 1:4, 2:24, 3:2-9, Jos. 12:2, 13:21). Their land was in the hill country of Canaan, an area well-fortified (Deut. 1:7, 19-20-44). This land, called Heshbon, once belonged to the Moabites (Num. 25-26). Later the tribe of Manasseh went to Gilead and "drove out the Amorites" living there (Num. 32:29). Another defeated king was Og of Bashan, but he will be discussed at the end of this chapter (Deut. 4:46-47, 31:4, Jos. 24:11-12).

While many nations to the west of the Jordan were afraid of Israel, mainly due to the defeat of Og, Sihon, and Jericho, other people, including the Amorites, set out to fight (Jos. 5:1, 9:1-10, 11:1-5). Five kings of the Amorites joined to attack Gibeon and were defeated by Israel (Jos. 10:5-12). When the Lord tells Israel of all the land left to be taken, He includes the land "of the Sidonians as far as Aphek, the region of the Amorites," though it is unclear if this includes or borders on that land (Jos. 13:4-10). Thus, not all of the Amorite territory was conquered by Israel, and the Amorite nation grew elsewhere (Num. 21:31-32, Jos. 5:1, 1Sa. 7:14). Many of the Amorites lived northeast of Israel, though at the time of the Judges some were still in Canaan.[71]

As understood from Scripture, the Amorites settled west of the Jordan and were slowly pushed northward during and after the conquest of Canaan. This is where they are found in records outside of Scripture. Their home, such as Hazezon Tamar, would have been in what is now the West Bank and Jordan, but they moved into the territory of Assyria, modern-day Syria (Gen. 14:7). Ein Gedi, an oasis, is another name for this place (2Ch. 20:2, Song. 1:14, Ezk. 47:10).[72,73] The Oak of Mamre, mentioned in the above with Abraham, is likely within the greater area of Hazezon Tamar, though the Ein Gedi is much smaller. The Arnon, the division between Moab and the Amorites, is known today as the Wadi Mujib.[74,75] The location of Gilead and Bashan is unclear, but it would have been in the northeast section of Israel, where Manasseh was located, as all the area from the Arnon to the Ammonites was Israel, and the Arnon divided Manasseh from Gad and Reuben.[76,77] Thus, the Amorites were pushed farther north over time, never fully wiped out, and they became a notable nation.

Some of the earliest attestations of the Amorites are in Sumerian texts, which called the land of the Amorites *Martu*, a land to the west.[78] The kingdom of Ebla, which the Amorites and Assyrians would later encompass, calls them the *Mar-tu* or *Mar-tu-am*, recognized by many scholars as the land of the Amorites.[79,80] The most famous of the Amorites may be Hammurabi.[81] King of Babylon, his name is said to be of both Amorite and Akkadian etymology.[81] He and his successors referred to themselves as the "king of the Martu," the land of the Amorites.[82] The Amorites at this time grew in power and held high positions in Assyria and Babylon.[83] Eventually, they fell to other nations, including the Hittites, Assyria, and Egypt.

Both Hittite treaties and the Amarna tablets contain references to a king of the *Mar.tu* or *Amurru* called *Azira/i* or *Aziras*.[84,85] Azira was a loyal subject, but eventually, he became a problem for others in the area.[84] In other letters, Azira was attacking the city Katna, and the writer, fearing capture while traveling through *Mar.tu*, requests assistance.[84] Writers from Dunip and Tyre also fear King Azira of the *Mar.tu*.[86] But it was the son of *Aziras*, *Duppit-tessub*, who reigned during the time of *Mursilis*, the Hittite king with whom the treaty was made.[85] Additionally, there is a bas-relief of seven kings subdued by Ramses III, including a Hittite, an Amorite, and five others from neighboring regions.[87] Tiglath-Pileser claims to have conquered the country of the *Amurru*.[88] Sennacherib's annals record the Amorites as the *MAR.TU.KI* or *Amurru* and define not only their land but also their distinct language.[89,90] The Chronicle of Nabonidus briefly mentioned the *Amurru* in a battle record.[91] *Amurru* means something like "the west" in Akkadian, which may have to do with its location west of the Euphrates in part of Assyria, putting them where the Israelites knew them to be.

The Amorites were well-known by all, if not well-loved. Though they were known to dwell in the western part of Mesopotamia, some resided in and even returned to Babylon, such as with Hammurabi's ancestors. But their nation eventually fell to the kingdoms that grew around them. They were Canaanites, but like the Hittites, were known as a separate, powerful group.

Girgashites

There is little known about the Girgashites, either within Scripture or outside. They are descended from the fifth son of Canaan, גִּרְגָּשִׁי in Hebrew (Gen. 10:16, 1Ch. 1:14).[92] As they are from Canaan, the Girgashites are among those whose land would be given as an inheritance to Israel (Gen. 15:21, Deu. 7:1, Jos. 3:10, Neh. 9:8). They are among the first tribes to face the Israelites after they crossed the Jordan, possibly placing them near the Jordan (Jos. 24:11). Their few appearances in Scripture may imply that they either were incorporated into another tribe of Canaan or were destroyed. Josephus renders the name for this son as Gergesus, but informs the reader that their people were overthrown completely by Israel and their cities destroyed, leaving no information "but their names."[15] Some scholars consider a personal name found in Ugaritic texts, *grgs* or *bn-grgs*, to be "son of Grgs or Girgash."[93,94,95,96] This may be the source of the spelling for the name used in the *Book of Jasher*: the Girgashi.[42,97] While the extra-biblical names for this people are inconclusive, it is reasonable to believe this was the nation that has since disappeared.

Hivites

The Hivites are descended from the sixth son of Canaan, likely called Hivi, חִוִּי in Hebrew (Gen. 10:17, 1Ch. 1:15).[98] Though they are not mentioned when God makes a covenant with Abraham, the land of Canaan is said to include the land of the Hivites, and God sends His angel to drive them out (Gen. 15:18-21).[69] One of Esau's wives is called a Hivite (Gen. 26:35, 27:46-28:9, 36:2). Shechem, a Hivite city, was known to Abraham and Jacob (Gen. 12:6, 33:18-19). Jacob bought land from the Hivite ruler there, named Hamor, and it was this man's son Shechem who violated Dinah, resulting in much death (Gen. 33:19-34:3-31). The Hivites, in general, were not dissimilar from nearby peoples and places that traded, shepherded, and had leaders at the city gate (Gen. 34:17-28).

When the Israelites came back from Egypt, they encountered a collection of the Canaanite tribes who "came together to make war against" Israel (Jos. 9:1). It is here that the Gibeonites are found to be

Hivites, though they deceived Israel into thinking they were a far-off nation so they would be protected (Jos. 9:1-16). At this point, their cities besides Gibeon were Kephirah, Beeroth, and Kiriath Jearim (Jos. 9:17). Because of their deception, Joshua made them woodcutters and water carriers for Israel (Jos. 9:17-27). Other Hivites joined with the northern kings of the Canaanites to attack Israel and Gibeon, but God delivered them into the hand of Israel (Jos. 11:1-19, 12:8, 24:11). Thus, they were not destroyed and even had cities in the days of David and Solomon (2Sa. 24:7, 1Kin. 9:20, 2Ch. 8:7-8). Saul, however, broke this treaty during his rule and put some of the Gibeonites to death, angering the Lord and leading to famine during David's reign (2Sa. 21:1-9).

The Hivites lived near Hermon, in Mizpah by the Phoenicians, and in the Lebanon mountains (Jos. 11:3, 2Sa. 24:7, Jdg. 3:3-5). This would place some Hivites in northern Israel, some in the mountains near Tyre and Sidon, some along the river Jordan in Shechem, and the rest likely around Jerusalem, which would have kept them quite near their brothers the Jebusites. Josephus states that the Israelites "overthrew" the cities of the Hivites, whom he calls Eudeus.[15,99] There is little known of the Hivites outside of Scripture. One inscription from Phoenicia mentions a land called *Hiyawa*, which may be the Hivites, but that hypothesis is tentative.[64,100,101] The same can be said for an inscription found among the records of Ramses II, who mentions the land of *hwt*, which is *Hiyawa*.[64,102] Scripture contains the most information on this small tribe of Canaan.

An additional tribe sometimes connected to the Hivites were the Horites in Seir. While the Hivites lived from the north to the south in Canaan, the Horites appear to have lived almost exclusively in the south. Their forefather was Seir the Horite, who is first mentioned during the time of Abraham and Kedorlaomer (Gen. 14:5-6). But the odd thing about Seir the Horite is that his son Zibeon is called the Hivite in a passage discussing his granddaughter's marriage to Esau (Gen. 36:2-25). In all other instances, these chiefs of Seir are called Horites and are said to have lived there until the Edomites drove them away (Gen. 36:20-30, Num. 13:5, Deut. 2:12-22). But why would they be called Horites if they are Hivites? It is possible they were renamed by Seir or his grandson Hori (Gen. 36:22).

Another possibility is that they were one tribe that originated in the north near Babel and split as they moved south and west. Some scholars have suggested that the Hurrians of northern Mesopotamia were the original sons of Hivi, and these became multiple groups – the Hurrians, the Hivites, and the Horites, among others – but how they are connected is unclear, if plausible.[103,104] The Hurrians were known as the *hurwi*, and these same scholars say the names of the Hivites and Horites came out of them.[103,104] The Horites were known as the *Khurru* by Thutmose IV.[105] All that can be known for sure about this group is that they appear to be related to the Hivites and they intermarried with the Edomites, who eventually expelled or wiped them out.

Arkites

The seventh son of Canaan gave rise to the people called the Arkites (Gen. 10:17, 1Ch. 1:15). Their name is עַרְקִי in Hebrew, Arkee in the *Book of Jasher*, and Arucas by Josephus, another name given to the city of Arce.[15,42,106] Like the Hivites, the Arkites are not mentioned in Genesis when God first promises the land of Canaan to Abraham (Gen. 15:17-21). While this word is not used outside of the chronologies, another is used for their territory and people. אַרְכִּי is translated as Arkite and found multiple times, though separate from the conquest.[107] It appears that this tribe never grew and was quickly overcome by other nations and tribes within or near Canaan. Going back to Josephus, the city Arce (Libanus) was once inhabited by the Arkites.[15] This city, located near Sidon, was renamed Libanus, Libanum, and Arca Caesarea when Greece and Rome controlled the area.[6,73,108,109]

Though the Arkites were still living in the land during the conquest, nothing seems to have been done about them. In fact, Joseph's sons' land was to include the land of the Arkites, yet this is the first time they are mentioned since Babel (Jos. 16:2). The next reference to the Arkites is of a certain man named Hushai. He was a friend of David who mourned for Absalom's conspiracy, though he obeyed David's command to go back and serve Absalom (2Sa. 15:32-37, 1Ch. 27:33). Hushai protected David against the plots of Absalom and his counselor Ahithophel (2Sa. 16:16-17:29). While the text is unclear, it is possible that one of Solomon's governors, Baana, was a son of this Hushai (1Ki. 4:7-16).

Two early references of the Arkites (perhaps to a city, an area, or both) are found in Assyrian and Egyptian records. Shalmaneser III fought troops that included those from Israel and Irqanata.[56] The *Execration Texts* speak of the city Irqartum as well.[110] Under the rule of Tiglath-Pileser III, Arqa was among his conquered cities.[23] The Amarna tablets speak of the same city, including people writing from *Ir-ka-ta* to Egypt.[111] In some of these letters, the writer is requesting aid from the Pharaoh. In another, the writer reports that the Habiri killed King Aduna of Irkata.[112] Thutmose III went to Irqata "in order to destroy the town" and those around it.[113] Other translations called the city *Erkatu* and placed it near the "coast road."[114] Because of its location, this city was likely also occupied by the Phoenicians. Today, this city clings to its roots and is known as Tell Arka.[115,116]

Sinites

The Sinites descended from the eighth son of Canaan, known as סִינִי in Hebrew, as Sini in the *Book of Jasher,* and Sineus by Josephus (Gen. 10:17, 1Ch. 1:15).[15,42,117] Their people are never mentioned elsewhere in Scripture, save the possibility they are included in the general Canaanites. There are, however, a few places in Scripture that infer where they went. There are also other extra-biblical sources that hint at other settlements. From these, it appears that the Sinites split up. They did not quite do what the Phoenicians did, to stay a nation spread throughout the Mediterranean, nor become a city like other brothers. Instead, some seemed to stay in Canaan, others settled near Egypt, and others went to a land that has been barely touched by this book so far.

First, there are references to a city in the northern Canaanite region that seems to imply at least some Sinites settled among their brothers post-Babel. Strabo, in his *Geography,* mentions a fortress called Sinna around Libanus, a mountainous region in modern-day Lebanon.[6] This area was also within the territory of the Sidonians, so perhaps some Sinites stayed with their more powerful brethren. Sin, as he likely was called, may have been the inspiration for a couple of Mesopotamian gods, particularly Isinu and Sin.[118,119,120] Sin was a common suffix in

Mesopotamian names, which could either be the result of this son or the nature of the language.

Bearing a comparable name to the Sinites, the Sinai Peninsula, once called the Desert of Sin, is located on the edge of Egypt, an area the Israelites spent considerable time in (Ex. 16:1, 17:1, Num. 33:11-12).[121] Here was a city called Pelusium, the same recorded by Strabo as being a border for the Phoenicians and one of the cities of Egypt.[37] In the book of Ezekiel, God speaks of the coming wrath for Egypt, including the city of Pelusium, "the stronghold of Egypt" (Ezk. 33:11-12). The word used for Pelusium is the same for the Desert of Sin. This city seems better connected to Mizraim and one of his sons, though it may have been founded by the Sinites. This area is known for Mt. Sinai, with an etymology that is similar to the Sinites and the desert land.[122] The mountain is said to be "between Elim and Sinai."[123] Before it was Pelusim to the Greeks, it was Sin to the Hebrews, *Seyan* to the Arabs, and *Per-Amun* to the Egyptians, for whom there was a temple.[124]

The last and most extreme location for the Sinites is in Asia, specifically China. China, while chosen mainly because of etymology and language, is plausible for other reasons. First, the Scriptural reference for this location is found in the book of Isaiah. Here, there is the word סינים or Sinim.[125] Various translations have different interpretations of how to translate this word, but most call it Sinim. Yet the Latin Vulgate translates the word as *australi*.[126] Why might this be? Well the chapter speaks on Israel's restoration, the verse saying, "See, they will come from afar – some from the north, some from the west, some from the region of (Sinim)."[126] Two clear directions are given, north and south, and a third is implied: Sinim. The Vulgate indicates that this is in the far east.[125,126]

Thus, there is a suggestion that some of the Sinites went far east and away from their brothers in Canaan. Regarding etymology, the word Sinim in Isaiah is related to those referenced earlier. But other nations had a similar name for this far east country. The Arabic word for China is *Sin* or *Tchin*.[127,128] Today, the western world, or at least those influenced by a Romance Language, refers to China as "sino-" or Sinitic.[129] But in ancient times, the East was called something like that found in Scripture. Ptolemy, in his *Geography,* called the land to the east both "Sera" and "Sinai."[130] He and others of the Roman Empire knew of a Chinese city called "Sera Metropolis."[131,132] Pliny is referring to these same people, known for their trade in cloth, when he speaks of the Seres, a group living near but separate from the Scythians.[133] He notes that while these people would trade the cloth they made, they were rather secluded.[133] This is specifically interesting, for as the Phoenicians were known for their clothmaking, so too were the Chinese known for theirs. Other works call the land Sinae and a city within called Thinae, which produced silk as Pliny described.[134]

A version of the name Thinae is found in Greek works, which called the land *Tsin* and *Thinae*, a name which seems to have originated with Eratosthenes.[128,135,136] Recent authors have written on a man called Cosmas who traveled to a place called *Tzinistae*, a land considered to be China.[137,138,139,140] Additionally, old Chinese, Japanese, and Sanskrit texts hold similar references to this ancient country, calling it *dzin, Shina,* and *Cina*, respectively.[141,142,143,144] While any number of coincidences could be named to explain why all these locations, not including others of a similar nature, have names for this distant land that are so similar, the name likely derived from a common ancestry, not just through etymology but genealogy. And regarding genealogy, these people likely did not stay here. Like their Japhetic cousins to the north, they too likely traveled farther than the connected continents of Eurasia.[145] Perhaps they too traveled to what became the Americas. And, as the Vulgate's language implies, they became the people of the islands south of Asia, Australia, and beyond.

Arvadites

The Arvadites, from the ninth son of Canaan and called אַרְוָדִי in Hebrew, are only mentioned twice in Scripture (Gen. 10:18, 1Ch. 1:16).[146] Scripture includes a city likely named from the founder only twice as well. In these verses, Arvad, or אַרְוָד in Hebrew, supports Tyre by giving the Phoenicians skilled oarsmen and soldiers (Ezk. 27:8-11).[147] Isidore connected this son, whom he called Arvadah, to the island city *Aradum*, near the coast of Phoenicia.[148] Josephus and the *Book of Jasher* renders the name *Arudeus* and *Arkee,* respectively, but Josephus adds that he inhabited the island *Aradus*.[15,42] Because of the connection to Tyre and its insignificant status, many ancient sources consider this to be a Phoenician city.

According to their records, the Assyrians encountered the Arvadites on various occasions. Sennacherib even directly names one *Arvadate*, *Abdi-li'ti*, in his annals.[19] Among the many cities of Phoenicia, Arvad, called *Ar-ma-da* "on the seashore," was a city from which Tiglath-Pileser I received tribute and boats.[56] Ashurnasirpal II comments on the tribute from the Phoenician cities, including the island of Arvad, which contained precious metals, colored cloth, and various animal and sea products.[17] Shalmaneser III fought the Arvadites and their brothers the Arkites.[56] Shalmaneser, Tiglath-Pileser III, and Esarhaddon mention someone named Matinu-ba'lu, Matan-be'l, and Matanba'al, respectively, as the governor of Arvad.[20,23,56] Assurbanipal mentions waring with Iakinlu, who ruled Arvad and dwelled "in the wide sea."[149] Iakinlu finally gave the king, among other things, dark-red wool as tribute, connecting them to the Sidonians.[149] Sargon II had to deal with a revolt by Arvad, Hamath, and Simirra.[58] Many other records contain Arvad, but Assyria dealt with them frequently.

Other sources focus on the city's connection to the sea. Pliny noted the city of *Arado* was an island at a distance from the coast.[150] The annals of Thutmose III recorded activities involving Arvad, called *3-r3-t-wt*, including its capture.[151] In the Amarna tablets, the writer asks Egypt to send someone to deal with the people of *Arwad* or *Ar-wa-da* who are causing trouble with Simyra "by way of the sea."[152] Surprisingly, one of the writers from Tyre is frustrated by the people of *Arwad* who were collecting ships and alliances.[153] Another reassures the ruler in Egypt that Arwad's ships are in Egypt.[154] Thus, many knew of Arvad and their people, though generally as Canaanites. They, too, would have been enveloped by the Phoenicians as their city and Arvad's people became a part of the greater nation.

Zemarites

The Zemarites, from the tenth son of Canaan, are also only found within the genealogies of Scripture; their name is צְמָרִים in Hebrew (Gen. 10:18, 1Ch. 1:16).[155] Josephus provides the name Samareus for this son of Canaan but states that their people were overthrown.[15] The *Book of*

Jasher calls this son Zimodi.[42] While this provides very little evidence for their location, Scripture gives one more clue. There was a city in the north, within Phoenicia, north of Sidon but south of Arvad, called Zemaraim (Jos. 18:22).[156] There was also a mountain by the same name (2Ch. 13:1-20). This is likely where the Zemarites settled. But as the Phoenicians grew, they fell under the rule of the Sidonians.

This city appears in various ancient records. Over time, this city came under the control of the Amorites, Hamathites, Egyptians, Assyrians, and Phoenicians.[24] The city of the Zemarites can be found along the one-time Phoenician coast, though known today as the site of Tell Kazel-Simyra.[157] This city, also found in the works of Pliny by the name Sumra, is a city located near Libanus along the coast, which is the ancient but renamed territory of the Arkites.[150] This coastal city, as shall be shown in the following, is often recorded alongside the cities of the Phoenicians, becoming one of their dependents.

Tiglath-Pileser III recorded two cities called Zimarra and Simirra, or Sumri, which were at this point under Phoenician control.[23,24] Sargon II mentions the city of Simirra, also called *si-mir-ra*, along with Arad, Damascus, and Samaria.[158,159] He also mentions a rebellion begun by a Hittite, looking for the throne of Hamath, who stirred up the cities of Arpadda and Simirra, among others.[57,58] In another record, Sargon recounts his visit to "the land of Zamua" and of a huge mountain called Mount Simirria, likely the same in Scripture.[160]

Another ancient name for this city and fortress is *Sumur*, not to be confused with the eastern Sumer and the Sumerians.[24] When writing to the Egyptians, the Akkadian Amarna tablets record the name of Zemaraim as *Sumur* or *Sumuri*, though translated into English as Simyra.[161] Other translations and records, however, give the city the name *Tsumuri*, which highly resembles the Hebrew name.[162] Still others provide the name Zemar.[162] In the Amarna tablets, we learn that the land of Simyra had grain, requested repairs from Egypt, and engaged in various battles.[111,161,163] There are also many times the writer reassures the receiver that Simyra is the servant of Egypt.[164] The annals of Thutmose III tell of the Pharaoh's travels to this Phoenician land. In fact, when the Pharaoh travels to the area, it is called the Phoenician harbor, though the coast of the city is Simyra.[151] This city seemed to be a convenient harbor for the Egyptians when they traveled to Kadesh.[151] The transcription for the city's Egyptian name is *D3-my-r3*.[151] The people of the area, who called themselves Simyra, were well known by other nations but appear to have been enveloped by the Phoenicians.

Hamathites

The Hamathites are from the eleventh son of Canaan; their name is חֲמָתִי in Hebrew (Gen. 10:18, 1Ch. 1:16).[165] While this specific name appears only twice in Scripture, a well-known city and nation were named after him in what is now in southern Syria.[166,167] While his people are never directly mentioned outside the collective Canaanites, his city is often found in Scripture. Hamath was one of the most northern Canaanite cities besides the territory of the Hittites.

Hamath is first mentioned during the exploration of Canaan, as Hamath would become the northern border of Israel (Num. 13:21, 34:8, Jos. 13:5, Ezk. 47:16-20, 48:1). The land of Naphtali was to include certain "fortified cities," one of which is Hammath, where some of Caleb's descendants lived (Jos. 19:35, 1Ch. 2:55).[168] Another city, Hammoth Dor, was given to the Levites within the land of Naphtali (Jos. 21:32).[169] When Israel settled in the land, Hamath's borders are provided along with a note that the Hivites lived nearby, though not expressly in it (Jdg. 3:3). It is implied that Damascus was a strong city for Hamath and Arpad (Jer. 49:23). While the book of Amos calls Hamath great, it also describes this city and others as complacent (Amo. 6:2).[170] The last mention and the clearest marker for the land of Hamath are in the book of Zechariah, where it says that Hamath borders on Israel around Damascus, Tyre, and Sidon (Zec. 9:1-2). King Jeroboam II restored the boundaries of Israel from "Lebo (or the entrance of) Hamath to the Sea of Arabah" (2Ki. 14:24-28). While the text is unclear, the land of Israel probably did not include most of the land of Hamath.

During the reign of David, there is evidence that the Hamathites still lived there. Their king, either Toi or Tou, sent gifts with his son to David as thanks for defeating Hadadezer's army, an enemy of Hamath (2Sa. 8:3-11, 1Ch. 18:3-10). Scholars identify this king as King Taita, who wrote in an inscription, "I (am) King Taita, the Hero, the King of [the Land?] PaDAsatini."[171,172] Taita controlled territory from Aleppo to Hama and included the kingdoms of Patin and Arpad in addition to Hamath.[171] When David brought back the Ark, he brought Israelites "from the Shihor River in Egypt to Lebo Hamath" (1Ch. 13:5). When Solomon held a festival for the Lord, people "from Lebo (or the entrance of) Hamath to Wadi Egypt" celebrated (1Ki. 8:65, 2Ch. 7:8). Later, Solomon captured Hamath Zorbah (2Ch. 8:3-4).

When the king of Assyria relocated Hamathites to "replace the Israelites," the Hamathites did not know how to serve the Lord and served other gods such as their Ashima (2Ki. 17:24-41, 18:34-19:13, Isa. 36:19, 37:13).[173] Neco of Egypt imprisoned King Jehoahaz of Judah at Hamath, and later, the king of Babylon executed captives from Judah and Zedekiah's sons there (2Ki. 23:33, 25:18-21, Jer. 39:5, 52:9-27). But God comforts His people, saying "the Root of Jesse will stand as a banner for the peoples; the nations will rally to him" – people from Africa, the islands of the sea, Babylon, and Hamath – and He will collect His scattered people (Isa. 11:9-12).

While the *Book of Jasher* calls this son Chamothi, Josephus calls him Amathus and his land Amathe, though later another descendant called it Epiphania.[15,42] Pliny recorded such a city, calling it Epiphanaenses, and placing it in Syria.[174] Both texts explain how the city was later known as Emath.[175,176] In texts closer to the region, however, the city is called Hamath. In annals of Shalmaneser III, Hamath is called *Amat* and seems to be a town under his control.[177] A king of Hamath, Irhuleni, and others nearby joined to fight Assyria.[177] Tiglath-Pileser III records an Enil and I'nil of Hamath as well as the defeat of this city, *Amatu*.[23,178] A man from Hamath, Ia'u-bi'di the Hittite, attempted to become king of Hamath, stirring up Arpadda, Simirra, Samaria, and Damascus against Assyria.[57,58,158] Sargon II eventually punished his crimes and, though Hamath proved troublesome for some time, he subdued it and relocated some inhabitants.[58,179,180] Babylonian inscriptions from Nabonidus mention the country of Hamath, yet they provide little information about the place.[91] Unsurprisingly, considering the city's proximity to Simyrra, the Egyptians dealt with Hamath, calling them *hwmwt* in the writings of Thutmose III.[181]

Lastly, there are a couple of brief inscriptions from the royal house Hamath.[182] These may be the most interesting of the texts regarding this onetime great people. Some want to call the hieroglyphic writing Hittite, others Hamathite, but either is definitely Canaanite.[183] Their word for *Hama*, which is Hamath, was *imatu*.[184] One inscription translates, "I am Urhilina son of Partas, Hamathite King."[185] Another text translates, "I am Uratamis Urhilina's son Hamathite king and I built this fortress."[186] This is intriguing since the name Hamath is linguistically linked to the Phoenician word *khamat* for "fort," and the city from Scripture was a fortified city.[187] These inscriptions mention three different kings of the Hamathites in their own language as well as document their city. Today, the city is known as Hama.[176,188]

Various People of Gigantic Proportion

A handful of tribes found in Scripture once dwelled near the Canaanites and seemed to be related to them. There is little to no specific ancestry found in Scripture, and yet they were important enough to include. Likely, they branched off from the Canaanites. These people are notable not only for their likely lineage but also due to their great height. They were giant people in what appears to be every sense of the word (Num. 13:31-32). Even the land around them was teaming with large produce (Num. 13:23). While I cannot define their direct ancestry, I decided, for the interest of research and curiosity's sake, to find them in history within and outside of Scripture.

The first group of giants, as they were called, were the Rephaites. The Israelites appear to have considered them to be a distinct tribe, even if descended from Canaan. Still, other tribes in the area seemed to have used the word Rephaim, which means giant, to name a larger group of Canaanites (Gen. 15:20, Psa. 135:11).[189] They are first mentioned when the kings of Mesopotamia and Canaan go to war, part of which included the Rephaites (Gen. 14:1-5). The Rephaites were said to live in Ashteroth Karnaim (Gen. 14:5).

Og, king of Bashan, ruling from Ashteroth and Edrei, was king of the Amorites, so it may be safe to assume that the Rephaites are a branch from the Amorites, and a tall one at that (Deut. 1:4, 4:47, 31:4, Jos. 2:10, 12:4). The book of Amos notes the Amorites for their height, comparing them to a cedar tree (Amo. 2:9). Their land, located in the northeastern part of Israel, was later given to Manasseh, Gad, Reuben, and a portion of Ephraim's tribe (Num. 32:33, Deut. 3:13, Jos. 17:15). Part of their land was the Valley of Rephaim, allowing that Rephaim could have been a person's name or that it simply meant giant (Jos. 15:8, 18:16, 2Sa. 5:18-22, 23:13, Isa. 17:5).

Og was notable for his great height – his bed was approximately thirteen by six feet – and for being the last of the Rephaites (Deut. 3:11, Jos. 12:4, 13:12). Even so, some Rephaites lived in Philistia (2Sa. 21:16). There was in Gath Ishbi-Benob, a descendant of Rapha but called a Philistine and a brother of Goliath; Saph of Rapha; and a twenty-four digited man, all who had massive weapons, but were killed by David's men (2Sa. 21:16-22, 1Ch 20:4-8). Perhaps this is how Goliath gained his great height (1Sa. 17:4-7).

The Ammonites called the Rephaites Zamzummites, but they were driven out by the Lord and the Ammonites took their land (Deut. 2:20-21). Here the people are called "as tall as the Anakites," another tribe that will be discussed (Deut. 2:21). The Emites also lived there, a group falling under the same description as the Zamzummites and Rephaites (Deut. 2:10-11). The Moabites drove out the Emites, though they seem to have just been a division of the Rephaites. The Emites and either the Zamzummites or a group similar called the Zuzites are included in the war of the Mesopotamian kings, living in Shaveh Kiriathaim and Ham, respectively (Gen. 14:5).

The last group of giants are the Anakites. Besides their notable height, the Anakites are intriguing because of their proposed connection to the Nephilim. However, they are related only through the meaning of their names and their stature. Anakim and Nephilim mean long-necked and giant, respectively.[190,191] The Nephilim of the pre-Flood world would have been wiped out along with everything that had "the breath of life in its nostrils" (Gen. 6:4, 7:22). In the post-Flood world, the Anakites are first mentioned during the exploration of Canaan (Num. 13:21-33, 14:7-8). In comparison with the Nephilim, the scouts say they "seemed like grasshoppers" (Num. 13:33). Here they are called the descendants of Anak, who come from the Nephilim (giants) living in Hebron (Num. 13:22-33). Their land included the hill country, like other

Canaanites, as well as Debir, though they remained in the Philistine cities Gath, Ashdod, and Gaza (Jos. 10:1-39, 11:21-22, 15:15).

The descendants of Anak are mentioned numerous times after this. Three of his descendants are Ahiman, Sheshai, and Talmai, who were driven out by Caleb from Kiriath Arba (Num. 13:22, Jos. 15:13-14, Jdg. 1:20). Additionally, the book of Joshua includes that the father of Anak was Arba, referred to as the "the greatest man among the Anakites" (Jos. 14:15, 15:13, 21:11). Scripture describes the Anakites as strong, taller than the Israelites, numerous, and builders of vast, tall cities (Deut. 1:28, 2:21, Jos 14:12). As with the other giants, the Anakites were used almost as a comparative measurement; they were significantly tall (Deut. 2:10-21). The Anakites are also called Rephaites, or giants (Deut. 2:11).

Outside of Scripture, there are accounts of people that may refer to a number of these giants. One group found in a text from Egypt mentions a people called the *Iy-'anaq*, recorded among a list of curses for "potential enemies of Egypt."[110,192] This text includes three rulers of the *Iy-'anaq*: Erum, Abi-yamimu, and Akirum.[110,192] Another group from these Egyptian texts is the *Shasu*, mentioned in the *Craft of the Scribe*, possibly the same as the *Shutu* in the *Execration Texts*, but they may be a separate tribe of the same area.[192,193] The first text describes the *Shasu* as having a height between 4 to 5 cubits, or 6'10"-8'7," tall enough to make them comparable to the giants of Scripture, including Goliath.[193,194] Interestingly, a man named Og is mentioned in a Phoenician inscription, the speaker stating that if someone were to "disturb" his bones, "the mighty Og will avenge" him.[195] The final connection between these Scriptural peoples and extra-biblical texts is found within a Ugaritic text. Here, there is a person referred to as "Rapiu, king of eternity."[196,197] This king is unique both because of his name and the place where he is found. In Ugaritic, his name is transcribed as *rpu,* and his throne was in Athtarat and Edrei.[196,198] Ashtaroth and Edrei were the cities that Og of Bashan ruled, and he was considered a Rephaite. Could the Rapiu king be Og? Possibly, and considering what we know, perhaps he was deified by his descendants.

21: Shem

Name

Shem is the third listed son of Noah in the Table of Nations, but he is first when the brothers are mentioned together (Gen. 5:32, 6:10, 7:13, 9:18, 10:1, 1Ch. 1:4). His name is שֵׁם in Hebrew.[1] Shem has been reasonably, though not certainly, established as the second son between Japheth and Ham. He is the only son whose age is known. The brothers were born after Noah was 500 years old (Gen. 5:32). Since Shem was 100 when he had his son Arphaxad, two years after the Flood, Shem was most likely born when Noah was 502 as Shem entered the Ark at 98 (Gen. 7:6, 8:13, 11:10). Shem's lineage is important because his people are part of Christ's earthly ancestry (Luk. 3:36).

Shem's people, along with other ancient peoples of the Middle East, are sometimes called Semites.[2] In addition, Hebrew comes from Shem's great-grandson Eber (Gen. 10:21-24).[3] The *Book of Jubilees* contains the supposed name of Shem's wife, Sedeqetelebab, whose name he used for a city he built near Noah's dwelling.[4] Also, it is Shem who joins Japheth to cover their father, and it is in Shem's tents that the descendants of Japheth were to dwell in (Gen. 9:18-27). But beyond these references, Shem is not mentioned again in Scripture. Instead, he is known by his sons and distant descendants.

The Table of Nations

Shem had five sons, each of whom were the progenitors of some rather sizable nations. These sons are Elam, Asshur, Arphaxad, Lud, and Aram (Gen. 10:22, 1Ch. 1:17). His line continues through to Abraham and continues in Scripture to connect with Christ. The books of *Jasher* and *Jubilees* records Shem's sons as well, but gives them slightly different names, like Ashur and Arpachshad, in addition to other supposed sons.[5,6] Josephus recorded similar names besides Ashur and Laud.[3] Arphaxad was born two years after the Flood, but he has two brothers listed before him. Two years is an awfully short time to have three children. Either the order does not matter, Elam was conceived before the Flood subsided, or there were multiple sons born at once. While Ham has more detail in his section of the Table of Nations than Japheth, Shem passes them all. Genesis includes multiple subsequent generations after two of his sons, and the line of Arphaxad led to many nations in addition to Israel (Gen. 10:26-29, 19:36-38, 25:1-16).

Where Was His Land?

Scripture largely indicates Shem's descendants' territory through the names of his sons. A couple of sons have other location indicators. For example, the descendants of Joktan dwelled "from Mesha toward Sephar, in the eastern hill country," but most do not (Gen. 10:30). While some of Arphaxad's family stayed in Ur and Shinar, others eventually went to the land of Canaan (Gen. 11:27-12:5). Though Lot separated from Abraham, his people remained near to his family, becoming the eastern nations of Moab and Ammon (Gen. 19:36-38). South of them was the land of Jacob's brother Esau: the Edomites (Gen. 36:9). The second wife of Abraham brought forth nations that possibly moved near to the Cushites, and Ishmael's people were not far off (Gen. 25:1-18).

The *Book of Jubilees* speaks on the division of the land. Where Japheth received the North and Ham the South, Shem received the middle land, though clearly these divisions were not always strictly adhered to.[7] In these writings, Shem's land is said to be a blending of cold and heat, a true middle ground between Ham and Japheth. His land reaches from the borders of Japheth's land – such as the Raffa mountains, the river Tina, and the Mediterranean Sea – and reaches south to the Egyptian sea, to name a few boundaries.[7] Each of his sons dwelled in the land and named his people after himself. As mentioned before, tribes, cities, and nations were named after a forefather. The names of his sons are what best define Shem's land in the Middle East.[7]

The *Book of Jubilees* and the *Antiquities* provide interesting additional information about the descendants of Shem, and thus his land. In the *Jubilees*, Madai marries a daughter of Shem and he remains near his wife's family rather than his own.[6] Josephus writes that the sons of Elam became the Elamites and later the Persians, a subject briefly touched on in the chapter on Madai as they lived south of him.[3,8] Next is Asshur, and his people became the Assyrians, preserving his name in the name of his people. They became one of the greatest empires of the ancient world.[3,8] Lud is likely the most northern-dwelling son of Shem as he appears to have settled in Anatolia; his people were called first Laudites, then Lydians.[3,8] Aram is said to have founded the Arameans, but both Josephus and Isidore say they were later called Syrians, perhaps because of the Assyrians.[3,8] Arphaxad is said to have founded the people in Chaldea.[3,8]

Though many nations were known by an ancestor, like the Assyrians, Medes, Israel, and others, the name Shem was not specifically used until a later date. Today, his name lives through the word Semite and includes more than the people of Israel.[2] Shem has been known both as Shem and Sem, illuminating why his people were known as Semites rather than Shemites. Works such as Camden's *Britannia* knew Shem as Sem, and Anderson's *Royal Genealogies* referred to him by both names.[9,10] Augustine calls him Sem and his father Noe.[11] Spain's histories even refer to Shem though he is not directly related to their people.[12] He was regarded as a forefather of earth's nations though his name was not well preserved.

Notable Mentions

One possible reason for his disappearance from history is that he may have quickly departed from the rest of the people at Babel. He is never mentioned again, even though he lived during Abraham's lifetime

(Gen. 11:10-31).[13] Some have speculated Shem to be Melchizedek, the king of Salem that Abraham meets after rescuing Lot (Gen. 14:18-20).[13,14] An intriguing fact of this account is that he is called the "Priest of God Most High" (Gen. 14:18). God gave the land of Canaan to Abraham and, according to other works, this middle land was to be Shem's. Why could Shem not have moved here? Could he have been a priest of God? Perhaps he did serve the Lord faithfully after the Flood. However, the book of Hebrews explains that Melchizedek was someone without ancestry and of a priestly order, of which Christ has been made "a priest forever" (Psa. 110:4, Heb. 7). This is likely someone greater than Shem (Heb. 7).

Evidence of Shem's descendants is also found outside of their land. In the most ancient sources, the descendants of Shem are known by a son's name. But in some texts, the people from the area of Canaan, Israel, and the surrounding region are referred to as Asiatics, notably in Egypt. The chapter on Mizraim deals briefly with this subject. Here, there is evidence of a Semitic presence around Kahun, markedly in the discovery of buried babies.[15] Other texts from Egypt during the reign of Thutmose III record bricklayers who appear to be of Semitic origin.[16] A mysterious group of Asiatics, or "C'mw" as the Egyptians called them, battled and even ruled Egypt for a time after the Exodus.[17] Even so, there are essentially no direct references to Shem outside of Scripture.

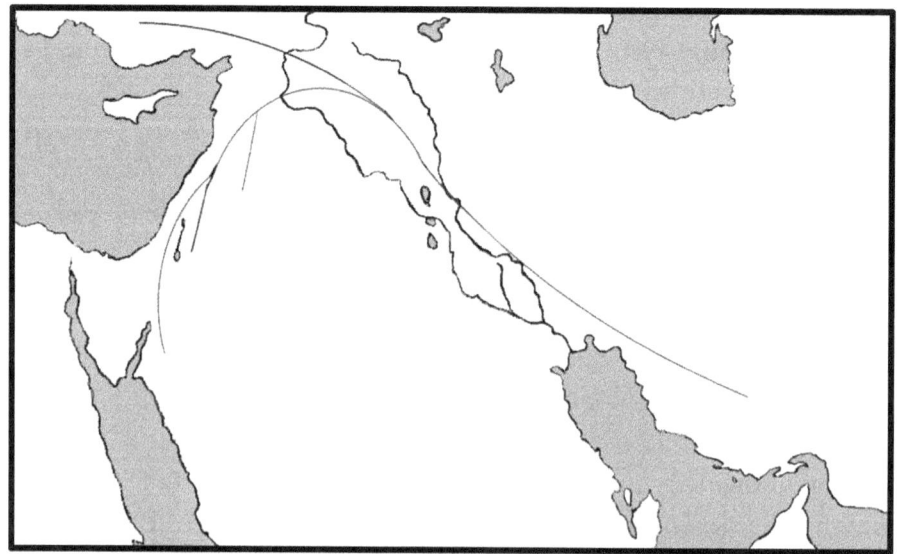

22: Elam

Eternity

Elam is the first of Shem's sons listed in Scripture (Gen. 10:22; 1Ch. 1:17). His name is עֵילָם in Hebrew.[1] Though it appears that at least his brother Arphaxad's family stayed in the general vicinity of Elam's territory, there is no extended record of Elam's family in Scripture. His nation, however, is mentioned frequently in Scripture, and his people played an important role in history. Indeed, there were Elamites with Medes and Parthians present on the day of Pentecost who heard the Gospel in their own language, and they probably brought that message back to their people (Acts 2:9).

Where is This Name Found?

The kingdom of Elam began not long after Babel, and it appears to have formed contemporaneously with Sumer. Though later events of their kingdom were well recorded in history, we know little about their origins outside of Scripture. Most of their texts come from their capital at Susa, but these are few, though we know they had a relationship with Shinar, Asshur, and Mesopotamia.[2,3,4,5]

One problem in learning about their beginnings is their language is an isolate, making it difficult to translate. The only surviving language that is close to Elamite is used by the Lurs, whose language is related to Persian.[4] Other languages, and especially Akkadian, were often used instead of Elamite, and Persian eventually won out.[4,6,7] But by the time of Abraham, the people of Elam had grown into a kingdom. Their King Chedorlaomer joined with those of Shinar, Ellasar, and Goiim to war with those in Canaan (Gen. 14:1-2). Chedorlaomer had subjugated the rulers in Canaan, but they rebelled (Gen. 14:3-12). During the battle, they took Lot's family; Abraham recovered everything and defeated Chedorlaomer and his allies (Gen. 14:13-17).

While the Elamite name for their people was *Haltamti* or *Hatamti*, other nations knew them by names similar to Hebrew, Babylonian, and Assyrian names.[2] The Sumerians called them *Alama*, Akkadians *Elamtu*.[2,3] So either we have not properly translated the Elamite name, or the other nations continued to use the older name while the Elamites changed their name, which they did on multiple occasions. Also, it is possible that while every other nation knew them as Elamites for Elam, the tribe or kingdom founded by Elam was replaced by one called the *Haltamti*. The Elamites came to be known as Persians when they changed their name to Paras.[8] Various texts connect the Elamites and the Persians. The *Book of Jubilees* provides in one passage the lands of Elam, Asshur, Babel, Susan, and Ma'edai together.[9] Susan may be from the supposed descendant of Elam named Shushan and may also be the Susa, the capital of Elam and Persia, mentioned in Scripture.[10] Lastly, both the works of Isidore and Josephus hold that the Elamites were the ancestors or "princes" of Persia.[11,12] Thus, Elam became Persia.

Scripture recorded multiple kings of Persia and Media, including Cyrus the Persian, Darius the Mede, and Artaxerxes (2Ch. 36:20-22, Ezr. 1:1-8, 3:7, 4:3-24, 6:14, 7:1, Dan. 6:28). As mentioned before, Elam was a neighbor to the Medes, and their nations were often recorded together within Scripture. The Median Empire joined with the Persian Empire, becoming the Medo-Persian Empire, though the latter name and language eventually won out.[8] The kingdoms of Elam and Madai were united by Cyrus the Achaemenid. Isaiah foretold that this joint empire would conquer Babylon and capture Jerusalem (Isa. 21:2, 22:6).

The book of Daniel chronicled the merging of the Persians and Medes and their takeover of the Babylonian empire. While Belshazzar was king in Babylon, an inscription was made on a wall during a banquet which read: "MENE, MENE, TEKEL, PARSIN" (Dan. 5:1-25). Daniel interprets the message, telling the king his reign is at an end and his kingdom "given to the Medes and the Persians" (Dan. 5:26-28). The prophecy comes true that night and Darius the Mede is made king (Dan. 5:30).

Once many of the exiles are back in Jerusalem, a letter written to King Artaxerxes includes a reference about Elamites of Susa, their onetime capital (Ezr. 4:9). God would call Israel out of Elam (Isa. 11:11). One of the more well-known stories involving both Persia and Susa is about Esther and King Ahasuerus or Xerxes (Est. 1-10). Persia is also included in many prophecies (Ezk. 27:10, 38:5, Dan 8:20, 10:1-20, 11:2). Elam is among many nations, such as Babylon and Madai, that would receive the wrath of God for their wickedness (Jer. 25:12-26, Ezk. 32:34). But though the Lord would destroy and scatter Elam, He would later restore their fortunes (Jer. 49:34-39).

Other ancient nations included the Elamites in their records. One of the closest nations to the Elamites were the Sumerians, calling the Elamites *ELAM(.Maki)*.[13] In Assyrian texts, the name for Elam often appears either as *Elamtu* or *e-lam-ti* and their people called *a-la-mu-u* or *e-la-me-e*.[14,15] Most Assyrian texts that include encounters with the Elamites imply that Assyria had conquered Elam, beginning possibly with Hammurabi and definitely during Sargon of Agad's reign.[16,17] The annals of Ashurbanipal note that Elam briefly rebelled.[18] A pattern of Elam rebelling and Assyria conquering continued for some time until they were finally their own nation, only to be taken over by Babylon and then joined to Media by Cyrus the Achaemenid.[19,20]

While the Elamites were no longer a nation by the time the Romans came into power, and the Persians were essentially ruined by Alexander the Great, there are a few records of Elam in the writings of these two nations. A state named Elymaei is where some of the Elamites in Acts likely came from (Acts 2:9).[21,22,23] Strabo recorded the Elymaei, but he also writes as though they are separate from the Persians and the Susii, with whom they bordered and warred.[24] But elsewhere, he notes a piece of land whom some said "belongs to Madai, but according to others, to Elymaea."[24] Strabo writes that the Susians and their neighbors were under the rule of Parthia, a group related to the Medes.[25] Though Strabo often refers to these people as separate – the Elymaea, Parthians, Susians – they all occupy the same general area and are undoubtedly descended from the same group of people, the Medo-Persians, and likewise, from Madai and Elam.[26] The book of Acts also records the Elamites, Parthians, and Medes as separate people and languages (Acts 2:9).

The writings of Livius, much like Strabo, state that the Medes and Elymaeans were a fierce people, enough to cause "terror," assumedly more so than the tribes in Europe.[27] In the book of Jeremiah, the Lord says that He would "break the bow of Elam" before restoring them, and Livius records that the Elymaeans had a sizable army of archers (Jer. 49:34-39).[28] Between Strabo, the Assyrian records, Livius, and Scripture, these people are clearly described as warlike. Plutarch recorded the Medes, the Elymaeans, and the Parthians as distinct and having their own king.[29]

Polybius simply notes the Elymaeans as a country near Media.[30] In Pliny's *Natural History*, Elymais is separated from Persis, which is likely Persia, but Pliny claims they changed their name to Parthia, making it a continuation of the Persian Empire but without its strength and size, though still controlling the same general area.[31] Yet in other records, such as those of Tacitus, the Elymaeans are given greater status than even the Parthians.[32] Perhaps these little states, as was often the case, joined and separated over the years as one rose and another fell. But while they never grew back to the strength of the Medo-Persian Empire, small states of Elam and Madai lasted a long time. And today, there is still a small district called Ilam.[33] Throughout this entire area, there are many different tar pits, or "springs" as they are sometimes called.[33] This is interesting, as their presence coincides with what is found in Genesis when men fleeing the king of Elam fell into tar pits in their haste (Gen. 14:10). Finally, the modern state of Iran rests upon what was the Persian kingdom, as mentioned in the chapter on Madai.

Notable Mentions

Though we know where Elam's people went, the man himself seems to have been lost. Many of the later kings of Elam are recorded in the Assyrian texts, but he appears to be absent.[19] One account from outside of the Elamite kingdom possibly mentions an Elamite king named Khumbaba whose reign coincided with Gilgamesh, though scholars are unsure if he was real, a deity, or both (besides which, he is portrayed as a dragon-like creature in the *Epic of Gilgamesh* and placed in a setting that is not Elam).[7,34] If this was an ancestor made deity – and made a monster by the Babylonians – it could be that the rival Sumer represented their neighbor's founder and king as a terror rather than the near cousins they were.[34] Elam could also be a king whose name was lost or never recorded at all. There is also the mystery of Chedorlaomer. Scholars have theorized Chedorlaomer as the Elamite King *Kutir-Lagamar*, but as we know little about the Elamites, this is only a suggestion.[35-37] Another proposed person is *Kudur-kumal* from another ancient text.[17] For sure, the name Chedorlaomer fits in the Elamite language, and *Lagamar* was an Elamite deity.[38,39]

As mentioned before, Susa was the capital of Elam. Susa is the city Esther was brought to and was where she would eventually marry the king. Daniel and Nehemiah were also in that city at some point during the captivity, and Daniel specifically mentions the "province in Elam" (Neh. 1:1, Dan 8:2). Both *Jasher* and the *Jubilees* include a descendant of Elam and an area within Elam's territory: Shushan and Susan, respectively.[9,10] In *Enmerkar and the Lord of Aratta*, Susin is the name of the city in Ansan, which is now within Iran.[40] This name is like another region: Susiana.[41] Sumerian texts know the city as *su-su-um*.[42] Assyrian texts imply that the Elamites were focused around "Susa and the Susian(s)," which may be mountains.[43] This city also hosted a temple to the god Inshushinak, a name incorporated into many different leader's names.[41] It appears that the Elamites began at or around Susa and moved south, forming a great nation that memorialized its ancestors for centuries to come.

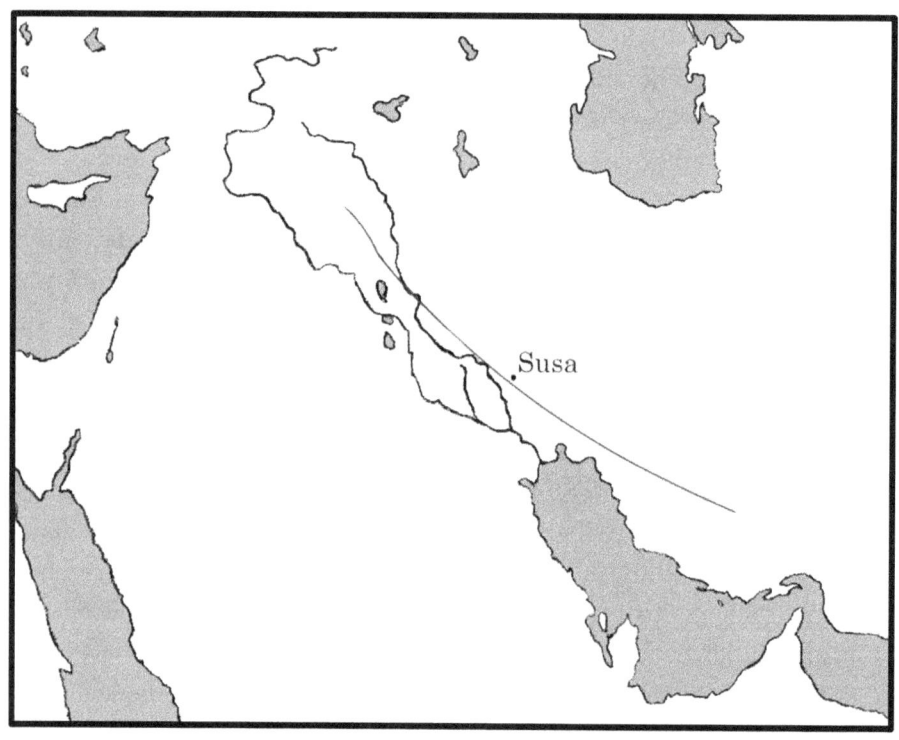

23: Asshur

Successful

Asshur was the second son of Shem listed in Scripture, his name appearing as אַשּׁוּר in Hebrew (Gen. 10:22, 1Ch. 1:17).[1] None of his descendants are in Scripture, but his people did not fade into obscurity. His people are best known as the Assyrians, the great kingdom north of Israel and neighbor to Babylon (Gen. 2:14). A few kings who interacted with Israel are in Scripture, and his people were a force to be reckoned with in the ancient world. As mentioned before, Nimrod settled in a part of his land, building the cities of Nineveh, Calneh, Rehoboth Ir, and Resen (Gen. 10:11). Assyria, of course, was one of two nations that the Lord used as a punishment for Israel. Even before the exile, Assyria often intimidated and antagonized the Israelites. In all, Asshur is mentioned over one hundred and fifty times in Scripture. His people would be among, though they are not explicitly mentioned, the "residents of Mesopotamia" in the account of Pentecost (Acts 2:9).

Where is This Name Found?

Other than the fact that Asshur was the second son of Shem and that his people were the Assyrians, we know little about the early years of his people. Josephus claims that Asshur went to Nineveh, calling his people Assyrians and claiming that his nation was "the most fortunate" of nations.[2] The *Book of Jubilees* notes little more of the land of Asshur than that there were mountains and it was within Shem's inheritance.[3] The *Book of Jasher* includes two sons of Asshur, but nothing is known of them or their legitimacy.[4] Asshur's people did not travel far from Babel, establishing themselves fairly quickly.

While the founder of Assyria is clearly Asshur, and Scripture repeatedly uses his name for this nation, one can only speculate about the early rulers of Assyria, as with most other nations. Even so, Assyria kept decent records of their people, and the annals from Assyria, Babylon, and other cultures agree with Scripture. Asshur, his deification, and the early rulers of his people shall be addressed after the discussion of the established Assyrian rulers found in Scripture and the extra-biblical references to his undoubtedly great nation. While Asshur is infrequently mentioned early in Scripture, many kings of Assyria played a significant role in the history of Israel.

The first reference to Asshur outside of chronology is in the book of Numbers when Moab calls Balaam to curse Israel, though he blesses them by command of the Lord instead (Num. 22-24). The only part of the oracle concerning Asshur involves their conquering the Kenites, and Asshur and Eber being subdued by the Kittim (Num. 24:22-24, Gen. 10:4). It is Balaam, though, who is more interesting. Balaam came from an area of the Euphrates called Pethor (Num. 22:5). A text from Deir 'alla, Israel, contained the names of a Balaam and his father Beor.[5] Some claim that Balaam was just a common name or that the biblical figure was from this southern city rather than from the north.[6] If it is about the biblical Balaam, this text from Deir 'alla was likely written during Balaam's trip to Moab. A record coming from a later time, during Shalmaneser III's reign, contains the city Pitru on the Euphrates, coinciding with Scripture.[7] Perhaps Balaam was Hittite, as Pitru was the Hittite name for Pethor, or perhaps he was Babylonian, but Assyria is the probable choice for his homeland (Num. 22:4-5).[7]

After Israel and Judah split, the Assyrian kings played a key role in the history of Israel and the world in general. The first king of Assyria directly mentioned in Scripture was called Pul, a king who may be Tiglath-Pileser III or a predecessor.[8] Sources such as the *Babylonian*

King List include a Pulu who may be this king, a separate Pul, or Tiglath-Pileser.[9] The reason that there may be two different people is two-fold. The first is that Menahem king of Israel and Tiglath-Pileser III, seemingly, lived at two different times.[10] Also, one verse could be translated as "the spirit of Pul king of Assyria (that is, Tiglath-Pileser king of Assyria)" or "the spirit of Pul king of Assyria and Tiglath-Pileser king of Assyria" (1Ch. 5:26).[11] The annals of Tiglath-Pileser III, however, contain a *Mi-in-hi-im-mu*, or Menahem, dwelling in Samaria, consistent with Scripture (2Ki. 15:17).[12] This king fled from Tiglath-Pileser III, according to Assyrian records, and Menahem sent tribute to Assyria (2Ki. 15:19-20).[12] Perhaps the dates for Tiglath-Pileser III were miscalculated and he reigned earlier than previously thought. But whomever this king was, King Menahem paid tribute to the Assyrian king to remove the Assyrians.

Tiglath-Pileser III invaded Israel and, as a result, claimed territories, namely those in the north such as Hazor and Kadesh, and areas such as Gilead, Galilee, and Naphtali's inheritance during the reign of Pekah of Israel (2Ki. 15:29). During his reign, Ahaz requested to meet Tiglath-Pileser III at Damascus, becoming Assyria's vassal and requesting help (2Ki. 16:7-18, 2Ch. 28:16-21; Hos. 5:13, 7:11, 8:9). Tiglath-Pileser III did not provide much aid, and accounts contain a campaign against Damascus or "*Di-mas-*qa."[13] Tiglath-Pileser III also took some people from Israel and moved them to Assyria (1Ch. 5:6-26).

Tiglath-Pileser III worked to expand the territory and increase the strength of the Assyrian Empire.[8] You will notice that Tiglath-Pileser III is frequently referenced in these chapters, for he kept extensive annals. The annals of Tiglath-Pileser III record the conquering of northern Israel, called "*Bit Hu-um-ri-a*" or "Omri-Land," from past-king Omri (1Ki. 16:21-23).[12] The text mentions a king of Judah, but his name is translated as Jehoahaz. However, his reign did not begin until after Tiglath-Pileser III, so this is likely a mistranslation between Hebrew to Assyrian and Assyrian to English.[14] Azariah's reign overlapped with Tiglath-Pileser's, and the annals include this fact.[15]

The last king of Israel was Hoshea, and he dealt with the Assyrians before the Northern Kingdom was taken into captivity. Shalmaneser V was king of Assyria during this time. He came to attack Israel because

Hoshea traitorously conspired with Egypt (2Ki. 17:3-4). After laying siege to Samaria for three years, Shalmaneser V takes the city and Israel, deporting many Israelites to Assyria and elsewhere, including, "Halah, in Gozano the Habor River and in the towns of the Medes" (2Ki. 17:5-6). This was the result of Israel's sin and rejection of the Lord's Word (2Ki. 17:21-23, Hos. 9:3, 10:6). After this, the king of Assyria took people from other lands, such as "Babylon, Cuthah Avva, Hamath and Sepharvaim," and relocated them to Samaria (2Ki. 17:22-24, 18:7-13). Terrible things befell the people who were resettled there, so the king of Assyria brought a priest to teach them "how to worship the Lord" (2Ki. 17:25-28).

We know of Shalmaneser V himself from texts outside of Scripture, but little of his reign is known besides the fact that he did reign. The *Babylonian King List* records Pulu and his son Ululaia, who is likely Shalmaneser V or IV, depending on interpretation.[16,17] Records of Tiglath-Pileser III mention a place called Shalmaneser, and perhaps this is the origin of his successor's name.[18,19] In addition, other records note a "Palace of Shalmaneser king of Assyria," which is likely the same place.[20]

Between the time that Shalmaneser V conquered Israel and the time of Sennacherib, who attempted to conquer Judah, there is a brief, fourteen-year period when Israel does not interact much with Assyria. This is during the reign of Sargon II, brother of Shalmaneser V and son of Tiglath-Pileser III.[21] From this time, Scripture has prophecies about Assyria, and Sargon's name is mentioned once in Isaiah after Sargon "attacked and captured" Ashdod in Philistia (Isa. 20:1). Isaiah mainly speaks on the coming of Assyria, whose king God will use as an instrument of wrath (Isa. 7:17-8:10).

> *"The Lord will bring on you and your people and on the house of your father a time unlike any since Ephraim broke away from Judah – he will bring the king of Assyria...therefore the Lord is about to bring against them the mighty floodwaters of the River – the king of Assyria with all his pomp. It will overflow all its channels, run over all its banks..." (Isa. 7:17, 8:7)*

Indeed, the Lord brought Assyria on Israel. But not all would go well for Assyria, for the kingdom was proud. So, the Lord spoke of their fall. The kings of Assyria were also haughty, naming themselves the "king of the world" and "king of the universe," ignoring the purpose the Lord set for them (Isa. 10:5-12).[22,23] Along the same vein, the Lord tells Israel not to fear Assyria, for a remnant would be brought out of exile (Isa. 10:24, 11:11-16, 27:13, Hos. 11:5-11, Mic. 7:12). Assyria's burdens would be taken off Israel (Isa. 14:24-27, 30:31, 31:8, Mic. 5:5-6). Additionally, the Lord says that Assyria and Egypt will "worship together," and Israel will join them to be "a blessing on the earth" and blessed by the Lord (Isa. 19:23-25).

Fourteen years after Shalmaneser V's attack on Israel, Sennacherib, son of Sargon II, attacked Judah during Hezekiah's reign (2Ki. 18:13, Isa. 36:1).[21] Sennacherib is mentioned numerous times in Scripture and was in regular contact with Hezekiah. Regarding the initial Assyrian attack, Hezekiah regained the cities that Sennacherib took, including Lachish, by giving the Assyrian king enormous amounts of gold and silver (2Ki. 18:14-16). Sennacherib taunted Hezekiah's people in Hebrew, claiming they have no confidence, strength, or security (2Ki. 18:17-37, 2Ch. 32:1-22, Isa. 36:2-22). His annals claim to have placed a yoke upon Hezekiah, king of Judah, but only so far as he imposed a tribute on Judah and destroyed Lachish, as seen in the Lachish reliefs.[24,25] The importance of connecting Lachish, Hezekiah, and Sennacherib is best explained by Austen Layard, who explains its significance is because this account was first found in Scripture:

> *Here, therefore, was the actual picture of the taking of Lachish, the city, as we know from the Bible, besieged by Sennacherib, when he sent his generals to demand tribute from Hezekiah and which he had captured before their return; evidence of the most remarkable character to confirm the interpretation of the inscriptions, and to identify the king who caused them to be engraved with the Sennacherib of Scripture.*[25]

Hezekiah turned to the Lord, asking for deliverance from Assyria, and the Lord answered him by destroying a portion of Assyria's army, leading to Sennacherib's withdrawal (2Ki. 19:14-36, Isa. 37:1-37, 38:6).

During the time of Sargon II, Isaiah recorded a prophecy that Assyria would conquer and exile Mizraim and Cush, an exile enacted by Sennacherib, who wrote, "I conquered Egypt (*Musur*) and Nubia (*Kusu*)" (Isa. 20:3-6).[26] Interestingly, the end of Sennacherib is recorded in Scripture as well. His reign ended because his sons Adrammelech and Shaezer murdered him in a temple, leaving his youngest son, Esarhaddon, to take his place as king (2Ki. 19:37, Isa. 37:38). Their names were likely Arda-Mulissi and Arad-Ninlil, the names found in Assyrian texts regarding the death of Sennacherib.[27,28,29] Sennacherib's death is in the annals of Esarhaddon, his son and successor.[30] Though these were his older brothers, it was Esarhaddon who was chosen to be king.[30] He writes that his brothers "went out of their senses, doing everything that is wicked" and killed their father.[30,31]

Esarhaddon ruled through Hezekiah's reign and did not trouble him or subsequent kings (2Ki. 20:6). Ashurbanipal followed Esarhaddon, bearing the name of his ancestor and god, and he attacked Judah (2Ch. 33:10-11). He is mentioned again in passing later in Scripture by the name of Osnapper (Ezr. 4:10). The king at that time was Manasseh, who Assyria briefly held captive (2Ch. 33:13). Manasseh and Judah, *Mi-in-si-e* and *Ia-u-di*, were found on a cylinder from Ashurbanipal's time.[32]

The final king of Assyria, Ashur-uballit II, mentioned, though not named, in Scripture ruled during the reigns of Josiah in Judah and Neco II in Egypt (2Ki. 23:29).[33] He is probably the same mentioned in the Amarna tablets, "To Naphuria…King of Egypt, my brother: · Ashur-uballit, king of Assur."[34] His rising to the throne is recorded in Babylonian records as well.[35] His reign marks the fall of Nineveh and, consequently, Assyria, as prophesied in Scripture (Nah. 3, Zep. 2:13-15).[36] The battle, which was later recorded by Herodotus and Josephus, ended poorly for both the Assyrians and Egyptians, who fell to Nebuchadnezzar.[37,38,39] Nebuchadnezzar was the son of Nabopolassar, the king who began the war with Assyria.[40] After Assyria, Nebuchadnezzar also conquered Judah (2Ch. 36:5-21, Jer. 50:17-18).[39]

Clearly, the kingdom of Assyria need not be established as having existed in history. Numerous sources could be provided in which other nations deal with the Assyrians – from the Cimmerians to Elamites. But that is not a necessary discussion. As shown with the sources from

Assyria and Babylon, the events outlined and prophesied in Scripture did come to pass, and these nations did interact with each other. Each king of Assyria is clearly in history just as they are found in Scripture. But what of Asshur himself? Obviously, the descendants of each son of Noah had peoples named after themselves. Asshur may be one of the most prominent as his name was immortalized in his nation, as a city, in his descendants, and most notably as a deity.

According to Assyrian records, it was *Ushpia* – ancestor to some of the rulers of Assyria, including Shalmaneser I and Esarhaddon – who built the first temple to Assur.[41,42] *Ushpia* was one of the "seventeen kings who dwelt in tents."[43] He was called the "priest of Assur" and the temple *Eharsagkurkurra*.[41] This temple was in the city of Assur along the Tigris below Nineveh, placing it near the later capital of Assyria and Babel, and its ruins are there today.[44]

Now there are a few interesting points about *Ushpia*. For one, he was of the kings "who dwelt in tents," implying that his people were still nomadic, placing him shortly after Babel and having yet to establish a city.[43] There is no surprise that the kings of Assyria were considered nomads so soon after leaving Babel. It was probably because of Ushpia that Asshur's people were no longer nomads. There were cities before the Flood, but they would have been destroyed, and that specific knowledge considered unimportant.

Also, the king list is strikingly similar to that found in Scripture. Some have noted that his name does not match the later imposed language group of the area, implying, if not proving, that the people coming from Babel were separate from those existing in later times.[45] The early names are bound to be more different. The language was completely changed from what existed pre-Babel. Additionally, Asshur's people and language would differ from Arphaxad's, who differed from Nimrod's, and he to Elam's. But over time, something of a common language, namely Akkadian, would equalize them. But the king list leads to the final point, which is the man who was king before *Ushpia*: *Azarah*.[43]

While happenstance might allow for a similar name to the Asshur of Scripture, it seems doubly unlikely that the following king would also set up a temple for a god whose name was also Assur. It was a practice to have gods made after great people. Thus, this *Ushpia* may have been a son or close descendant of Asshur who deified the forefather posthumously. Later, the city and nation would be named after their patron god, as the land of Assyria was called, "the Land of [the god] Assur" or "KUR.[DINGIR} *assur*.KI."[46,47] Either would be suitable, but both hold a strong connection to their founder Asshur.

The onetime Assyrian Empire is now part of Syria and Iraq, though the extent of their land included parts of modern-day Turkey, Egypt, and beyond.[48] To say that today the land once inhabited by Assyria is a mix of peoples is easily understood. Still, note that even during the early days of Assyria, the empire contained a variety of people, though brothers. Aram lived in what became the southwestern part of Assyria. Assyrian kings claimed parts of Babylon, the Babylonians conquered Assyria, and the Amorites claimed these northern thrones on multiple occasions.[49,50] Finally, the Israelites, descendants of Arphaxad, also mixed with the Assyrians when they were exiled. But to this day, some tribes hold on to their Assyrian origins, going directly back to the original ancestor proven not only by location and language but also by genetics.[51,52,53] Today the name of Asshur lives on through the Assyrians and the name Syria.[54]

Notable Mentions

Here we continue the conversation on *Ushpia* and *Azarah*. The records of ancient Assyria contain a list of seventeen men: *Tudiya, Adamu, Yangi, Harharu, Mandaru, Imsu, Harsu, Didanu, Danu, Zuabu, Nuabu, Abazu, Belu, Azarah, Ushpia,* and *Apiasal,* all of whom "dwelt in tents" or were nomads.[43] The *Sumerian King list* is like this one. Both section off a certain number of kings, not only as nomads but by a flood that "swept over (the earth)."[55] The names of the Sumerian kings beginning at Eridu were *Al-lulim, Alalgar, En-men-lu-Anna, Wn-men-gal-Anna, Dumu-zi, En-sipa-zi-Anna, En-men-dur-Anna, Ubar-Tutu,* and then the flood "swept over," after which "*Gal[...]ur*" ruled in Kish and the list continues.[55] Three things are intriguing about these lists: the number, names, and nomadic nature of these people.

While the lists are not exact, which should not be expected considering their age and the nature of their composition, they are analogous to Scripture's account. Both lists include a man whose name resembles that of the Scriptural Adam. The first and most obvious is that of Adamu of the Assyrian list and then Al-lulim, who could be based on Adam. From Adam to Noah, there are ten people or generations, with the generation of Shem, Ham, and Japheth being the eleventh (Gen. 5:1-32). There are seventeen in the king list of Assyria and eight in the king list of Sumer. Of course, there are numerous other king lists, but these two are particularly fascinating in that they include information directly relating to early history.

Again, the number of kings is noteworthy. One may wonder how that can be true when the numbers seem different, yet they work well. Though they are missing two generations, perhaps the numbers were confused, a generation lost, or they considered Noah as one "reigning" after rather than before the Flood. Let us say Nuabu is Noah. If this is the case, there are ten generations between Adamu and Nuabu, allowing for the first person to be God, as He is included in the genealogy of Adam (Gen. 5:1-3, Luk. 3:38). The inclusion of a god may be partly why the Assyrian kings referred to themselves as the "king of the universe" or "king of the earth" if they considered themselves descendants of deities.[22,23,41,56] After Babel, and these nomads ceased their wanderings, Ushpia built a temple in what became a city named after the deity worshiped, the father.

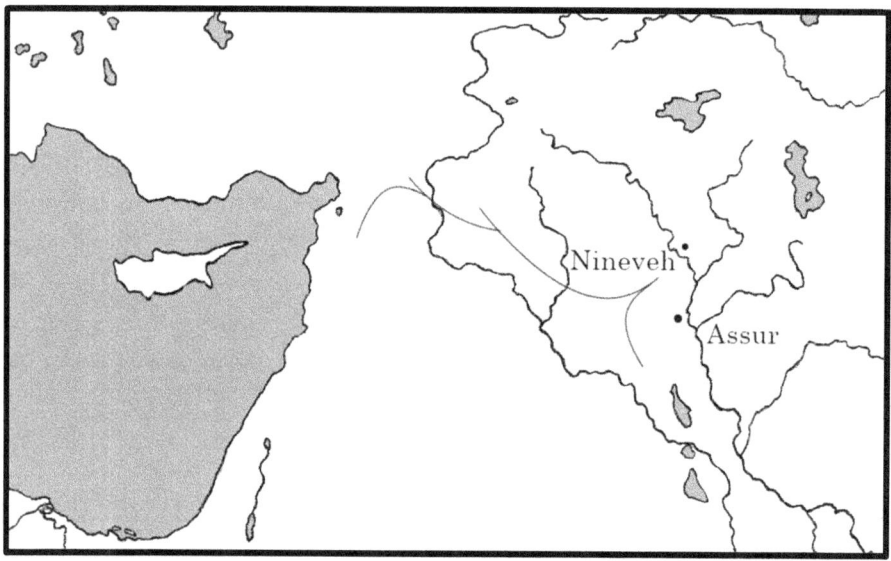

24: Arphaxad

Stronghold of Chaldees

Arphaxad, or Arpakshad, was the third son of Shem recorded in Scripture, and his name is אַרְפַּכְשַׁד in Hebrew (Gen. 10:22).[1] Unlike the previous genealogies, assumed to be in birth order, the line of Arphaxad comes after his presumed youngest brother Aram's descendants (Gen. 10:22-24). Arphaxad is singled out as having been born two years after the Flood, perhaps making Elam and Asshur twins or implying one was born shortly after the Ark landed (Gen. 11:10).[2] The reason his line is listed last is because Arphaxad's line connects Shem to Israel and thus to Christ, the focal point of Scripture.

Scripture includes only one son of Arphaxad: Shelah, whose name means "spear" or "branch" (Gen. 10:24).[3,4] This line continues to Shelah's son Eber, to his sons Peleg and Joktan, and concluding with Joktan's sons (Gen. 10:24-29). Following the account of Babel, which is thought to have occurred around the time of Peleg, the line from Peleg to Abraham is completed and immediately followed by Abraham's call (Gen. 11:10-12:1). Within the Ebla Tablets, there is a city called *Phaliga*, or *Phalga*, which some scholars have suggested is derived from Peleg.[5,6] This city was found in Mesopotamia on the Euphrates, placing it within the vicinity of Babel. However, though the names are similar, we cannot be sure that Peleg founded this city, though the possibility is there. Besides in genealogies, Arphaxad is never again specially named in Scripture (Gen. 10:22-24, 11:10-13, 1Ch 1:17-24, Luk. 3:36).

Where is This Name Found?

Arphaxad had other sons and daughters besides just Shelah and became the father of a people separate from Abraham's (Gen. 11:12-13). Within the *Antiquities,* Josephus states that Arphaxad fathered "the Arphaxadites, who are now called the Chaldeans."[7] This name should look familiar, for Abraham was called from the land of Ur of the Chaldeans (Gen. 11:31). Other texts record additional sons of Arphaxad, such as *Anar* and *Ashcol,* and *Kainam.*[8,9] A wife of *Arpachshad* was a daughter of Susan and granddaughter of Elam.[10] These texts continue with naming Peleg in response to the division.[11] Kainam is said to have married a daughter of Madai, who had married a sister of Arphaxad, and had a brother named Kesed, the probable line for the Chaldeans.[12] Kesed is said to be the father of a man named Ur, who built the city Ur Kasdim after himself and his father.[13] Kesed is also the name of a nephew of Abraham, so it could have been a family name (Gen. 22:22).

Thus, it is safe to assume that Josephus was correct in naming Arphaxad as the father of the Chaldeans. These people were often mentioned in Scripture, certainly far more than by the name of their forefather. The *Book of Jubilees* notes that Arpachshad received the third portion of land from Shem, including the land of the Chaldees "east of the Euphrates" to the Red Sea and the sea by Egypt, and "all the land of Lebanon and Sanir and 'Amana to the border of the Euphrates."[14] The land of the Chaldeans was centered around Ur Kasdim (Gen. 11:28-31, 15:7, Neh. 9:7).

Chaldea is first mentioned as the location of Abraham's family. His family included his father, Terah, his brothers – Nahor and Haran – Nahor's wife Milcah, both brother's children – Milcah, Iscah, and Lot – and Sarai (Gen. 11:27-29). After Haran died in Ur, Terah moved his family to Harran and died there (Gen. 11:28-32). Scripture is clear that it was the Lord who called Abraham out of the land of the Chaldeans (Gen. 15:7, Neh. 9:7, Acts 7:4). Chaldea is also referenced outside of this Abrahamic connection. Chaldea is one of the few nations mentioned in the book of Job (Job 1:17). The Hebrew used here, and for most of the references to Chaldea, is כַּשְׂדִּימָה, or *Kasdiy*, related to Kesed, a name for Abraham's nephew and possible son of Arphaxad.[15,16] These related words translate as Kasdite, Chaldean, Chaldea, and astrologer, a common profession in Babylon.[17,18] The word for Chaldean is translated as astrologer in Daniel (Dan. 2:5-10, 3:8, 4:7, 5:7-11).

While certain translations of Scripture display the word for Chaldean as Babylonian, the Hebrew word is still referring to the Chaldeans, such as the case of an attack recorded during the reign of Jehoiakim. This passage deals with descendants who are all from Shem: Arameans, Moabites, Ammonites, and the Chaldeans (2Ki. 24:2). During the reign of Zedekiah, Scripture specifically separates Nebuchadnezzar of Babylon from the Chaldeans.[19] But because of the location and the strength of Babylon compared with that of Chaldea, it is under the name Babylon these people were known. Marduk-Baladan was a Chaldean king of Babylon, and Nebuchadnezzar is called Chaldean and king of Babylon, but his successor Belshazzar is called king of the Chaldeans (2Ki. 20:12, Ezr. 5:12, Dan. 5:30).[20] The books of Isaiah and Jeremiah record the fall of Babylon using both the word for Babylon and the Chaldeans, subtly distinguishing them and implying the dominance of one group (Isa. 13:19, 23:13, 43:14, 47:1-5, 48:14-20, Jer. 25:12). Also, the Babylonians may have originally come from Nimrod while the Chaldeans came from Arphaxad. Both dwelled in basically the same area yet were somewhat distinct from one another.

Now both Arphaxad and Kesed's names were used to name places and people after themselves. Both became the Chaldees. The Chaldeans kept very few records of themselves, possibly because they were nomadic, as Abraham and his family were. As will be discussed in the following chapter, their people were noted for having chieftains rather than a king. And while a handful of cities bear the name of Arphaxad, the people took a name derived from Kesed.

The Assyrians knew the descendants of Arphaxad as the KUR.*kaldi* or simply the *Kaldi* and of the land *Kaldu*.[21,22,23] Babylon is also distinguished as they called it "KUR.*kar-dun-ia-as*" or *Kardunias*.[24] At the time of Tiglath-Pileser III, the Chaldeans were ruled by chieftains and had fallen to Assyria.[21,24] During the reign of Nabopolassar of

Babylon, the Assyrians attacked a city near Arraphu in northern Assyria, which is modern-day Kirkuk, Iraq.[25,26] Near this city was Nuzi, now called Torgan Tepe, where several texts were found, one of which contains the name *Arip-hurra*.[27,28] While this person, whose son, *Hupita*, is also mentioned, is probably not Arphaxad, the location and similarity of the name Arrapha to Arphaxad may imply a connection to him.[28] Nabonidus, Nebuchadnezzar's successor, dealt with enemies who moved to Arrapha.[29] The Assyrians knew the city as *ar-rap-ha-ia* or *Arraphayu*.[30] Records from Sennacherib include the city as *Arrapkha*.[31] In one record, the name *Kidite* is mentioned as the "provincial gove[rnor of ...] and of the (the city) Arrapha."[30] This area was known as *Arrapichi'tis* by Ptolemy and connected to Arphaxad and the Chaldeans by Bochart, Isidore, and others.[32,33,34,35] A relatively new site, found near Nineveh, north of Arrapha, is Tell Arpachiyah.[36] To the surprise of some researchers, but expected in light of Scripture, the site displays excellent structures and city systems that would be found post-Babel.[37]

Notable Mentions

As Abraham was from Ur of the Chaldees, it is likely that Arphaxad lived nearby. But this is not necessary as Arphaxad's people covered a great area. Over time, his people filled the land along with Nimrod's descendants. Asshur and Arphaxad's people eventually ruled Nimrod's northern cities. Yet a city called Ur remained for a time, and up until Abraham's time was known by the biblical name *Ur Kasdiy* or *Kasdim* (Gen. 11:28). This is like the name used by the Assyrians: *mat Kaldi*.[38] As mentioned before, Kesed is said to have had a son named Ur who built a city after himself, called "'Ara of the Chaldees."[13] While the land of Ur Kasdim encompassed most of the land in the southern part of the Babylonian Empire, Ur itself is likely one of three places within the region: Ur, Urfa, or Uruk.[38] These are along the Euphrates and are just as likely, or unlikely, to be the city of Abraham.

First is Uruk, the Erech of Scripture, the homeland and center of the kingdom of Gilgamesh, the great warrior of the Sumerian epic of the same name, and Enmerkar, whose tale holds a similar account to the Babel event (Gen.7, 10:10, 11).[39,40,41] Because Uruk is specifically known as Erech, this is not likely Ur Kasdim.

The second option is the location known as the Royal Tombs of Ur. Sir Leonard Wooley, the man credited with the discovery of the Royal Tombs, wrote about a ziggurat found at the current archaeological site of Ur, saying that some clay tablets,

> "not only gave [them] the first information obtained about the Ziggurat itself, but identified the site, called by the Arabs al Mughair, the Mound of Pitch, as Ur 'of the Chaldees', the biblical home of Abraham."[42]

These Ziggurats, along with other similar structures found around the world, may have been based on the original Tower of Babel. A third location, much farther north than either of these cities, is a place once called Urfa, now named Sanliurfa in Turkey, and near to the ancient kingdom of Urartu.[43,44] This city is also mentioned in the Ebla Tablets, and it is not far from the city of Harran.[45]

Ur of the Chaldeans could have simply been a name for the territory controlled by the other descendants of Arphaxad rather than a distinct city, of which the above are only three candidates. The post-Flood people chose the plain of Shinar to build the Tower of Babel, an area often associated with Babylon and Chaldea (Gen. 11:1-9, 14:1). However, Shinar was not isolated south of the Euphrates and Tigris but included the whole plain within the rivers, which would include Urfa.[46] In fact, there is reason to believe Shinar included the area of what is still known as Sinjar, Iraq.[46]

Placing the tower of Babel closer to the "mountains of Ararat" would make sense for the Dispersion as that location is a bridge-point for the Far East, Middle East, Africa, Europe, and many different sea points (Gen. 8:4, 9:19, 11:1-9). Even so, we simply do not know how far east people went from the Ark to start building Babel. Thus, as each location is plausible but unconfirmed, I am reluctant to make a definite claim. All we know is that Abraham was called from Ur of the Chaldees and that there are archaeological sites within Sumer and Mesopotamia that fit the descriptions we have.

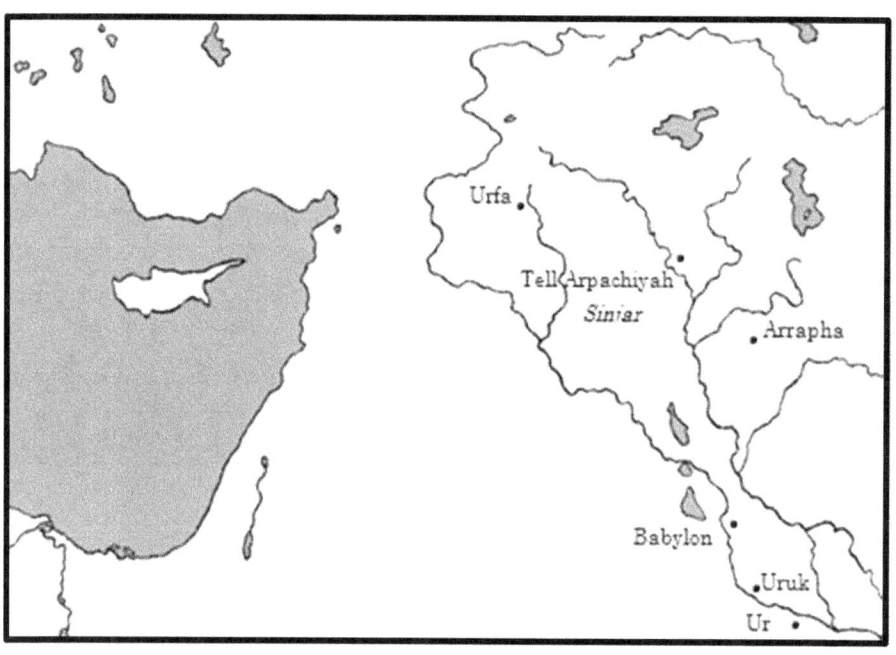

25: The Descendants of Arphaxad

In contrast to the previous chapters where only the direct sons and their descendants would be discussed, this chapter will deal with numerous generations of people. While Arphaxad likely stayed in Ur of the Chaldees, or nearby, the Chaldees were not the only identifiable descendants of Arphaxad. Though much due focus is given to Abraham, and sometimes Edom and Ishmael, few know the full extent of those who came from Shem's son Arphaxad. Shelah, son of Arphaxad, had a son named Eber and his line produced numerous people, more than the Hebrews. There were the sons of Joktan, the descendants of Lot, the Edomites, the Ishmaelites, and other descendants from Abraham's family. The descendants of Arphaxad made up many of the people of Mesopotamia and the nearby regions. His people can be included as the ancestors of those "residents of Mesopotamia" and Judea mentioned in Acts on Pentecost (Acts 2:9). The people were numerous, their language and culture similar to other descendants of Arphaxad, and their history important. This and more will be discussed in the following.

Eber

Unlike some of the other people discussed so far, we know quite a bit about Eber and his family. His father was Shelah and his sons were Peleg and Joktan (Gen. 10:24-25). Shelah was 30 years old when he fathered Eber, and Eber was 34 when he fathered Peleg, placing them approximately one hundred years after the Flood (Gen. 11:10-17). Like the other sons discussed thus far, Eber is important because of his name and the people who claimed it. Though many of his people did not have a land to call their own until the time of Moses, we have a definite time that their people were founded.

As mentioned in the previous chapter, Eber's people appear to have mainly lived in Ur of Chaldees. The name Eber is עֵבֶר in Hebrew and means "across."[1,2] The word Hebrew or עִבְרִי, literally "Eberite," is etymologically related to Eber.[3,4,5] The word Hebrew is used numerous times in Scripture to denote the descendants of Eber via Abraham. The name is first used when the Mesopotamian kings attacked Canaan and carried off Abraham's nephew Lot with his family (Gen. 14:13). The name Eber, however, is almost strictly used in the genealogies, and Shem is called the "ancestor of all the sons of Eber" (Gen. 10:21, 1Ch. 1:18-25, Luk. 3:35).

While Eber is undoubtedly known best for his fathering the Hebrews, as mentioned before, other nations came from Eber in addition to Peleg and Joktan's descendants. That is not to say that other "Hebrews" of Abraham arose elsewhere, rather, that others also bore his name. One such possibility is the 'Apiru. But a clearer connection is found at Ebla, one of the oldest cities in Mesopotamia.

The Eblaites were found at the site now called Tell Mardikh-Ebla, located in northern Syria today.[6] Researchers found a king list at this site, common enough in the region, but it included the name Ebrum.[6] This King Ebrum was prosperous and powerful, and he interacted with the kings of Assyria and Akkad.[7] There are two ways to translate this name: *Eb-ru-um* and *Eb-ri-um*.[6] Both are reminiscent of the Hebrew name, though the latter is quite similar to the name "Hebrew" or "Eberite. While we cannot say for sure that this is the Eber of Scripture, the similarity is striking, and the location and timing make the connection plausible. Additionally, a handful of gods worshiped in Ebla seem to have been a corrupted form of Yahweh with adopted deities from Assyria, Babylon, or the Canaanites.[6] Researchers found other names that resemble Hebrew names from Scripture, indicating a similar heritage.[6]

Peleg and Joktan

Peleg is remembered for his name, not because of a people named after him, but because his name is the best indicator of when the Tower of Babel event occurred. Scripture writes of Eber's sons, "he was named Peleg, because in his time the earth was divided; his brother was Joktan" (Gen. 10:25). It is the division that is key, for that is what his name means in Hebrew, which is פֶּלֶג, derived from the word "to split."[8,9] Josephus writes that Phaleg was "born at the dispersion of the nations."[4] The *Book of Jasher* recorded something similar, stating, "the name of one was Peleg, for in his days the sons of men were divided."[10] The *Book of Jubilees* says Eber had a wife named 'Azurad and she had a son Peleg, "for in the days when he was born the children of Noah began to divide the earth amongst themselves: for this reason he called his name Peleg."[11] While this account gives an additional reason for the divided nations, it is clear that Peleg was thus named because the people split by language across the earth (Gen. 11:1-9).[12]

Tablets from Ebla and elsewhere contain names like Peleg's – *Phaliga* –but there is not sufficient evidence to say that this is certainly Peleg.[13, 14] Scripture says he was thirty when his son Reu was born and lived two hundred and nine years afterwards, having other children as well (Gen. 11:18-19, 1Ch. 1:19-25, Luk. 3:35). This line continues from Reu to Terah, the father of Abraham, the father of the Israelites and part of the lineage of Christ (Gen. 11:20-28, Luk. 3:23-38).

The second of these brothers is Joktan, sometimes called Yoktan, whose name means "he will be made little" in Hebrew יָקְטָן (Gen. 10:25).[15] Like Peleg, he is only mentioned within the genealogies, but the Table of Nations records many of his sons (Gen. 10:26-29). People have speculated on Joktan's name and location, but most places are based on myth and prejudice rather than biblical truth. Because of the lack of solid evidence for his name found anywhere, the extent of the

Joktanite tribes will be examined in light of his sons. Most, or perhaps all, of his sons are found in the Arabian Peninsula. Despite his name, his descendants were numerous, and he had thirteen known sons: Almodad, Sheleph, Hazarmaveth, Jerah, Hadoram, Uzal, Diklah, Obal, Abimael, Jobab, Sheba, Ophir, and Havilah. (Gen. 10:26-29, 1Ch. 1:20-23). These sons gave rise to the many people in the southern portion of the Arabian Peninsula, most of whom dwelled near the sons of Cush.

The names Sheba and Havilah are recognizable as their names are the same as Cush's sons and a grandson (Gen. 10:7). Considering where their generation falls, these sons were likely named after the descendants of Cush, located in modern-day Yemen and the surrounding area in the Arabian Peninsula, as discussed in the chapters on Cush's sons.[16,17,18] Joktan's sons quite possibly settled in this area. In Josephus' works, Sheba's name is recorded as Sabeus, indicating that these people were likely related to the Seba, Sabei, or Sheba of Cush, found today in Yemen.[19] While Ham's descendants would have named the land, the language of Joktan with elements of Cush's people remained.[20] And this is likely the case for most of Joktan's sons. They mixed with those of the vast Arabian Peninsula. But Havilah and Sheba, however, might indicate where the majority of the Joktanite tribes settled.

Josephus records Almodad as Elmodad, and the *Book of Jasher* calls him Almodad.[19,21] Bochart and Ptolemy place this tribe, which they categorize as Arabic, in the southern part of the Arabian Peninsula and called them the "Almodaei, or Allumaeotae."[22] Jerah is rather well known in Arabic sources. One writer collects the many names of a region that bears the name of Joktan,

> *"Following the line of settlements southward, by Baisath Joktan, or Beishe, and the Kithebanitae or Beni Kahtan of Ptolemy and Burckhardt, the name of the Father of Yemen reappears, in that of Hud-Jerah, a town on the mountain chain."*[23]

Kahtan is the Arabic name for the biblical Yoktan or Joktan, which – though the account has been somewhat confused with time or intent – connects the lineage from Joktan to these Arab tribes.[24] In the name *Hud-Joktan*, *Hud* is to be the Arabic name for Heber, father of Joktan, who was the father of *Kahtan*, father of *Yarab* or Jerah.[25] They gave rise to a people in the lower part of the Arabian Penninsula.[25] Beni Kahtan is the name of a place and a collection of tribes, which are said to have dwelled near Mekka.[26,27] Near them, that is, within the region of *Baisath Joktan*, were the *Iobaritae* or *Beni-Jubbar* who were likely named after another brother called Jobab.[28] It was this tribe, and later kingdom, that centered around Mecca.[29] The Arabian accounts of these tribes provided names similar to Scripture's account: Jorham, Yarab, Yareh, and Yobab.[24,30,31]

Considering that his brother's tribes are found along the edges of the Arabian Peninsula, we can assume that Abimael's people would be found here as well. Indeed, writers have compared Abimael's people to the Minaei, as they were later called, who sometimes lived in the city of Karn-al-Manzil, which is near Mecca.[32,33] Strabo recorded that the Minaei lived near the Red Sea in the city Carna, which is known as Charmaei, Carman Regia, and of course Karn-al-Manzil.[32,34] These people, unsurprisingly, were "next to...the Sabaeans" according to Strabo.[34] Both Bochart and Pliny mention that some people once believed this tribe descended from Minos of Crete, though that was not the case.[35,36] Yet it must be noted that while the connection of Abimael and the Minaei is believable, any number of Arabian tribes could have arisen from them as any other, much like the Canaanite tribes.

Hadoram and Hazarmaveth appear to have dwelled together. Josephus knew them as Asetmoth and Adoram.[19] While one bears the name "village of death," the people became quite prosperous.[37] Pliny mentions two tribes in one account: the Chatramotitae and the Atramitae.[36,38] They were known for their frankincense.[38] These two tribes inhabited a prosperous land in southern Yemen farther east than their brothers called Hadramaut.[39] This name and the tribes' names could have come from Hadoram and Hazarmaveth, transliterated as *Hadowram* and *Chatsarmaveth*, respectively.[37,40] Though Hadoram is considered to be the father of the Atramitae, these two brothers appear to have joined together to become the people of Hadramaut.[41] Ashurbanipal's annals mention a city far in the south of Arabia called Hurarina that may have been within this land.[42] The name Hadramaut, appearing as *hdrmt*, is frequently found in Hadramitic texts in the region of Yemen once inhabited by this people.[43] And the *HDRMT* land "still today carries the ancient name Hadramawt."[44]

Another son known for riches is Ophir. In Scripture, the land of Ophir was known to be rich with gold, even as early as the time of Job (Job 22:24, 28:16, Psa. 45:9). King Hiram of Tyre sent ships to Ophir to bring back precious metals and algum wood to Solomon for the Temple, and before that, David had gold from that land (1Ki. 9:28, 10:11-12, 1Ch. 29:4, 2Ch. 8:18, 9:10). King Jehoshaphat attempted to send many ships to Ophir for their gold, but the ships never made it (1Ki. 22:48). Because ships were sent, Ophir must have been best reached by water. By the time of Isaiah, Ophir's gold had become scarce (Isa. 13:12). The location of Ophir, however, has been much debated, with claims from southern Arabia to India to possibly a new world altogether.[45] There are as many different places suggested for the location of Ophir as there are texts about those places. To list them all would be tedious. Yet as most of these other sons are found in and around Arabia, it is relatively safe to assume that Ophir remained here as well.

To begin, an ostracon from Tell Qasile, Israel contains a record of gold from Ophir sent to Beth-horon.[223] Josephus says Ophir, once called Aurea Chersonesus, was a place in India.[45] Diodorus wrote that Arabia was ripe in gold and other precious items.[46] The Egyptians never mention Ophir by name, but they spoke of a place they called Amau that held "gold in enormous quantities" and was accessible by water.[47,48] An Ethiopian text tells of a journey to Saphir for gold.[49] An Arabic text, seemingly based on Scripture, puts Sheba, Ophir, and Havilah together, noting that Ophir, called Send, has gold.[50] A Greek text mentions an island called *Ourphe*, located in the Red Sea.[51] Most of these locations place Ophir near the western coast of Arabia or the eastern coast of Africa. Perhaps the land was in India, as some authors suggest. Still, coupling what most scholars say with the location of other Joktanites leads to the conclusion that the land was near Seba and Havilah in Arabia.

Unlike most of his brothers, Uzal is mentioned outside of the genealogies. Uzal was a place where Danites and Greeks bought wares such as iron, cassia, and cane to trade with Tyre (Ezk. 27:19). Scholars have identified the city now called Sanaa, once called Azal, as the location of Uzal.[52,53] This name is quite similar to what Josephus provides, who renders it *Aizel*.[19] According to legends from the surrounding region, the city was built by Shem and then named after his descendant Uzal, calling it Azal.[54] While we cannot know the truth regarding Shem's architectural pursuits, Uzal's identification appears to be accurate.

The remaining sons have relatively few mentions in recorded history, yet what can be known will be discussed. Sheleph, also known as Sheaf and Saleph, possibly left his name in the city known as Al-Salif, Yemen.[55] A tribe thrice attested to known as the Saleph and the Salapheni lived in Yemen.[56,57,58] Diklah, or Decla, is scarcely known outside of Jewish works.[19,21] While a handful of scholars have given him patronage of a Yemeni tribe called the Duklaite, no outside sources of the tribe have been found.[59,60] Lastly is Obal with עוֹבָל used in the first genealogy and עֵיבָל in the second with no other uses in context of this son.[61,62] This reflects what is found in the *Book of Jasher* and Josephus' works, who record him as Ebal and Obal.[19,21] While he likely had a tribe of his own, he probably joined a stronger brother and faded from record.

Haran and Nahor

While Abraham is the best-remembered son of Terah, his brothers also played an important role in history, both for Israel and the Middle East. The order of the brothers in Scripture is Abraham, Nahor, and Haran. Any of these brothers could have been eldest, but Haran and his people will be discussed first in this section because his death is mentioned first (Gen. 11:27-31). Haran had his son Lot while still in Ur of the Chaldees as well as a daughter named Milcah – the wife to Nahor – and another child named Iscah (Gen. 11:27-29). Josephus recorded these children as Lot, Milcah, and Sarai.[63] The descendants of Lot will be discussed in a following section, but Lot is the nephew who follows Abraham to the promised land (Gen. 12:1-14:16). But before Terah and his family leave Ur of the Chaldees, Haran dies (Gen. 11:28). Once they leave, they settle in a city called Haran, Harran for clarity, staying even after Terah's death (Gen. 11:31-12:4).

Despite the similarity of the names, the city Harran and the man Haran seem to be unconnected, mainly because the etymologies of their names are different. The man Haran is הָרָן in Scripture, meaning "mountaineer," and comes from the Hebrew words for "mountain" or "range of hills."[64,65,66] The city Harran is חָרָן in Scripture, which appears similar to the previous name, but instead comes from a word meaning to "glow, ...melt, burn, ...or incite passion."[67,68]

The place Harran is important to Nahor's family. While Haran never arrived, and Abraham left, Nahor and his family stayed in Harran. This city can be found today in Turkey, not far south from the historic site of Urfa, the city which may be where Abraham and his family were from.[69,70] The Ebla tablets contain the name Harran as *Ha-ra-an*[ki] and sometimes *Ha-ra-nu*[ki] or *Kar-ra-nu*[ki]."[70] This city was home to a deity known as the moon-god by the Mari, Hittites, and Babylonians, each noting the "temple of Sin of Harran," the "Harranian Moon-god," and "the temple of e.hil.hil in Harran."[70,71,72] Idol-worship was so common that it even affected Abraham's extended family (Gen. 31:30-35). Nahor, however, is specifically said to have worshiped the Lord (Gen. 31:53). The family of Nahor was still living in Harran when Jacob fled from Esau to Laban's home (Gen. 27:43). But for this area and lineage to be fully understood, Nahor's family must be discussed.

Like his brothers, Nahor was also born in Ur of the Chaldees and left with his father's family to Harran, where they settled (Gen. 11:27-31). Nahor was likely named after his grandfather, but perhaps the meaning of the name, which is "snorer" or "snorting," had something to do with it (Gen. 11:22-26).[73,74] As mentioned before, his wife was Haran's daughter Milcah and together they had "Uz, Buz, Kemuel, Kesed, Hazo, Pildash, Jidlaph and Bethuel" (Gen. 22:21-22). This Buz perhaps was the father of the Buzites mentioned in the book of Job (Job. 32:2-6). Nahor also had a concubine, Reumah, who bore him, "Tebah, Gaham, Tahash and Maacah" (Gen. 22:24). Kemuel was the father of a man named Aram; Bethuel was the father of Rebekah and Laban (Gen. 22:21-22, 24:15-47, 29:5). Rebekah, of course, was the wife of Isaac and Laban the father of Rachel and Leah, who married Jacob (Gen. 24:1-67, 28:1-29:30). The sons would have built up communities for themselves as Nahor and Abraham did.

The land that Nahor's family lived in, however, was called by a variety of names. His family also did not remain in the city of Harran permanently, and they eventually moved outside of the city. Evidence for this is found in a reference to a town of Nahor mentioned in Genesis (Gen. 24:10). In the "Harran Census," found in the region of Harran, there was a city titled "Til-nahiri."[75,76] A city called Nahur is frequently mentioned in the Mari texts, though whether it is the same as Til-nahiri or the town of Nahor, as its location is east of Harran, is less certain.[77] There were also towns nearby known as *Sarugi, Til-Turakhi, Til-sa-Turah,* and *Nakhur* which could be connected to this family.[14,78] Aram Naharaim was the name the greater area was known by, though more commonly as Mesopotamia. This location is mentioned in the same passage as the town of Nahor, the land of Nahor's family (Gen. 24:10). Aram Naharaim, mentioned a handful of times in Scripture, is clearly part of Mesopotamia as the name means "Aram of the two rivers" (Deut. 23:4, Jos. 24:2, Jdg. 3:8-10, 1Ch. 19:6).[79] The Egyptians referred to the land, and possibly a city, as "Naharin."[80] In the Amarna letters, the land was known as "Na-ah-ri-ma" or "Nahrima."[81]

Within the land of Aram Naharaim was Paddan Aram, meaning field or "table-land of Aram," the final identifiable location of Nahor's family.[82] This is where Isaac's wife, Rebekah, is from (Gen. 25:20). Again, it is to Paddan Aram Jacob is sent when he flees Esau and finds Laban (Gen. 28:1-7, 29:6-12). Jacob stays here, marries, and raises sheep and sons until he flees Laban and returns to his homeland (Gen. 29-31, 33:18, 35:9-26, 46:15, 48:7). Laban's land was in Aram Naharaim and near to Harran (Gen. 29:1-4). Between Harran and Nahur is a well called "Bir Yaqub" or "Jacob's Well."[83] These are the cities and areas in which Abraham's family began.

Abraham and Israel

Anyone who has read Scripture should have recognized an emphasis on the history of the people of Israel throughout the text. While every detail of their history cannot be discussed here, many of their interactions with other nations have been previously discussed and many shall be discussed. To avoid their history would be inappropriate, for without it, there would be almost nothing known about many of the nations discussed in this work, let alone their origins. Additionally, it was through Israel that "all of the nations of the world would be blessed," and this through Christ (Gen. 12:3).

Of all the descendants of Shem and Arphaxad, Abraham is the best-known. It is his lineage that connects to Christ, his that the nation of Israel arose from, his that is the secondary focus of the Old Testament. The *Book of Jubilees* holds that Abraham was named after his maternal grandfather.[84] Additionally, Abraham's family remained in Ur Kesdim for many generations after Babel until Terah's family moved to Harran (Gen. 11:31).[85] Nahor, Abraham, and Terah are said to have served the Lord (Gen. 31:53). God called Abraham to an unknown promised land where he would become a great nation through whom all people would be blessed, though at the time, he and his wife Sarah were childless (Gen. 12:1-3, 17:19-21, 21:1-7). During this time, he watched over his nephew Lot, who fathered the Moabites and Ammonites (Gen. 12:4, 13:1-14:16, 19:36-38). God made a covenant with Abraham and changed his and his wife's names (Gen. 17:1-16). This was the covenant made with all descendants of Israel, one that only God could perfectly keep and was fulfilled with Christ's ultimate sacrifice (Gen. 15:4-21, 17:1-27, Isa. 53:1-12, Rom. 3:21-31).

Though Isaac is remembered best for his almost being sacrificed, he was not Abraham's only son (Gen. 22:1-18). Abraham also had Ishmael with Hagar (the handmaiden of Sarai from Egypt) and Zimran, Jokshan, Medan, Midian, Ishbak, and Shuah with Keturah, his wife after Sarah's death (Gen. 16:1-16, 25:1-11). Isaac married Nahor's granddaughter Rebekah (Gen. 24:1-67). Together, Isaac and Rebekah had twin boys: Jacob and Esau (Gen. 25:19-34, 33:1-16). When Jacob fled to Harran, he received a vision at Bethel that the Lord would bless him (Gen. 27:41-28:22). Jacob married the daughters of his mother's brother Laban: Rachel and Leah (Gen. 29:1-30). After wrestling with God, the Lord renamed him and his people Israel, a name coming from Hebrew words meaning power and God (Gen. 32:22-32).[86]

In all, Jacob had thirteen children. Leah gave him Reuben, Simeon, Levi, Judah (who is of the line of Christ), Issachar, Zebulun, and Dinah, the only daughter of Jacob; Bilhah, Rachel's handmaiden, had Dan and Naphtali; Zilpah, Leah's handmaiden, had Gad and Asher; finally, Rachel had Joseph and Benjamin, though she died giving birth to her younger son (Gen. 29:31-30:24, 35:16-26). These sons became the twelve tribes of Israel. Consequently, they did not remain in Harran but returned to Abraham's promised land (Gen. 30:25-34:31). During this time, Isaac, and presumably Rebekah, died, and they were buried in the cave with Abraham and Sarah (Gen. 23:1-20, 25:7-11, 35:27-29).

As was common in this family, there was jealousy and favoritism among the sons of Jacob (Gen. 37:3). The brothers sold Joseph to Midianites and Ishmaelites, leading to the series of events that brought Israel to the heart of Egypt (Gen. 37:1-36, 39:1-47:31). Israel stayed in Egypt for a couple of hundred years, where Israel was enslaved until the Lord delivered them (Ex. 1:1-3:22, 12:1-42). The twelve tribes of Israel then wandered in the desert for four decades, received the Law, and eventually were allowed into the promised land of Abraham (Ex. 15:22-Deut. 34:12, Num. 14:26-35).

This land initially was to stretch from the Euphrates, the Hittite or Canaanite country, to the Mediterranean, the Negev, and Gilead (Deut. 34:1-4). The land that was taken encompassed most of this area, but the Israelites failed to take all the territory and drive out all the people (Jos. 12:1-22:34, Jdg. 1:1-3:6). Dan and Beersheba are often used to describe the northern and southern ends of Israel, respectively (Jdg. 20:1, 1Sa. 3:20, 2Sa. 3:10, 17:11, 24:2-15, 1Ki. 4:25, 1Ch. 21:2, 2Ch. 30:5). The Lord commanded the Israelites to drive out and completely destroy many Canaanite nations, and this was not arbitrary. This was done to keep Israel unadulterated by foreign gods and to punish the nations who had rejected God (Gen. 15:16, Deut. 20:16-18). Still, they were to leave Edom, Moab, and Ammon as God's inheritance to the descendants of Lot and Esau, though they were not without conflict (Deut. 2:4-19).

Though Israel was ruled by God, and the Lord raised up judges, eventually, the people wanted a king (Rth. 1:1, 1Sa. 8:1-9). This united kingdom was short-lived, and Israel divided into the Northern Kingdom of Israel and the Southern Kingdom of Judah (1Sa. 10:1-27, 16:13, 2Ch. 10:1-19). Eventually, the Northern Kingdom fell in 720 B.C. to the Assyrians and Judah to the Babylonians in 586 B.C. (2Ki. 17:6-24, 2Ch. 36:15-21).[87,88] Some of Israel remained in the land, and some were relocated in the surrounding nations; but eventually, a remnant was allowed to rebuild under Cyrus (2Ch. 36:22-23, Ezr. 1:1-4). They remained this way under the Greeks and the Romans until they were destroyed in 70 A.D.[89,90] Though not under the same governance as they were in the Old Testament, after enduring many horrors over the centuries in the various places they dwelled, the people of Israel became a nation once more.[91]

Now that the history of Israel and their territory has been established, the extra-biblical references to them, their nation, and the kings can be discussed. Israel is mentioned in several texts from surrounding nations. Israel and Israelite settled areas, like Samaria, also have a collection of texts such as the ostracon of Samaria and Lachish that, though they do not always specifically reference Israel, mention places in Israel and Yahweh.[88] Artifacts from Moab, a neighbor and relative of Israel, includes references not only to Israel but also King Omri and his son, who would have been Ahab; under Ahab's son Jehoram's rule, Mesha and Moab revolted (2Ki. 3:1-27).[92] The Mesha Stele also mentioned the tribe of Gad, a "Davidic altar hearth," and a reference to the House of David.[93] One of the well-known discoveries from this area is the Tel-Dan fragment containing the name of King Hadad of Aram – whose people this fragment likely came from – the name Israel, and the "the House of David," which is the "dynastic name of the kingdom of Judah" as compared to "*Bit Humrī*" for the Northern Kingdom.[94]

Ahab king of Israel, son of Omri, was known to the Assyrians as "*A-ha-ab-bu* ^{mat}*Sir-Tla'-a-a*" or Ahab the Israelite.[95] The House of Omri would entitle the line of Israel's kings, that is, the Northern Kingdom, for some time in extra-biblical texts, even when the king of the time was not of the line of Omri. Such is the case of King Jehu of Israel, a man who killed Ahab's family (2Ki. 9:1-10:36). On the Black Obelisk from Shalmaneser III's reign, Jehu or *Ia-u-a* is called a son of Omri, or *Hu-um-ri-a*, when he ruled Israel.[96] The annals of Adad-nirari III at Calneh record Israel or ^{mat}*Hu-um-ri* among the various nations that had submitted to Assyria.[96] Jehoahaz, *Ia-u-ha-zi*, of Judah, *Ia-u-da-a-a*, is recorded in an inscription attributed to Tiglath-Pileser III which mentions a Azriau of *Ia-u-da-a-a*.[97] Another record from Assyria calls Israel *Bit Hu-um-ri-a*, referring to King Omri (1Ki. 16:16-28).[97]

Sargon II names himself the "conqueror of Samaria (*Sa-mir-i-na*) and of the entire (country of) Israel (*Bit-hu-um-ri-a*)" and the "subduer of the country of Judah (*Ia-u-du*)."[97,98] While the annals of Sennacherib make great boasts of subduing King Hezekiah, *Ha-za-qi-a-a-a*, the Lord delivered him from Assyria, and Assyria's king was assassinated by his older sons and succeeded by Esarhaddon (2Ki. 19:1-37).[99] Both Esarhaddon and Ashurbanipal dealt with Manasseh, *Me-na-si-i*, king of *Ia-u-di*.[100] Shortly thereafter, Nebuchadnezzar of Babylon invaded Judah, and his records contain *Ia-'-kin* a son of Judah's King *Ia-ku-u-ki-nu* of *amel Ia-a-hu-da-a-a* or *Ia-ku-du*, who are likely Jehoiakim and Jehoiachin of Judah (2Ki. 23:26-25:26).[101] This event seems to have also been recorded in the Merneptah Stele, which says, "Israel is laid waste."[102,103] Though most of the extra-biblical references are not positive, they do show the significance of Israel among the nations of the Middle East.

Hagar and Ishmael

Ishmael and his people come from the relationship of Abraham and his wife's maidservant Hagar when Sarah was impatient for a son (Gen. 16:1-4). While Sarah became jealous of Hagar and Ishmael, the Lord had mercy on Abraham's son (Gen. 16:4-15, 17:23-27, 21:8-21). The Lord promised that Ishmael would become the father of a great nation and of twelve rulers (Gen. 17:19-20, 21:12-13). After they were sent away, Hagar got Ishmael a wife from her homeland Egypt (Gen. 21:9-21, 25:9-10). Scripture says he lived in the Desert of Paran, the area along the Red Sea's eastern coast, and became an archer (Gen. 21:20-21).

Ishmael had twelve sons: Nebaoith, Kedar, Adbeel, Mibsam, Mishma, Dumah, Massa, Hadad, Tema, Jetur, Naphish, and Kedemah (Gen. 25:13-16, 1Ch. 1:29-31). He also had a daughter named Mahalath, also known as Basemath, the wife of Esau, and possibly other children in addition to those listed (Gen. 28:9, 36:3). His people were known as Ishmaelites. Another name for the descendants of Ishmael is Hagrite, from Hagar, his mother (Psa. 83:6). Some Ishmaelites were defeated by the tribes of Reuben and Gad during the Conquest, though a few remained, for a Hagrite named Jaziz served under David (1Ch. 5:10-20,

27:30-31). Ishmael lived to be one hundred and thirty-seven (Gen. 25:17).

At the time of his death, Ishmael's sons had settled from Havilah to Egypt, though other records show that in later times they roamed the Middle East (Gen. 25:18, 16:11-12). They were merchants and nomads, moving about the Sinai Peninsula, Egypt, Havilah, Gilead, and even up into Assyria (Gen. 37:25-28, 39:1). Joseph was sold to a group of Midianite and Ishmaelite merchants by his brothers (Gen. 37:28). These two groups seemed to have lived close together and possibly even intermarried (Jdg. 8:22-24). Two notable Ishmaelites during the times of the kings were Amasa, the son of David's sister Abagail, and Jether (2Sa. 17:25, 1Ch. 2:16-17). Another Ishmaelite specifically mentioned was Obil, who tended the king's camels (1Ch. 27:30). Besides these references, and one mentioning the enmity of other nations towards Israel, the Ishmaelites are not mentioned again by that name (Psa. 83:6). Ishmael, called *Su-mu-il* in Assyrian texts, is a land synonymous with Arabia, whose king was Uate' during the time of Ashurbanipal.[104] This record says King Uate' of Arabia and Ishmael was a son of Hazai, brother of Uate', and grandson of Bir-Dadda.[104] Thus, his people were often called Arabians.

Nebaioth is the firstborn of Ishmael, specifically stated twice in Scripture (Gen. 25:13, 1Ch. 1:29). Additionally, we know Basemath is the daughter of Ishmael as she is called the sister of Nebaioth (Gen. 28:9, 36:3). There is a question to whether Nebaioth is a son or a daughter, for the name is feminine.[105] The people descended from Nebaioth are the Nabaiti found in the Assyrian records, also called Nabaiateans, whose king was Natnu.[104] The king of Arabia fled to their land for a time.[104] The land of Qedar, called *Qi-id-ri*, and its King Ammuladi dwelled near the Nabaiateans.[104] Egypt interacted with Nebaioth's descendants, calling their city Baabayt.[106]

While there is no consensus, it appears that Nebaioth's people are connected to the *NBYT,* from an Arabian inscription from Jebel Ghunaym, and were mentioned alongside Massa, Dedan, and Tema, all of whom appear to be at war.[107,108] Massa and Tema are siblings of Nebaioth, and Dedan has previously been noted as a tribe on the eastern border of Saudi Arabia, placing Nebaioth in the midst of Saudi

Arabia. This fits with the marriage of Esau to Nebaioth's sister. The association of these names, which has been made since the days of Josephus and Jerome, may join the Nebaioth to the Nabateans of Nabataea, a prominent group of Arabs in the Middle East after the exile of Israel and before the rise of Greece.[109,110] The Nabateans may be the combination of multiple Ishmaelite tribes, such as the Nebaioth and Kedarites. [110]

Despite his status as second-born, Kedar gave rise to possibly the greatest of the Ishmaelite tribes (Gen. 25:13, 1Ch. 1:29). Though this may have had to do with the combining of Kedar and Nebaioth at some point in their history, the Kedarites were a sizable tribe in their own right. For example, a Psalmist aligned them with Meshech and described them as those who hate peace (Psa. 120:5-7). Like their father, they were great archers and warriors, but Scripture notes the end of their greatness (Isa. 21:16-17, Jer. 49:28-32). These people were nomads, living in dark tents, and were perhaps a dark people, who dwelled in the desert and raised flocks and camels alongside Nebaioth (Sng. 1:5, Isa. 42:11, Jer. 2:10, 49:28-32, Ezk. 27:21, Isa. 60:7).[111] Yet in one passage, the flocks are not only referring to actual livestock but to the people of Nebaioth and Kedar who are gathered to the Lord, serving and sacrificing to Him, as they too would be saved (Isa. 59:21-60:7).

While the name Kedar means "dark" in Hebrew, elsewhere, the name Qedem, or words like it, meant "the East" as the Kedarites were possibly the greatest of the tribes of the East and of Arabia.[111,112] In Egyptian records, Qedem was an encompassing name for the people and land of the East.[112] A failed attack by the Qedarites is mentioned alongside the Mas'a tribe in the letters of Nabu-sum-lisir.[113] The name "QDRYN," an Aramaic transcription for the Qedarites, is found on the Mareshah onomasticon.[114] Pliny knew them as the Cedrei and placed them near Egypt in Petra, alongside the Nabataei.[115] In much later accounts of the region, travelers noted the similarity of the Bedouins to the Kedarites as they were nomads in the desert who lived in black tents and specifically called Kedar their father.[116] The extent of their wanderings stretched from Assyria to Babylon, from the west of Madai to the south near the Red Sea, and to the east of Egypt in Petra.[42,117,118] Their capital was at some point placed at Dumah, called Adummatu in

Assyrian records, and today is known as Dumat al-Jandal (Gen. 25:14, 1Ch. 1:30, Isa. 21:11).[119,120]

The first ruler of the Arabs in known records is Gindibu', who aided Hadadezer or Ben Hadad against Assyria (1Ki. 11:23).[121,122] The first record of Qedar in Assyrian records is from the time of Tiglath-Pileser III in a text saying Assyria conquered "KUR.*qid*-ri KUR.*a*-*ri*-bi" which is Qedar and Arabia.[123] The leader of the Arabs during that time was "*za-bi-be-e sar-rat*," that is Zabibe the queen, and she was followed by Queen Samsi.[123,124] During the time of Sennacherib of Assyria and Merodach-Baladan of Babylon, queen Iati'e ruled Qedar and Arabia.[117] When they rebelled, her brother Baskanu was captured along with Adinu, wife of Babylon's king, and their armies by Sennacherib.[117] Two queens ruled during the time of Esarhaddon, Talhuna and Tabua, the latter made queen by Esarhaddon.[125] Esarhaddon named Adummatu (Dumah) as the "stronghold" or capital of the Arabs and Qedar, whose king at the time was Hazail, possibly the same Hazael in Scripture (2Ki. 8:15).[119,126] Afterwards, Esarhaddon recognized his son Ia'lu, or Uate', son of Hazail, as king.[125] King Ammuladi of Qedar, or *qi-id-ri*, was recorded when he revolted against Ashurbanipal, a revolt which ended in defeat and the capture of him and Aidia, wife of Uate'.[127]

Following these revolts, Abiate', son of Te'ri, became king of Kedar and Arabia, though his brother Aamu was caught in battle and "flayed in Nineveh"; these two brothers are mentioned among the letters of Nabu-sum-lisir.[104,113] A number of different leaders ruled the Qedarites after this point, including: Mati-il and his son Kabaril in Dedan; Nabonidus of Babylon at Tema; Mahlay and his son Iyas of Qedar; and Shahru in Tema, evidenced by an Egyptian inscription at Tell el-Maskuta.[128,129,130,131] The final two recorded kings of Qedar are Gashmu and his son Qainu from the Tell el-Maskhuta site.[128,130] Gashmu is the same man called Geshem the Arab in the book of Nehemiah, who is one of the leaders of the people surrounding Israel after the Exile (Neh. 2:19, 6:1-2).[114,130]

Note that in many of these texts, the Nebaioth, Kedarites, and Arabs are often considered synonymous, especially the latter two. While the Arabs were made up of many different tribes, the strongest of these groups were the Kedarites, thus rendering the name of many Arabs as

Kedarites and those of Kedar Arab. After the decline of the Kedarites, a group called the Nabateans rose to power in the same vicinity as Kedar and Nebaioth. While some do not consider the lineage to be direct, to completely exclude the Ishmaelites would be erroneous as they rose to power at this time, their culture and language are comparable, and they dwelled in the same regions.[110,132]

Additionally, while the various tribes of Ishmael are seldom mentioned, the kings of Arabia are included on many occasions when interacting with the following: Solomon, when the Arabs brought gold; Jehoshaphat, who received rams and goats; Jehoram, who was attacked by the Arabs near Cush; Ahaziah, who was the only son of Jehoram's left by Arab raiders; and Uzziah, who was delivered from the Arabs at Gur Baal (1Ki. 10:15, 2Ch. 9:14, 17:11, 21:16, 22:1, 26:7).

The Arabs are also often part of prophecy. They are mentioned in the destruction of Babylon, where "no Arab will pitch his tent" (Isa. 13:20). All of Arabia is prophesied against, including Dedan, Kedar, and Tema, when the "pomp...will come to an end" and the "survivors...will be few" (Isa. 21:13-17). In one part of Scripture, the word for Arab is translated instead as nomad, for that is what most of them were; elsewhere, they and their cities are part of the "distant places" in the desert (Jer. 3:2, 25:23-24, Ezk. 30:5). Though each son started his own tribe, by the end of the fifth and fourth centuries B.C., they were collectively known as Kedarites or Arabs.

Tema was not only a tribe of Ishmael but also was the name of a city (Gen. 25:15, 1Ch. 1:30). In one of Job's distressed replies, he mentions the caravans of Tema searching for water in the desert (Job 6:19-19). In the prophecy against Arabia, Tema is mentioned as a city alongside Sheba (Isa. 21:14, Jer. 25:23). Tema and its people are mentioned alongside Saba', that is Sheba, and Mas'a, which is Messa, in a record of Tiglath-Pileser III.[97] The Jebel Ghunaym inscription mentions Tema' alongside Nebaioth.[107] In the annals of Sennacherib, Tema's people are included with those of Sumu'el, which is Ishmael and the Arabs.[133] The name is transliterated as URU.te-ma-a-a and LU.te-e-me.[133,134] At the end of his rule, and after killing the Arab leader, Nabonidus stayed at Tema while his kingdom fell to the Medo-Persian Empire.[135] Pliny refers to them as the Thimanai, connected to the Nabataei.[36] The city was known for trade, conveniently placed on a desert oasis, and to this day is known by the name Teima.[136]

Naphish is only mentioned three times in all of Scripture. Two of those are within the genealogies, and the only thing known about them is that they were an Arab tribe (Gen. 25:15, 1Ch. 1:31, 5:19). Yet in each passage that they are mentioned, Jetur is also mentioned alongside them. Regarding Scripture, these two brothers are named together when the Reubenites, Gadites, and Manassites fought the Hagrites, Jetur, Naphish, and a people called Nodab, placing them northeast of Israel (1Ch. 5:18-22). Nothing more is known about Nodab save that they appear to be another Arab tribe. Jetur has quite soundly been identified with Ituraea.[137] Ituraea, found in Syria, is described as mountainous, difficult to navigate, and dangerous to travel through.[138] Their land stretched from "the Lake of Tiberias to Damascus," north of Israel, the land Philip the tetrarch governed (Luk. 3:1).[139] The Ituraeans and Arabians there were called raiders, known for archery.[138,140]

Massa is found alongside Tema and Saba in the annals of Tiglath-Pileser III and was known as Mas'a and Mas'ai in these records.[97] Massa is also mentioned in the Jebel Ghunaym inscription alongside Tema.[107] Additionally, the Nabu-sum-lisir letters notes an attack by chief Ayakabaru of Massa on Assyria, a record that aides in placing Massa in northern Arabia alongside Tema.[107,141] Within these letters and among some Nabataean inscriptions are names such as Agur, Jakeh, and Lemuel, associated with Arab kings in Massa and both kings and sages in Scripture (Pro. 30:1, 31:1).[107,141] While these extra-biblical texts do not necessarily contain the same people found in Proverbs, they do show that the wisdom of Arab sages was admired by Israel.[141] These also point to the location of Massa, which is in northern Arabia.[107]

As for the remainder of Ishmael's sons, besides grouping them alongside the general people of Ishmaelites and Arabs, there is relatively little known about each individual. For example, though there are multiple people found in Scripture and ancient inscriptions with the name of Hadad, such as the Hadadezer and Ben-Hadad, not to mention gods with the same name, none of them coincide with the tribe of Hadad, son of Ishmael (Gen. 25: 15, 1Ki. 11:23, 15:18).[142] Some have conjectured that there was an Arab tribe called Hadad whose name was used for the city of Hadedda in Yemen, but that is a tentative conclusion.[143] One of the Ishmaelite tribes, descended from Adbeel, is connected to the Idiba'ilean tribe in Assyrian records.[97] They were a people "whose countries [(are) far away], towards the West" in Arabia, possessing goods such as camels, spices, and precious metals, and who gained status in the eyes of Tiglath-Pileser III to be made "Warden of Marches on (the frontier of) Musur" which is Egypt.[97,134,144] Either or both Mibsam and Mishma could be found in either of two cities called Jebel Misma in the northwestern part of Saudi Arabia.[145] Kedemah is mentioned in Scripture by name only in the genealogies, yet his name is similar to the word used for eastward or antiquity (Gen. 25:15, 1Ch. 1:31).[146,147] Additionally, his name is related etymologically with Kedemoth, a wilderness east of Israel near Heshbon, and it is to the people of the East that Moab and Ammon's land would be given (Deut. 2:26, Ezk. 25:10).[148] While there is little specifically known about these final tribes of Ishmael, his descendants are clearly documented throughout history and archaeology as existing where Scripture says.

Sons of Keturah

After Sarah's death, Abraham took another wife named Keturah and had six more sons (Gen. 25:1). These were: Zimran, Jokshan, Medan, Midian, Ishbak, and Shuah (Gen. 25:2, 1Ch. 1:32). Little is known about most of these sons, and they are rarely mentioned again, save two of them. Most, however, likely became part of the many tribes of the Middle East. Scripture states that Abraham sent them "to the land of the east" away from Isaac (Gen. 25:6). Josephus writes that Abraham sent these sons to Trylodytis and Arabia Felix, "as far as it reaches to the Red Sea," placing these sons in the mid to southern part of the Arabian Peninsula.[149] Again, the *Book of Jasher* holds that Abraham sent them "to the mountain at the east" so they would be far from Isaac.[150] The *Book of Jubilees* records that the sons of Ishmael and Keturah "went together and dwelt from Paran to the entering in Babylon in all the land which is towards the East facing the desert. And these mingled with each other" and were called both Arabs and

Ishmaelites.[151] Though not all the sons stayed in the same location, all appear to have dwelled within the Middle East.

The first son is Zimran, or Zambran (Gen. 25:2, 1Ch. 1:32).[149] The only place that scholars have connected him to is a city near Mecca, within Arabia Felix, called Zabram.[152,153,154] The second son, Jokshan, had two sons named Sheba and Dedan (Gen. 25:2-3, 1Ch. 1:32). As Ham's descendants came first, Jokshan's sons were likely named after them. Scripture records three sons of Dedan: Asshurim, Letushim, and Leummim (Gen. 25:3). The wilderness of Shur, located near Kadesh and Egypt, could possibly be where the Asshurim settled at some point, for a tribe called A'shar dwelt there (Gen. 16:7, 20:1, Ex. 15:22).[155] It is from the two latter sons that perhaps the Lihyan kingdom in Arabia arose, located just south of Edom.[156] While these people probably did not originate there, it is near the other Dedan, Sheba, and Joktan that the Lihyanites later settled. These people joined the Ishmaelites and other sons of Shem and Ham.

While little is known about the two previous sons, there is almost nothing known about Medan, Ishbak, and Shuah. Like many ancient tribes, their existence is only known because of Scripture or an ancient text. For Medan, the only extra-biblical connections are to two cities called Madanu and Badana in Arabia.[97,157] Ishbak may be connected to the Iasbuq or Iasbuk of Assyrian records.[158] Another translation renders the name "Iasbukite."[159] In this text, a man called Bur-Anate from Iasbuq is called by a leader in Hattina to fight, perhaps against Shalmaneser III of Assyria.[158] A possible tribe of Shuah is found in the Book of Job. Bildad, a friend of Job, is a Shuhite (Job. 2:11). The annals of Ashurnasirpal II record that Assyria defeated the people in the country of Suhu near the city Anat, now called Anah, along the Euphrates.[160,161,162] Later, they in the city of Rahilu became subject to Nabopolassar.[157,163]

Midian is the most recognizable son, and there is a relative abundance of information about him. He had five sons: Ephah, Epher, Hanoch, Abida, and Edaah (Gen. 25:4). Only one of these sons, Ephah, is mentioned again in Scripture, alongside his father Midian, from whom come camels to Israel and praise to the Lord (Isa. 60:6). Either the man or the country is mentioned among the list of kings over Edom when a king named Hadad is said to have "defeated Midian in the country of Moab" (Gen. 36:35).[164] Joseph was sold to a group of Midianite merchants, though some translations call them Medanites (Gen. 37:28). When Moses fled from Egypt, he went to Midian and married Zipporah, a daughter of Jethro, or Reuel, the priest of Midian and mentor to Moses (Ex. 2:15-3:1, 4:19, 18:1). Additionally, Moses asks his brother-in-law, Hobab, to remain with Israel as he knew where to camp in the desert (Num. 10:29).

Despite the renewed familial connection between Israel and Midian via the marriage of Moses and Zipporah, Midianites near Moab joined in the Moabites' fear that the Israelites would "lick up everything" as they had with the Canaanites, leading them to summon Balaam (Num. 22:4-7). Balaam blessed Israel instead of cursing them, but the Moabites and Midianites led Israel into idolatry, and Cozbi, daughter of a Midianite tribal chief, was killed with Zimri the Simeonite along with 24,000 in a plague (Num. 25:1-18). These two peoples were enemies after this point, and at the end of Moses' life, Israel killed five Midianite kings, Evi, Rekem, Zur, Hur, and Reba, and the men were allowed to keep the virgins they captured (Num. 31:1-24). The 'land' of these Midianites, as will be explained, overlapped with the land of the Amorites and Moabites east of the Jordan (Jos. 13:16-21). Later, the Midianites oppressed Israel until the Lord used Gideon to overthrow them and their leaders: Oreb, Zeeb, Zebah, and Zalmunna (Jdg. 6:1-8:28, 9:17).

During the time of the Exodus and the Judges, there were tribes of Midian in Moab and south of Edom. One city connected with the Midianites is Madyan Shu-aib near the Gulf of Aqaba.[165] But their territory expanded farther than this, for Midian was said to be near Egypt with respect to the information found in Exodus. But specifically, Midianite pottery has been found all over the Middle East: from northern Saudi Arabia to the Negev, to the south near the Dead Sea, Sinai, Petra in Edom, and to the east in Moab.[166] Additionally, the Shasu, a wandering desert tribe mentioned in Egyptian texts may have been Midianites that lived near Egypt in the Negev.[167,168,169,170] Clearly, the Midianites were nomadic. And yet, the Midianites were not a single tribe but a collection. Much like how only certain tribes of the Edomites gained special recognition, as shall be explained below, so too only certain tribes were encountered by Israel. This would explain why Jethro and his people were so friendly towards Moses and Israel and why others were hostile. In addition, some Medanites may have joined the Midianites, making the people rather dynamic.

Edom

Of Isaac and Rebekah's twins, Jacob is the better known for becoming Israel, yet Esau also had a great nation. Scripture provides a detailed description of him: he was hairy, red, and liked to spend his days hunting (Gen. 25:25-30). He was the favored son of his father but is known as the man who "despised his birthright" for a bowl of stew (Gen. 25:30-34). When Jacob gets the blessing intended for Esau, the older brother plots to kill the younger, though they later reconcile (Gen. 27:41, 33:1-15). When the Israelites returned to their land, they were told not to "abhor the Edomite, for he is your brother" (Deut. 23:7). The Lord saved this land for Edom's descendants (Deut. 2:4-29, Jos. 24:4).

Esau married two Canaanite women, Hittites named Judith and Basemath, who brought grief to his parents (Gen. 26:34-35). But upon learning of his father's command that Jacob marry from among family, he took Mahalath from the children of Ishmael (Gen. 28:8-9). Esau dwelled in the land of Seir and the "country of Edom," away from Jacob (Gen. 32:3, 33:16, 36:6-9). This land was called Edom, a nickname of Esau's which meant red (Gen. 25:30, 36:1-8, Num. 21:4). But this land was once called Seir (Gen. 32:3, 33:14, 36:8, Num. 24:18, Jdg., 5:4). The land was named after Seir the Horite, a people who lived in the hill country of Seir and who were among those attacked by Kedolaomer, possibly making Seir a descendant of Canaan considering the time period, his tribe name, and location (Gen. 14:6, 36:20). It is possible that Esau's wives are from the people of Seir (Gen. 36).

The borders of Edom or Seir are included in Scripture, such as Mount Hor, the Negev, and the Desert of Sin, which is in the "extreme south" of both Israel's and Edom's land (Num. 33:37, 34:3, Jos. 15:1-21). Another territory marker is Ezion Geber, a place near Elath (1Ki. 9:26, 2Ki. 16:6). Mount Halak "rises toward Seir," and there is a mountain called Seir (Jos. 11:17, 2Ch. 20:22). Among the prophecies about the people of Seir and Edom, one says they will be desolate.[171] Yet there is hope for Edom, and a remnant would remain (Dan. 11:41, Amo. 9:12). While each prophecy mentions the land, one prophecy marks their territory as stretching from Teman to Dedan (Ezk. 25:12-14). These descriptions help define the general area of Edom.

The leaders of Seir and Edom were known as chiefs (Gen. 36:18-43, Ex. 15:15). In Genesis, it appears the chiefs of Seir were current or ruled just before Edom's chiefs began their rule. The sons of Seir the Horite, also clan chiefs, were: Lotan, Shobal, Zibeon, Anah, Dishon, Ezer, and Dishan (Gen. 36:20-30). Though Scripture includes the descendants of each of these sons, only a handful are pertinent to Esau's descendants.

Esau had many wives and sons. The daughter of Ishmael, sister of Nebaoith, was known as both Mahalath and Basemath (Gen. 28:9, 36:3). Her son was Reul, whose sons were Nahath, Zerah, Shammah, and Mizzah, men who were chiefs (Gen. 36:10-17). Esau had two other wives before he married Ishmael's daughter. The first was Judith, also known as Oholibamah, said to be Hittite and Hivite but has an ancestry that resembles the sons of Seir the Horite (Gen. 36:2-24). Under one record, she is a daughter of Beeri the Hittite; under the other, daughter of Anah the Hivite (Gen. 26:34, 36:2). How can this be? Perhaps the ancestry of the Horites was a mix of both Hittites and Hivites. Also, Beeri was quite possibly her mother, and her father was Anah, making her a "granddaughter of Zibeon" who, assuming they are the same person, was a son of Seir the Horite (Gen. 36:2-20). Her sons, also chiefs, were Jeush, Jalam, and Korah (Gen. 36:5-18). Lastly, his wife Basemath, or Adah, is said to be a daughter of Elon the Hittite (Gen. 26:34, 36:2). Adah's son was Eliphaz, and he had: Teman, Oman, Zepho, Gatam, and Kenaz (Gen. 36:11). Eliphaz also had a concubine named Timna, possibly the same Timna who was a chief and a sister to Lotan, son of Seir, and she bore Amalek, a chief of Edom (Gen. 36:12-40). At the end of the chiefs of Edom is this list; Timna, Alvah, Jetheth, Oholibamah, Elah, Pinon, Kenaz, Teman, Mibza, Magdiel, and Iram (Gen. 36:40-43, 1Ch. 1:51-54). All these ruled in the land of Esau, father of the Edomites.

After the Exodus, the Israelites encountered a king of Edom, who refused them passage (Num. 20:14-21, Jdg. 11:17-18). Much later, Edom became subject to David, though Edom set up kings again (1Sa. 14:47, 2Sa. 8:14, 2Ki. 8:20-22, 14:7). A man of Edom's royal line, named Hadad, revolted against Solomon, fled to Egypt, and married the sister of Pharaoh's wife (1Ki. 11:14-22). Yet the kings of Israel, Judah, and Edom were often at peace (2Ki. 3:12-26). Saul's head shepherd was an Edomite named Doeg (1Sa. 21:7, 22:9, 18, 22). There were also Edomites among Solomon's wives (1Ki. 11:1). But by the time of the Babylonian exile, there was no longer a king in Edom (1Ki. 22:47).

As mentioned before, some landmarks of the land of Seir and Edom help identify its present location. For example, Mount Hor has since been identified as Jebel Maderah, a mountain southwest of Israel, near Kadesh and Moab, with Edom found between the two.[172] Mount Seir is not a single mountain but a range within the middle of Edom, found today in southern Jordan.[172,173] Mount Halak is identified as Jebel Yelek, south of Israel.[174] Ezion Geber and Elath are two markers that partly show the extent of Edom's territory. Ezion Geber has been identified as Tell el-Kheleifeh on the Gulf of Aqabah, a location housing Elath, once called Eilat (among other names), and is now Aqaba.[175,176] While this does not identify the entirety of Edom's land, it gives a decent picture.

Considering their proximity to Egypt, there is no surprise to find that Egypt knew of Edom, called *S-m-sw-y- tw-my* or *S>-mys-y-t-my*, that is, Shemesh Edom.[177] As mentioned before, although Israel had subjugated Edom, they rebelled and set up their own king. These kings were recorded in Assyria, such as one named Quas-malaka who reigned at the same time as Jehoahaz, Aya-ramu during the time of Sennacherib, and Qa'us-gabri during the time of Esarhaddon, all of whom paid tribute to Assyria.[178,179,180] The Assyrians knew the land of Edom as "KUR.*u-du-mu-a-a*" or "Udummaya."[181] During the time of the Greeks and the Romans, Edom was known as Idumea. Josephus explains the situation clearly, calling Edom *Adom* and informing the reader his country was called, "*Adom*, for the Hebrews call what is red *Adom*;...but the Greeks gave it a more agreeable pronunciation, and named it *Idumea*."[182]

Another record tells of the subjection of various areas in the Middle East, including Idumea.[183] And it was from among this region that people came to listen to Jesus (Mar. 3:8). Regarding Edom's own records, few ostraca have been found, though their script is, unsurprisingly, quite similar to Hebrew and could be considered more of a dialect rather than a completely separate language.[184,185] Though they kept few records, or few have been found, the Edomites were a very real people known throughout the Middle East.

While the Edomites are obviously the primary nation descended from Esau, they were not the only nation. Esau's son Eliphaz had two nations: the Temanites and the Amalekites. While one is much better known than the other, both are important to the Biblical narrative and to history. Eliphaz's firstborn son, Teman, called Theman by Josephus, was the father of the Temanites. Teman was chief in the land of Edom for a time (Gen. 36:11-42, 1Ch. 1:36-53).[186] Later, a man named Husham "from the land of the Temanites" succeeds as king in the land of Edom (Gen. 36:34, 1Ch. 1:45). In later prophecies, Teman is joined with Edom and appears to have greater importance among the Edomites (Jer. 49:7-20, Ezk. 25:13). These tribes were not separate territories, but rather, chiefs of Edom ruled over different sections of Edom and a king, possibly elected, ruled over the whole land.

Within Scripture, the Temanites are described as being wise and fierce warriors, though the prophecies say their wisdom and strength are gone (Jer. 49:7, Oba. 1:9). Teman was located south of, or "to the right of," Edom, possessing a mountain called Mount Paran (Ezk. 20:46, Amo. 1:12, Hab. 3:3).[187] This wisdom, or perceived wisdom, is given in the book of Job when Eliphaz the Temanite, friend of Job, visits, comforts, and attempts to instruct Job (Job 2:11, 42:7-9). These two men are the only ones named Eliphaz in Scripture. Perhaps Eliphaz the son of Esau was a forefather of Eliphaz the friend of Job as Elihu, son of Barakel, may have descended from Buz of Nahor. During the time of Adad-Nirari II, multiple Temanites revolted against Assyria: Nur-Adad; Mamli, who had taken the cities of Mount Kashiari; and Mukuru, who fought against Assyria with the Arameans.[188]

The youngest son of Eliphaz, or the last mentioned, was Amalek, a chief among the Edomites (Gen. 36:12-16). Two names, עֲמָלֵק and עֲמָלֵקִי, are used for the Amalekites.[189,190] The latter is derived from the former and is less frequently used. Though Teman seemed to have had great importance among the Edomites, the Amalekites were one of the great enemies of the Israelites. Their land was in the Negev, part of which would belong to Ephraim, and included the land which stretched "to Shur and Egypt" (Num. 13:29, Jdg. 5:14, 1Sa. 27:8). Josephus writes that while Edom "was a large country," many of its tribes "kept the names of its peculiar inhabitants," one of which was Amalek.[186] While it seems apparent that the Amalekites of Scripture after this point are descended from Amalek, there is one mention of the Amalekites prior to his birth, during the battle led by the kings of Mesopotamia down to the edge of the Sinai Peninsula, the home of the Amalekites (Gen. 14:1-7). How can there be Amalekites prior to Amalek? As these people are not mentioned until the Exodus and they neighbored Edom, it is likely that Moses simply called the area by this name because that is who lived there presently, or Amalek's name came from a former people, which is not improbable.

The Amalekites are known for their many battles with Israel, often joining other nations in hopes of overcoming Israel (Psa. 83:7). Living in the Negev, they were the first to war with the Israelites as they came out of Egypt, attacking them before they entered the land.[191] In one battle, the Lord says that He "will completely blot out the memory of Amalek" and "The Lord will be at war with the Amalekites from generation to generation" (Ex. 17:14-16, Deut. 25:19). Among the last of Balaam's oracles is this: "Amalek was the first among the nations, but he will come to ruin at last" (Num. 24:20).

During the time of the Judges, the Amalekites attacked Israel many times. King Eglon of Moab gathered nations to him, including the Amalekites, to help him subdue Israel; during Gideon's day, they invaded Israel (Jdg. 3:13, 6:3-7:12, 10:12). Even to the time of Saul, the Amalekites brought trouble to Israel, and Samuel killed their king, Agag, when Saul disregarded his duty to completely destroy them (1Sa. 14:48, 15:1-32, 28:18). Agag, however, may not be the name of the king but the title, as it is used earlier in Scripture before this king (Num. 24:7). Additionally, Haman in Esther was called an Agagite, either making him descended from or subject to Agag of Amalek (Est. 3:1-10, 8:3-5, 9:24). After an Amalekite raid in the Negev, a slave of an Amalekite aided David in finding his people and family (1Sa. 30:1-20,

2Sa. 8:12, 1Ch. 18:11). Yet another Amalekite boasted, falsely, of killing Saul during the battle, so David slew him (2Sa. 1:1-16). Simeonites are said to have killed the Amalekites living in Seir (1Ch. 4:43). As the Lord commanded them to be wiped out, there is little to find in the way of their existence in ancient records. In many ways, they truly were blotted out of memory in history.

Moab and Ammon

Among the various descendants of Arphaxad, the parentage of Moab and Ammon is probably the most infamous. These two great nations come from Lot, son of Haran and nephew of Abraham. Though they set out together, Lot and Abraham separated, resulting in Lot going to "the plain of the Jordan" by Sodom (Gen. 13:1-18). Lot and his family were kidnapped by invaders from Mesopotamia, and Abraham pleads with the Lord that He would spare Sodom for the sake of Lot (Gen. 14:12, 18:16-33). God did destroy the city, but He first saved Lot and his family (Gen. 19:1-25). Only Lot and his daughters survived and fled to Zoar, a city that later would be part of Moabite territory (Gen. 19:26-29). They soon left Zoar for a cave, during which time these two sons were born (Gen. 19:30). This was the way it came about: the older sister convinced the younger to join her in getting her father drunk, two separate times, and conceive children with him (Gen. 19:31-35). Thus, Moab was born of the older daughter and Ben-Ammi of the younger (Gen. 19:36-38). These men became the fathers of Moab and Ammon.

The Moabites were sometimes enemies and other times friends of Israel. The most notable encounter was when King Balak of Moab and the Midianite leaders summoned Balaam to curse Israel (Num. 22:1-24:14). In return, Balaam blessed Israel and cursed Israel's enemies, including Moab, though Moab later led Israel into idolatry (Num. 24:15-25, 25:1-5). During the time of the Judges when Israel rebelled, they were subjected to Moab, whose king at the time was Eglon (Jdg. 3:12-30, 1Sa. 12:9). As He often did with other nations, the Lord used the Moabites to discipline Israel (2Ki. 24:2-4). Still, the Lord commanded the Israelites to not provoke Moab, for He had given "Ar to the descendants of Lot" (Deut. 2:9, Jdg. 11:15).

Israelites Elimelech and Naomi moved their two sons to Moab during a famine, during which time they married Moabite women – Orpah and Ruth (Rth. 1:1-4). After the men died, Naomi moved back home with Ruth, who married Boaz, becoming the great-great-grandmother of David and part of the earthly line of Christ (Rth. 1:5-4:22). Though he later defeated Moab and subjected them to Israel, David had his family stay with the king of Moab, and one of his "mighty men," Ithmah, was a Moabite (1Sa. 22:1-4, 2Sa. 8:2, 1Ch. 11:46).

Some of Solomon's wives were Moabite women; these led him astray with their gods, namely the god Chemosh (1Ki. 11:1-33). As Ashur was called both god and father in Assyria, Chemosh was called the father of King Mesha of Moab on the famous Mesha Stele, or Moabite Stone, found in Jordan.[92] Scripture includes a Mesha king of Moab who may be the same Mesha of the stele. Reigning during and after Ahab, he rebelled against Israel, and, in an effort to gain favor from a god for the failing rebellion, he sacrificed his firstborn son (2Ki. 3:1-27). A Moabite named Jehozabad, son of Shimrith, conspired against Joash king of Israel, ultimately leading to his death (2Ch. 24:26). Scripture also contains prophecies stating that Moab will be ruined but, though her "survivors will be few and feeble," eventually their land will be restored (Isa. 15:1-16:14, Jer. 25:21, 27:3, 48:1-47, Dan. 11:41).

The location of Moab is well established. The Wadi Mujib is "almost certainly" the biblical Arnon river and valley, dividing Ammon and Moab, which is near to the Valley or Plains of Moab, found today in the Jordan Rift Valley, northeast of the Jordan River and Dead Sea (Num. 21:11-20, 26:3, 33:48-49, Deut. 1:5).[192] One of the chief cities of Moab was called Ar and perhaps was on the slopes surrounding the Arnon (Num. 21:14-28, Deut. 2:9-29). While the location of this town is uncertain, a possible site is in a town called Aroer, today the modern city of 'Ara'ir (Jer. 48:19).[92,193] A ruined site then and gone now was Iye Abarim, located in the Abarim mountain range east of the Jordan where Mount Nebo, the mountain where Moses dies, is located (Num. 33:44-48, Deut. 32:49, 34:1-6). In addition to Ar, one of Moab's great strongholds was Kir Hareseth (Isa. 15:1-16:12, Jer. 48:1-47). It was to this city that the king of Assyria sent exiles when he took Damascus

(2Ki. 16:9, Amo. 1:5, 9:7). A Moabite inscription found in the modern city of Al-Kerak recorded a King K]msyt of Moab who served Kemosh.[194]

Moab was also identified from ostraca and steles, such as the Moabite Stone, which is most likely the most famous and crucial Moabite artifact. Though many cities of Moab have been found, not all have been located. Some in Scripture have yet to be found: Zoar, Beer Elim, Eglaim, Holon, Eglath Shelishiyah, Jahaz, Jahzah, Beth Diblathaim, and Mephaath (Num. 21:30, Isa. 15:1-16:12, Jer. 48:1-47). The Mesha Stele lists these cities: Karhah, Medeba, Ball-Meon, Kiriathaim, Kerioth, Shiran, Sharath, Mt. Nebo, Jahaz, Dibon, Beth-Bamoth, Bozrah, Diblathaim, and Horonaim.[92] The cities that can be found and their modern locations are: Tell Hisban, near Mt. Nebo; Medeba, or Madaba, a plain with settlements; Dibon, or Dimon, modern-day Dhiban; Elealeh, the tell in El'Al; "Beth" Baal-meon, modern-day Ma'in; Jazer, possibly Khirbet Jazzir; Beth Gamul at Khirbet el-Jemeil; Nimrim, a Tell, where an Aramaic ostracon was found; Buseirah stands next to the site of Bozrah; Kiriathaim, considered by scholars to be "the ruins of 'el Kureiyat'" between Dhibon and Madaba; Horonaim, in the Wadi Ghueir; Beth Jeshimoth, tell Khurbet Sueimeh north of the Dead Sea; and lastly, Sibmah or Shibmah is likely Sumia near Nebo in Jordan (Isa. 15:1-16:12, Jer. 48:1-47).[195-202]

The annals of Tiglath-Pileser III record a man named Salamanu of Moab, possibly a king, rendering the land's name as *Ma'abaya*.[178,203] Another transliteration is ᵐᵃᵗ *Mua'aba-a-a*.[204] Sargon II recorded that Moab brought tribute to Ashur, Sennacherib recorded a king named Kammusunadbi, and Esarhaddon mentions a king named Musuri.[205] Two different artifacts from Egypt record the name *mwib* or Moab and the city of Dibon.[206] Though Moab was a small nation, surrounded by brothers and enemies, Moab was known in history and, like the nations around them, helped make up the people that dwell there to this day.

The younger son, born of the younger daughter, was Ben-Ammi, who became the father of the Ammonites (Gen. 19:38). The Ammonites had become a sizable nation, enough so that their border was well fortified (Num. 21:24). Like Moab, the land of the Ammonites was not to be taken by Israel, for the Lord gave the land to Lot's people, though they did take some land (Deut. 2:19-37, Jdg. 11:15). Even so, the

Ammonites, sometimes with their brother Moab or other neighbors, attacked Israel many times, oftentimes in Gilead and usually as a judgment from the Lord (Jdg. 3:13, 10:6-33, 1Sa. 14:47, 2Ki. 24:2-4, 2Ch. 20:1-23). One of these provocations mentions a King Nahash of Ammon (1Sa. 11:1-11, 12:12). Later, Nahash showed kindness to David, yet his son Hanun acted disgracefully (2Sa. 10:1-19). This led to the subjection of his people by Israel, though they retained a king (1Ch. 19:1, 20:1-3, 2Ch. 26:8, 27:5).

Many other Ammonites are also specifically mentioned in Scripture, some of which may have been related to Nahash. Two daughters – Abigail and Zeruiah – of a man named Nahash were the wife of an Israelite and the mother of Joab, respectively (2Sa. 17:25). A fourth child of a Nahash of Rabbah in Ammon was a son named Shobi (2Sa. 17:27). Baalis, an enemy of Israel, is a third king of Ammon (Jer. 40:14).[224] One of David's mighty men was Zelek the Ammonite (2Sa. 23:37). Ammonite Zabad son of Shimeath led to the fall of King Joash (2Ch.24:26). Among Solomon's wives were Ammonites, and they were among those who led Solomon and Israel astray with their gods, their contribution being Molech (1Ki. 11:1-33, 2Ki. 23:13). Solomon's son Rehoboam was the son of an Ammonite named Naamah, and other Israelites married them as well (1Ki. 14:21-31, 2Ch. 12:13, Ezr. 9:1-2, Neh. 13:1-28). One of the leaders Israel dealt with after returning from exile was Tobiah, an Ammonite (Ezk. 11:41, Neh. 2:10-19, 4:3-7). Though the Ammonites were often rebuked, the Lord promised to restore them (Jer. 9:26, 25:21, 27:3, 49:1-6, Ezk. 21:29-32, 25:1-7).

Only a handful of references are given to locate Ammon. Rabbah, a city in Scripture, was Ammon's capital (Deut. 3:11, Jos. 13:25, 2Sa. 11:1, 12:26, 17:27, Ezk. 21:20). This city is currently the capital of Jordan.[207] The city went through a number of name changes, including Rabbath Ammon, Philadelphia, and finally Amman after the original founder of the land – Ben Ammi.[207,208] This city's name means "capital of the sons of Ammon."[209] This city holds one of the great archaeological finds in the Middle East, housing statues, figurines, and even burial sites.[210] In this same area, a temple was found with evidence of cremated human remains.[211,212] Ammon worshiped a god named Molech, whose sacrifices were often children, which this site evidences. One city or area that was sometimes under Ammonite control is Heshbon, the same Tell Hisban found today (Jer. 49:3).[196] The Jabbok River is also a significant landmark of Ammon, a northern boundary at different times of Ammon's history, found alongside Gilead to the Jordan, and today is the Zarqa of Jordan (Deut. 3:16, Jos. 12:2, 13:10).[213,214]

One of the unique aspects of the country and people of Ammon is in the name. In Scripture, the father of Ammon is בֶּן־עַמִּי or Ben-Ammiy, which translates to "son of my people."[215] On some ostraca from Ammonite territory is the phrase "*bn 'm[n]*" – the people of Ammon.[216] This form of the name frequently appears in more ancient texts. For example, the name of their capital city Rabbath Ammon literally means the capital of Ammon's sons.[209] Ugaritic inscriptions contain names such as "*'my*" and "*bn'myn*" that refer to Ben-Ammiy.[216,217] The people of Ammon, like their brother, were subject to Assyria, who called them *mat Bit-Am-man-na-a-a*, translated as either Beth- or Bit-Ammon.[178,218] Assyrian records contain the name Beth-Ammon many times along with their kings.[98,100,119,127,205] Clearly, the Ammonites were known as the sons of Ammon.

The Ammonites continued long after the Assyrian and Babylonian captivities of Israel and Judah, and even beyond their return. I and II Maccabees even recount a conflict between Israel and the Ammonites.[219] Additionally, pottery from 'Umayri, within Ammon, was found from this time in addition to stamps with the names *sb' 'mn* and *'mn 'y'*, which translate to *Shuba' 'Ammon* and *'Ammon 'Aya'*.[220,221] They are written in Aramaic as the land was later taken over by multiple other nations and empires, yet this evidences that the Ammonites, along with their brothers, were not completely wiped out. Instead, they are among the early nations that make up the people of modern-day Jordan.[221,222]

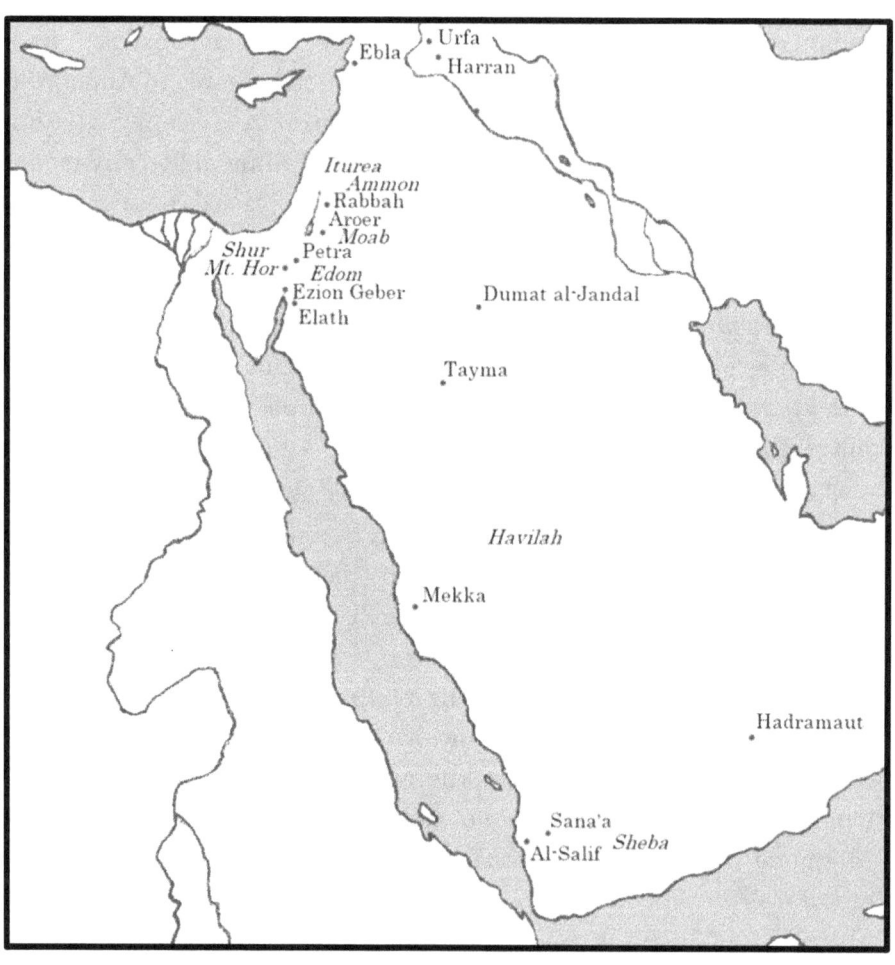

26: Lud

Lud is the fourth listed son of Shem in Scripture, his name appearing as לוּד in Hebrew (Gen. 10:22, 1Ch. 1:17).[1] Scripture rarely mentions Lud and his people. This is likely due to their proximity to Abraham's descendants. Lud and his people seemed to have moved far from the rest of his brothers and were consequently influenced by Japheth's sons. They are often confused with their cousins the Ludim, the Libyans, but they were not near each other in the slightest – on the opposite sides of the Mediterranean, in fact. The Lydians, as the descendants of Lud were called, are mentioned in the books of Ezekiel and Isaiah. Within a prophecy about Egypt, Ezekiel writes, "The allies of Egypt will fall," allies which include Lydia (Ezk. 30:5-6). The Lydians served in the army of Tyre, who hung "their shields and helmets" on the walls of the city, for they were skilled archers (Ezk. 27:10, Isa. 66:19). They are also included among those who will hear proclaimed the glory of God (Isa. 66:19).

Where is This Name Found?

While we know little about Lud and his people from Scripture, other nations recorded parts of their history under similar names. Josephus knew Lud as Laud and his people as the Laudites and the Lydians.[2] The *Book of Jasher* knew him as Lud and son of Shem, yet also gave him two unknown sons: Pethor and Bizayon.[3] If Pethor was real, he may have founded the city of the same name on the Euphrates, settling there instead of with his father (Num. 22:5).[4] The *Jubilees* says the portion of land for Lud was northwest of his brother Asshur, placing him in Anatolia, modern-day Turkey.[5] *The Etymologies* by Isidore states Lud was the ancestor of the Lydians.[6]

Due to their immersion with the people of Anatolia, who were mainly of Japhetic descent, there are relatively few records of the early Lydians. You may have noticed that Anatolia was prime ground for early settlements. Descendants of Javan, Gomer, Asshur, and obviously Lud, among others, settled in this area at one time or another. This land choice is unsurprising as this area was part of a crossway into much of the north and east. But back to the Lydian records, the texts that exist are difficult to translate, and the writing, though distinct, resembles more of Japheth's people than of Shem's.[7,8]

According to Herodotus, the Lydians received their name from a man named Lydus, descended from a man born of a god – perhaps extrapolating from Lud's history – and were previously called Meiones.[9,10] The Assyrians knew the Lydians as "*matu* Lu-ud-di," during the reign of King Gyges of Lydia.[11] Though a few other texts mention the Lydians, they are given so little notice that one may assume Lydia was rather insignificant to the vast scope of history. The Babylonians called the Lydians "uru Lu-u-du."[12] Texts from Babylon during the reign of Nabonidus state that he killed the king of Lydia; during Nebuchadnezzar's reign, there is a record of oil sent to a Lydian named Zabiria.[13] Furthermore, while one nation claimed the name of Lydia, there may have very well been other nations that split off from Lud's descendants on the peninsula of Anatolia.

Notable Mentions

While Lydia appears inconsequential in history, and Lud is infrequently mentioned in Scripture, many cities within the land were important to the early Church. Sardis, the "royal city of the Lydians," was home to one of John's seven churches (Rev. 1:11, 3:1-6).10

Philadelphia was also under Lydian rule and housed a church (Rev. 1:11, 3:7-13).14 Ephesus and Smyrna both were under the control of Lydia for a time and held churches, the former of which also has an epistle (Rev. 1:11, 2:1-11, Eph. 1:1-6:24).15 Paul and Silas met a purple cloth-maker from Thyatira named Lydia (Acts 16:14).16 Lydia was opened to the Gospel, and she "and her whole household were baptized" (Acts 16:15). Thyatira would later house a church and receive a letter from John (Rev. 1:11, 2:18-29). Last is the Lydian city Laodicea, the last of John's seven churches and likely recipient of a letter from Paul (Col. 4:16, Rev. 1:11, 3:14-22).17 In addition, due to their location and language, it is likely that the Pamphylians present at Pentecost were related to Lud (Acts 2:10). So while we do not know much of Lud, his people were part of the early Church, and the land housed many of God's people.

27: Aram

Highland

Aram is the fifth and final son of Shem recorded in Scripture; his name is אֲרָם in Hebrew (Gen. 10:22, 1Ch. 1:17).[1] He had four sons recorded in Scripture: Uz, Hul, Gether, and Mash (Gen. 10:23, 1Ch. 1:17). Though only four of his direct descendants are mentioned, Scripture includes multiple kings from his people. His name is remembered best today in the Aramaic language and in the past as Aram, the land of Arameans. A common phrase used to describe Aram is "Syria of Damascus" as Damascus was the capital of Aram (2Sa. 8:6). His people are now called Syrians, even in Scripture.

Where is This Name Found?

The land of Aram is soundly established in Mesopotamia around Damascus and the surrounding area. Before, during, and for a time after the days of Abraham, part of the land of Aram was known as Aram Naharaim and Paddan Aram in northwestern Mesopotamia, in which part of Abraham's family settled (Gen. 24:10, 28:2). This is the land that Balaam of Peor is from (Num 23:7, Deut. 23:4-5). Damascus was also the land of Eliezer, Abraham's former heir (Gen. 15:2). Bethuel, father of Rebekah, Isaac's wife, is called an Aramean because he lived in the land of Aram (Gen. 25:20, 28:2-7, 31:20-49).[2] Additionally, Jacob is inferred as being an Aramean, possibly for having lived in Paddan Aram for so long (Gen. 31:18, Deut. 26:5). The names Aram Naharaim and Paddan Aram mean "Aram of the two rivers" and "table-land of Aram," respectively.[3,4] The Egyptians and the writers of the Amarna letters knew this land as *Naharin* and *Na-ah-ri-ma*.[5,6]

The *Book of Jasher* claims that Aram and his four sons, "Uz, Chul, Gether and Mash," each built cities and named them after themselves.[7] The *Book of Jubilees* says that Aram received the fourth portion of land from his father, Shem.[8] The land of Aram is part of Mesopotamia, though it would be centered around Damascus, north of Israel (2Sa. 8:6). Josephus confirms again that it was Aram who gave rise to the Aramites, called Syrians by the Greeks.[9] Additionally, he notes that Damascus, the chief city of Aram for hundreds of years to come, was founded by his son Uz.[9]

Many of the surrounding kingdoms knew of and recorded the land of Aram in their texts. Among the most ancient, the tablets from Ebla contain the names *Armi* and *A-ra-mu*[ki].[10,11] The nearby kingdom of Urartu had a leader whose name *Ar(r)amu* possibly meant Aramean.[12] The stele of Naram-Sin records the capture of Simrrum and Aram, called *A-ra-me*[ki] in the text, which included the name of its ruler: Dubul.[13,14] In one story, the god Nergal gives Naram-Sin the cities of *Arman* and *Ibla*, which are Aram and Ebla in northwest Mesopotamia.[15] Babylon, under the reign of Adad-apla-iddina, encountered the Arameans when they, along with a group called the Suteans, both called "hostile," attacked Babylonian cities and carried off goods.[16] The letters from Amarna recorded two names – *Ti-ma-as-gi* and *Di-mas-ka* – for Damascus, the capital of Aram.[17] Texts from the reign of Amenhotep III record the "*p3-34m(w)*," that is, "the one from Aram."[18] While these letters focused more on politics and uneasy agreements, we know from Scripture that Egypt traded with Aram, which is how the Arameans acquired chariots (1Ki. 10:29).

In the Akkadian language, utilized by the Assyrians, Aram and the Arameans were known as KUR.*a-ri-me* and KUR.*a-ru-mu*.[19, 20] Other transliterations are *ah-la-mi-i* KUR and *ar-ma-ia*.MES.[18] Additionally, these Assyrian texts frequently mention the capital of Aram. Though this city eventually became the capital of Aram, it was once its own province (Gen. 14:15, 2Sa. 8:6, 2Ki. 5:12, Isa. 7:8, 17:1-3).[21] This is why it is often called Aram Damascus. The Egyptians knew Damascus as "*tmsq*."[22] Assyria's name for Damascus is somewhat obscure, for it appears as "KUR.*sa*-ANSE.NITA-*su-a-a*," that is *Sa-imerisuaya*, identified by its King Rahianu, or Rezin.[23] Aram and Damascus also did business with Tyre. Scripture recorded their trade of "turquoise, purple fabric, embroidered work, fine linen, coral," rubies, wine, and wool for Tyre's goods (Ezk. 27:16-18). A record from the reign of Shalmaneser IV stated that Damascus held riches such as silver, gold, and copper.[24]

Scripture records Israel's encounters with the Arameans on many occasions, some of which were pleasant. The first is Cushan-Rishathaim of Aram Naharaim, whom the Lord subjected Israel to for eight years (Jdg. 3:7-11). The annals of Shalmaneser I mention the *Ahlami*, which are the Arameans, alongside the Hittites, all of whom Assyria overcame.[25] Tiglath-Pileser I recorded multiple battles with the *Ahlami*, who at this time lived in the north near the Amorites but south of the Euphrates.[26,27] At one time, the land of Aram-Damascus was known as *[Bit]ᵐHaza'ili* or Beth Hazael, for Hazael was one of the Aramean kings.[28] Another text from Nippur called the Arameans "LUE *a-[ram]*" or "the people of Bit-Aram."[18]

David dealt with a king of Zobah named Hadadezer (2Sa. 8:5). The Arameans of Damascus are mentioned separately from Hadadezer, implying that the Arameans either were not all under one king or different cities had their own rulers under a king ruling from Damascus (2Sa. 8:3-12, 1Ch. 18:3-9). This Hadadezer, a son of former King Rehob, ruled from Zobah, a city that seems to be near Hamath (2Sa. 8:9-12). David again dealt with Arameans from Zobah, Aram Maacah, Aram Naharaim, and Beth Rehob when the Ammonites hired them to fight Israel, led by Hadadezer and his commander Shobach (2Sa. 10:1-19, 1Ch. 19:6-19). One of David's mighty men, Igal son of Nathan, was from Zobah (2Sa. 23:36). During the time of Saul, Zobah, or Aram-tsoba, was possibly ruled by chiefs, who we might think of as lords under the rule of a prince with a king over him (Psa. 60:1, 1Sa. 14:47). The city of Rehob, first mentioned during the exploration, was located in the north near Hamath (Num. 13:21). The city of Dan in northern Israel, first called Laish, was in a valley near Beth Rehob (Jdg. 18:27-29).

A contemporary of this Hadadezer was a man named Rezon, son of Eliada (1Ki. 11:23). He fled from his "master" Hadadezer of Zobah, gathered rebels in the aftermath of Aram's loss, "settled and took control of" Aram-Damascus where he began to rule and became an adversary for Solomon (1Ki. 11:23-25). Later, during the time of Asa king of Judah, Rezon is called Hezion king of Aram at Damascus, father of Tabrimmon, whose son was Ben-Hadad, contemporary of Asa (1Ki. 15:18). Outside of Scripture, we know nothing else about Tabrimmon. His son Ben-Hadad, however, made a beneficial treaty with Asa king of Judah (1Ki. 15:18-22, 2Ch. 16:2-6). Later, Ben-Hadad attacked Samaria during the reign of Ahab, king of Israel, though eventually he made a treaty with Ahab and allowed markets in Damascus as Aram had in Samaria (1Ki. 20:1-43).

There was no war with the Arameans again until the reign of Jehoshaphat of Judah when he requested the aid of Ahab of Israel to regain Ramoth Gilead from Aram, resulting in Ahab's death (1Ki. 22:1-38, 2Ch. 18:10-34). Perhaps one reason why they had peace until this time, besides a treaty, was because the Arameans were fighting with the Assyrians. The annals of Adad-Nirari II records "The defeat of the desert folk, the Ahlame Arameans" and a city they had taken along the Euphrates, called Gidara by Assyria and Ratammatu by Aram.[29] Two other fortresses, Sinabu and Tidu, were held by the *Arumu*, ruled by "Ammiba'li, son of Zamani" at that time, but were retaken for Assyria by Assur-Nasir-Pal.[30] Shalmaneser III fought with the Hatti, Hamathites, and the Arameans, ruled by someone named Hadad-ezer, or "Adad-'idri," in Aram Damascus, and he appears to be the same Ben-Hadad of the days of Asa, Ahab, Jehoshaphat, and Ahaziah (1Ki. 22:51).[31,32] Assyria recorded an additional "royal city of Arame" called *Arzashkunu*, found today in Turkey.[33,34]

During the time of Elisha, Joram ruled Israel and the same Ben-Hadad briefly continued as king of Aram (1Ki. 22:50, 2Ki. 1:17, 3:1). One of the commanders of the Aramean army at this time was a man named Naaman. Scripture gives many details about this great man (2Ki. 5:1). But besides his standing as a great officer, Naaman is known for having leprosy (2Ki. 5:1). Additionally, he had an Israelite slave girl who advised him to go to Elisha (2Ki. 5:3). He listened and asked his "master," the king of Aram, if he could go, and wrote a letter to the king of Israel, who consequently suspects war (2Ki. 5:2-7).

Elisha heard of the king's distress and requested that Naaman come to him (2Ki. 5:8-9). Instead of healing Naaman with some great ritual, as expected, Elisha commanded him to wash seven times in the Jordan River. This angered Naaman, comparing the Jordan to two rivers of Damascus: Abana and Pharpar, known today as Barada and 'Awaj (2Ki. 5:11-12).[35,36] But after his servants plead with him, Naaman washes and is healed (2Ki. 5:13-14). He then says to Elisha, "Now I know there is no God in all the world except in Israel" (2Ki. 5:15-16). He asks forgiveness for bowing in the temple of Rimmon with his master and is sent away in peace (2Ki. 5:17-19).

A short time later, the king of Aram, Ben-Hadad, warred with Israel, though Elisha continually informed the king of Israel of their locations (2Ki. 6:8-10). The frustrated king tried to capture Elisha (2Ki. 6:11-14). But the Lord sent "horses and chariots of fire" and struck the army blind, allowing Elisha to lead them into Samaria (2Ki. 6:15-19). Elisha then fed them and sent them back to Ben-Hadad, who ceased that raid (2Ki. 6:20-23). Soon after, Ben Hadad laid siege to Samaria (2Ki. 6:24). There was a famine, and the people were starving to the point of cannibalism (2Ki. 6:25-32). Elisha warned them to wait, for by the next day, food would be cheap and plentiful (2Ki. 6:32-7:2). The next day, the Lord caused the Arameans to hear the coming of a great army, and they fled, leaving everything behind, which a handful of leprous men found and told the people in the city (2Ki. 7:3-20).

After Ben-Hadad, Hazael was anointed as king of Aram. Now the Lord had commanded Elijah, the predecessor of Elisha, to anoint Hazael as king of Aram along with Jehu over Israel (1Ki. 19:15-17, 2Ki. 9:1-13). Later, when Elisha was in Damascus, Ben-Hadad was ill and asked Hazael to go to Elisha (2Ki 8:7-8). He asked Elisha if the king would get better, and Elisha told Hazael to say, "'You will certainly recover,' but the Lord has revealed to me that he will in fact die" (2Ki. 8:9-10). Hazael felt ashamed as Elisha stared at him and wept. Hazael questioned him, and Elisha admitted that Hazael would become king of Aram and inflict harm to Israel (2Ki. 8:11-13). Hazael went home, spoke what Elisha told him, smothered Ben-Hadad, and became king of Aram (2Ki. 8:14-15). This appears to be the same Hazael of Aram Damascus mentioned in the annals of Shalmaneser III.[37]

Before Jehu, Ahaziah and Joram were kings in Judah and Israel, and they went to war with Hazael of Aram, though Joram was wounded (2Ki. 8:25-29). Afterward, Jehu conspired against and killed Joram, Ahaziah, and Jezebel (2Ki. 9:1-37; 2Ch. 22:1-12). While Jehu ruled, the Lord "reduced the size of Israel," and Hazael captured much territory, including land from Gilead to Aroer in Ammon (2Ki. 10:32-33). This may aid in identifying when the Tel-Dan Stele, possibly the most significant Aramaic artifact and inscription found so far, was erected in Dan.[38] During the reign of Joash, Hazael attacked Gath and attempted to attack Jerusalem, but Joash, though wounded in the war, appeased him with gifts from the temple (2Ki. 12:17-18, 2Ch. 24:23-25). Israel fell again under Hazael during the reign of Jehoahaz. Though the Lord delivered them, Israel returned to false gods and Aram destroyed their army (2Ki. 13:1-9).

After Hazael, his son Ben-Hadad reigned in Aram (2Ki. 13:3-25). Adad-Nirari III records fighting Aram and Damascus during this time, but he could have fought either of these two kings, for the man named is Mari', whom he "[...shut up] in Damascus, [his royal city]," though this may have simply been an honorific.[39] The end of Shalmaneser IV's reign was marked by a campaign into Damascus, led by the "*tutanu*" or commander Shamshi-ilu to Damascus, after which they received tribute from "Hadyan of the Damascene."[24] This campaign as recorded in the "Eponym Chronicle" includes the name Hadyan II.[24] Jehoahaz's son Jehoash defeated Aram three times and recaptured towns from Ben-Hadad that Hazael had taken (2Ki. 13:9-25). There are prophecies against Damascus, the fortress of Ben-Hadad – mentioned with Hazael – that it would be destroyed, which causes distress to cities such as Hamath and Arpad (Jer. 49:23-27, Amo. 1:3-5).

Rezin ruled during the days of Pekah in Israel and Jotham in Judah (2Ki. 15:32-37). During the reign of Ahaz in Judah, Rezin attacked Jerusalem along with Pekah, though they were mostly unsuccessful (2Ki. 16:5, Isa. 7:1-8). They did take some people from Israel to

Damascus, for Ahaz and Judah had turned to foreign gods (2Ch. 28:4-5, 23). Rezin did, however, regain the city of Elath, where the Edomites moved (2Ki. 16:6). Tiglath-Pileser III reigned in Assyria at this time, and he fought with Menahem and Pekah (2Ki. 15:19-29).[40,41] When Rezin attacked Jerusalem, Ahaz asked Tiglath-Pileser III to aid him, attacking Damascus and sending the "inhabitants to Kir" and putting Rezin to death (2Ki. 16:7-9).[42] This fulfilled prophecies by Amos and Isaiah, which said Assyria would attack Damascus, burn the city, and send its people to Kir (Isa. 8:4-8, 17:1-14, Amo. 1:3-5). The annals of Tiglath-Pileser III recorded that only Aram was attacked this way.[43,44] The account of Tiglath-Pileser III has a most unflattering record of Rezin, called "*Ra-hi-a-nu*," likening him to a mongoose (a coward) as Assyria brutally killed his men, laid siege to Damascus, captured "the ancestral home...of Rahianu (Rezin) or the land of Damascus," and carried off captives.[41,44,45]

Though Damascus was basically destroyed and the people of Aram captured, some people remained in the land, and these returned to being tribes. Even so, the people retained their spirit and caused problems for Sargon in later years.[46] These were the Arameans who dwelled along the Tigris.[47] These Arameans were among the tribes the Lord sent to raid Judah under Jehoiakim's reign before the Babylonian captivity (2Ki. 23:36-24:2, Jer. 35:11).

Long after the Assyrian takeover, and not to mention changing hands between empires from Babylon to Rome, Damascus played its part again in Scripture. While Damascus and Aram were not the powers that they once had been, they were still formidable. By the period of the New Testament, Rome controlled the area. Phoenicia, founded by Canaan's sons, was referred to as Syrian Phoenicia as it was in the general area of old Aram, though Syria included more land than just Phoenicia (Mat. 4:24, Mar. 7:26). Even Naaman, called an Aramean in the Old Testament, is referred to as a Syrian in the New Testament, for Syrian was the Greek name for Aramean (Luk. 4:27).[9] When Jesus was born, Quirinius was the governor of Syria (Luk. 2:2).[48,49]

Yet the account that is best known and possibly most crucial in the New Testament concerning Aram and its great city is of the conversion of Saul. Now Scripture recorded that the Jews had synagogues not only in Israel but also in various parts of the Roman Empire, like Damascus (Act. 9:2). In Damascus, there were followers of "the Way," which was the way of Christ, and Saul desired to go and arrest them (Act. 9:1-2). But before he reached the city, he was blinded on the road as the Lord spoke to him (Act. 2:3-9). In the meantime, the Lord spoke to a believer named Ananias to find Saul of Tarsus and "restore his sight," for the Lord had chosen Saul to share the Gospel to Israel and the Gentiles (Act. 9:10-16). So Ananias did as the Lord asked, and Saul's sight was restored, after which he was baptized and began to preach in Damascus about Christ (Act. 9:17-27; 2Co. 11:32-33).

At a later point, the council in Jerusalem sent a letter of instruction and encouragement to the believers in Antioch, Cilicia, and Syria, the latter of which Paul preached to (Act. 15:1-29, 41, 18:18, 20:3, 21:3). When Paul was arrested, he had multiple opportunities to tell of his journey to Damascus and spoke in Aramaic (Act. 22:1-21, 26:1-32). Paul visited Damascus numerous times in addition to other travels through Syria (Gal. 1:17-21). Though Aram fell off the map in name and his people scattered, the Lord did not forget them, sending His missionaries and apostles so that they too might hear the Gospel.

Notable Mentions

Though the Arameans were scattered during and after the reign of Tiglath-Pileser III, the people and their language continued even into the present day. After Akkadian faded from use, Aramaic became the lingua franca of the Middle East. Even portions of Scripture are written in Aramaic, such as Daniel and Ezra.[50] This began during the height of Aram and continued even through the time of the Persians.[51,52] The vast majority of the texts found with Aramaic inscriptions are on many papyri from Elephantine, dating from the exile into the intertestamental period.[51] As they were deported throughout Assyrian controlled lands, the Arameans were gradually referred to as Syrians, for with time, the land of Assyria was called Syria.[9,53,54] Aram's language lived on in various dialects and is still spoken today, sometimes bearing the name of Aramaic, Syrian, or as the "Assyrian language."[55,56] Today, there are still small pockets of ethnic, Christian

Arameans in the world who refer to themselves as the descendants of Aram, though they are mainly found in and recognized by Israel.[57]

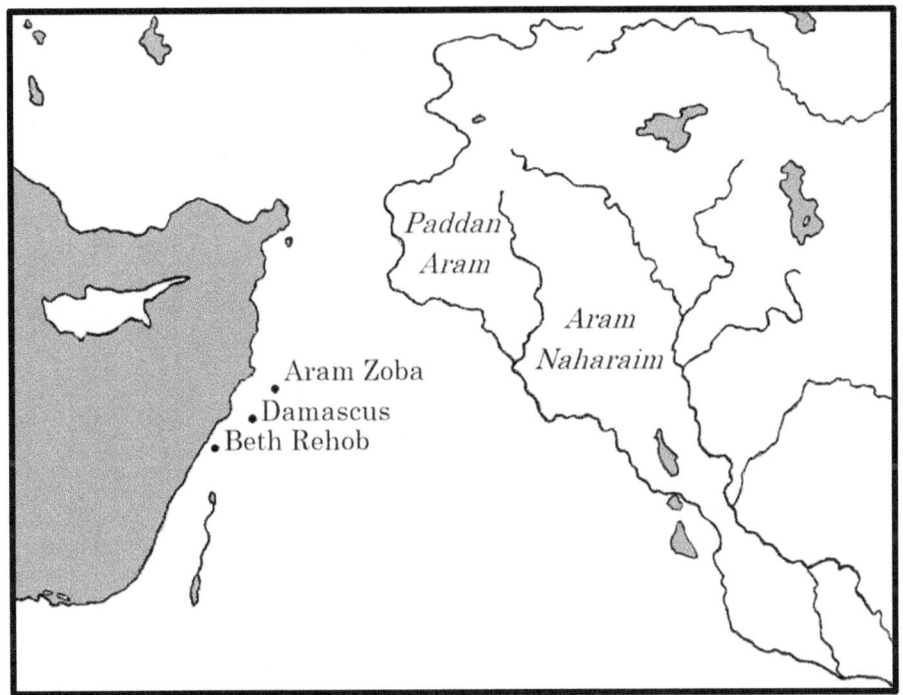

28: The Sons of Aram

The sons of Aram are best known collectively by their father's name: the Arameans. Yet they are not entirely without mention in the histories outside of Scripture. Though they are more elusive to discovery than their well-known father, they left their mark in the various locations they settled. The Arameans were a great nation, known by many of the surrounding nations and empires that encountered them. Though eventually these stronger nations overcame and conquered them, the people have remained essentially as they were and where they were from shortly after Babel to this day.

Uz

The first son of Aram recorded in Scripture is Uz, whose name in Hebrew is עוּץ and means "consultation" (Gen. 10:23, 1Ch. 1:17).[1] The *Book of Jasher* includes that Aram's sons built cities named after themselves, and Josephus said Uz built Trachonitis and Damascus.[2,3] There are two other people by the name of Uz besides the son of Aram: one is descended from Seir the Horite, living in Edom's land, and the other is a son of Nahor, whose brother was Buz, father of the Buzites (Gen. 22:21, 36:28, Job 32:2-6). While these two could have given their name to the land of Uz, the son of Aram is much more probable as he came before. Uz is mentioned two other times in Scripture. The prophet

Jeremiah recorded that the nations would drink the cup of the Lord's wrath, including all the kings of Uz (Jer. 25:15-31). In a similar passage, the people of Edom are said to dwell in the land of Uz (Lam. 4:21). From these passages, we find Uz in Arabia.

A couple of other records and writers speak on the location of Uz. The "War Scroll," as it is sometimes called, found among the Dead Sea Scrolls contains a passage on "the sons of Aram" who are "Uz and Hul and Togar and Mesha beyond the Euphrates."[4] While the first two and possibly the fourth son fit with the sons of Aram, the third does not. Instead, it is likely that "Togar and Mesha" are the sons of Gomer who lived north of the Euphrates, whereas Uz lived south of or near to Damascus in Aram. Additionally, Ptolemy associated Uz with a tribe called the Aesitae in the "Arabia Deserta" near "Chaldea and the Euphrates."[5]

Perhaps his land once extended to a portion of Edom's territory, implied by the above passages from the prophets, but Edomites also lived in the north later in their history. This is, of course, coupled with passages in Job where Sabeans and Chaldeans raided the land of Uz, and neighbors included people descended from both Edom and Keturah. These passages and general locations help point to the location of the land of Uz, but the extent of his territory may remain a mystery. After all, Chaldea was in the northeast, and the Sabeans and Edomites were in the southern parts of the Middle East. While it is good to know that Edom's descendants dwelled in Uz, that does not mean that Uz dwelled in Edom. The best indicator for the land of Uz comes from Josephus, who says Uz founded Damascus and Trachonitis.[3]

Uz was likely the first ruler of Damascus. Damascus was a center of Aram, and the land of Aram was often referred to as Aram-Damascus (Gen. 14:15, 2Sa. 8:6, Isa. 7:8). The city was known as *Ti-ma-as-gi* and *Di-mas-ka* to the writers of the Amarna Letters, *tmsq* in Egyptian inscriptions, and sometimes as *Sa-imerisuaya* to Assyria.[6,7,8] While Uz settled just south of his father in Damascus and Trachonitis, being that these people are one family, there is little wonder why they eventually became one kingdom under the greater name of Aram. And even today, Damascus is an important, middle eastern city.

Trachonitis was known as Argob in Scripture. Indeed, the surrounding land was known as Argob, Trachonitis, and Lajah, which was a rocky region.[9] During the time of the Israelite Conquest, Argob was a whole region, not only a city (Deut. 3:4). This part of the land, which was also held by the Rephaites and Og of Bashan, was given in part to the tribe of Manasseh and was later governed by Ben-Geber under Solomon (Deut. 3:13-15, 1Ki. 4:13). The name Argob means "stony" in Hebrew, like Trachonitis, the name given by the Greeks, means "rocky."[10,11] During the year of Tiberius, Philip, brother of Herod, was "tetrarch of Ituraea and Trachonitis" (Luk. 3:1). The mountain range Coele-Syria ends just above Damascus and *Trachones*, according to Strabo, an area that is populated by Arabians and Ituraeans.[12,13] The city is found below Damascus and known today by the Arabic name El-Leja, meaning "refuge."[14] Outside of these two Mesopotamian cities, there is little information as to Uz's location.

Though these two great cities are pertinent to the history of the Middle East, this is not what Uz is best recognized for. Instead, his land is best remembered as the home of Job (Job. 1:1). Job was an "upright" man who "feared God and shunned evil," noted alongside Noah and Daniel in other parts of Scripture (Job. 1:1, Ezk. 14:14, 20). He had a rather large family, consisting of seven sons and three daughters, all of whom were killed early in his account (Job. 1:2-19). There is a passage in Genesis of a man named Jobab who ruled in Seir-Edom who could be associated with Job (Gen. 36:33-34). He was succeeded by a Temanite and lived in what is modern-day Jordan, but their names derive from two different Hebrew words; Job means "persecuted," and Jobab means "howler," so they were not necessarily the same people.[15,16]

Job had a great deal of wealth in the form of sheep, camels, oxen, donkeys, and servants, most of which were carried off or killed by the Sabeans and Chaldeans (Job 1:3, 13-17). These people would have been to the far south and north of Uz. Three of his four friends were from the Buzites, Shuhites, and Temanites (Job 2:11, 32:2). Job is known for his trials, the dialogue between him and his friends, and the Lord's words to these five men. Scripture also records that Job had brothers and sisters (Job 42:11). After his trials, the Lord blessed Job with more than he had before (Job 42:12-15). Though nothing explicitly says he was a descendant of Uz, Job lived in his land, and perhaps that land was the better for it.

Hul

The second son of Aram was Hul, who is only mentioned within the genealogies (Gen. 10:23, 1Ch. 1:17). His name is חוּל in Hebrew and means "a circle."[17] The *Book of Jasher* records Hul as Chul; Josephus knew him as Ul and stated he founded the Armenians to the north, a suggestion made again by Isidore.[2,3,13] This may fit with what is found in the *Book of Jubilees*, which states that Aram's land stretched "to the north of the Chaldees to the border of the mountains of Asshur and the land of *'Arara*," which may be Ararat.[18] Finally, a modern account claims that Hul was the father of the Armenians, indicated by an area called Cholbeth, or "Hul's Houfe," whose people were the Cholobetene.[19]

Now, most of the people in northern Turkey and Armenia seem to have come from the descendants of Japheth, and specifically Gomer. The previous chapters of this book already discussed this. Perhaps some of the people of Hul traveled north into southern Armenia. Probably what truly happened – that these people were a mixture of different descendants of Noah – was confused with time and language. The Armenian tradition is that Hayk, considered the founder of Armenia, had a descendant named Aram, who gave "birth to Ara the Beautiful."[20] There was, according to some scholars, a city in Syria named Chollae that may have been founded by Hul.[21] This city may have led rise to the people of Cholbeth, called the Cholobetene, who traveled north from Syria or Aram. Many scholars attest that this son of Aram, son of Shem, gave rise to these people in Armenia.[21,22,23,24] Even so, the Armenians are not named after Aram but rather after the above-mentioned Hayk. Hul was simply one of the tribes of Aram who, though a possible founder of Chollae, fell into obscurity within the greater scope of Aram.

Gether

Aram's third son is Gether, whose name is גֶּתֶר Hebrew, and he only appears in the genealogies (Gen. 10:23, 1Ch. 1:17).[25] While Josephus places Hul in an unlikely location, his placement of Gether is even more dubious. He says that the Bactrians arose from *Gather*, and this is highly implausible.³ Gether, instead, likely settled closer to his brother Uz, south of Damascus and near Israel. The tribe and city that fits this best are the Geshurites of Geshur found in Scripture. They are first mentioned during the Israelite Conquest when Jair, a descendant of Manasseh, conquered land to the "border of the Geshurites and the Maacathites" (Deut. 3:14). The land of "Geshur and Maacah" was in Manasseh's territory, but the people remained (Jos. 13:11-13).

The people of Geshur, along with the people of Maacah, lived in the general region of King Og of Bashan, bordering his kingdom (Jos. 12:5). Whether the Geshurites mentioned alongside the Philistines in the book of Joshua are the same Geshurites living in the north by Gilead is uncertain; it appears there may have been two tribes by the same name, but their relation, if any, is unclear (Jos. 13:2, 1Sa. 27:8). Geshur, possibly a city, is said to be in Aram during the reign of David and was previously a territory distinct from Aram proper (2Sa. 15:8, 1Ch. 2:23). David married a woman named Maacah, who was daughter to Talmai, king of Geshur, and Absalom' mother (2Sa. 3:3, 1Ch. 3:2). Talmai's father was Ammihud, mentioned in the story of Absalom's flight to his maternal grandfather's city, Geshur (2Sa. 13:37-38, 14:23-24).

The Geshurites and their land are found in separate, extra-biblical texts as well. The Amarna letters mention that "all the towns of Garu" or ^{KUR}Gar-ri were hostile and placed Geshur just to the east and north of the Sea of Galilee, but south of Damascus.[26,27] Scholars consider the capital of Geshur to be at a site called et-Tell, which is in Bethsaida.[28,29] Tel Dover is deemed to be a settlement on the southwest border of Geshur's territory, located on the southeastern shore of the Sea of Galilee.[28,29] Other cities within their region are known as Tel Hadar, Tel 'En gevv, Tel Soreg, Ashtaroth, and Pihilu.[28,29] While Israel mostly left Geshur alone for much of its existence, the kingdom became part of and was associated with Aram. Assyria eventually subjected Aram and the Geshurites, ruled then by Ba'il, under the reign of Shalmaneser III.[29,30] There is a modern city called both *Rafid* and *Gshur* within Golan that is near ancient Geshur but lacks records connecting the ancient kingdom with the modern city.[31]

Mash

Mash, also called Meshech in one genealogy, is the fourth and final son of Aram recorded in Scripture; his name is מַשׁ in Hebrew (Gen. 10:23, 1Ch. 1:17).[32] While Mash and his people were a tribe of Aram, where his people settled is disputed. Josephus claims Mesaas, another name for Mash, founded a people called the Mesaneans in Charax Spasini, but this location seems to be too far to the southeast.[3] Isidore writes that Mash was the progenitor of the Maonnes, but these are located far west in Turkey.[13] A record by King Tukulti-urta II of Assyria mentions a city north of the Euphrates called *Mashkite*.[33] More recent scholars identify Mash with a mountain called Mount Masius, found within the Gordiaean range and near two cities between the Tigris and the Euphrates: Nisbis and Tigranocetra.[19,22,34,35,36] The *Gilgamesh* epic mentioned "twin mountains" called Mashu within Mesopotamia.[37] This fits with the description found in the *Book of Jubilees*, which writes that Aram's inheritance included "all the land of Mesopotamia between the Tigris and the Euphrates to the north of the Chaldees," though Assyria eventually dominated this region.[18] Whether he remained with his people or joined Meshech in the north is unclear. Any of these locations within Mesopotamia may have been the land of Mash.

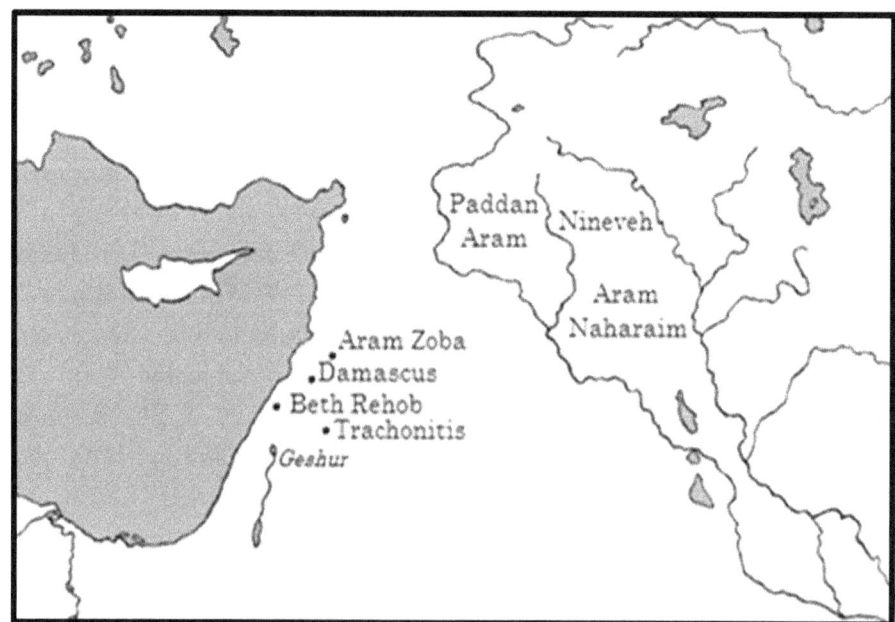

29: Words and Wanderings

Stories of Babel from around the World

The account that follows the Table of Nations in Scripture is on the Tower of Babel. Here, the descendants of Noah are divided because they deliberately disobeyed God's command to fill the earth (Gen. 1:28, 9:1-17). When the Lord divided them by language, they spread out over the face of the whole earth, bringing with them their own language, becoming more separate as they traveled. Now, there are various theories as to how many languages there were and how they were divided. While there is the possibility that we will never know the whole story nor exactly how the Lord divided the nations and their languages, perhaps these theories will shed light on this historic event.

One theory on how the languages were divided among the people at Babel is to make the breaks with the three sons of Noah. This could be so. The languages of the people who came from Japheth seem to follow similar constructs, writing systems, grammar systems, and phonology. Those of Ham seem to follow similar traditions, sound mechanisms, and use of oral records. Between the two is Shem, whose people tend to have similar writing systems, circular histories, and phonologies. And yet, there are many ancient base language points – that is, languages with nothing before them – that there were likely more than three divisions.

Were they divided by each of the people listed in the Table of Nations? Many have attempted to divide up the languages that way. In fact, many mythologies have said that after the division, one group had the "original" language, or they made up their own aside from Babel. While it appears that some of these languages derived from a single group or descendent, it is hard to distinguish which are the original languages present at Babel and which are the offshoots. After all, while some languages survived, some died off or were changed by neighboring languages. And this is not to say that any language, living or dead, found today is an original, unchanged language from Babel. Yet, this is just as likely. For example, among the oldest languages of the world are Gaelic, Cuneiform, Assyrian, Eblatic, Hebrew, Aramaic, Elamite, Egyptian, and a handful of others. Scholars assign various dates to each of them, and many have changed with time. Each has the credibility to be among the original languages from Babel, changed, dead, or otherwise, and each has language branches.

But how many were present at the start? There is no way to know for sure just how many people were present at Babel. After all, this event happened about a hundred years post-Flood, and Noah's sons started having children soon after. Including Shem, there were at least five generations from the Flood to Babel (Gen. 10). Estimating a number would be futile. We only know what Scripture provides. While we do not know if these were the only tribes, each of the listed sons had perhaps dozens of clans or tribes with them, and we do not know how many languages would have been found between them.

What we know is that we can trace many languages to a certain point, and then the trail just stops. There is nothing more. There are no proto-languages nor any naturalistic explanation for why they arose as they did. Furthermore, these languages are often more complex than modern languages. This is highly indicative of a Babel-like event and contradictory to an evolutionary model of language formation, which is highly improbable anyway considering the necessities of speech and grammar. As we learned in the first chapter, mankind had the ability to speak from the beginning. Thus, at the Babel Dispersion, people would have left with fully formed languages and no proto-languages before them, which is just what we find in the study of linguistics.

Noah

Japheth
- **Gomer** — Celtic, Scythian, Caucasus, Anatolia
- **Magog** — Germanic
- **Madai** — Indo-Iranian
- **Javan** — Hellenic
- **Tubal** — Italic, Iberian
- **Meshech** — Balto-Slavic
- **Tiras** — Thracian, Italic, Alpine

Shem
- **Elam** — Elamite (Persian)
- **Asshur** — Assyrian, Mesopotamian
- **Arphaxad** — Mesopotamian, Arabic, Hebrew, Akkadian, Ammonite, Moabite, Idumæan
- **Lud** — Southern Anatolian
- **Aram** — Aramaic, Arabic

Ham
- **Cush** — Cushitic (Ethiopic, Sudan), Arabic, Far East, Mesopotamian
- **Mizraim** — Egyptian, Philistic, Mycenean
- **Put** — Berber, West African
- **Canaan** — Canaanite, Phoenician, Ugaritic, Ammonite, Hittite, Far East

The Table of Nations was not put together with the descendant's chosen land in mind. Rather, it was a post-Flood genealogy of the actual descendants of Noah. Thus, it is difficult to claim with absolute certainty that any one language is for sure an original from a particular son. Perhaps it was that Gomer and his sons had similar languages, Asshur and his sons' languages were similar to the rest of the family, and the same among the individual sons of Ham. It might very well be that every individual family had their own language, every person in the Table of Nations had their own, or it was broken down by clans. I find the latter two suggestions plausible. Perhaps these answers will never be found, and we can be content with that. In the meantime, there are other fascinating details related to the Tower. The following will attempt to divulge information of the Tower of Babel known from Scripture and various accounts from around the world.

The Biblical Account

To begin a discussion on the origin of languages, we must first go to the Biblical or Judeo-Christian account. The history of Israel and Christianity is drawn from Scripture, which recorded the actual event. While the entire world derives its history and language from this event, not everyone accepts this account. Genesis recorded what happened:

> *"Now the whole world had one language and a common speech. As men moved eastward, they found a plain in Shinar and settled there. They said to each other, 'Come, let's make bricks and back them thoroughly.' They used brick instead of stone, and tar for mortar. Then they said, 'Come, let us build ourselves a city, with a tower that reached to the heavens, so that we may make a name for ourselves and not be scattered over the face of the whole earth. But the Lord came down to see the city and the tower that the men were building. The Lord said, 'If as one people speaking the same language they have begun to do this, then nothing they plan to do will be impossible for them. Come, let us go down and confuse their language so they will not understand each other.' (Continued on following page)*

> *So the Lord scattered them from there over all the earth, and they stopped building the city. That is why it was called Babel – because there the Lord confused the language of the whole world. From there the Lord scattered them over the face of the whole earth." (Gen. 11:1-9)*

So language was divided because of man's disobedience. It appears the language spoken before Babel no longer exists. Thus, God made mankind and scattered them across the earth (Acts 17:26). And in these scattered nations, we search for accounts of this momentous event.

Accounts from Around the World

We now know the account of Babel and the Dispersion of nations that Scripture provides for us. But what about records found throughout the world? Are there any? In brief, yes, and there are many of them. Each reflects Scripture to varying degrees. Many tell of building a tower, others simply of some sort of structure. When a story includes a tower, and not all do, the construction and appearance often differ. Some stories have a tower, but no language division. Most stories contain a dispersion, usually through a divine cause. Some stories claim their people kept the original language.

The point is that we can find the story of Babel throughout the world. Although the account changed, often in rather creative ways, the central, memorial theme remained: a great event separated people. Keep an open mind as you read. Though the stories may seem strange, they would have been quite normal in their culture. As with Creation and Flood accounts, some of which will be included for context, these various myths, legends, and records appear to be speaking of the same event. And why would people not have some stories? Like the Flood, what happened at Babel shaped mankind.

There are various retellings, found in works such as the *Antiquities*, the *Book of Jasher*, and the *Book of Jubilees*, that are not the Word of God, but typically align with Scripture. The account from the *Jubilees* begins with Peleg, his wife Lomna, and their son Reu, named so because of how evil mankind had become.[1] Scripture implies that Reu would have been born after the Dispersion. The account has them leaving Ararat for Shinar to build the city and tower with fire-baked bricks and asphalt, which is tar, found plentifully after the Flood.[1] The account claims they built for forty-three years until God spoke against their actions, stating that mankind needed to be "dispersed into cities and nations."[1] The Lord went down to see what man has built and confused their language.[1] So Shinar is called Babel. The people stopped building, and they dispersed by language and tribe.[1] The account is similar to Scripture but embellished with the tower's destruction.[1]

The *Book of Jasher* specifically calls out Nimrod, the king of the earth, for bringing the people together to build the tower unto heaven.[2] The account is similar to Scripture in that they did not want to be scattered, but the text adds that the people wanted to make themselves famous and kings of the earth.[2] Of all the places on the Earth, they chose Shinar to dwell in and began baking bricks.[2] While they were building, they divided into three groups: one to fight God, one to go to heaven and make new gods, and one to kill God.[2] The people were so evil that they mourned when a brick broke but not if someone fell and died.[2] God saw this and, speaking to angels, said that they should go down and confound their tongues.[2] Once they could not understand each other, they began to fight and kill each other.[2] So the people stopped building and scattered across the earth as the Lord designed.[2] Like *Jubilees*, this story includes the destruction of the tower.[2] Though the account adds unscriptural elements, it contains the general story.

Josephus also takes some liberty with the account. Again, Josephus names Nimrod as the instigator, a tyrant of great strength, a king that wanted to avenge mankind against God.[3] He places the people's first settlement in Shinar.[3] Josephus says that God wanted them to go abroad so they would not be evil together but enjoy the fruits of the earth.[3] Instead, they built a tower of "burnt brick" and "bitumen," solid and waterproof.[3] Now God did not want to destroy them, so He "caused a tumult," dividing their language so they could not understand each other.[3] Josephus places the Tower in Babylon and says that it was originally called Babel by the Hebrew word for confusion.[3] Josephus also tells of a Sibyl's accounting:

> "When all men were of one language, some of them built a high tower, as if they would thereby ascend up to heaven; but the gods sent storms of wind and overthrew the tower, and gave everyone his peculiar language...."[4]

Of all the extra-biblical accounts of a language dispersion event, the legend from ancient Sumer is the best known. Though *Enmerkar and the Lord of Aratta* contains legends beyond language confusion, this Sumerian account speaks of a peaceful time in "harmony-tongued Sumer."[5] The text also says, "the whole universe, the people in unison,/To Enlil in one tongue," implying the same unity that existed after the Flood during the building of Babel.[5] But after this, their god Enki came down and confused their language:

> "Enki a-da the lord, a-da the prince, a-da the king,
> Enki, the Lord of abundance, (whose) commands are trustworthy,
> The lord of wisdom, the l[ord] of Eridu,
> Changed the speech in their mouths, [brought?] contention into it,
> Into the speech of man that (until then) had been one."[5]

Though there is no tower in this story, the theme of unity followed by a divine confusion of tongues corresponds to Scripture. Additionally, it was written near to and soon after the Babel event. In Babylon, a later kingdom south of Sumer, the tower and city of Etemenanki, meaning "foundation of heaven on earth," was rebuilt by Nebuchadnezzar.[6] Nebuchadnezzar says this tower, called the "Stages of the Seven Spheres," was built long ago by another king, but never finished and, "from the lapse of time it had become ruined... the casing of burnt brick had bulged out, and the terraces of crude brick lay scattered in heaps."[7] This may be the same ziggurat whose instructions are in the *Enuma Elis*, Sumer's creation story.[8] Many additional ziggurats have been found in Babylon, the most famous being Etemenniguru, the Great Ziggurat of Ur, whose name has a similar meaning to Etemenaki.[9] Another ruined tower was found at Borsippa, or Birs Nimrud, which is sometimes referred to as the Tower's (unproven) ruins.[10]

George Smith discovered a collection of fractured tablets that contained a similar Babel account to that found in Sumer.

> "... against the father of all the gods was wicked,
> ... of him, his heart was evil, ...
> ... Babylon brought to subjection,
> small and great he confounded their speech.
> All the day long they continued building their high Tower;
> But in the night He made an end of their Tower entirely.
> In his anger he determined
> to scatter them abroad on the face of the earth
> This He ordained; their course was confused
> ... He broke up their course
> ... fixed the sanctuary."[11]

Here is a man with evil intentions, a tower is built to a great height, and the divine confounds speech, dividing the people.

A later retelling of the Tower of Babel translated into Ge'ez, or Ethiopic, from Arabic is most like the account found in Scripture, for it was likely taken from the original. The text begins in the "days of Phalek" when the "earth was divided... among the three sons of Noah...."[12] The sons were unhappy for the division, for they had been "fathered together" beforehand.[12] Nevertheless, God divided their "tongues" since they built a tower "in Sennaar," which was destroyed.[12]

> "...and what remained of them He dispersed over the earth.... Therefore God dispersed them and scattered them, and brought upon them the division of their languages; until if one of them spake, no other understood what he said."[12]

The Georgian and Armenian tradition holds that their ancestor Hayk, a descendant of Gomer, slew Nimrod after the destruction of the Tower. While the chronicle gives little information on its construction, it does mention the language division, the dispersion of nations, and Nimrod as the key player.[13] Hayk and his people fought Nimrod and his giants, though Hayk was also a giant, and they defeated Nimrod when Hayk "struck Nimrod's chest" with an arrow that went "through [his] plate of bronze, and came out behind."[14]

Unsurprisingly, the Greeks have as many ideas on how language formed as there are those who wrote on the origin of language, but only a couple are pertinent. While they have gods seemingly based on Javan, Japheth, and Noah, as mentioned in the chapters on Japheth and Javan, their mythos on language does not stop with these three. Instead, they say Hermes divided language among men and men into diverse peoples.[15,16] In Roman mythology, which heavily borrows if not completely steals from the Greek, it is Mercury who divides the languages of men, who before had lived without "cities or laws" and spoke one language, causing confusion among people.[15] In his description of Babylon, Herodotus describes a great "tower of solid masonry, a furlong in length and breadth, upon which was raised a second tower, and on that a third, and so on up to eight."[17] Babylon built many such ziggurats, which were likely based on the Tower.

The British Isles also have their share of Babel stories, but it is hard to distinguish which were influenced by monks and which are myth from old. Camden's *Britannia* is most probably derived, in part, from Scripture as he talks about "Noe" and his three sons who spread out "after the division of tongues" and they "increased and multiplied more and more."[18] Another text mixed with legend and Scripture is the *Lebor Gabala Erenn,* which explains the founding of Ireland by the descendants of Japheth after Babel, though the text tries to explain that not everyone was part of the building.[19] Additionally, the document describes the founding of the Scots and Gaels, the latter of whom descend from Goidal Glas who they claim created Gaelic.[19] The last Iles text discussing the origin of language is the *Auraicept Na n-Eces*, which explains that Ireland's founder Fenius invented Gaelic:

> *"...every obscure sound that existed in every speech and in every language was put into Gaelic so that for this reason it is more comprehensive than any language. ...it was the first language that was brought from the Tower."*[20]

The text tells of another account that claims Gaedel wrote his Gaelic language on "tablets and stones" in Calcanesis.[20] The text further explains the story of Nimrod and the Tower, who became a king during a time when there were only "counselors and chiefs," of which he was one of seventy-two.[20] Nimrod, a mighty man, united these men, and this angered the "King of Heaven," who said,

> "...come that we may see and confound those men's speech. Now great was the power of Adam's seed and their strength at that time in making the Tower, that they might know thus whether the power of heaven's King was over them, He confounded them, that is, He confused them."[20]

But how much of this myth is original? One cannot say for sure. Likely, the original tale was mixed with the Biblical account, though Fenius Farsid is still remembered as the originator of the Gaelic language.

The eastern European myth of the *Feher Szarvas*, or the *White Stag*, contains an account of Nimrod, "the mighty hunter, son of Kush, great-grandson of Noah, king of the land of Shinar."[21] Nimrod married a woman named Eneth and they have twin sons: Hunor and Magor.[21] These, of course, are to become the Huns and the Magyars according to tradition.[21] This myth tells the story of the Huns, who they came from, and how they came to their land. Russia has a similar white stag story, but in theirs, the Russians, Poles, and Lechs were given from heaven.[22] Both accounts refer to Nimrod as a king and that his people wandered for a time. In the North, the Estonians have a story called the "cooking of languages" in which people, wanting to "become blessed," sought to reach heaven by building a tower.[23] But the god, fearing they would raid heaven, "played a trick on them" by confusing their language "so that one had not understood the other's language, so that it was properly confused."[23] The workers could neither give nor receive commands to build.[23] Thus, the people separated by language and left the tower.

Norse mythology has a somewhat familiar story on how the earth and mankind were created, though the story is slightly different than the scriptural account. The three sons of Borr, Woden, Vili, and Ve, made everything.[24,25] They made the earth and skies from the giant Ymir's body.[24] First, they formed the earth, then the seas, then the trees and sky.[24] The "earth and heaven were made, and the sun and the constellations of heaven were fixed," and days were divided, very much like what Genesis describes.[24] After this, the first two people were created: the man was Askr and the woman Embla.[24] They were made of two trees and given spirit, life, wit, feeling, "form, speech, hearing, and sight," and the three gods gave them clothing.[24,25] The people were given Midgard to live in, and from them arose mankind.[24] The gods also made Asgard, which men call "Troy," the author says, as described in Tiras' chapter.[24] Though differing from Scripture, this story shows how even after Babel, the nations held onto their history. Mankind was created, and God gave them their being.

The people of the Americas also have their origin stories. Like the rest, they vary in how and why people were created and how and why they gained languages and were separated. In what is now California, there were people called the Maidu who had a legend of their creator making the earth out of water and mud, forming the heavenly bodies, and then making animals and people, the latter of which he tried to make immortal.[26] But because the Coyote opposed this, he failed to make them immortal, so Coyote's son died because he brought death to earth.[26] After this, mankind spoke many languages and the first man, Kuksu, sent the tribes away "with directions as to their life and customs."[26] The Yuki people had a similar creation story with a watery earth, a creator, Coyote, and the introduction of death, though people are made by placing sticks in houses.[27] The people traveled the earth, creating new tribes by laying sticks in houses and giving "them their customs and mode of life, and each their language."[27]

There is a tribe of Alaska called the Tlingit, whose legends include a god named El who created the earth, people, and plants, though he "obtained the sun, moon, and stars."[28] He loves the people he made, but is often angry with them; his son loves them more.[28] The legend also briefly mentions a flood.[28] The Salishan of northwest America and southwest Canada have a story on the division of tribes and languages that began over a silly argument and drove the people apart.[29] As they separated and created new tribes, they added new words as they discovered new things, causing the language to change.[29]

> *"Each split in the tribe made a new division and brought a new chief. Each migration brought different words and meanings. Thus the tribes slowly scattered; and thus the dialects, and even new languages, were formed."*[29]

While there is no tower, like other legends, there is a confusion of tongues and an argument that precedes the division.

The Blackfoot people of North America also have stories about their origins. Their flood story says that someone called Old Man sat atop the highest mountain with every animal.[30] While he waited, he sent down an otter, a beaver, and a duck, hoping one would bring up dirt.[30] Finally, he sent a muskrat, which brought up dirt, and everything could grow on the earth.[30] It was because of Old Woman that people "died forever" instead of only for a brief time.[30] After the deluge, Old Man mixed different colors with water on the mountain and brought people together.[30] Old Man gave different men different cups and made them chiefs of different people.[30] When they drank, they spoke differently, except those with the black water.[30]

The Iroquois have a particularly relatable account of creation and division. They hold that the "good mind" or "Got-ti-gah-rak-senh" made many things: the sun, moon, and stars; water over the earth; land for people to live on; and man and woman from earth, giving them life, calling them "Ongwahonwd, that is to say, a real people."[31] There was a battle between the "Good Mind" and the "Bad Mind," with the former prevailing and the latter becoming an "Evil Spirit of the world of despair."[31] After a period of war and a catastrophe, "six families took refuge in a large cave in a mountain" and stayed there for some time until they were led out by the "Holder of the Heavens" who gave them ways to live.[31] During this time, the people had one language.[31] But the "Holder of the Heavens" led six families down a river and had them settle at different parts of it.[31] Soon, each family's language changed, though they had agreed to remain unified.[31]

The Choctaw of Louisiana have a flood legend. Their god, Aba, told them to "build a large boat...away from any water" and to put in it all of the animals and food, enough to feed them for a time.[32] Most people left off from building the boat, but one family was faithful, though they did not know why they were to build it.[32] They built the boat, gathered the animals, collected the food, and boarded the boat.[32] Only this Choctaw family survived the terrible flood, and when the rain stopped, they saw there was no land or life left.[32] The family sent a dove and crow to look for land before the boat finally landed.[32] The Choctaw also have a language myth. The account talks of "Aba," a good spirit that "created many men" who all spoke the same language: Choctaw.[32] The story of their attempted "tower" begins when the people came together and wondered at what the sky was made of.[32] To find out, they stacked rocks atop one another to touch heaven.[32] But while they slept, a wind knocked the mound down.[32] This happened for three nights, with the rocks landing on the builders the final night.[32]

> *"The men were not killed, but when daylight came and they made their way from beneath the rocks and began to speak to one another, all were astounded as well as alarmed – they spoke various languages and could not understand each other."*[32]

Thus, the people were unable to continue. According to the legend, those that became the Choctaw held onto the original language.[32] But since they could not understand each other, they began to quarrel and so had to separate into many different groups throughout the land.[32]

The tribes of the southwestern United States and parts of Mexico told of a great demi-god named Montezuma. He was a great man that existed before the Great Spirit made people.[33] Montezuma made the various tribes and taught them everything.[33] They with the animals had one language.[33] Then a flood came over the earth, though Coyote warned Montezuma of the coming flood and thus he had a boat to survive while everything else was destroyed.[33] Eventually the flood ended, and Montezuma and the Great Spirit made new people and animals in the new world with Montezuma leading and dividing them into tribes.[33] But he was prideful and said that they did not "need a Creator" and named himself Creator instead, ignoring the advice of Coyote.[33] So Montezuma proceeded to gather the nations, told them of his greatness, and commanded them to make him a great, multi-floored house "rising into the sky, rising far above this earth into the heavens, where [he] shall rule as Chief of the Universe."[33] The Great Spirit tried to tell Montezuma "to stop challenging that which cannot be challenged."[33] Montezuma would have none of it, calling himself "almighty" and "the Great Rebel."[33] Because of his arrogance, the Great Spirit destroyed the house with lightning and confused language.[33]

In Mesoamerica, the Quiche-maya have a legend in their *Popol Vuh* of four men who traveled to Tulan-Zuiva to meet the gods; while they were there, they befell "a peculiar misfortune of the confusion of tongues."[34] Similarly, the Nahua say a flood covered even the tallest mountains, and only a few families escaped.[35] Afterward, those families grew and built a tower.[35] But their languages were confused and the people scattered, save for a small group who spoke the same language that stayed together as they wandered the land.[35]

The Toltecs claim that after the flood, surviving men multiplied and built a "zacuali" for if the world was destroyed again, but there was a confusion of languages, so the people dispersed across the earth.[36,37] Noah is called Coxcox in a South American myth where, after the flood, his children were born without speech, so the "great spirit" sent a dove to teach them.[37] In North America, the Kaska people have a creation legend in which the earth began as water and was made in six days.[38] There was a flood, so the people made rafts to escape, but were separated as the water receded.[38]

> "...when in their wanderings they met people from another place, they spoke different languages, and could not understand one another. This is why there are now many different centres of population, many tribes, and many languages. Before the flood, there was but one centre; for all the people lived together in one country, and spoke one language."[38]

Asia also has a variety of origin legends and accounts. As mentioned in the chapter of Madai, the Gaikho of India claim that they descend from Adam, or *Ai-ra-bai*, and Eve, *Mo-ra-mu*, and the Sgaus and Red Karens have a similar record.[39] After a long list of descendants of Adam, clearly taking tips from Egypt and Babylon's king lists, there is a man called Pan-dan-man who may be based on someone like Peleg or Nimrod.[39] During his time, the people built "a pagoda that should reach up to heaven," but half-way through construction, a god confused their speech; as they could not understand each other, they stopped building and spread out.[39,40] Afterwards, a man named Than-man-rai founded their tribe.[39] In the north, the Tharu of Nepal tell of the "fall of Chittone," where the tribes started as one but were separated.[41]

The Makir in Bengal have their own creation story that, though unique, tells of the creation of the earth, plants, animals, and people: a man named Bamon-po and his wives Assamese and Mikir.[42] The second wife had a strong and brave son named Ram who could defeat demons.[42] He was made a god of the Hindus, his descendants.[42] This "mighty race of men" was eventually discontented with "the mastery of the earth" and decided to "conquer heaven" by building a tower.[42]

> "Higher and higher rose the building, till at last the gods and demons feared lest these giants should become the masters of heaven, as they already were of earth. So they confounded their speech, and scattered them to the four corners of the earth. Hence arose all the various tongues of men."[42]

Like in Scripture, they abandoned the structure and dispersed.

A story from Hindu mythology says the world tree was "so tall that it reached almost to heaven" that it decided to reach its branches across the earth and "gather all men together... [to] protect them, and prevent them from separating."[43] But the god Brahma punished the tree's pride by cutting up its branches and throwing them across the earth where sprung "wata trees, and made differences of" languages and beliefs, dividing mankind.[43] The Kacha Naga of Assam claim that all people came from one man and were divided, though not at a tower.[44] Instead, strangely enough, languages were formed when a group of men, who were looking for a daughter, attacked a python and, while they hacked at it, their languages and visage changed, so they separated.[44]

The African continent has several language and tower stories, though most are similar. David Livingstone met a tribe near Lake Ngami who had a story about people who built a great structure much like the Tower, but their heads were "cracked by the fall of the scaffolding."[45] In the central part of Africa, the Babala have a story about the Wangongo who "wanted to know what the moon was" and preceded to find out by balancing poles atop another.[46] Once they got too high, they all fell.[46] The A-Louyi of Zambesi wanted to kill their god Nyambe, who had fled earth on a spider-web.[47] So they made "masts to reach up to heaven" and climbed up the stack, but they died when it collapsed.[47] Many other tribes have stories of trying to get to the moon or sun via a wooden structure.[47] Kenya has a story from the Wa-sania that says in early times, all tribes spoke one language, yet "during a severe famine the people went mad and wandered in all directions, jabbering strange words," which became different languages.[44]

In the Pacific Ocean, a tribe of the Admiralty Islands tells of a chief named Muikiu of the Lohi.[40] He told the people to build a house "as high as heaven."[40] Before they finished, a man warned them to stop.[40,44] Muikiu was prideful and boastful, but he listened, sprinkling water on the people so their languages were confused and they dispersed.[44] A tribe of the Andaman Islands claims that all "their accounts of creation" and the rest of their history from before the Flood comes from To'mo, their "first parent."[48] They believe that their god, Pu'luga, is eternal and the creator.[48] In their version of Eden, where there was death, the first man was very tall, had a beard, and was told to not eat of a certain tree within that place.[48] To-ma lived a long time, but his descendants were too many to stay where they lived.[48] So Pu'luga gave them what they needed and sent them off in pairs by language.[48]

The collective peoples of Ngarrindjeri from southern Australia have a unique story on the origin of language.[49] These believe that once there was an obnoxious older woman whose death brought delight.[49] All the people came to see her and proceeded to eat her. Each tribe ate a different part of her and began to speak a different language.[49] Finally, the Polynesians say their forefather Rata, his wife, and their three sons survived a "great flood."[50] Some time afterward, those sons "attempt to erect a building to reach the sky" to see Vatea, their creator and god.[50] Yet Vatea was angry, drove the builders away, destroyed their structure, and confused their language so that they could not understand one another.[50]

Even though not all these stories mention a tower, it is curious that so many places around the world have built structures that reached towards or are aligned with the heavens, and the people worshiped the heavens. Think of the ziggurats of the Middle East or the pyramids of Africa, which the temples of South America mimic. There are the pagodas and stupas in Asia, and the stone-circles found not only in the United Kingdom but also in Europe and Africa. There are also similar structures in North America. Mankind has had a fascination with the heavens since Babel, so it is no coincidence that they built structures to worship them. In the same way, the "tower" at Babel seemed to be a popular structure. These are odd and often useless constructions unless one considers their origin.

What does this mean? Simply, there was a great event in the past that divided languages and people. As they went their separate ways and formed new cultures, these people passed down this event to their children. Over time, as the game of telephone usually goes, some information was lost, and embellishments were made to the original story. Though the stories often differ from the true record found in Scripture, sometimes making the story logistically impossible, the general theme remains the same.

One could make the argument that, instead of being inspired by God, the writers of Scripture took these stories from the mythology of other nations, but this argument is weak. Two groups could copy off each other, and maybe even a handful more. Still, it is highly improbable that every continent and dozens of tribes with different languages and cultures would come up with basically the same story. Language formation stories are one thing, but saying there was one language and then an incredible event happened that led to the often deliberate confusion of them? And so many that involve building a great structure, often to the heavens out of pride? Then each of these people groups separated by language? No, these people did not arrive at these legends by chance. People recorded them because all nations came from the people who were at Babel and descended from Adam and Eve through Noah and his sons.

Part 3

THE NEW TESTAMENT

30: To All Nations

Now that we have followed the ancestry of the nations and know their origins, what does that mean for people today? How does knowing the ancestry of every person on earth relate to our lives? The answer is simple: it is the reason why we have worth and why we are saved. Scripture tells us that in the beginning, when God made all things, He made one man and one woman: Adam and Eve (Gen. 1:1-2:25). Despite living in a perfect world, mankind rebelled against God and were cast out of paradise and sin entered in (Gen. 3). Yet God did not leave them and their descendants without hope. God promised to send a Savior to redeem mankind from sin (Gen. 3:15). After many generations, God decided to wipe man from the earth because of their wickedness, save one righteous man: Noah (Gen. 4:1-6:9). Noah and his family were saved from the Flood on the Ark along with a remnant of God's creation (Gen. 6:10-8:22). From these people, God repopulated mankind on earth (Gen. 9:1-10:32, Acts 17:26). Mankind did not obey God for long, and they soon rebelled. This rebellion ended with the division of language and the dispersion across the earth (Gen. 11:1-9).

> "And I, because of their actions and imaginations, am about to come and gather all nations and tongues, and they will come and see my glory. I will set a sign among them, and I will send some of those who survive to the surrounding nations – to Tarshish, to the Libyans and Lydians (famous as archers), to Tubal and Greece, and to the distant Islands that have not heard of my fame or seen my glory. They will proclaim my glory among the nations."
>
> ~ Isaiah 66:18-19 ~

Here are two crucial points: God promised to send a Savior, and all mankind came from Adam and Eve via Noah's descendants. We are saved because Christ came to save sinners, the sons of Adam. He came because He loved us and promised from the creation of the world to do so. Yet in every century of history, we find mankind rebelling against what God commanded from the beginning. Mankind has forgotten where we came from and whom we are to serve. This is in spite of the fact that, as the last chapter demonstrated, nearly every nation that descended from Noah's sons had an origin account like Scripture. This should not come as a surprise to us but as greater evidence of the unity of mankind.

How do we know that Christ came to save all people? Christ's earthly lineage was of Abraham. Since we know that Christ came to save sinners, and we know that all people descend from Adam through whom all were made unrighteous and dead in sin, then we know that Christ came to save us, too (Gen. 3:15, Col. 2:13, 1 Tim. 1:15, 1Co. 15:21-22). God chose Israel to be the people from whom Christ came. The Lord tells Abraham multiple times that "all nations of the earth will be blessed through" him (Gen. 12:3, 18:18, 22:18, 26:4, Gal. 3:8). The blessing for all nations is Christ. Mankind is not left without hope. The Psalmist asks that the Lord would be gracious and give His blessings so that His "ways may be known on earth, [His] salvation among **all nations**" (Psa. 67:2). The Lord told Israel that they would be "a covenant for the people, a light for the gentiles" through the Lord and that the Lord's house "will be called a house of prayer for all nations" and that "righteousness and praise will spring up before all nations" (Isa. 42:6, 56:7, 61:11).

> "It is too small a thing for you to be my servant to restore the tribes of Jacob and bring back those of Israel I have kept. I will also make you a light for the Gentiles, that you may bring my salvation to the ends of the earth."
>
> ~ Isaiah 49:6 ~

These promises were foretold hundreds of years before they were fulfilled, and many people looked for His coming (Isa. 7:14, 9:1-7, 11:1-10, 40:1-31, Mic. 5:2-5, Psa. 74:12, Heb. 11:13-16). They knew what His Salvation promise meant for all people.

> "For my eyes have seen your salvation, which you have prepared in the sight of all people, a light for revelation to the Gentiles and for glory to your people Israel."
>
> ~Luke 2:30-32~

The promised Messiah finally came to those who did not recognize Him, to those who did not know they needed Him. The whole world was in darkness and has now seen the light (Isa 9:2, Mat. 4:16). While He was on earth, Christ reminded the apostles that, though they would start in Jerusalem, they would also witness to the Gentiles (Mat. 10:18, 24:14, Luk. 24:46-49). His last commands were to "go and make disciples of all nations, baptizing them in the name of the Father and of the Son and of the Holy Spirit, and teaching them to obey everything" He commanded (Mat. 28:18-20, Acts 1:1-8).

On the Day of Pentecost, the day on which the Holy Spirit filled the disciples, they began to speak in various tongues "as the Spirit enabled them" (Acts 2:4). At this time, "God-fearing Jews from every nation under heaven" were in Jerusalem (Acts 2:5). They heard the disciples and were astonished, for "each one heard them speaking in his own language" (Acts 2:6-7). Amazed, the people asked,

> *"Then how is it that each of us hears them in his own native language? Parthians, Medes and Elamites; residents of Mesopotamia, Judea, and Cappadocia, Pontus, and Asia, Phrygia and Pamphylia, Egypt and the parts of Libya near Cyrene; visitors from Rome (both Jews and converts to Judaism); Cretans and Arabs – we hear them declaring the wonders of God in our own tongues!" (Acts 2:8-11)*

This amazing event was an act of God. Just as in the days of Babel, when God confounded language and separated people, so too did He join people back together through language! One may even call it a reversal of Babel, though it is not as though He made all people speak one language again. Instead, He gifted the disciples with the means to share the Gospel with all nations. But notice, now, the nations mentioned. These are the descendants of Madai, Elam, Arphaxad, Asshur, Lud,

> "I have made you a light for the Gentiles, that you may bring salvation to the ends of the earth."
>
> ~ Acts 13:47 ~

Put, Mizraim, Javan, Gomer, Ashkenaz, Abraham, representatives of Shem, Ham, and Japheth. These people would have brought the message to their homelands, to all the children of the nations.

After the martyrdom of Stephen, the Church finally left Jerusalem (Acts 8:1). Philip, on the road to Gaza, met an Ethiopian, a descendant of Cush (Acts 8:26-27). After Philip explained the words of Isaiah on the Messiah, the Ethiopian was baptized into Christ (Acts 8:28-39). Then Philip was taken by the Lord and sent to Azotus, the Philistine Ashdod, to preach the Word on his way to Caesarea (Acts 8:40). Cornelius, a centurion at Caesarea, called for Peter, and Peter had just received a vision from the Lord that told him all things, or people, are clean because God made them so (Acts 10:1-16). At Cornelius' house, Peter finally realized, "God does not show favoritism but accepts men from every nation who fear him and do what is right" (Acts 10:17-34). Though many of the believers did not first accept that the Lord would pour His Spirit on Gentiles, they finally say that God "granted even the Gentiles repentance unto life" (Acts 10:44-46, 11:1-18, 13:26-48, 26:23).

During this time, the Church spread out to Cyprus, Phoenicia, and Antioch (Acts 11:19-26). Paul preached throughout the Roman world with his companions, sharing the Gospel to all people, Jew and Gentile alike (Acts 9:15). Many of the disciples preached the Gospel beyond the Greco-Roman world. Paul writes near the beginning of his epistle to the Romans that all are sinners saved by grace, and reminds us, "Is God the God of the Jews only? Is he not the God of the Gentiles too? Yes, of the Gentiles too, since there is only one God, who will justify the circumcised by faith and the uncircumcised through that same faith" (Rom. 3:29-30). Though God made Israel the starting place and ancestry for His Gospel, He wanted all men to be saved and adopted to sonship as heirs in His kingdom with Christ (Rom. 8:15, 1Cor. 15:23, Eph. 1:5, 3:6).

> "'After this I will return and rebuild David's fallen tent. Its ruins I will rebuild, and I will restore it, that the remnant of men may seek the Lord, and all the Gentiles who bear my name, says the Lord, who do not know these things' that have been known for ages."
>
> ~ Acts 15:16-18 ~

Since then, missionaries have gone into all the earth to share the Word of God that everyone might hear the

Gospel. Because of them, people from the East to the West have heard. There are churches from the North to the South. Though the work to reach all people is still ongoing, one can imagine what it will be like when we are together with Christ. At the end of days, people from every nation, tribe, and tongue will be joined in worship to our God, King, and Savior.

> *"In my vision at night I looked, and there before me was one like a son of man, coming with the clouds of heaven. He approached the Ancient of Days and was led into his presence. He was given authority, glory and sovereign power; all peoples, nations and men of every language worshiped him...." (Dan. 7:13-14)*
>
> *"After this I looked and there before me was a great multitude that no one could count, from every nation, tribe, people and language, standing before the throne and in front of the lamb. They were wearing white robes and were holding palm branches in their hands. And they cried out in a loud voice:*
> *'Salvation belongs to our God,*
> *Who sits on the throne,*
> *And to the Lamb.'" (Rev. 7:9-10)*

Sadly, many people now follow the doctrine of evolution, which stands in opposition to God and His Word. This belief replaces the fact that mankind came from Adam and Eve through Noah, stating instead that mankind evolved over millions of years to their present state. This doctrine teaches that some people are more valuable than others. It is not within the scope of this book to disprove evolution through science. Many others have done so before; the evidence is there. But what does the archaeological and textual evidence presented in this book show? They demonstrate that mankind did descend from these sons, that they were separated at Babel, and they indeed came from Adam and Eve, who were created by God to serve Him. Because of our descent from Adam, Christ came to save us, too.

If mankind did not come from the sons of Noah, if they did not come from Adam, if God did not create Adam, then for what reason did Christ come to us? If Adam did not sin, then for what reason did Jesus have to die? But Adam did sin, and he did father all mankind. Because of this, we may share in the Riches of Christ. Not only this, but as Christians, we are called to share this Good News, this Gospel, with the whole world, not only to one particular place or people. God told us how He made the world and how the nations came from those first two people. He told us it was because of man's sin the nations were divided. But not everyone knows this, and they certainly do not think that we were created in the image of God. Jesus did not come to save apes or something that evolved via the godless, purposeless process of evolution. He came to save people by His death and resurrection. He came to save those He loved. He came for those He made.

> "From one man he made all the nations, that they should inhabit the whole earth; and he marked out their appointed times in history and the boundaries of their lands. God did this so that they would seek him and perhaps reach out for him and find him, though he is not far from any one of us. 'For in him we live and move and have our being.' As some of your own poets have said, 'We are his offspring.'"
>
> ~ Acts 17:26-28 ~

All of this – the Table of Nations, Genesis, origins – matters because it explains how God made you and all mankind, and how He wants you, and all mankind, to be saved and come to a knowledge of the truth. Salvation is why it matters that all the nations are related. All the information presented in this book is more than trivia. It is to show you that you were created in the image of God, and every person you meet is your brother or sister. This is not to separate you by Noah's sons, but to show how you are among the children of Adam through Noah.

We are all brothers and sisters. We are all of one blood (Acts 17:22-31). If we are not children of Adam and his sin, then Christ did not come to save us. But if we are – and we are – then He did come for us. Christ came to save the children of Adam. We are all one. Thus, go into all the world and preach the Gospel, baptizing them into the Father, Son, and Holy Spirit, and teach those people everything He has commanded us so that they may know that, no matter name or nation, we are loved by this same Savior.

> "For God so loved the world, that he gave his only begotten Son, that whosoever believeth in him should not perish, but have everlasting life. For God sent not his Son into the world to condemn the world; but that the world through him might be saved."[1]
>
> ~ John 3:16-17 ~

Source Notes and Further Reading

Towards the end of writing this book, it was brought to my attention that some readers may wonder why I included old writing scripts and why or how I chose the sources I used. I will attempt to explain this in the following as well as suggest further reading. As I mentioned in my preface, I am a layperson, and I wanted a book for laypeople that drew from various scholarly sources to explain the origins of mankind as we find them in the Bible. To that end, my primary source and the foundational document for this book is the Bible, as should be clear from my writing. But I also used a variety of extra-biblical sources from various points in history. As most people do not wish to read such texts, I collected and presented them in a format I thought would be engaging and useful. That said, how did I choose the sources that I did?

This is a tricky question to answer, for I did not always use all the same criteria for choosing a source. Typically, my critique would factor in when the reference was written, who wrote it, and what the purpose was for writing it. I also considered the opinion of scholars, especially when the authenticity of a text was in question. These criteria would help me judge whether or not I should accept or discard a specific text. Also, I would look for and choose the oldest texts I could find because the older the text, the closer to the original source the writer would be.

These texts could be originals, side by side translations, or excerpt translations from multiple books. I would find genealogies, cultural and national histories, and annals, the older, the better. Often, I referenced dictionaries, concordances, and etymological resources to help in determining what certain names meant as well as the history, location, and nature of a person or people group. I also thought it would be useful to include the original script (especially the Hebrew and Greek from the Bible) or a transcription to show similarities between languages and people groups, which is helpful in tracing travels.

In addition, I referenced various genetic and linguistic sources, not all of which I expound upon in my book, for brevity's sake. I used secular, religious, and seemingly neutral sources for my book, from the ancient world to the present. They were typically authors or scholars that are generally accepted, respected, or devoted to a particular subject. Some of these you may recognize if you peruse the End Notes section, others, perhaps not. I tried to use the most well-known and authoritative sources as I could; however, some will appear (or are) obscure to most people. Some people may question some of my choices, but to not include them in this discussion would be to ignore valuable and long-held resources heedlessly, and that I simply could not do.

Regardless of the source, the goal was to show that we all use the same evidence and often come to similar conclusions. While all the sources are found in the End Notes section, I will include a brief list of works that you will perhaps find helpful in understanding a couple of specific subjects I touched on that I think would be profitable to read:

- The Bible with a concordance. I would suggest *Strong's*.
- "Ancient Human DNA: Neandertals and Denisovans" by Jeffrey Tomkins
- "The Genesis 10 Table of Nations and Y-Chromosomal DNA" by Richard Aschmann
- "Where in the World Is the Tower of Babel?" by Anne Habermehl
- *Enmerkar and the Lord of Aratta*
- *Ancient Near Eastern Texts Relating to the Old Testament* by James Pritchard
- *The Antiquities of the Jews* by Flavius Josephus
- *Britannia* by William Camden
- *Unwrapping the Pharaohs* by John Ashton and David Down

Acknowledgments

No book is written without the help and encouragement of many people, and I would like to thank a few of those people here.

My husband, Josh, whose encouragement, feedback, and patience kept me going even when I was discouraged. Your support means the world to me!

My editor, Rachel, whose enthusiasm, skills, and hard work helped make this book into something I can be proud to share. I could not have finished this book without you!

My beta readers, who helped make sense of my writing for more people than just myself! Your feedback and willingness to read my work have been such an encouragement to me. A special note of thanks to Chris and Keryn. You both helped clarify my writing so much, and for that, I am grateful.

And finally, to all the family, friends, and acquaintances along the way, whose involvement and ideas helped shape the vision for this book. There are too many to name after all these years, but without your knowledge, interest, and input, this book would not be what it is.

About the Author

Madelyn Rose Craig is an award-winning author and speaker from Southeast Michigan. She has been an avid scholar of creation research for over a decade and enjoys sharing the message of the Gospel through the written word. Madelyn began writing at a young age, but her passion for writing and sharing her work grew when she was 16. She received her Bachelor's degree in English and Art from Concordia University, Ann Arbor, in 2016. Madelyn is wife to an adoring husband, mother to a beautiful daughter, and owner of a rambunctious Labrador. If she is not writing or reading, then she is probably on a walk with her family, painting, or playing guitar. For more information about the author and her work, check out her website madelynrosecraig.com!

Chapter Notes

Chapter 1
1. John D. Morris, Ph.D. 1995. "Did the Evolutionists Present a Good Case at the Scopes Trial?". *Acts & Facts.* 24 (8).
2. Brian Thomas, M.S. 2017. "Who Were Cro-Magnon People?". *Acts & Facts.* 46 (12).
3. Carl Wieland, Ph.D. Oct. 1978. "Cro-Magnon – not a club-wielding brute". *Creation.* 1(2):24-26.
4. Brian Thomas, M.S. "New Finds Reveal Fully-Human Neandertal". *Institute for Creation Research.* 25 Aug. 2014. Accessed 22 Dec. 2017.
5. Jeffrey P. Tomkins, Ph.D. 2014. "Ancient Human DNA: Neandertals and Denisovans". *Acts & Facts.* 43 (3).
6. Jeffrey P. Tomkins, Ph.D. "DNA Proof that Neandertals Are Just Humans". *Institute for Creation Research.* 21 Feb. 2014. Accessed 22 Dec. 2017.
7. John D. Morris, Ph.D. 1997. "Is Neanderthal in Our Family Tree?". *Acts & Facts.* 26 (9).
8. D. Phillips. 2000. "Neanderthals Are Still Human!" *Acts & Facts.* 29 (5).
9. Nicholas Wade. "Fossil DNA Expands Neanderthal Range." *The New York Times.* 2 Oct. 2007. science ed., p. F3. Accessed 22 Dec. 2017.
10. Carl Wieland and Robert Carter. "Not the Flintstones – it's the Denisovans". *Creation Ministries International.* 25 Jan. 2011. Accessed 22 Dec. 2017.
11. Johannes Krause, Qiaomei Fu, Jeffrey M. Good, Bence Viola, and Michael V. Shunkov, Anatoli P. Derevianko, and Svante Paabo. "The complete mitochondrial DNA genome of an unknown hominin from southern Siberia." *Nature.* no. 464. 8 Apr. 2010. pp. 894-97. doi:10.1038/nature08976. Accessed 22 Dec. 2017.
12. Kate Ravilious. "Neandertals Ranged Much Farther East Than Thought." *National Geographic News.* 1 Oct. 2007. Accessed 22 Dec. 2017.
13. Greg Beasley. "A Possible Creationist Perspective on the Tyrolean (Oetztaler) Ice Man". *Journal of Creation.* 8(2):179-191. Aug. 1994. Accessed 22 Dec. 2017.
14. "1101." The New Strong's Complete Dictionary of Bible Words. 1996.
15. "894." The New Strong's Complete Dictionary of Bible Words. 1996.
16. Anne Habermehl. "Where in the World Is the Tower of Babel?" *Answers Research Journal.* vol. 24. 2011. pp. 30-31. Accessed 18 Sept. 2018.
17. Elizabeth Mitchell. "Doesn't Egyptian Chronology Prove That the Bible is Unreliable?". *The New Answers Book 2.* Ed. Ken Ham. Green Forest: Master Books. 2010. p. 256.
18. Flavius Josephus. "The Antiquities of the Jews". *The Works of Josephus Complete and Unabridged.* Peabody: Hendrickson Publishers. 1987. 1.8.166-68.

Chapter 2
1. "3315." *The New Strong's Complete Dictionary of Bible Words.* 1996.
2. Flavius Josephus. "The Antiquities of the Jews". The Works of Josephus Complete and Unabridged. Peabody: Hendrickson Publishers. 1987. 6.1.122.
3. "The Book of Jubilees." *The Apocrypha and Pseudepigrapha of the Old Testament in English.* ed. R H. Charles. Oxford: Clarendon Press. 1913.7.15-16.
4. Josephus 6.1.124-5.
5. "The Book of Jubilees," 9.
6. *The Book of Jasher.* Salt Lake City: J. H. Parry & Company. 1887. http://www.sacred-texts.com/chr/apo/jasher/. Accessed 25 Jan. 2017. 10.
7. Josephus 6.1.126.
8. Josephus 6.1.127-8.
9. "The Book of Jubilees," 9.8.
10. "The Book of Jubilees," 8-9.
11. "The Book of Jubilees," 8.

12. "The Book of Jubilees," 8.10.
13. "The Book of Jubilees," 8.12.
14. "The Book of Jubilees," 8.29-30.
15. Ammianus Marcellinus. *The Roman History of Ammianus Marcellinus, During the Reign of the Emperors Constantius, Julian, Jovianus, Valentinian, and Valens.* Trans. C D. Yonge. London: George Bell & Sons. 1902. Accessed 23 Feb. 2017. 580.
16. James Anderson. *Royal Genealogies: or, the Genealogical Tables of Emperors, Kings, and Princes from Adam to thefe Times; In Two Parts.* Vol. I. London: James Bettesworth, 1732. II parts. Accessed 27 Jan. 2017.
17. William Camden. Dana F. Sutton, ed. Trans. Philemon Holland. *Britannia*. The Philological Museum. 2004. www.philological.bham.ac.uk/cambrit/. Accessed 27 Jan. 2017.
18. John Stevens. *A Brief History of Spain* London: Nutt. 1701. 2-4.
19. Homer. *The Iliad*. Trans. Ennis Rees. New York: Barns & Noble. 2005. VIII.46.
20. Robert Graves. *The Greek Myths*. New York: Penguin Classics. 2012. Accessed 13 Apr. 2017. 89.
21. *The Sibylline Oracles*. Trans. Milton S. Terry. New York: Eaton & Mains. 1899. www.sacred-texts.com/cla/sib/sib.pdf. Accessed 7 Feb. 2017. 24.
22. Isidore of Seville. *The Etymologies of Isidore of Seville*. Trans. Stephen A. Barney, W J. Lewis, J A. Beach, and Oliver Berghof. Cambridge: Cambridge University Press. 2006. IX.ii.25
23. *Le Voyage de la Terre Sainte*. 1532. Geneve: Slatkine Reprints. 1971. p. 155.
24. *The Pylgrymage of Sir Richard Guylforde to the Holy Land, A.D. 1506*. 1506. London: Longmans. 1851. p. 16.
25. Le Strange, Guy. *Palestine Under the Moslems: A Description of Syria and the Holy Land from A.D. 650 to 1500*. London A.P. Watt, 1890, p. 550.

Chapter 3

1. Flavius Josephus. "The Antiquities of the Jews". *The Works of Josephus Complete and Unabridged*. Peabody: Hendrickson Publishers. 1987. 1.6.123.
2. *The Book of Jasher*. Salt Lake City: J. H. Parry & Company. 1887. http://www.sacred-texts.com/chr/apo/jasher/. Accessed 25 Jan. 2017. 7.2.
3. "The Book of Jubilees." *The Apocrypha and Pseudepigrapha of the Old Testament in English.* ed. R H. Charles. Oxford: Clarendon Press. 1913.7.19.
4. "1586." *The New Strong's Complete Dictionary of Bible Words*. 1996.
5. "The Book of Jubilees," 9.7-8.
6. William Camden. *Britannia*. Dana F. Sutton, ed. Trans. Philemon Holland. The Philological Museum. 2004. www.philological.bham.ac.uk/cambrit/. Accessed 27 Jan. 2017. 17.
7. "Galatia." *The American College Dictionary*. 1958. 498.
8. Pausanias. *Pausanias Description of Greece with an English Translation by W. H. S. Jones, M.A.* Vol. I. London: William Heinemann. 1918. VI vols. p. 19.
9. J P. Mallory and Douglas Q. Adams. "Hallstatt." *Encyclopedia of Indo-European culture*. pp. 254, 344. Accessed 19 Mar. 2017.
10. Peter B. Ellis. *The Ancient World of the Celts*. New York: Barnes & Noble Publishing. 1999. pp. 7, 22-26. Accessed 12 Oct. 2018.
11. "Gaul." *The American College Dictionary*. 1958. p. 503.
12. Aaron Arrowsmith. *A Grammar of Ancient Geography*. London: S. Arrowsmith, Soho Square. 1832. The Internet Archive. p. 8. Accessed 27 Jan. 2017.
13. Arrowsmith, 48.
14. Strabo. *Geography*. Trans. H C. Hamilton and W Falconer. London: George Bell & Sons. 1903. The Perseus Project. Accessed 27 Jan. 2017. 4.1.
15. Julius Caesar. *Caesar's Gallic War*. Trans. W A. McDevitte and W S. Bohn. New York: Harper & Brothers. 1869. The Perseus Project. Accessed 27 Jan. 2017. 1.1.
16. Isidore of Seville. *The Etymologies of Isidore of Seville*. Trans. Stephen A. Barney, W J. Lewis, J A. Beach, and Oliver Berghof. Cambridge: Cambridge University Press. 2006. IX.ii.115.
17. John Stevens. *A Brief History of Spain*. London: Nutt. 1701. p. 4.

18. Strabo, 4.1.1.
19. Anthony King. *Roman Gaul and Germany.* Oakland: University of California Press. 1990. pp. 31-32. Accessed 12 Oct. 2018.
20. Julius Caesar, 2.3.
21. James Anderson. *Royal Genealogies: or, the Genealogical Tables of Emperors, Kings, and Princes from Adam to thefe Times; In Two Parts.* Vol. I. London: James Bettesworth. 1732. p. 442. Accessed 27 Jan. 2017.
22. Anderson, 2.
23. Juansheriani, Juansher. *Concise History of the Georgians* or *The Kingdom of Abkhazia.* Trans. Robert Bedrosian, 1991. www.conflicts.rem33.com/images/Georgia/KArtlis%20Tskhovreba.htm. Accessed 27 Jan. 2017.
24. Strabo, 4.2.
25. The Cambrian Institute. *The Cambrian Journal.* Vol. III. London: LONGMANS & Company. 1856. p. 314. Accessed 28 Jan. 2017.
26. Edwin Guest. *Origines Celticae (A Fragment) and Other Contributions to the History of Britain.* Vol. II. London: Kennikat Press. 1883, 1971. II vols. Accessed 27 Jan. 2017. 38.
27. Samuel J. Evans. *Drych y Prif Oesoedd.* 2nd ed. London, Bangor: Jarvis & Foster: J. M. Dent & Co. The Internet Archive. pp. 7, 8, 148-9. Accessed 28 Jan. 2017.
28. J.C. Zeuss, Ed. H Ebel. *Grammatica Celtica.* Paris: Maisonneuve & Co. 1868. Accessed 28 Jan. 2017. 207.
29. "Cambrian." *The Online Etymology Dictionary.* 2017. Accessed 28 Jan. 2017.
30. Isidore IX.ii.104
31. Isidore IX.ii.101-105
32. Koch, John T. *Celtic Culture.* Vol. 1-2. Santa Barbra: ABC-CLIO. 2006. Accessed 13 Apr. 2017. 198.
33. Koch, 739.

Chapter 4

1. "813." *The New Strong's Complete Dictionary of Bible Words.* 1996.
2. *The Book of Jasher.* Salt Lake City: J. H. Parry & Company. 1887. http://www.sacred-texts.com/chr/apo/jasher/. Accessed 25 Jan. 2017. 7.3.
3. Flavius Josephus. "The Antiquities of the Jews." *The Works of Josephus Complete and Unabridged.* Peabody: Hendrickson Publishers, Inc. 1987. 1.6.126.
4. Josephus, 1.3.90.
5. M. Chahin. *The Kingdom of Armenia.* 2nd ed. London: Routledge. 2001. p. 25. Accessed 28 Jan. 2017.
6. Martti Nissinen, C S. Seow, and Robert K. Ritner. Ed. Peter Machinist. *Prophets ad Prophecy in the Ancient Near East.* Atlanta: Society of Biblical Literature. 2003. p. 156. Accessed 28 Jan. 2017.
7. Pavel Dolukhavnov. *The Early Slavs: Eastern Europe from the Initial Settlement to the Kievan Rus.* New York: Routledge. 2013. p. 119. Accessed 3 Nov. 2018.
8. W. W. How and J. Wells. *A Commentary on Herodotus.* Oxford: Oxford University Press. 2000. The Perseus Project. Accessed 28 Jan. 2017. 1.15.2.
9. Herodotus. *Herodotus, The Histories.* Trans. A D. Godley. Cambridge: Harvard University Press. 1920. Accessed 8 Feb. 2017. Rpt. of *The Histories.* 440. 4.1.1-2.
10. Muhammad A. Dandamaev, and Vladimir G. Lukonin. *The Cultural and Social Institutions of Ancient Iran.* Cambridge: Cambridge University Press. 2004. Accessed 22 Mar. 2017.
11. Brentjes, Burchard. *Arms of the Sakas.* Varanasi: Rishi Publication. 1996. Accessed 22 Mar. 2017.
12. James B. Pritchard, ed. Trans. Albrecht Goetze. *Ancient Near Eastern Texts Relating to the Old Testament.* 3rd ed. Princeton: Princeton University Press. 1969. p. 316. Accessed 15 Feb. 2017.
13. Pliny the Elder. *The Natural History.* Trans. John Bostock and H T. Riley. London: Taylor and Francis. 1855. The Perseus Project. Accessed 27 Jan. 2017. 4.25.
14. John E. Hill. "*The Western Regions according to the Hou Hanshu The Xiyu Juan 'Chapter on the Western Regions' from Hou Hanshu 88'*". Trans. John E. Hill. 2nd ed., 2003.

https://depts.washington.edu/silkroad/texts/hhshu/hou_han_shu.html. Accessed 21 Feb. 2017. Sec19.
15. Anthony François Paulus Hulsewé. *China in Central Asia: The Early Stage: 125 BC-AD 23; an Annotated Transl. of Chapters 61 and 96 of the History of the Former Han Dynasty*. Leiden: E. J. Brill. 1979. Accessed 21 Feb. 2017. 129.
16. Ammianus Marcellinus. *The Roman History of Ammianus Marcellinus, During the Reign of the Emperors Constantius, Julian, Jovianus, Valentinian, and Valens*. Trans. C. D. Yonge. London: George Bell & Sons. 1902. pp. 580-82. Accessed 23 Feb. 2017.
17. Pliny, 6.1.
18. R. T. S. *The New Biblical Atlas and Scripture Gazeteer; with Descriptive Notices of the Tabernacle and the Temple*. London: The Religious Tract Society. 1851. p. 2. Accessed 27 Jan. 2017.
19. John T. Painter. *Ethnology or the History & Genealogy of the Human Race*. London: Bailliere, Tindall & Cox. 1880. Accessed 27 Jan. 2017. 103.
20. Strabo. *Geography*. Trans. H.C. Hamilton and W. Falconer. London: George Bell & Sons. 1903. The Perseus Project. Accessed 27 Jan. 2017. 7.3.
21. James Anderson. *Royal Genealogies: or, the Genealogical Tables of Emperors, Kings, and Princes from Adam to thefe Times; In Two Parts*. Vol. I. London: James Bettesworth. 1732. p. 2. Accessed 27 Jan. 2017.
22. Strabo, 12.3.
23. "ASCA'NIA LACUS." *Dictionary of Greek and Roman Geography*. 1854. Accessed 8 Feb. 2017.
24. Anderson, 442.
25. *The New Strong's Complete Dictionary of Bible Words*, "7384.".
26. *The Book of Jasher*, 10.9.
27. "The Book of Jubilees." *The Apocrypha and Pseudepigrapha of the Old Testament in English*. ed. R H. Charles. Oxford: Clarendon Press. 1913. 8.12, 8.16, 8.28
28. Painter, 112.
29. "RIPHATH." *Encyclopaedia Britannica*. 6th ed. Vol. 18. 1823. Accessed 9 Feb. 2017.
30. Edward Wells. *An Historical Geography of the Old and New Testament*. Vol. 1. Oxford: Clarendon Press. 1809. p. 64. Accessed 10 Feb. 2017.
31. Pliny, 6.7, 14.
32. Joseph Mede and John Worthington. *The Works of Ioseph Mede, B. D. In Five Books*. 3rd ed. London: Roger Norton, for Richard Boyston. 1672. p. 280. Accessed 10 Feb. 2017.
33. Pliny, 4.24, 6.7.
34. Strabo, 11.2.
35. *The New Strong's Complete Dictionary of Bible Words*, "8425.".
36. *The Book of Jasher*, 10.10.
37. *The Annals of Sennacherib*. Trans. Daniel D. Luckenbill. Chicago: The University of Chicago Press. 1924. p. 9. Accessed 14 Feb. 2017.
38. *The Annals of Sennacherib*, 62.
39. *The Annals of* Sennacherib, 77, 86.
40. Henry W.F. Saggs. "SAA 01 001: The Correspondence of Sargon II, Part I: Letters from Assyria and the West." *The ORACC*. Edited by Steve Tinney and Eleanor Robson, SimoParpola and the Neo-Assyrian Text Corpus Project. 2001. oracc.museum.upenn.edu/saao/saa01/pager. Accessed 14 Feb. 2017.
41. Daniel D. Luckenbill. *Ancient Records of Assyria and Babylonia*. Chicago: The University of Chicago Press. 1927. II vols. p. 12. Accessed 15 Feb. 2017.
42. Pritchard, 318.
43. *Biblia Hebraica Stuttgartensia*. Stuttgart: Deutsche Bibelgesellschaft, 1997. 967.
44. *The New Strong's Complete Dictionary of Bible Words*, "1004.".
45. Daniel I. Block. *The Book of Ezekiel, Chapters 25-48*. Grand Rapids: William B. Eerdmans Publishing Company. 1998. p. 74. Accessed 16 Feb. 2017.
46. Juansher Juansheriani. *Concise History of the Georgians* or *The Kingdom of Abkhazia*. Trans. Robert Bedrosian, 1991. www.conflicts.rem33.com/images/Georgia/KArtlis%20Tskhovreba.htm. Accessed 27 Jan. 2017.
47. George A. Bournoutian & Jamal J. Qarabaghi. *Two Chronicles on The History of Karabagh*. Trans. George A. Bournoutian. Cost Mesa: Mazda Publishers. 2004. p. 20. Accessed 17 Feb. 2017.

48. *The Chronicles of Jerahmeel; or, The Hebrew Bible Historiale.* Trans. M. Gaster. London: Oriental Translation Fund. 1899. www.sacred-texts.com/bib/coj/ coj000.htm. p. 67. Accessed 16 Feb. 2017.
49. Strabo, 11.5.
50. Amjad Jaimoukha. *The Chechens: A Handbook.* New York: Routledge. 2004. p. 29. Accessed 17 Feb. 2017.
51. George Anchabadze. *THE VAINAKHS (THE CHECHEN AND INGUSH).* Trans. T. Paichadze. Tbilisi: Caucasian House. 2009. p. 17. Accessed 17 Feb. 2017.
52. Peter B. Golden, Haggai Ben-Shammai, and Andras Rona-Tas, eds. *The World of the Khazars: New Perspectives.* Leiden: Brill. 2007. p. 14. Accessed 19 Feb. 2017.
53. Josephus, 1.6.122.
54. Scharlipp, Wolfgang-Ekkehard. *Die Frühe Türken in Zentralasien.* Darmstadt: Wissenschaftliche Buchgesellschaft. 1992. Accessed 19 Feb. 2017. 18.
55. Twitchett, Denis C., Herbert Frank, and John K. Fairbank. *The Cambridge History of China: Volume 6, Alien Regimes and Border States, 907-1368.* Vol. 6. Cambridge: Cambridge University Press. 1994. Accessed 21 Feb. 2017. 397.
56. "Bulgar." *Encyclopaedia Britannica.* 2015. Accessed 21 Feb. 2017.
57. Peter B. Golden. *Studies on the Peoples and Cultures of the Eurasian Steppes.* Braila: Bucurest. 2011. p. 23. Accessed 19 Feb. 2017.
58. Peter B. Golden. "OQ AND OĞUR ~ OĞUZ.". LN Gumilyov Eurasian National University. p. 15. Accessed 21 Feb. 2017.
59. Peter B. Golden. *An Introduction to the History of the Turkic Peoples.* WIESBADEN: OTTO HARRASSOWITZ. 1992. pp. 96, 100, 116-117, 264, 381.
60. O. Pritsak. *THE PECHENEGS A Case of Social and Economic Transformation.* The Peter de Ridder Press. 1976. s155239215.onlinehome.us/turkic/22Kangars/ PritsakPechenegs.htm. Accessed 21 Feb. 2017.
61. Victor Spinei. *The Great Migrations in the East and South East of Europe from the Ninth to the Thirteenth Century.* Romanian Cultural Inst.: Center for Transylvanian Studies. 2003. p. 96. Accessed 21 Feb. 2017.
62. Volodymyr Kubiĭovych, ed. *Ukraine: a concise encyclopedia.* Vol. 1. Toronto: University of Toronto Press. 1963. p. 929. Accessed 21 Feb. 2017.
63. Carl Waldman and Catherine Mason. *Encyclopedia of European Peoples.* Broj Stranica: Infobase Publishing. 2006. p. 106. Accessed 21 Feb. 2017.
64. Victor Spinei. *The Romanisn and the Turkic Nomads North of the Danube Delta from the Tenth to the Mid-Thirteenth Century.* Vol. 6. Leiden & Boston: Brill. 2009. pp. 183-4. Accessed 21 Feb. 2017.
65. "Oguz." *Encyclopaedia Britannica.* 2015. Accessed 21 Feb. 2017.
66. "The Bilge Kagan Inscription". TÜRIK BITIG: Абай атындағы Қазақ Ұлттық педагогикалық университет. Accessed 21 Feb. 2017.
67. Ross, E. Denison, and Vilhelm Thomsen. "The Orkhon Inscriptions: Being a Translation of Professor Vilhelm Thomsen's Final Danish Rendering." *Bulletin of the School of Oriental Studies, University of London,* vol. 5, no. 4. 1930. pp. 861–876. www.jstor.org/stable/607024.
68. Luckenbill, 297, 352.
69. Daphne Machin Goodall. *A History of Horse Breeding.* London: Hale. 1977. Accessed 12 Apr. 2018.
70. Waldman, 476.
71. "The Kultegin Inscription". TÜRIK BITIG: Абай атындағы Қазақ Ұлттық педагогикалық университет. Accessed 22 Feb. 2017.

Chapter 5
1. "4031." *The New Strong's Complete Dictionary of Bible Words.* 1996.
2. *The New Strong's Complete Dictionary of Bible Words, "3098.".*
3. *The Book of Jasher.* Salt Lake City: J. H. Parry & Company. 1887. http://www.sacred-texts.com/chr/apo/jasher/. Accessed 25 Jan. 2017. 7.2-4, 10.7.
4. "The Book of Jubilees." *The Apocrypha and Pseudepigrapha of the Old Testament in English.* ed. R H. Charles. Oxford: Clarendon Press. 1913. 9.8-9.

5. Isidore of Seville. *The Etymologies of Isidore of Seville*. Trans. Stephen A. Barney, W J. Lewis, J A. Beach, and Oliver Berghof, Cambridge: Cambridge University Press. 2006. IX.ii.89-90.
6. St. Jerome. *Jerome: The Principal Works of St. Jerome*. Ed. Philip Schaff. Trans. W H. Freemantle. vol. 3. Grand Rapids: Christian Classics Ethereal Library. 1892. 6 vols. p. 335. Accessed 24 Feb. 2017.
7. Karl Blind. "The Teutonic Kinship of the Skythians." *The Academy*. vol. 36. 18 Jan. 1900. pp. 11-12. Accessed 19 Apr. 2018.
8. C. E. Snowden. *A Brief Survey of British History*. London: Methuen & Co. 1905. pp. 5-7. Accessed 18 Apr. 2018.
9. Flavius Josephus. "The Antiquities of the Jews". *The Works of Josephus Complete and Unabridged*. Peabody: Hendrickson Publishers. 1987. 1.6.123.
10. Strabo. *Geography*. Trans. H C. Hamilton and W Falconer. London: George Bell & Sons. 1903. The Perseus Project. Accessed 27 Jan. 2017. 7.3.2.
11. Herodotus. *The Histories*. Trans. A D. Godley. Cambridge: Harvard University Press. 1920. Accessed 18 Apr. 2018. 1.15, 2.22, 4.8-11, 4.20.
12. *Preservation of the Frozen Tombs of the Altai Mountains*. Ed. David Tresilian. Paris: UNESCO. 2008. pp. 19-30. Accessed 19 Apr. 2018
13. Andrew Curry. "Frozen Siberian Mummies Reveal a Lost Civilization." *Discover*. 25 June 2008. Accessed 18 Apr. 2018.
14. Emma Watts-Plumpkin. "The Scythians; discovering the nomad-warriors Siberia." *Current World Archaeology*. No.84. 25 July 2017. Accessed 19 Apr. 2018.
15. Johannes Magnus. *Historia de omnibus Gothorum Sueonumque regibus*. Rome: Johannem Mariam de Viottis. 1554. pp. 22-23. Accessed 24 Feb. 2017.
16. James Anderson. *Royal Genealogies: or, the Genealogical Tables of Emperors, Kings, and Princes from Adam to thefe Times; In Two Parts*. Vol. I. London: James Bettesworth. 1732. II parts. p. 2. Accessed 27 Jan. 2017.
17. Jordanes. *The Origin and Deeds of the Goths*. Trans. Charles C. Mierow. Princeton: Princeton University Press. 1915. Accessed 25 Feb. 2017. IV.
18. Jordanes, XVII.
19. *Guta Saga: The History of the Gotlanders*. vol. 12, London: Viking Society for Northern Research. 1999. p. 3. Accessed 24 Feb. 2017.
20. Bosse Carlgren. "Om Det Gutniska Språket." *Gutamålsgillet*. Gutamålsgillet, 10 Jan. 2013. Accessed 25 Feb. 2017.
21. Ptolemy. *The Geography of Claudius Ptolemy*. Dover Publications. 1991. Accessed 28 Feb. 2017. II.X.
22. Anderson, 107.
23. Tacitus. *The Agricola and Germania of Tacitus*. Trans. K B. Townshend. London: Aberdeen University Press. 1894. p. 92. Accessed 24 Feb. 2017.
24. Noel D. Broadbent. *Lapps and Labyrinths: Saami Prehistory, Colonization and Cultural Resilience*. Washington, D.C.: Smithsonian Institution Scholarly Press. 2010. p. 12. Accessed 24 Feb. 2017.
25. "Finnish Genetics: Abstracts and Summaries." *Khazaria*. Kevin A. Brook, ed. Family Tree DNA. 2000. www.khazaria.com/genetics/finns.html. Accessed 25 Feb. 2017.
26. "Russia." *Online Etymology Dictionary*. Accessed 25 Feb. 2017.
27. Broadbent, 15.
28. Virpi Laitinen. "Y-Chromosomal Diversity Suggests that Baltic Males Share Common Finno-Ugric-Speaking Forefathers." *Human Heredity*. vol. 53. no. 2. May 2002, doi:10.1159/000057985. Accessed 25 Feb. 2017.
29. Mary K. Simmons, editor. *Unrepresented Nations and Peoples Organization: Yearbook 1995*. The Hague: Kluwer Law International. 1996. p.141. Accessed 25 Feb. 2017.
30. Cornelis Dekker. *The Origins of Old Germanic Studies in the Low Countries*. Leiden: Brill. 1999. p. 210. Accessed 18 Apr. 2018.
31. "Swedish." Simons, Gary F. and Charles D. Fennig (eds.). 2017. *Ethnologue: Languages of the World, Twentieth edition*. Dallas: SIL International. Accessed 25 Feb. 2017. Online version: http://www.ethnologue.com.
32. Richard P. Aschmann. *The Genesis 10 Table of Nations and Y-Chromosomal DNA*. 10 Nov. 2016. pp. 1-30. Accessed 11 Jun 2018.

33. "Teutonic (Germanic) Languages." *Encyclopaedia Britannica*. Eds. John V. Dodge, John Armitage. 1960. pp. 973-74.
34. John McWhorter. Preface. *Our Magnificent Bastard Tongue*. New York: Penguin Group. 2008. p. XXI.
35. *The Anglo-Saxon Chronicle*. Trans. & Ed. Michael Swanton, New York: Routledge. 1998. p. 67. Accessed 18 Apr. 2018.
36. Snorri Sturluson. *The Prose Edda*. Trans. Rasmus B. Anderson. Chicago: Scott, Foresman and Company. 1901. pp. 44-45. Accessed 18 Apr. 2018.
37. Bill Cooper. *After the Flood*. Chichester: New Wine Press. 1995. pp. 83-102. Accessed 18 Apr. 2018.
38. James Orr. "MAGOG." *The International Standard Bible Encyclopaedia Vol. 3*. Eds. James Orr, John L. Nuelsen, and Edgar y. Mullins. 1915. Accessed 27 Feb. 2017.
39. Geoffrey of Monmouth. *The British History of Geoffrey of Monmouth: In Twelve Books*. Ed. J. A. Giles. Trans. A. Thompson. London: William Stevens. 1842. pp. 22-23. Accessed 27 Feb. 2017.
40. James Heywood and Thomas Wright. *Cambridge University Transactions During the Puritan Controversies of the 16th and 17th Centuries*. Vol. 1. London: Henry G. Bohn. 1854. p. 160. Accessed 27 Feb. 2017.
41. W R. Cooper. *The Chronicle of the Early Britons*. Trans. W R. Cooper. Cooper. 2002. pp. 9-10. Accessed 27 Feb. 2017.
42. *Lebor Gabála Érenn: Book of the Taking of Ireland Part 1-5*. Ed. and Trans. R. A. S. Macalister. Dublin: Irish Texts Society. 1941.
43. Jürgen Beyer. "Ist maarahvas (,Landvolk'), die alte Selbstbezeichnung der Esten, eine Lehnübersetzung? Ein e Studi e zu r Begriffsgeschicht e de s Ostseeraums." *Zeitschrift für Ostmitteleuropa-Forschun.* vol. 56. 2007. pp. 570, 593. Accessed 27 Feb. 2017.
44. Riho Grünthal. "Suomalais-Ugrilainen Seura." *Suomalais-Ugrilainen Seura*. 29 Feb. 2008. 27 Feb. 2017. http://www.sgr.fi/ct/ct51.html.
45. Elias Lönnrot. *Kalevala: the Epic Poem of Finland*. Trans. John M. Crawford, vol. 01. Project Gutenberg. 1888. Accessed 27 Feb. 2017.
46. *THE HERO OF ESTONIA AND OTHER STUDIES IN THE ROMANTIC LITERATURE OF THAT COUNTRY*. Trans. W F. Kirby. London: John C. Nimmo. 1895. 2 vols. Accessed 27 Feb. 2017. Rpt. of *KALEVIPOEG*.
47. "Kalevala." *Online Etymology Dictionary*. 2017. Accessed 27 Feb. 2017.
48. "kalevala". *Dictionary.com Unabridged*. Random House, Inc. 27 Feb. 2017.
49. "KALEVA." *Behind the Name*. 1996. Accessed 27 Feb. 2017.

Chapter 6

1. "4074-7." *The New Strong's Complete Dictionary of Bible Words*. 1996.
2. *The New Strong's Complete Dictionary of Bible Words* "3370.".
3. "The Book of Jubilees." *The Apocrypha and Pseudepigrapha of the Old Testament in English*. ed. R H. Charles. Oxford: Clarendon Press. 1913. 8.19.
4. Flavius Josephus. "The Antiquities of the Jews". *The Works of Josephus Complete and Unabridged*. Peabody: Hendrickson Publishers. 1987. 1.6.124.
5. *The Lutheran Study Bible, English Standard Version*. Concordia Publishing House. 2009. pp. 29-31.
6. Josephus, 1.6.143.
7. "The Book of Jubilees," 8.1-5.
8. "The Book of Jubilees," 10.35-36.
9. "The Book of Jubilees," 9.9-10.
10. Illya Gershevitch, ed. *The Cambridge History of Iran*. Vol. 2. London: Cambridge University Press. 1985. p. 74. Accessed 1 Mar. 2017.
11. Gershevitch, 75
12. John Muir. *Original Sanskrit Texts on the Origin and History of the People of India*. 3rd ed.vol. 2. London: Trubner & Co. 1871.pp. 290-93. Accessed 27 Mar. 2018.
13. Xavier S Nayagam. Thani. *Tamil Culture*. Academy of Tamil Culture. 1963. 1-10 vols. Accessed 1 Mar. 2017. 127.
14. Sebastian C Adams. *Adams' Syn Chronological Chart or Map of History*. Chart. 1871. Attic Books. 2013.

15. Gershevitch, 54.
16. *The Sculptures and Inscription of Darius the Great on the Rock of Behistûn in Persia.* Translated by L W. King and R C. Thompson. London: LONGMANS & Company. 1907. Accessed 1 Mar. 2017. i.6.
17. "Aryan." *Online Etymology Dictionary.* 2017. Accessed 1 Mar. 2017.
18. Josef Wiesehofer. *Ancient Persia from 550 bc to 650 ad.* Trans. Azizeh Azodi. New York: I.B. Tauris Publishers. 2001. pp. Preface XI, 56. Accessed 1 Mar. 2017.
19. "Iran." *Online Etymology Dictionary.* 2017. Accessed 1 Mar. 2017.
20. Martin van Bruinessen. "Kurdistan in the 16th and 17th centuries, as reflected in Evliya Çelebi's Seyahatname". *The Journal of Kurdish Studies* 3 (2000), 1-11.
21. "Medeia." *A Dictionary of Greek and Roman biography and mythology.* 1813-93 Accessed 28 Feb. 2017. 1003-04.
22. Rhodius Apollonius. *The Argonautica.* Trans. R C. Seaton. London: Heinemann. 1912. p. 225. Accessed 1 Mar. 2017.
23. "Medius." *A Dictionary of Greek and Roman biography and mythology.* 1813-93. Accessed 28 Feb. 2017. 1004.
24. Hesiod. *Theogony.* Trans. High G. Evelyn-White. Cambridge: Harvard University Press. 1914. p. 1000. Accessed 28 Feb. 2017.
25. C. Gilhodes. *The Kachins Religions and Customs.* New Delhi: Mittal Publications. 1922. pp. 10, 108-10. Accessed 1 Mar. 2017.
26. Mason, F. "On the dwellings, works of Art, Laws, &c. of the Karens." *Journal of the Asiatic Society of Bengal.* vol. 37, pt. 2. 1868. pp. 125-71. Accessed 9 Jan. 2018.

Chapter 7

1. "3120." *The New Strong's Complete Dictionary of Bible Words.* 1996.
2. *The New Strong's Complete Dictionary of Bible Words* "3125.".
3. Flavius Josephus. "The Antiquities of the Jews". *The Works of Josephus Complete and Unabridged.* Peabody: Hendrickson Publishers. 1987. 1.6.124 & 127-128.
4. Isidore of Seville. *The Etymologies of Isidore of Seville.* Trans. Stephen A. Barney, W J. Lewis, J A. Beach, and Oliver Berghof. Cambridge: Cambridge University Press. 2006. IX.ii.28.
5. "The Book of Jubilees." *The Apocrypha and Pseudepigrapha of the Old Testament in English.* ed. R H. Charles. Oxford: Clarendon Press. 1913. 9.10-11.
6. *The Book of Jasher.* Salt Lake City: J. H. Parry & Company. 1887. http://www.sacred-texts.com/chr/apo/jasher/. Accessed 25 Jan. 2017. 7.1-6
7. *The Book of Jasher,* 10.13.
8. James Anderson. *Royal Genealogies: or, the Genealogical Tables of Emperors, Kings, and Princes from Adam to thefe Times; In Two Parts.* Vol. I. London: James Bettesworth. 1732. II parts. p. 2. Accessed 27 Jan. 2017.
9. Isaac Kalimi. *The Reshaping of Ancient Israelite History in Chronicles.* Winona Lake: Eisenbrauns. 2005. p. 396. Accessed 23 Apr. 2018.
10. "Esarhaddon 060." *Open Richly Annotated Cuneiform Corpus.* Royal Inscriptions of the Neo-Assyrian Period (RINAP) Project. 2017.
11. Daniel D. Luckenbill. *Ancient Records of Assyrian and Babylonia.* Chicago: University of Chicago Press. 1927. pp. 31,40, 46, 61, 105. Accessed 23 Apr. 2018.
12. John P. Brown. *Israel and Hellas.* Berlin: Walter de Gruyter. 1995. p. 82. Accessed 6 Mar. 2017.
13. Callimachus. *The Hymns of Callimachus.* Trans. William Dodd. London: T. Waller & J. Ward. 1755. p. 5. Accessed 6 Mar. 2017.
14. Michael Wood. *In Search of the Trojan War.* Berkley: University of California Press. 1998. p. 219.Accessed 6 Mar. 2017.

Chapter 8

1. "473." *The New Strong's Complete Dictionary of Bible Words.* 1996.
2. Flavius Josephus. "The Antiquities of the Jews". *The Works of Josephus Complete and Unabridged.* Peabody: Hendrickson Publishers. 1987. 1.6.127.
3. Strabo. *Geography.* Trans. H C. Hamilton and W Falconer. London: George Bell. 1903. Accessed 8 Mar. 2017. 5.2.4.

4. James Anderson. *Royal Genealogies: or, the Genealogical Tables of Emperors, Kings, and Princes from Adam to thefe Times; In Two Parts.* Vol. I. London: James Bettesworth, 1732. p. 2. Accessed 27 Jan. 2017.
5. Donald C. Haggis and Carla M. Antonaccio, eds. *Classical Archaeology in Context.* Berlin: Walter de Gruyter. 2015. p. 196. Accessed 6 Mar. 2017.
6. Virgil. *The Aeneid of Virgil.* Trans. Allen Mandelbaum. New York: Bantam Dell. 1971. V.967.
7. Homer. *The Iliad.* Trans. Ennis Rees. New York: Barnes & Noble Classics. 2005. II.582.
8. Shelley Wachsmann. "Is Cyprus Ancient Alashiya? New Evidence from an Egyptian Tablet." *The Biblical Archaeologist.* vol. 49, no. 1. Mar. 1986. pp. 37-39.
9. Alexander Zephyr. *State of Israel. its Friends and Enemies. Prophetic Future.* Bloomington: iUniverse. 2013. Accessed 6 Mar. 2017.
10. Amador Arraes. *Dialogos de dom Frey Amador Arraiz Bispo de Portalegre.* na oddicina de Diogo Gomez Lovreyro. 1604. p. 21. Accessed 6 Mar. 2017.
11. Sir Richard Francis Burton. *Os Lusiadas (the Lusiads).* Vol.1. London: Bernard Quaritch, 1880. 2 vols. pp. 255, 289. Accessed 6 Mar. 2017.
12. *The New Strong's Complete Dictionary of Bible Words,* "8659."
13. Julia Montenegro and Aracadio Del Castillo. "The Location of Tarshish: Critical Considerations." *RB.* vol.123. no.2. 2016. pp.239-68. doi:10.2143. Accessed 7 Mar. 2017.
14. Barry J. Beitzel. *The New Moody Atlas of the Bible.* Chicago: Moody Publishers. 2009. Accessed 7 Mar. 2017.
15. Arie Van Der Kooij. *The Oracle of Tyre: The Septuagint of Isaiah Xxiii As Version and Vision.* Vol. 71. Leiden: Brill. 1998. pp. 44-47. Accessed 7 May 2018.
16. Frank M Cross. "An Interpretation of the Nora Stone." *Bulletin of the American Schools of Oriental Research.* no. 208. 1972. pp. 13–19. doi: 10.2307/1356374. Accessed 7 Mar 2017.
17. "Sardinian." *Dictionary of History.* 2011. Accessed 7 Mar. 2017.
18. Jeffrey P. Emanuel. "Sea Peoples, Egypt, and the Aegean: the Transference of Maritime technology in the Late Bronze-Early Iron Transition." *Aegean Studies.* no.1. 2014. p. 35. Accessed 7 Mar. 2017.
19. Herodotus. *The Histories.* Trans. A D. Godley. Cambridge: Harvard University Press. 1920. Accessed 7 Mar. 2017. 1.163.1.
20. Pausanias. *Description of Greece.* Trans. W.H.S. Jones and H.A. Ormerod. London: Harvard University Press. 1918. Accessed 7 Mar. 2017. 6.19.3.
21. J.G. Frazer, trans. and comment. *Pausanias's Description of Greece.* vol. IV. London: The MacMillan Company. 1898. VI vols. Accessed 7 Mar. 2017. 59.
22. William Ward. *The Ships of Tarshish. A Discourse.* Bungay: C. Brightly. 1805. p. 10. Accessed 7 Mar. 2017.
23. Strabo, 3.1-2.
24. "Tartessus." *Dictionary of Greek and Roman Geography.* 1854. Accessed 8 Mar. 2017.
25. *The New Strong's Complete Dictionary of Bible Words,* "3794."
26. *The New Strong's Complete Dictionary of Bible Words,* "2953."
27. *The New Strong's Complete Dictionary of Bible Words,* "2954."
28. "CITIUM." *Encyclopaedia Britannica.* 1911. Accessed 11 Mar. 2017.
29. *The Catholic Study Bible: The New American Bible.* Oxford: Oxford University Press. 2011. p. 621. Accessed 11 Mar. 2017.
30. Henry M. Morris. *The Genesis Record.* Grand Rapids: Baker Book House. 1976. p. 248.
31. John H. Hill. *Foundations: A Commentary of Genesis 1-10.* John H. Hill. 2006. p. 398. Accessed 11 Mar. 2017.
32. *The New Strong's Complete Dictionary of Bible Words,* "1004."
33. Daniel 11:29-30. *Concordia Self-Study Bible, New International Version.* St. Louis: Concordia Publishing House. 1984. 1320
34. "Note on 11:30". *Concordia Self-Study Bible, NIV.*
35. Polybius. *Histories.* Trans. Evelyn S. Shuckburgh. London: Macmillan. 1889. Accessed 11 Mar. 2017. 29.27.
36. Michael O. Wise Martin G. Abegg, and Edward M. Cook. *The Dead Sea Scrolls - Revised Edition: A New Translation.* San Francisco: Harper Collins. 2005. p. 31. Accessed 11 Mar. 2017.

37. Menahem MANSŪR. *The Dead Sea Scrolls: A College Textbook and Study Guide.* Leiden: E. J. Brill. 1964. p. 66. Accessed 11 Mar. 2017.
38. *Directory of a Dead Sea Scroll The Pesher to Habakkuk.* Trans. Fred P. Miller. 1999. Accessed 11 Mar. 2017.
39. Mireille Hadas-Lebel. *Jerusalem Against Rome.* Leuven-Dudle: Peeters Publishers. 2006. p. 24. Accessed 11 Mar. 2017.
40. Geza Vermes. *The Dead Sea Scrolls in English.* 4th ed., Sheffield, Sheffield Academic Press, 1995, pp. 33-34. Accessed 7 May 2018.
41. *The New Strong's Complete Dictionary of Bible Words,* "1721."
42. *The New Strong's Complete Dictionary of Bible Words,* "4499."
43. Giannis Giannopoulos (2006). "Δωδεκάνησος, η γένεση ενός ονόματος και η αντιμετώπισή του από τους Ιταλούς". *Ἑῶα καὶ Ἑσπέρια* (in Greek). 6:275–296. doi:10.12681/eoaesperia.78. Accessed 13 Mar. 2017.
44. "Dodona." *A Greek-English Lexicon.* 1940. Accessed 14 Mar. 2017.
45. Plutarch. *Pyrrhus.* Trans. Bernadotte Perrin. Cambridge: Harvard University Press. 1920. Accessed 14 Mar. 2017. 1.1.
46. William W. Tarn. *Antigonos Gonatas.* Oxford: Clarendon Press. 1913. p. 60. Accessed 14 Mar. 2017.
47. Richard Abbott. *Triumphal Accounts in Hebrew and Egyptian.* Lean Publishing. 2012. Accessed 14 Mar. 2017.
48. Alan Gardiner. *The Kadesh Inscriptions of Ramesses II.* Oxford: University Press. 1960. p. Accessed 14 Mar. 2017.
49. "Dardanus." *Dictionary of Greek and Roman Geography.* 1854. Accessed 14 Mar. 2017.
50. *Dictionary of Greek and Roman Geography,* "Dardania."
51. Pliny. *The Natural History.* Trans. John Bostock and H T. Riley. London: Taylor and Francis. 1855. Accessed 14 Mar. 2017. 5.33.
52. *Pentateuchal Targumim.* Trans. J.W. Etheridge. 1862. Accessed 14 Mar. 2017. II.X.
53. Virgil, I.698, 790, 846, 865.
54. Sebastian C. Adams. *Adam's Syn Chronological Chart or Map of History.* Chart. 1871. Attic Books. 2013.
55. John Hooper. "The enigma of Italy's ancient Etruscans is finally unraveled." *The Guardian,* 18 June 2007. Accessed 14 Mar. 2017.
56. Virgil, V.1050, VII.
57. William Shepherd. "Reference map of Italy. Northern Part; The Growth of Roman Power in Italy; Reference map of Italy. Northern part." Map. *Historical Atlas.* New York: Henry Holt and Company. 1911. pp. 27, 29, 31. Accessed 14 Mar. 2017.
58. Alfanso X. *General Estoria I.* Trans. P. Sanchez-Prieto Borja, Rocío D. Moreno, and Elena T. Belso. REAL ACADEMIA ESPAÑOLA: Banco de datos (CORDE) [en línea]. p. 69. Accessed 17 Mar. 2017.

Chapter 9
1. "8422." *The New Strong's Complete Dictionary of Bible Words.* 1996.
2. "The Book of Jubilees." *The Apocrypha and Pseudepigrapha of the Old Testament in English.* ed. R H. Charles. Oxford: Clarendon Press. 1913. 9.11.
3. *The Book of Jasher.* Salt Lake City: J. H. Parry & Company, 1887. http://www.sacred-texts.com/chr/apo/jasher/. Accessed 25 Jan. 2017. 10.13.
4. Pliny. *The Natural History.* Trans. John Bostock and H T. Riley. London: Taylor and Francis. 1855. Accessed 17 Mar. 2017. 3.19.
5. *The Annals of Sennacherib.* Trans. Daniel D. Luckenbill. Chicago: The University of Chicago Press. 1924. pp. 77, 86. Accessed 14 Feb. 2017.
6. Henry W.F. Saggs. "SAA 01 001: The Correspondence of Sargon II, Part I: Letters from Assyria and the West." *The ORACC.* Eds. Steve Tinney and Eleanor Robson, SimoParpola and the Neo-Assyrian Text Corpus Project. 2001. oracc.museum.upenn.edu/saao/saa01/pager. Accessed 14 Feb. 2017.
7. John M Ruthven. *The Prophecy That Is Shaping History.* Fairfax: Xulon Press. 2003. Accessed 16 Mar. 2017. p. 68.
8. Flavius Josephus. "The Antiquities of the Jews". The Works of Josephus Complete and Unabridged. Peabody, Hendrickson Publishers. 1987. 1.6.124.

9. Bodie Hodge. *Tower of Babel: The Cultural History of our Ancestors*. Green Forest: Master Books. 2013. pp. 170-72.
10. Annick Payne. *Iron Age Hieroglyphic Luwian Inscriptions*. Atlanta: Society of Biblical Literature. 2012. pp. 8, 9. Accessed 16 Mar. 2017.
11. James Anderson. *Royal Genealogies: or, the Genealogical Tables of Emperors, Kings, and Princes from Adam to thefe Times; In Two Parts*. Vol. I. London: James Bettesworth. 1732. p. 2. II parts. Accessed 27 Jan. 2017.
12. James Anderson, 67.
13. Stevens, John. *A Brief History of Spain*. London: Nutt. 1701. pp. 4, 138.
14. Nennius. The "Historia Brittonum". Ed. Mark the Hermit. London: John and Arthur Arch, Cornhill. 1819. p. 11. Accessed 17 Mar. 2017.
15. Pedro IV. *The Chronicle of San Juan de la Peña*. Trans. Lynn H. Nelson: Philadelphia. University of Pennsylvania Press. 1991. p.1. Accessed 17 Mar. 2017.
16. Alfanso X. *General Estoria I*. Trans. P. Sanchez-Prieto Borja, Rocío D. Moreno, and Elena T. Belso, REAL ACADEMIA ESPAÑOLA: Banco de datos (CORDE) [en línea]. pp. 69-70. Accessed 17 Mar. 2017.
17. R.L. Trask. *The History of Basque*. London: Routledge. 2013. p. 36. Accessed 2 Apr. 2018.
18. Carl Waldman and Catherine Mason. *Encyclopedia of European Peoples*. Ed. Claudia Schaab. 2006. pp. 61, 129, 411, 572, 886. Accessed 2 Apr. 2018.
19. Strabo. *Geography*. Trans. H. L. Jones. Cambridge: Harvard University Press. 1924. Accessed 3 Apr. 2018. 6.4.
20. *La Verdadera historia del rey don Rodrigo*. Valencia: Pedro Patricio Mey and S. Martin. 1606. p. 69.

Chapter 10

1. "4902." *The New Strong's Complete Dictionary of Bible Words*. 1996.
2. "The Book of Jubilees." *The Apocrypha and Pseudepigrapha of the Old Testament in English*. ed. R H. Charles. Oxford: Clarendon Press. 1913. 9.12-13.
3. Flavius Josephus. "The Antiquities of the Jews". *The Works of Josephus Complete and Unabridged*. Peabody: Hendrickson Publishers. 1987. 1.6.125
4. "Mazaca." *Harpers Dictionary of Classical Antiquities*. 1898. Accessed 21 Mar. 2017.
5. "Kayseri." *The Concise Dictionary of World Place-Names*. 2nd ed. 2014. Accessed 21 Mar. 2017.
6. Isidore of Seville. *The Etymologies of Isidore of Seville*. Trans. Stephen A. Barney, W J. Lewis, J A. Beach, and Oliver Berghof. Cambridge: Cambridge University Press. 2006. p. 193.
7. Robert F. Harper. *Assyrian and Babylonian Literature: Selected Translations*. New York: D. Appleton and Company. 1901. p. 59-60. Accessed 21 Mar. 2017.
8. Daniel D. Luckenbill. *Ancient Records of Assyria and Babylonia*. Vol. I. Chicago: University of Chicago Press. 1926. pp. 74, 132, 144. Accessed 8 May 2018.
9. Herodotus. *The Histories*. Trans. A D. Godley. Cambridge: Harvard University Press. 1920. Accessed 21 Mar. 2017. 3.94.
10. Pliny the Elder. *The Natural History*. Trans. John Bostock and H T. Riley. London: Taylor and Francis. 1855. Accessed 21 Mar. 2017. 6.4.
11. Xenophon. *Anabasis*. Trans. Carleton L. Brownson. vol. 3. Cambridge: Harvard University Press. 1922. 7 vols. Accessed 21 Mar. 2017. 5.4.33.
12. Strabo. *Geography*. Trans. H.C. Hamilton and W. Falconer. London: George Bell & Sons. 1903. 3 vols. Accessed 21 Mar. 2017. 11.2, 14.
13. James Anderson. *Royal Genealogies: or, the Genealogical Tables of Emperors, Kings, and Princes from Adam to thefe Times; In Two Parts*. Vol. I. London: James Bettesworth. 1732. II parts. p. 2. Accessed 27 Jan. 2017.
14. Serhii Plokhy. *The Origins of the Slavic Nations*. Cambridge: Cambridge University Press. 2006. p.262. Accessed 22 Mar. 2017.
15. Richard Hakluyt. *The Principal Navigations, Voyages, Traffiques, and Discoveries of the English Nation*. 1616. New York: E. P. Dutton & Co. 1907. p. 49. Accessed 22 Mar. 2017.
16. Robert Collis. *The Petrine Instauration*. Leiden: Brill. 2011. p. 248. Accessed 22 Mar. 2017.

17. Vsevolod Holubnychy. *Selected Works of Vsevolod Holubnychy.* Alberta: CIUS Press. 1982. p. 60. Accessed 22 Mar. 2017.
18. В. КОлиаКУ эНАНий. *Какие существуют гипотезы о происхождении слова «Москва»?* ОКАиJНи УАиUBI МОСКВЫ. Accessed 22 Mar. 2017
19. Michael Oard. "The Ice Age and the Genesis Flood". *Acts & Facts.* 16 (6). 1987.
20. Bodie Hodge *Tower of Babel: The Cultural History of our Ancestors.* Green Forest: Master Books. 2013. pp. 174-75.
21. Brian Thomas, M.S. "DNA Trends Confirm Noah's Family". *Acts & Facts.* 45 (7). 2016.
22. Nathaniel T. Jeanson. "On the Origin of Human Mitochondrial DNA Differences." *Answers Research Journal.* vol. 9. 27 Apr. 2016. 123-30. Accessed 22 Mar. 2017.
23. Jennie Cohen. "Native Americans Hailed from Siberian Highlands, DNA Reveals." *History.com.* 26 Jan. 2012. Accessed 22 Mar. 2017.
24. Maanasa Raghavan, Pontus Skoglund, Kelly E. Graf, Mait Metspaulu, et al. "Upper Paleolithic Siberian genome reveals dual ancestry of Native Americans." *Nature.* vol. 505. 20 Nov. 2013. pp. 87-9. doi:10.1038/nature12736. Accessed 22 Mar. 2017.
25. Brian Handwerk. ""Great Surprise"—Native Americans Have West Eurasian Origins." *National Geographic.* 22 Nov. 2013. Accessed 8 May 2018.
26. Richard P. Aschmann. *The Genesis 10 Table of Nations and Y-Chromosomal DNA.* 10 Nov. 2016. pp. 1-30. Accessed 11 Jun 2018.

Chapter 11

1. "8494." *The New Strong's Complete Dictionary of Bible Words.* 1996.
2. "The Book of Jubilees." *The Apocrypha and Pseudepigrapha of the Old Testament in English.* ed. R H. Charles. Oxford: Clarendon Press. 1913. 9.13.
3. Flavius Josephus. "The Antiquities of the Jews". *The Works of Josephus Complete and Unabridged.* Peabody: Hendrickson Publishers. 1987. 1.6.125.
4. Strabo. *The Geography of Strabo.* Trans. H L. Jones. Cambridge: Harvard University Press. 1924. Accessed 23 Mar. 2017. 6.4.
5. Isidore of Seville. *The Etymologies of Isidore of Seville.* Trans. Stephen A. Barney, W J. Lewis, J A. Beach, and Oliver Berghof. Cambridge: Cambridge University Press. 2006. Accessed 24 Mar. 2017. IX.ii.31.
6. Gocha T. Tsetskhladze, ed. *North Pontic Archaeology: Recent Discoveries and Studies.* Leiden: Brill. 2001. p. 52. Accessed 24 Mar. 2017.
7. Strabo, 2.5.
8. John T. Painter. *Ethnology: or the History & Genealogy of the Human Race.* London: Bailliere, Tindall & Cox. 1880. pp. 152-54. Accessed 15 May 2018.
9. Strabo, 7.3.
10. Euripides. *The Alcestis of Euripides.* Trans. H B. L. London: Richard Bentley and Son. 1884. p. 95. Accessed 23 Mar. 2017.
11. Julia Valeva, Emil Nankov, and Denver Graninger, eds. *A Companion to Ancient Thrace.* Chichester: John Wiley & Sons, Inc. 2015. p. 28. Accessed 24 Mar. 2017.
12. Xenophanes. *Xenophanes of Colophon: Fragments: a Text and Translation with a Commentary.* Ed. James H. Lesher. Toronto: University of Toronto Press. 2001. p. 90. Accessed 23 Mar. 2017.
13. *A Companion to Ancient Thrace,* 13-14.
14. J. Herrmann and E Zürcher, eds. *History of Humanity: From the Seventh Century B.C. to the Seventh Century A.D.* Paris: UNESCO. 1996. pp. 219-23. Accessed 15 May 2018.
15. "TYRANGI'TAE." *Dictionary of Greek and Roman Geography.* 1854. Accessed 15 May 2018.
16. Herodotus. *The Histories.* Trans. A D. Godley. Cambridge: Harvard University Press. 1920. Accessed 24 Mar. 2017. 1.57.
17. Thucydides. *The Peloponnesian War.* Trans. J M. Dent. New York: E. P. Dutton. 1910. Accessed 24 Mar. 2017. 4.109.
18. J.B. Lightfoot, F.J.A Hort, and J.E.B Mayor, eds. *The Journal of Classical and Sacred Philology.* Vol. 2. Cambridge: Cambridge University Press. 2012. pp. 1-19, 176. Accessed 24 Mar. 2017.
19. Herodotus, 6.137.

20. Strabo, 5.2.
21. Richard Stillwell and William L. MacDonald. "Lemnos." *The Princeton Encyclopedia of Classical Sites.* Ed. Marian H. McAlister. 1976. Accessed 24 Mar. 2017.
22. "Tyrrhenian Sea." *Encyclopaedia Britannica.* 2012. Accessed 24 Mar. 2017.
23. Titus Livius (Livy). *The History of Rome, Book 26.* Trans. Frank G. Moore. Cambridge: Harvard University Press. 1943. Accessed 24 Mar. 2017. 26.19.
24. Titus Livius (Livy). *The History of Rome.* Trans. Canon Roberts. New York: E. P. Dutton. 1912. Accessed 24 Mar. 2017. 5.33.
25. Polybius. *Histories.* Trans. Evelyn S. Shuckburgh. London: Macmillan Company. 1962. Accessed 12 May 2017. 34.10.
26. *Dictionary of Greek and Roman Geography,* "Etruria.".
27. Roger D. Woodard, ed. *The Ancient Languages of Europe.* Cambridge: Cambridge University Press. 2008. p. 7. Accessed 24 Mar. 2017.
28. Philip Baldi. *The Foundations of Latin.* Berlin & New York: Mouton de Gruyter. 1999. p. 111. Accessed 14 Mar. 2017.
29. Robert Drews. *The End of the Bronze Age: Changes in Warfare and the Catastrophe ca. 1200 B.C.* Princeton: Princeton University Press. 1995. p. 54. Accessed 15 May 2018.
30. Eliezer D. Oren. *The Sea Peoples and Their World: A Reassessment.* Philadelphia: University of Pennsylvania Press. 2000. p. 67. Accessed 15 May 2018.
31. Henry M. Morris. *The Genesis Record.* Grand Rapids: Baker Book House. 1976. p. 249.
32. Bill Cooper. *After the Flood.* Chichester: New Wine Press. 1995. p. 204.
33. Bodie Hodge. *Tower of Babel: The Cultural History of our Ancestors.* Green Forest: Master Books. 2013. pp. 177-78.
34. Plato. *Plato in Twelve Volumes.* Trans. R G. Bury. vols. 10 & 11. Cambridge: Harvard University Press. 1968. 12 vols. Accessed 25 Mar. 2017. 1.637.
35. "Tyr." *Merriam-Webster.* 1828. Accessed 25 Mar. 2017.
36. Snorri Sturluson. *The Prose Edda.* Trans. Arthur G. Brodeur. Oxford: Oxford University Press. 1916. p. 6, 21, 39, 113. Accessed 25 Mar. 2017.
37. "Tuesday." *Online Etymology Dictionary.* 2017. Accessed 25 Mar. 2017.
38. Anonymous. *Floamanna Saga.* p. 21. Accessed 25 Mar. 2017.
39. "Thursday." *Online Etymology Dictionary.* 2017. Accessed 25 Mar. 2017.
40. Eric Gaba. "Satellite caption of the Mediterranean Sea." Screenshot from *NASA.* Jun 2007. Accessed 7 May 2018.

Chapter 12

1. "The Book of Jubilees." *The Apocrypha and Pseudepigrapha of the Old Testament in English.* ed. R H. Charles. Oxford: Clarendon Press. 1913. 7.13-15.
2. "2526." *The New Strong's Complete Dictionary of Bible Words.* 1996.
3. *The New Strong's Complete Dictionary of Bible Words.* "1990."
4. William Camden. Sutton, Dana F., editor. trans. Philemon Holland. *Britannia.* The Philological Museum, 2004. www.philological.bham.ac.uk/cambrit/. Accessed 27 Jan. 2017.
5. Richard P. Aschmann. *The Genesis 10 Table of Nations and Y-Chromosomal DNA.* 10 Nov. 2016. pp. 1-30. Accessed 11 Jun 2018.
6. *The Book of Jasher.* Salt Lake City: J. H. Parry & Company. 1887. http://www.sacred-texts.com/chr/apo/jasher/. Accessed 25 Jan. 2017. 7.10-13, 10.19
7. *The Book of Jasher,* 10.20.
8. "The Book of Jubilees," 8.8-10.
9. "The Book of Jubilees," 8.30.
10. "The Book of Jubilees," 8.22-25.
11. Flavius Josephus. "The Antiquities of the Jews". *The Works of Josephus Complete and Unabridged.* Peabody: Hendrickson Publishers. 1987. 1.6.130-139.
12. David McIntee. *The War of Horus and Set.* New York: Bloomsbury Publishing. 2013. pp. 4, 6. Accessed 29 Mar. 2017.
13. "Seth." Donald B. Redford. *The Oxford Encyclopedia of Ancient Egypt: P-Z.* 2001. p. 269. Accessed 29 Mar. 2017.
14. *Epics of Sumerian Kings.* Trans. H L. Herman and L J. Vanstiphout. Leiden: Brill. 2004. p. 174. Accessed 29 Mar. 2017.

15. *Epics of Sumerian Kings*, 65.

Chapter 13

1. "The Book of Jubilees." *The Apocrypha and Pseudepigrapha of the Old Testament in English*. ed. R H. Charles. Oxford: Clarendon Press. 1913. 10.30-34.
2. "3568." *The New Strong's Complete Dictionary of Bible Words*. 1996.
3. Biblical References from *The Holy Bible, New International Version*: Isa. 11:11, 18:1, 20:3-5, 37:9, 43:3, 45:14, Jer. 46:9, Ezk. 29:10, 30:4-9, 38:5, Nah. 3:9, Zep. 3:10.
4. *The New Strong's Complete Dictionary of Bible Words*, "3569."
5. *The New Strong's Complete Dictionary of Bible Words*, "3571."
6. William G. Dever. *Who were the Early Israelites and Where did they come from?* Grand Rapids: William B. Eerdmans Publishing Company. 2006. p. 34. Accessed 30 Mar. 2017.
7. *The New Strong's Complete Dictionary of Bible Words*, "3572."
8. I.E. Edwards, C.J. Gadd, and N.G.L Hammond, eds. *The Cambridge Ancient History*. Cambridge: Cambridge University Press. 1971. p. 100. Accessed 30 Mar. 2017.
9. *The Sumerian King List*. trans. Thorkild Jacobsen. Chicago: The University of Chicago Press. 1939. p.77. Accessed 30 Mar. 2017.
10. Karen R. Nemet-Nejat. *Daily Life in Ancient Mesopotamia*. Westport: Greenwood Press. 1998. p. 20. Accessed 30 Mar. 2017.
11. *The Book of Jasher*. Salt Lake City: J. H. Parry & Company. 1887. http://www.sacred-texts.com/chr/apo/jasher/. Accessed 25 Jan. 2017. 10.20.
12. *History of Assurbanipal*. Trans. George Smith. London: Williams and Norgate. 1871. pp. 34, 38. Accessed 31 Mar. 2017.
13. James H. Breasted. *Ancient Records of Egypt: The eighteenth dynasty*. Chicago: University of Illinois Press. 2001. p. 32. Accessed 31 Mar. 2017.
14. George Steindorff and Keith C. Steele. *When Egypt Ruled the East*. Chicago: University of Chicago Press. 2014. p. 39. Accessed 31 Mar. 2017.
15. Breasted, 17, 212-217.
16. Robert Draper. "The Black Pharaohs." *National Geographic*. Feb. 2008. Accessed 31 Mar. 2017.
17. Percy Handcock. *Selections from the Tell El-Amarna Letters*. "From Abdi-hiba of Jerusalem to the King". Trans. Keilinschriftliche niblio-thek Winkler. New York: Macmillan Company. 1920. Accessed 31 Mar. 2017.
18. Steindorff, 101.
19. Margaret Bunson. "Wawat." *Encyclopedia of Ancient Egypt*. 2nd ed., 2002. p. 429.
20. A. Paul. *A History of the Beja Tribes of the Sudan*. Cambridge: Cambridge University Press. 1954. p. 20. Accessed 31 Mar. 2017.
21. Flavius Josephus. "The Antiquities of the Jews". *The Works of Josephus Complete and Unabridged*. Peabody: Hendrickson Publishers. 1987. 1.6.130-131.
22. *The New Strong's Complete Dictionary of Bible Words*, "128."

Chapter 14

1. "5434." *The New Strong's Complete Dictionary of Bible Words*. 1996.
2. Flavius Josephus. "The Antiquities of the Jews". *The Works of Josephus Complete and Unabridged*. Peabody: Hendrickson Publishers. 1987. 1.6.134-35.
3. James Anderson. *Royal Genealogies: or, the Genealogical Tables of Emperors, Kings, and Princes from Adam to thefe Times; In Two Parts*. Vol. I. London, James Bettesworth. 1732. p. 4. II parts. Accessed 27 Jan. 2017.
4. Isidore of Seville. *The Etymologies of Isidore of Seville*. Trans. Stephen A. Barney, W.J. Lewis, J.A. Beach, and Oliver Berghof. Cambridge: Cambridge University Press. 2006. IX.ii.10-18.
5. *The New Strong's Complete Dictionary of Bible Words*, "2341."
6. *The New Strong's Complete Dictionary of Bible Words*, "5454."
7. Strabo. *Geography*. Trans. H C. Hamilton and W Falconer. London: George Bell & Sons. 1903. 3 vols. Accessed 4 Apr. 2017. 16.4.
8. Sir Walter Raleigh. Eds. Thomas Birch and William Oldys. *The Works of Sir Walter Raleigh*. Vol. 2. Oxford: Oxford University Press. 1829. 8 vols. p. 317. Accessed 5 Apr. 2017.

9. *The New Strong's Complete Dictionary of Bible Words*, "7484."
10. *The New Strong's Complete Dictionary of Bible Words*, "7483."
11. *The New Strong's Complete Dictionary of Bible Words*, "7482."
12. Job 39:19. *Holy Bible, New King James Version*. Nashville: Thomas Nelson Publishing. 1982. p. 366.
13. Maurice Sartre. *The Middle East Under Rome*. Cambridge: Harvard University Press. 2005. p. 66. Accessed 7 Apr. 2017.
14. Jean-François Breton. *Arabia Felix from the time of the Queen of Sheba*. Notre Dame: University of Notre Dame Press. 1999. p. 71. Accessed 7 Apr. 2017.
15. Jean-Jacques Glassner and Benjamin R. Foster, eds. *Mesopotamian Chronicles*. Leiden: Brill. 2005. p. 217. Accessed 7 Apr. 2017.
16. *The New Strong's Complete Dictionary of Bible Words*, "7614."
17. *The New Strong's Complete Dictionary of Bible Words*, "7652."
18. "H7652 - sheba` - Strong's Hebrew Lexicon (KJV)." *Blue Letter Bible*. 4 Apr. 2017.
19. "NIV Search Results for "sheba"." *Blue Letter Bible*. 4 Apr. 2017.
20. *The New Strong's Complete Dictionary of Bible Words*, "884."
21. *The New Strong's Complete Dictionary of Bible Words*, "5436."
22. *The New Strong's Complete Dictionary of Bible Words*, "7615."
23. Robert D. Burrowes. *Historical Dictionary of Yemen*. 2nd ed. Plymouth: Rowman & Littlefield. 2010. p. 319. Accessed 4 Apr. 2017.
24. Augustus. *The Deeds of Divine Augustus*. Trans. Thomas Bushnell. The Internet Classics Archive. 1998. p. 26. Accessed 4 Apr. 2017.
25. Kenneth A. Kitchen. *On the Reliability of the Old Testament*. Grand Rapids: William B. Eerdmans Publishing Company. 2003. p. 437. Accessed 4 Apr. 2017.
26. Ragaei el Mallakh. *The Economic Development of the Yemen Arab Republic (RLE Economy of Middle East)*. New York: Routledge. 2014. p. 4. Accessed 4 Apr. 2017.
27. Pliny. *The Natural History*. Trans. John Bostock and H T. Riley. London: Taylor and Francis. 1855. Accessed 4 Apr. 2017. 6.32.
28. *The New Strong's Complete Dictionary of Bible Words*, "1719."
29. *The New Strong's Complete Dictionary of Bible Words*, "1720."
30. "Dedan." *Dictionary of the Ancient Near East*. 2010.
31. "Dedan." *Dr. William Smith's Dictionary of the Bible*. 1868.
32. *The New Strong's Complete Dictionary of Bible Words*, "5455."
33. "Middle East geographic." *NASA*. 16 Jun. 2005. CC. Accessed 18 May 2018.

Chapter 15

1. "5248." *The New Strong's Complete Dictionary of Bible Words*. 1996.
2. *The Book of Jasher*. Salt Lake City: J. H. Parry & Company. 1887. http://www.sacred-texts.com/chr/apo/jasher/. Accessed 25 Jan. 2017. 7.23.
3. "H894 - Babel - Strong's Hebrew Lexicon (KJV)." Blue Letter Bible. Accessed 7 Jun. 2018. https://www.blueletterbible.org//lang/lexicon/lexicon.cfm?Strongs=H894&t=KJV
4. *The Book of Jasher*, 9.
5. Flavius Josephus. "The Antiquities of the Jews". *The Works of Josephus Complete and Unabridged*. Peabody: Hendrickson Publishers. 1987. 1.4.113-19.
6. K. van der Toorn and P.W. van der Horst. "Nimrod Before and After the Bible." *Harvard Theological Review*. vol. 83, no. 1. Jan. 1990. pp. 1-29. Accessed 7 June 2018.
7. *The New Strong's Complete Dictionary of Bible Words*, "894."
8. *The New Strong's Complete Dictionary of Bible Words*, "895."
9. I.J. Gelb. "The Name of Babylon." *I Studied Inscriptions from Before the Flood*. Vol. 4. Richard Hess and David Toshio, eds. Winona Lake: Eisenbrauns. 1994. pp. 266-69. Accessed 7 Jun. 2018.
10. James B. Pritchard, ed. *Ancient Near Eastern Texts Relating to the Old Testament*. 3rd ed. Princeton: Princeton University Press. 1969. p. 315. Accessed 11 Apr. 2017.
11. A.R. George. *Babylonian Topographical Texts*. Louvain: Peeters Publishers. 1992. p. 255. Accessed 10 Apr. 2017.
12. "Babylonians." *Encyclopedia of the Peoples of Africa and the Middle East*. Jamie Stokes, ed. 2009. pp. 83-85. Accessed 7 June 2018.

13. Wilfred G. Lambert. "Babylon: Origins". in: Eva Cancik-Kirschbaum, Margarete van Ess and Joachim Marzahn, eds. *Babylon. Wissenskultur in Orient und Okzident/ Science Culture Between Orient and Occident.* Berlin: De Gruyter. 2011. pp. 71–76. Accessed 7 Jun. 2018.
14. Josephus, 1.6.135.
15. "MERODACH-BALDAN." *The International Standard Bible Encyclopedia.* Geoffrey Bromiley, ed. 1995. pp. 325-26. Accessed 7 June 2018.
16. Albert K. Grayson. *Assyrian and Babylonian Chronicles.* Winona Lake: Eisenbrauns. 2000. pp. 73-75. Accessed 7 Jun. 2018.
17. *International Standard Bible Encyclopedia* "NABOPOLASSAR." p. 470.
18. Grayson, 88-100.
19. *International Standard Bible Encyclopedia* "NEBUCHADREZZER." pp. 506-08.
20. Ronald H Sack. *Amel-Marduk: 562-560 B.C.* Kevelaer: Butzon und Bercker. 1972. pp. 3-26. Accessed 7 June 2018.
21. *International Standard Bible Encyclopedia,* "NERGAL-SHAREZER." p. 520.
22. *International Standard Bible Encyclopedia* "NABONIDUS". pp. 468-70.
23. Pritchard, 306, 312.
24. Keaton Halley. "Belshazzar: The second most powerful man in Babylon." *Creation.* July 2015. Vol. 37, no. 3. pp. 12-15. Accessed 7 June 2018.
25. Thorkild Jacobsen. *The Sumerian King List.* Chicago: The University of Chicago Press. 1939. pp. 77, 87, 120. Accessed 10 Apr. 2017.
26. Pritchard, 265.
27. Albrecht Goetze. "The Kassites and Near Eastern Chronology." *Journal of Cuneiform Studies.* vol. 18. no. 4. 1964. pp. 97–101.
28. Frank R. Allchin and Stanley A. Wolpert. "India." *Encyclopaedia Britannica.* 2018. Accessed 7 June 2018.
29. H L. Herman and L J. Vanstiphout. *Epics of Sumerian Kings: The Matter of Aratta.* Leiden: Brill. 2004. p. 65. Accessed 10 Apr. 2017.
30. "The Epic of Gilgamesh". Benjamin R. Foster, Trans. *The Norton Anthology of World Literature.* vol. 1. 2nd ed. New York: W. W. Norton & Company. 2009. XI.
31. Wilfred G. Lambert and A.R. Millard. *Atra-ḫasīs: The Babylonian Story of the Flood.* Winona Lake: Eisenbrauns 1969, Rpt. 1999. pp. 59, 129. Accessed 10 Apr. 2017.
32. "The Epic of Gilgamesh.", I.
33. Walther Sallaberger and Aage Westenholz. *Mesopotamien: Akkade-Zeit und Ur III-Zeit.* Orbis Biblicus et Orientalis. 160/3. Göttingen: Vandenhoeck & Ruprecht. 1999. pp. 31-32. Accessed 7 Jun. 2018.
34. Christophe Wall-Romana. "An Areal Location of Agade." *Journal of Near Eastern Studies.* vol. 49, no. 3. 1990. pp. 205–245. *JSTOR.* JSTOR. www.jstor.org/stable/546244.
35. *The New Strong's Complete Dictionary of Bible Words,* "3641."
36. *The New Strong's Complete Dictionary of Bible Words,* "8152."
37. Samuel N Kramer. *The Sumerians: Their History, Culture, and Character.* Chicago: University of Chicago Press. 2010. pp. 33-36, 166. Accessed 8 Jun. 2018.
38. William. W Hallo and William K. Simpson. *The Ancient Near East: A History.* San Diego: Harcourt Brace College Publishers. 1998. p. 29. Accessed 8 Jun. 2018.
39. J. N. Postgate. *Early Mesopotamia: Society and Economy at the Dawn of History.* London: Taylor & Francis. 2015. p. 38. Accessed 8 Jun. 2018.
40. "Ninua." *Open Richly Annotated Cuneiform Corpus.* Royal Inscriptions of the Neo-Assyrian Period (RINAP) Project. 2017.
41. *The International Standard Bible Encyclopedia,* "NINEVEH." pp. 538-39.
42. Daniel D. Luckenbill. *The Annals of Sennacherib.* Vol. II. Chicago: The University of Chicago Press. 1924. pp. 34, 60, 101, 113, 152, 154. Accessed 11 Apr. 2017.
43. Pritchard, 303-05.
44. N. G. L. Hammond. *The Cambridge Ancient History.* 2nd ed. vol. III. Cambridge: Cambridge University Press. 1982. p. 80. Accessed 11 Apr. 2017.
45. Luckenbill, *ARAB* Vol. II, 23, 74, 240.
46. Luckenbill, *ARAB* Vol. II, 72, 408.
47. Carsten Niebuhr. *Carsten Niebuhrs Reisebeschreibung nach Arabien und andern umliegenden Ländern.* Vol. 2. Hamburg: Kopenhagen. 1778. p. 355. Accessed 12 Apr. 2017.

48. Stephen Bertman. *Handbook to Life in Ancient Mesopotamia.* Oxford: Oxford University Press. 2003. p. 122. Accessed 12 Apr. 2017.
49. Pritchard, 165.
50. Luckenbill, *ARAB* Vol. II, 25, 113.
51. Tamara M. Green. *The City of the Moon God.* Leiden: E. J. Brill. 1992. p. 34. Accessed 12 Apr. 2017.
52. W. W. How and J. Wells. *A Commentary on Herodotus.* Oxford: Oxford University Press. 1989. Accessed 12 Apr. 2017. 1.181.
53. "Ninurta." *Dictionary of the Ancient Near East.* 2000. Accessed 12 Apr. 2017.
54. Pritchard, 93, 95, 161, 300.
55. Dominik Bonatz. *The Archaeology of Political Spaces.* Berlin: Walter de Gruyter. 2014. pp. 12, 20. Accessed 12 Apr. 2017.
56. *The Book of Jasher,* 11.
57. Pritchard, 62, 64-65.
58. Pritchard, 68.
59. *The Seven Tablets of Creation.* Trans. Leonard W. King. London: Luzac. 1902. Accessed 12 Apr. 2017.
60. Anne Habermehl. "Where in the World Is the Tower of Babel?" *Answers Research Journal.* vol. 24. 2011. pp. 25-35. Accessed 18 Sept. 2018.

Chapter 16

1. "The Book of Jubilees." *The Apocrypha and Pseudepigrapha of the Old Testament in English.* ed. R H. Charles. Oxford: Clarendon Press. 1913. 9.1.
2. Flavius Josephus. "The Antiquities of the Jews". *The Works of Josephus Complete and Unabridged.* Peabody: Hendrickson Publishers. 1987. 1.6.132-34.
3. "4714." *The New Strong's Complete Dictionary of Bible Words.* 1996.
4. *The New Strong's Complete Dictionary of Bible Words,* "4713."
5. "H4713 - Mitsriy - Strong's Hebrew Lexicon (KJV)." *Blue Letter Bible.* Accessed 17 Apr. 2017.
6. BLB, "H4714 - Mitsrayim - Strong's Hebrew Lexicon (KJV)."
7. Daniel D. Luckenbill. *Ancient Records of Assyria and Babylonia.* Vol. II. Chicago: The University of Chicago Press. 1927. p. 224. Accessed 12 Apr. 2017.
8. Daniel I. Block. *The Book of Ezekiel, Chapter 25-48.* Grand Rapids & Cambridge: William B. Eerdmans Publishing Company. 1998. p. 166. Accessed 18 Apr. 2017.
9. *The Tell-El-Amarna Letters.* Trans. Hugo Winkler. London: Luzac & Co. 1896. pp. 12-13, 28-29. Accessed 18 Apr. 2017.
10. "msrm." *A Dictionary of the Ugaritic Language in the Alphabetic Tradition.* 3rd ed., 2015. Accessed 18 Apr. 2017.
11. John F. Ashton and David Down. *Unwrapping the Pharaohs.* Green Forest: Master Books. 2006. pp. 11, 194-211. Accessed 19 Apr. 2017.
12. "Egypt." *The Online Etymology Dictionary.* 2017. Accessed 18 Apr. 2017.
13. Simson R. Najovits. *Egypt, Trunk of the Tree.* Vol. I. New York: Algora Publishing. 2003. p. 85. Accessed 18 Apr. 2017.
14. I. E. S. Edwards, C J. Gadd, and N. G. L Hammond, eds. *The Cambridge Ancient History.* Vol. 1. Cambridge: Cambridge University Press. 1971. pp. 14-15. Accessed 19 Apr. 2017.
15. Emily Teeter, ed. *Before the Pyramids.* Chicago: The University of Chicago Press. 2011. p. 33. Accessed 19 Apr. 2017.
16. Lyla P. Brock. *Egyptology at the Dawn of the Twenty-first Century.* Vol. 2. Cairo & New York: American University in Cairo Press. 2003. pp. 173-74. Accessed 19 Apr. 2017.
17. Josephus, 1.8.166-68.
18. Ian Shaw. *The Oxford History of Ancient Egypt.* Oxford: Oxford University Press. 2003. pp. 90-93. Accessed 19 Apr. 2017.
19. "Aegyptus." *Harpers Dictionary of Classical Antiquities.* 1898. Accessed 19 Apr. 2017.
20. Elizabeth Mitchell. "Doesn't Egyptian Chronology Prove That the Bible is Unreliable?". *The New Answers Book 2.* Ed. Ken Ham. Green Forest: Master Books. 2010. p. 256.
21. Ashton and Down, 83.
22. Erasmus Wilson. *The Egypt of the Past.* London: Kegan Paul, Trench, and Company. 1881. p. 158. Accessed 19 Apr. 2017.

23. Heinrich K. Brugsch. *A History of Egypt under the Pharaohs, Derived Entirely from the Monuments.* Trans. Philip Smith. 2nd ed., vol. I. London: John Murray. 1881. pp. 157-58. Accessed 19 Apr. 2017.
24. Fritz Hommel. *The Ancient Hebrew Tradition Illustrated by the Old Monuments.* Trans. Edmund McClure and Leonard Crossle. Brighton: Society for Promoting Christian Knowledge. 1897. p. 227. Accessed 21 Apr. 2017.
25. "MOSCHA PORTUS." *Dictionary of Greek and Roman Geography.* 1854. Accessed 21 Apr. 2017.
26. James M. Miller, J.A. Dearman, and M P. Graham, eds. *The Land that I Will Show You.* Sheffield: Sheffield Academic Press. 2001. pp. 264-66. Accessed 21 Apr. 2017.
27. A. Rosalie David. *The Pyramid Builders of Ancient Egypt.* London & New York: Routledge. 2002. pp. 190, 249. Accessed 19 Apr. 2017.
28. Mitchell, 257.
29. Ashton and Down, 91.
30. David, 137, 170.
31. Ashton, 95.
32. K.S.B. Ryholt and Adam Bülow-Jacobsen. *The Political Situation in Egypt During the Second Intermediate Period, C. 1800-1550 B.C.* Copenhagen: Museum Tusculanum Press. 1997. pp. 213, 294. Accessed 19 Apr. 2017.
33. Mitchell, 258-59.
34. Ashton and Down, 215.
35. Ashton and Down, 100.
36. William C Hayes. *The Scepter of Egypt.* Vol. 1. 1978. Accessed 20 Apr. 2017. 149-50.
37. David, 195, 199.
38. Kathryn A. Bard. *An Introduction to the Archaeology of Ancient Egypt.* Chichester: John Wiley & Sons, Inc. 2015. p. 213. Accessed 20 Apr. 2017.
39. David M. Rohl. *Pharaohs and Kings: A Biblical Quest.* Crown Publishers. 1995. p. 279. Accessed 20 Apr. 2017.
40. Hayes, 135.
41. Hayes, 351.
42. Ashton and Down, 121-22.
43. Mitchell, 260.
44. David Down. *Unveiling the Kings of Israel: Revealing the Bible's Archeological History.* Green Forest: Master Books. 2011. p. 102. Accessed 20 Apr. 2017.
45. Catharine H. Roehrig, Renee Drefus, and Cathleen A. Keller, eds. *Hatshepsut: From Queen to Pharaoh.* New Haven: Yale University Press. 2005. p. 202. Accessed 20 Apr. 2017.
46. Rhoehrig, et al., 3.
47. James B. Pritchard, ed. *Ancient Near Eastern Texts Relating to the Old Testament.* 3rd ed. Princeton: Princeton University Press. 1969. pp. 234-39. Accessed 11 Apr. 2017.
48. Ashton and Down, 128.
49. Miriam Lichtheim. *Ancient Egyptian Literature.* vol. II. Berkeley: University of California Press. 1976. p. 77. Accessed 20 Apr. 2017.
50. Mitchell, 261.
51. Mitchell, 262.
52. Ashton and Down, 191, 209.
53. Edward Lipinski. *On the Skirts of Canaan in the Iron Age.* Louvain: Peeters Publishers. 2006. p. 157. Accessed 21 Apr. 2017.
54. Herodotus. *The Histories.* Cambridge: Harvard University Press. 1920. Accessed 21 Apr. 2017. 2.159
55. Josephus, 10.5.74-10.6.98.
56. Herodotus, 2.161-69.
57. Bill T. Arnold. *Who Were the Babylonians?* Atlanta: Society of Biblical Literature. 2004. p. 95. Accessed 21 Apr. 2017.
58. Josephus, 10.7.108-115.

Chapter 17
1. "3866." *The New Strong's Complete Dictionary of Bible Words.* 1996.

2. *The New Strong's Complete Dictionary of Bible Words*, "3864."
3. Flavius Josephus. "The Antiquities of the Jews". *The Works of Josephus Complete and Unabridged.* Peabody: Hendrickson Publishers. 1987. 1.6.132.
4. Josephus, 1.6.136-37.
5. *The New Strong's Complete Dictionary of Bible Words*, "6047."
6. Pliny. *The Natural History.* Trans. John Bostock and H T. Riley. London: Taylor and Francis. 1855. Accessed 4 Apr. 2017. 5.1
7. James H. Breasted. *Ancient Records of Egypt: From the Earliest Time.* Vols. 1 & 2. Chicago: The University of Chicago Press. 1906. pp. 234-35. Accessed 25 Apr. 2017.
8. J. Desmond Clark. *The Cambridge History of Africa.* Cambridge: Cambridge University Press. 1982. p. 919. Accessed 25 Apr. 2017.
9. Alan H. Gardiner. *Egypt of the Pharaohs.* Oxford: Clarendon Press. 1961. p. 273. Accessed 25 Apr. 2017.
10. Stanley Mayes. *The Great Belzoni.* London & New York: Tauris Parke Paperbacks. 2003. pp. 9, 160. Accessed 25 Apr. 2017.
11. Strabo. *The Geography of Strabo.* Trans. H. L. Jones. Cambridge: Harvard University Press. 1924. Accessed 25 Apr. 2017. 13.1.
12. Pliny, 5.4.
13. W.F. Albright. "New Light on Magan and Meluha." *Journal of the American Oriental Society.* vol. 42. 1 Jan. 1922. pp. 317-22. doi:10.2307/593644. Accessed 25 Apr. 2017.
14. *The New Strong's Complete Dictionary of Bible Words*, "5320."
15. Luckenbill, Daniel D. *Ancient Records of Assyria and Babylonia.* Vol. II. Chicago: The University of Chicago Press. 1927. p. 293. Accessed 25 Apr. 2017.
16. Samuel Shuckford. *The Sacred and Profane History of the World.* Vol. 1. Oxford: Clarendon Press. 1810. p. 128. Accessed 25 Apr. 2017.
17. *The New Strong's Complete Dictionary of Bible Words*, "5297."
18. *The New Strong's Complete Dictionary of Bible Words*, "4644."
19. Breasted, 30, 92, 96, 188, 224, 262.
20. Bridget McDermott. *Decoding Egyptian Hieroglyphs.* New York: Chartwell Books. 2016. p. 130. Accessed 25 Apr. 2017.
21. Victor Hamilton. *The Book of Genesis.* Grand Rapids: William B. Eerdmans Publishing Company. 1990. p. 337. Accessed 25 Apr. 2017.
22. Breasted, 36.
23. *The New Strong's Complete Dictionary of Bible Words*, "6625."
24. *The New Strong's Complete Dictionary of Bible Words*, "6624."
25. *The Book of Jasher.* Salt Lake City: J. H. Parry & Company. 1887. http://www.sacred-texts.com/chr/apo/jasher/. Accessed 25 Jan. 2017. 10.23.
26. "Esarhaddon 060." *Open Richly Annotated Cuneiform Corpus.* Royal Inscriptions of the Neo-Assyrian Period (RINAP) Project. 2011. oracc.museum.upenn.edu/rinap/Q003289/html. Accessed 26 Apr. 2017.
27. Luckenbill, 274.
28. James B. Pritchard, ed. *Ancient Near Eastern Texts Relating to the Old Testament.* 3rd ed. Princeton: Princeton University Press. 1969. pp. 262, 290. Accessed 26 Apr. 2017.
29. Luckenbill, 286.
30. John A. Wilson. *Studies in Honor of John A. Wilson.* Chicago: The University of Chicago Press. 1969. p. 40. Accessed 26 Apr. 2017.
31. *The New Strong's Complete Dictionary of Bible Words*, "3695."
32. *The New Strong's Complete Dictionary of Bible Words*, "3732."
33. *The New Strong's Complete Dictionary of Bible Words*, "3731."
34. *The New Strong's Complete Dictionary of Bible Words*, "6429."
35. *The New Strong's Complete Dictionary of Bible Words*, "6430."
36. James B Pritchard. "The Israel Stele Pharaoh Merneptah Translation." *The Ancient Near East - An Anthology of Texts and Pictures.* Princeton: Princeton University Press. 1958. Accessed 27 Apr. 2017.
37. *The New Strong's Complete Dictionary of Bible Words*, "5512."
38. Biblical References from *The Holy Bible, New International Version:* Jos. 13:2-3, Jdg. 3:3-31, 10:6-11, 13:1-5, 14:1-4, 15:3-20, 16:5-30, 1Sa. 4:1-17, 5:1-11, 6:1-21, 7:3-14, 9:16, 10:5, 12:9, 13:3-23, 14:1-52, 17:1-57, 18:6-30, 19:5-8, 21:9, 22:10, 23:1-28, 24:1, 27:1-11, 28:1-19, 29:1-11, 30:16, 31:1-11, 2Sa. 1:20, 3:14-18, 5:17-25. 8:1-12, 19:9, 21:12-19, 23:9-16,

1Ki. 4:21, 15:27, 16:15, 2Ki. 8:2-3, 18:8, 1Ch. 1:12, 10:1-11, 11:13-18, 12:19, 14:8-16, 18:1-11, 20:4-5, 2Ch. 9:26, 17:11, 21:16, 26:6-7, 28:18.

39. Biblical References from *The Holy Bible, New International Version:* Isa. 2:6, 9:12, 11:14, Jer. 25:20, 47:1-4, Ezk. 16:27-57, 25:15-16, Amo. 1:8, 6:2, 9:7, Oba. 1:19, Zep. 2:5, Zec. 9:6).
40. Trevor Bryce. *Ancient Syria: A Three Thousand Year History.* Oxford: Oxford University Press. 2014. p.110. Accessed 27 Apr. 2017.
41. Trevor Bryce. *The World of the Neo-Hittite Kingdoms.* Oxford: Oxford University Press. 2012. p. 13. Accessed 27 Apr. 2017.
42. *ORACC*, "Sennacherib 1015."
43. Luckenbill, 105.
44. Hans Wildberger. *Isaiah 13-27: A Continental Commentary.* Trans. Thomas H. Trapp. Minneapolis: Fortress Press. 1997. p. 95. Accessed 23 May 2018
45. John Strange. *Caphtor Keftiu: A New Investigation.* Leiden: Brill. 1980. p. 43, 72. Accessed 27 Apr. 2017.
46. Pritchard, 138.
47. Strange, 12, 185.
48. Avrāhām Malāmāṭ. *Mari and the Bible.* Leiden: Brill. 1998. p. 35. Accessed 27 Apr. 2017.
49. James Hastings, ed. *The Expository Times.* Vol. 8. Edinburgh: T. & T. Clark. 1897. p. 181. Accessed 27 Apr. 2017.
50. Strange, 36.
51. "Notes for 17:4". *Concordia Self-Study Bible, New International Version.* Concordia Publishing House. 1984. p. 399.
52. Strange, 112, 147-184.

Chapter 18

1. "6316." *The New Strong's Complete Dictionary of Bible Words.* 1996.
2. "The Book of Jubilees." *The Apocrypha and Pseudepigrapha of the Old Testament in English.* ed. R H. Charles. Oxford: Clarendon Press. 1913. 9.1.
3. Flavius Josephus. "The Antiquities of the Jews". *The Works of Josephus Complete and Unabridged.* Peabody: Hendrickson Publishers. 1987. 1.6.132-33.
4. Pliny. *The Natural History.* Trans. John Bostock and H T. Riley. London: Taylor and Francis. 1855. Accessed 4 Apr. 2017. 5.1.
5. John R. Miles. *Scripture Geography.* Manchester: S. Johnson. 1838. p. 328. Accessed 2 May 2017.
6. William Sime. *Sacred Geography.* Edinburgh: William Oliphant and Son. 1835. p. 461. Accessed 2 May 2017.
7. Paul L. MacKendrick. *The North African Stones Speak.* Chapel Hill: The University of North Carolina Press. 1980. p. 188. Accessed 1 May 2017.
8. John C Ridpath. *With the World's People.* Washington D. C.: Clark E. Ridpath. 1916. p. 563. Accessed 1 May 2017.
9. James H. Breasted. *Ancient Records of Egypt: The nineteenth dynasty.* Chicago: University of Illinois Press. 1906. p. 254. Accessed 2 May 2017.
10. Kathryn A Bard. "Libya." *Encyclopedia of the Archaeology of Ancient Egypt.* 2005. p. 445. Accessed 2 May 2017.
11. James H. Breasted. *Ancient Records of Egypt: The twentieth to the twenty-sixth dynasties.* Chicago: University of Chicago Press. 1906. pp. 392-93. Accessed 2 May 2017.
12. Breasted, *Ancient Records of Egypt: The nineteenth dynasty*, 72.
13. Ernst Herzfeld. *The Persian Empire.* Wiesbaden: Franz Steiner Verlag. 1968. p. 283. Accessed 2 May 2017.
14. Breasted, *Ancient Records of Egypt: The nineteenth dynasty.* 195, 250, 262.
15. Breasted, *Ancient Records of Egypt: The twentieth to the twenty-sixth dynasties*, 24.
16. "Nebuchadnezzar." *A Dictionary of the Bible.* 1902. Accessed 2 May 2017.
17. Hugo Winkler. *The History of Babylonia and Assyria.* New York: Charles Scribner's Sons. 1907. p. 317. Accessed 2 May 2017.
18. *Faith and Thought: Journal of the Victoria Institute.* vol. 91-94. 1959. p. 178. Accessed 2 May 2017.

19. Royal Historical Society. *Transactions of the Royal Historical Society.* Vol. 4. London: Longmans. Green and Co. 1889. p. 316. Accessed 2 May 2017.

Chapter 19

1. "3667." *The New Strong's Complete Dictionary of Bible Words.* 1996.
2. John W. Lea. *The Book of Books and Its Wonderful Story.* Philadelphia: J. L. Winston Company. 1922. p. 8. Accessed 5 May 2017.
3. Flavius Josephus. "The Antiquities of the Jews". *The Works of Josephus Complete and Unabridged.* Peabody: Hendrickson Publishers. 1987. 1.6.142.
4. Josephus, 1.6.134 & 138-39.
5. "The Book of Jubilees." *The Apocrypha and Pseudepigrapha of the Old Testament in English.* ed. R H. Charles. Oxford: Clarendon Press. 1913. 10.28-33.
6. "The Book of Jubilees,"9.1-2.
7. *The Book of Jasher.* Salt Lake City: J.H. Parry & Company. 1887. http://www.sacred-texts.com/chr/apo/jasher/. Accessed 25 Jan. 2017. 10.24-29.
8. *The New Strong's Complete Dictionary of Bible Words*, "3669."
9. "כְּנַעַן." *Gesenius Hebrew Chaldee Lexicon Old Testament Scriptures.* 1857. Accessed 4 May 2017.
10. *Gesenius Hebrew Chaldee Lexicon Old Testament Scriptures,* "כְּנַעַן."
11. Biblical References from *The Holy Bible, New International Version*: Ex. 3:8-17, 6:4-15, 13:5-11, 15:15, 16:35, 23:23-28, 33:2, Lev. 14:34, 18:3, 25:38, Num. 13:2-29, 14:25-45, 21:1-3, 26:19, 32:30-49 33:40-51, 34:2-29, 35:10-14, Deu. 1:7, 7:1, 11:30, 20:17, 1Ch. 16:18, Psa. 105:11, 135:11, Oba. 1:20.
12. Biblical References from *The Holy Bible, NIV:* Jos. 3:10, 5:1-12, 7:9, 9:1, 11:3,12:8, 13:3-4,14:1,16:10,17:12-18,21:2, 22:9-32, 24:3-11, Jdg. 1:1-33, 3:1-5, 4:2-5:19, 21:12.
13. *The Tell-El-Amarna Letters.* Trans. Hugo Winkler. London: Luzac & Co. 1896. p. 277. Accessed 18 Apr. 2017.
14. Carl Bezold and Ernest A. W. Budge. *The Tell El-Amarna Tablets in the British Museum.* London: Harrison and Sons. 1892. pp. xiii-xv. Accessed 5 May 2017.
15. *The Tell-El-Amarna Letters,* 210, 276, 282-83.
16. *The Tell-El-Amarna Letters,* 273.
17. Robert Drews. "Canaanites and Philistines." *Journal for the Study of the Old Testament.* vol. 23, no. 81. 1 Dec. 1998. pp. 47-48. Accessed 2 May 2018.
18. Michael C. Astour. "The Origin of the Terms "Canaan," "Phoenician," and "Purple"." *Journal of Near Eastern Studies.* vol. 24, no. 4. Oct. 1965. pp. 346-50. Accessed 5 May 2017.
19. Maria E. Aubet. *The Phoenicians and the West: Politics, Colonies and Trade.* Cambridge: Cambridge University Press. 2001. p. 10. Accessed 5 May 2017.
20. The American University of Beirut. *Berytus: archeological studies published by the Museum of Archeology of the American University of Beirut.* Copenhagen: Munksgaard. 1970. p. 26. Accessed 5 May 2017.
21. Niels P. Lemche. *The Canaanites and Their Land.* 1991. Sheffield: Sheffield Academic Press. 1999. pp. 26, 55-57. Accessed 5 May 2017.
22. Gösta W. Ahlström. *The History of Ancient Palestine.* Minneapolis: Fortress Press. 1993. p. 141. Accessed 2 May 2018.
23. Jonathan N. Tubb. *Canaanites.* Norman: University of Oklahoma Press. 1998. p. 15. Accessed 2 May 2018.
24. Ahlström, 59.

Chapter 20

1. "The Book of Jubilees." *The Apocrypha and Pseudepigrapha of the Old Testament in English.* ed. R H. Charles. Oxford: Clarendon Press. 1913. 8:13, 10:28-33.
2. Flavius Josephus. "The Antiquities of the Jews". *The Works of Josephus Complete and Unabridged.* Peabody: Hendrickson Publishers. 1987. 8.13.316-18.
3. Flavius Josephus. "Flavius Josephus Against Apion". *The Works of Josephus Complete and Unabridged.* Peabody: Hendrickson Publishers. 1987. 1.17-18.
4. Glenn E. Markoe. *Phoenicians.* Berkley: University of California Press. 2000. p. 33. Accessed 8 May 2017.

5. Isidore of Seville. *The Etymologies of Isidore of Seville*. Trans. Stephen A. Barney, W.J. Lewis, J.A. Beach, and Oliver Berghof. Cambridge: Cambridge University Press. 2006. IX.ii.22
6. Strabo. *The Geography of Strabo*. Trans. H C. Hamilton and W Falconer. London: George Bell & Sons. 1903. Accessed 9 May 2017. 16.2.
7. "6721." *The New Strong's Complete Dictionary of Bible Words*. 1996.
8. *The New Strong's Complete Dictionary of Bible Words*, "6722."
9. *The New Strong's Complete Dictionary of Bible Words*, "*4606*."
10. *The New Strong's Complete Dictionary of Bible Words*, "*4605*."
11. *The New Strong's Complete Dictionary of Bible Words*, "6865."
12. *The New Strong's Complete Dictionary of Bible Words*, "*5183*."
13. *The New Strong's Complete Dictionary of Bible Words*, "*5184*."
14. *The New Strong's Complete Dictionary of Bible Words*, "*5403*."
15. Josephus, *Antiquities*, 1.6.138-39.
16. James B. Pritchard, ed. *Ancient Near Eastern Texts Relating to the Old Testament*. 3rd ed. Princeton: Princeton University Press. 1969. p. 145. Accessed 26 Apr. 2017.
17. Pritchard, 275-76, 280-81.
18. Pritchard, 288.
19. Daniel D. Luckenbill. *Ancient Records of Assyria and Babylonia*. Vol. II. Chicago: The University of Chicago Press. 1927. p. 119. Accessed 16 May 2017.
20. Pritchard, 290-91.
21. Pritchard, 258.
22. *The Tell-El-Amarna Letters*. Trans. Hugo Winckler. London: Luzac & Co. 1896. pp. 116, 198-99, 266-67. Accessed 18 Apr. 2017.
23. Pritchard, 282-83.
24. Trevor Bryce. *The Routledge Handbook of the Peoples and Places of Ancient Western Asia*. London: Routledge. 2009. pp. 654, 672. Accessed 11 May 2017.
25. "GEBAL." *Eerdmans Dictionary of the Bible*. 2000. p. 487. Accessed 11 Jun. 2018.
26. *The New Strong's Complete Dictionary of Bible Words*, "1380."
27. *The New Strong's Complete Dictionary of Bible Words*, "1382."
28. Niels P. Lemche. *The Canaanites and Their Land*. 1991. Sheffield: Sheffield Academic Press. 1999. pp. 25-26, 55-57. Accessed 5 May 2017.
29. Michael C. Astour. "The Origin of the Terms "Canaan," "Phoenician," and "Purple"." *Journal of Near Eastern Studies*. vol. 24, no. 4. Oct. 1965. pp. 346-50. Accessed 5 May 2017.
30. Charles R. Krahmalkov. *A Phoenician-Punic Grammar*. Leiden: Brill. 2000. pp. 137, 143, 184, 207, 269, 293. Accessed 9 May 2017.
31. Brian R. Doak. *Phoenician Aniconism in Mediterranean and Ancient Near Eastern Contexts*. Atlanta: Society of Biblical Literature. 2015. p. 137. Accessed 9 May 2017.
32. Henry C. Rawlinson. *A Commentary on the Cuneiform Inscriptions of Babylonia and Assyria*. Cambridge: Cambridge University Press. 2014. p. 30. Accessed 9 May 2017.
33. "Phoenicia." I & II. *Dictionary of Greek and Roman Biography and Mythology*. 1870. Accessed 9 May 2017.
34. Mabel Moore. *Carthage of the Phoenicians in the Light of Modern Excavation*. London: W. Heinemann. 1905. p. 37. Accessed 9 May 2017.
35. Maria E Aubet. *The Phoenicians and the West: Politics, Colonies and Trade*. Cambridge: Cambridge University Press. 2001. p. 11. Accessed 5 May 2017.
36. Markoe, 64, 190-91.
37. Strabo, 16.
38. Josephus, *Antiquities*, 11.8.313-25.
39. Arrian. *Alexander the Great: The Anabasis and the Indica*. Trans. Martin Hammond. Oxford: Oxford University Press. 2013. pp. 58-66. Accessed 9 May 2017.
40. *The New Strong's Complete Dictionary of Bible Words*, "2850."
41. *The New Strong's Complete Dictionary of Bible Words*, "2845."
42. *The Book of Jasher*. Salt Lake City: J. H. Parry & Company. 1887. http://www.sacred-texts.com/chr/apo/jasher/. Accessed 25 Jan. 2017. 7.13.
43. *The New Strong's Complete Dictionary of Bible Words*, "2865."
44. Biblical References from *The Holy Bible, New International Version:* Gen. 15:20, Ex. 3:8-17, 13:5, 23:23-28, 33:2, 34:11, Deut. 7:1, 20:17, Jos. 3:10, Neh. 9:8.

45. Carl S. Ehrlich. From an Antique Land: An Introduction to Ancient Near Eastern Literature. Plymouth: Rowman & Littlefield. 2009. p. 236. Accessed 24 May 2017.
46. Luckenbill, 26, 29.
47. Pritchard, xxiii, 190.
48. Trevor Bryce. *The Kingdom of the Hittites.* Oxford: Oxford University Press. 1999. p. 9. Accessed 24 May 2017.
49. Gerard Gertoux. *Abraham and Chedorlaomer: Chronological, Historical and Archaeological Evidence.* lulu.com. 2015. p. 87. Accessed 24 May 2017.
50. Pritchard, 255.
51. Winckler, 33, 99, 107, 109, 111, 237, 277.
52. James H. Breasted. *Ancient Records of Egypt: The Eighteenth Dynasty.* Vol. 2. Chicago: University of Illinois Press. 2001. Rpt. 1906. pp. 204, 213, 301. Accessed 18 Jun. 2018.
53. Marc Van De Mieroop. Cuneiform Texts and the Writing of History. London & New York: Routledge. 2005. p. 67. Accessed 24 May 2017.
54. Pritchard, 199-203.
55. "Tiglath-Pileser III 13." *Open Richly Annotated Cuneiform Corpus.* Royal Inscriptions of the Neo-Assyrian Period (RINAP) Project. 2017.
56. Pritchard, 275, 279.
57. Luckenbill, 27.
58. Pritchard, 285-87.
59. *The New Strong's Complete Dictionary of Bible Words* "2982."
60. *The New Strong's Complete Dictionary of Bible Words* "2983."
61. Theophilus G. Pinches. *The Old Testament in the Light of the Historical Records and Legends of Assyria and Babylonia.* Brighton: Society for Promoting Christian Knowledge. 1902. p. 324. Accessed 10 May 2017.
62. Winckler, 306-07.
63. Edward Lipinski. *Itineraria Phoenicia.* Paris: Peeters. 2004. p. 502. Accessed 13 June 2018.
64. Silvin Košak. *Tabularia Hethaeorum.* Wiesbaden: Otto Harrassowitz Verlag. 2007. pp. 154-55. Accessed 11 May 2017.
65. Gwilym H. Jones. *The Nathan Narratives.* Sheffield: Sheffield Academic Press. 1990. p. 122. Accessed 18 Jun. 2018.
66. *The New Strong's Complete Dictionary of Bible Words,* "567."
67. Isidore, IX.ii.23.
68. Detlef Jericke. *Abraham in Mamre: Historische Und Exegetische Studien Zur Region von Hebron Und Zu Genesis 11, 27-19, 38.* Leiden: Brill. 2003. pp. 1-3. Accessed 11 June 2018.
69. Biblical References from *The Holy Bible, New International Version:* Ex. 3:8-17, 13:5, 23:23, 33:2, 34:11, Deut. 7:1, 20:17, Jos. 3:10, 24:8-18, Neh. 9:8.
70. Biblical References from *The Holy Bible, New International Version:* Num. 13:29, Deut. 20:17, Jos. 3:10, 7:7, 24:15, Jdg. 1:34-46, 3:5, Ezk. 16:3-45.
71. Biblical References from *The Holy Bible, New International Version:* Jdg. 1:34-36, 6:10, 1Ki. 9:20, 21:26, 2Ki. 21:11, 2Ch. 8:7, Ezr. 9:1.
72. "Ein Gedi." *Jewish Virtual Library.* Ed. AICE. 26 May 2017.
73. Pliny. *The Natural History.* Trans. John Bostock and H T. Riley. London: Taylor and Francis. 1855. Accessed 12 May 2017. 5.15.
74. Paul J Ray. "Dibon: Its Archaeological and Historical Setting in Old Testament Times.". Institute of Archaeology Andrews University. 20 Nov. 2006. p. 27. Accessed 26 May 2017.
75. Friedbert Ninow. "In Search of the "City Which is in the Middle of the Valley"." *Andrews University Seminary Studies.* vol. 40, no.1. 2002. pp. 125-29. Accessed 26 May 2017.
76. "Map 4: Land of the Twelve Tribes." Map. Gen. Ed. Hoerber, Robert G. *Concordia Self-Study Bible, NIV.* Colorado Springs: International Bible Society. 1984.
77. "GILEAD." II & III. The International Standard Bible Encyclopedia Vol. IV. 1998. Accessed 26 May 2017.
78. Herman Vanstiphout. *Epics of Sumerian Kings: The Matter of Aratta.* Atlanta: Society of Biblical Literature. 2003. pp. 64-65, 152-53. Writings from the Ancient World 20. Accessed 12 June 2017.
79. Archi, Alfonso. "Mardu in the Ebla Texts." *Orientalia.* vol. 54, no. ½. 1985. pp. 7–13. *JSTOR.* www.jstor.org/stable/43075305.

80. Cyrus H. Gordon and Gary A. Rendsburg, eds. *Eblaitica: Essays on the Ebla Archive and Eblaite Language.* Vol. 4. Winona Lake: Eisenbrauns. 2002. p. 116. Accessed 26 May 2017.
81. Marc Van De Mieroop. *King Hammurabi of Babylon: A Biography.* Malden: Blackwell Publishing. 2008. pp. 2-3. Accessed 27 May 2017.
82. Hammurabi. *The Letters and Inscriptions of Hammurabi, King of Babylon, about B.C. 2200.* Trans. L W. King. London: Luzac & Co. 1900. pp. 170, 196, 207-08. Accessed 27 May 2017.
83. Marc Van De Mieroop. *A History of the Ancient Near East, ca. 3000-323 BC.* Chichester: John Wiley & Sons, Inc. 2015. pp. 95, 115. Accessed 30 May 2017.
84. Winckler, 105, 255.
85. Pritchard, 203.
86. Winckler, 103, 275.
87. James H. Breasted. *Ancient Records of Egypt: The twentieth to the twenty-sixth dynasties.* Vol. IV. Chicago: The University of Chicago Press. 1906. pp. 75-76. Accessed 30 May 2017.
88. Pritchard, 274-75.
89. *ORACC,* "Sennacherib 004."
90. *ORACC,* "Sennacherib 015."
91. Pritchard, 305.
92. *The New Strong's Complete Dictionary of Bible Words,* "1622."
93. Jesus-Luis Cunchillos, Juan-Pablo Vita, and Jose-Angel Zamora. *Ugaritic Data Bank.* Madrid: Laboratorio de Hermeneumatica. 2003. pp. 740, 767. Accessed 10 May 2017.
94. Cyrus H. Gordon. *Ugaritic Textbook.* Rome: Editrice Pontificio Istituto Biblico. 1998. pp. 177, 198, 211, 223. Accessed 10 May 2017.
95. "GIRGASHITE." *The International Standard Bible Encyclopedia Vol. II.* Editors Geoffrey W. Bromiley et al. 1995. Accessed 10 May 2017. 472.
96. "grgs." A Dictionary of the Ugaritic Language in the Alphabetic Tradition. 2015. Accessed 10 May 2017.
97. Billie J. Collins. *The Hittites and Their World.* Atlanta: Society of Biblical Literature. 2007. p. 203. Accessed 10 May 2017.
98. *The New Strong's Complete Dictionary of Bible Words,* "2340."
99. Josephus, *Antiquities,* 5.1.49-57.
100. Bryce, *Routledge Handbook,* 318, 383.
101. Annick Payne. *Iron Age Hieroglyphic Luwian Inscriptions.* Atlanta: Society of Biblical Literature. 2012. p. 44. Accessed 11 May 2017.
102. W. Hovestreydt and L.M.J. Zonhoven. *Annual Egyptological Bibliography.* Leiden: Brill. 1980. p. 92. Accessed 11 May 2017.
103. "HIVITES." *The International Standard Bible Encyclopedia Vol. II,* 724.
104. John Bright. *A History of Israel.* London: Westminster John Knox Press. 2000. pp. 116-17. Accessed 18 Jun. 2018.
105. "GEZER." III. *The International Standard Bible Encyclopedia Vol. II,* 458.
106. *The New Strong's Complete Dictionary of Bible Words,* "6208."
107. *The New Strong's Complete Dictionary of Bible Words,* "757."
108. Polybius. *Histories.* Trans. Evelyn S. Shuckburgh. London: Macmillan Company. 1962. Accessed 12 May 2017. 5.59.
109. Pliny, 5.16, 5.48.
110. Robert K Ritner. "Execration Texts (1.31)." *In the Context of Scripture: Canonical Compositions from the Biblical World.* Vol. I. Ed. W. W. Hallo. Brill: Leiden. 1997. Accessed 2 Jun 2017. 50-52.
111. Winckler, 170-71, 232-33.
112. Winkler, 172-73, 228-29.
113. Pritchard, 241.
114. James H. Breasted. *Ancient Records of Egypt: From the Earliest Time.* Vol. 2. Chicago: The University of Chicago Press. 1906. p. 214. Accessed 16 May. 2017.
115. "ARCA." Dictionary of Greek and Roman Geography. 1854. Accessed 16 May 2017.
116. Shigeo Yamada. *The Construction of the Assyrian Empire.* Leiden: Brill. 2000. pp. 158-59. Accessed 16 May 2017.
117. *The New Strong's Complete Dictionary of Bible Words,* "5513."

118. Samuel N. Kramer. *Sumerian Mythology*. Philadelphia: University of Pennsylvania Press. 1972. pp. XV, 47-48. Accessed 31 May 2017.
119. "Isinu." The Routledge Dictionary of Gods and Goddesses, Devils and Demons. 2004. Accessed 31 May 2017.
120. "Sin." 1 & 2. The Routledge Dictionary of Gods and Goddesses, Devils and Demons. 2004. Accessed 31 May 2017.
121. *The New Strong's Complete Dictionary of Bible Words*, "5512."
122. *The New Strong's Complete Dictionary of Bible Words*, "5514."
123. Biblical References from *The Holy Bible, New International Version*: Ex. 16:1, 19:1-34:32, Lev 7:38, 25:1, 26:46, 27:34, Num. 1:1-19, 3:1-14, 9:1-5, 10:12, 26:64, 28:6, 33:15-16, Deut. 33:2, Jdg. 5:5, Neh. 9:13, Psa. 68:8-17.
124. Plutarch. *Iside e Osiride*. Via Volga: Harmakis Edizioni. 2017.
125. *The New Strong's Complete Dictionary of Bible Words*, "5515."
126. "Yeshaiya (Isaiah) 49:12 (VUL) - ecce isti de longe venient." Blue Letter Bible. 18 Jun. 2018. <https://www.blueletterbible.org/vul/isa/49/12/t_conc_728012>.
127. V.V. Barthold. *Four Studies on Central Asia*. Vol. I. Leiden: Brill. 1962. p. 27. Accessed 1 June 2017.
128. Oxford. *The Oxford Review*. Vol. 1, no. 1-2. Oxford: Slatter and Munday. 1807. p. 841. Accessed 1 June 2017.
129. "Sino-." *Merriam-Webster*. 1828. Accessed 1 June 2017.
130. Ptolemy. *Ptolemy's Geography: An Annotated Translation of the Theoretical Chapters*. Trans. J L. Berggren and Alexander Jones. Princeton: Princeton University Press. 2000. Accessed 1 June 2017. 71. 79.
131. M. Rollin. *The History of the Arts and Sciences of the Ancients*. Glasgow: Blackie, Fullarton, & Co. 1829. p. 594. Accessed 1 June 2017.
132. William Vincent, ed. *The Periplus of the Erythrean Sea*. Vol. II. London: T. Cadell and W. Davis. 1805. p. 491. Accessed 1 June 2017.
133. Pliny, 6.20.
134. William D. Cooley. *The History of Maritime and Inland Discovery*. Vol. 1. London: Longman, Rees, Orme, Brown, and Green. 1830. p. 117. Accessed 1 June 2017.
135. Vincent, 493.
136. Carl F. Gutzlaff and Andrew Reed. *China Opened*. London: Smith, Elder and Co. 1838. p. 45. Accessed 1 June 2017.
137. William Vincent. *The Commerce and Navigation of the Ancients in the Indian Ocean*. Vol. II. London: T. Cadell and W. Davies. 1807. p. 600. Accessed 1 June 2017.
138. Paramita Mukherjee, Arnab K. Deb, and Miao Pang. *China and India: History, Culture, Cooperation and Competition*. Los Angeles: Sage. 2016. p. 19. Accessed 1 June 2017.
139. Charles R. Beazley. *The Dawn of Modern Geography*. London: John Murray. 1897. pp. 193-94. Accessed 1 June 2017.
140. *The Chinese Repository*. Vol. XIII. Victoria, Hongkong. 1844. p. 119. Accessed 1 June 2017.
141. Geoff Wade. *The Polity of Yelang and the Origins of the Name China*. Ed. Victor H. Mair. Philadelphia: University of Pennsylvania Press. 2009. pp. 7, 10, 18. Accessed 1 June 2017.
142. Joshua A. Fogel. *Between China and Japan*. Leiden: Brill. 2015. p. 25. Accessed 1 June 2017.
143. Kautilya. *Arthashastra*. Trans. R Shamasastry. p. 110. Accessed 1 June 2017.
144. *China Archaeology and Art Digest*. Vol. 4, no. 1-2. Hong Kong: Art Text. 2000. p. 159. Accessed 1 June 2017.
145. Richard P. Aschmann. *The Genesis 10 Table of Nations and Y-Chromosomal DNA*. 10 Nov. 2016. pp. 1-30. Accessed 11 Jun 2018.
146. *The New Strong's Complete Dictionary of Bible Words*, "721."
147. *The New Strong's Complete Dictionary of Bible Words*, "719."
148. Isidore, IX.ii.24.
149. Luckenbill, 296-97, 325, 352-53.
150. Pliny, 5.17.
151. Breasted *Ancient Records of Egypt: From the Earliest Time*, 168, 194, 196-198.
152. Winckler, 180-81.
153. Winckler, 274-75.
154. Winckler, 234-35.

155. *The New Strong's Complete Dictionary of Bible Words*, "6786."
156. *The New Strong's Complete Dictionary of Bible Words*, "6787."
157. Leila Badre. "Tell Kazel-Simyra: A Contribution to a Relative Chronological History in the Eastern Mediterranean during the Late Bronze Age." *Bulletin of the American Schools of Oriental Research*. no. 343. 2006. pp. 65–95.
158. Luckenbill, 3.
159. "Tiglath-Pileser III 46." *ORACC.*
160. Luckenbill, 74.
161. Winckler, 100-03.
162. William M.F. Petrie. *A History of Egypt during the XVIIth and XVIIIth Dynasties*. Vol. II. New York: Charles Scribner's Sons. 1896. pp. 279, 280, 283-85, 292-93.VI vols. Accessed 17 May 2017.
163. Winckler, 112-13, 122-23, 186-87.
164. Winckler, 229, 269, 275.
165. *The New Strong's Complete Dictionary of Bible Words*, "2477."
166. *The New Strong's Complete Dictionary of Bible Words*, "2574."
167. *The Book of Jasher*, 10.33.
168. *The New Strong's Complete Dictionary of Bible Words*, "2575."
169. *The New Strong's Complete Dictionary of Bible Words*, "2576."
170. *The New Strong's Complete Dictionary of Bible Words*, "2579."
171. Trevor Bryce. *The World of the Neo-Hittite Kingdoms: A Political and Military History*. Oxford: Oxford University Press. 2012. p. 129. Accessed 14 Jun. 2018.
172. The University of Haifa. "The history of King David." ScienceDaily. *ScienceDaily*. 15 December 2014. Accessed 14 Jun 2018.
173. *The New Strong's Complete Dictionary of Bible Words*, "2578."
174. Pliny, 5.19.
175. Ross Burns. *Monuments of Syria: A Guide*. London: I. B. Tauris & Co. 2009. p. 162. Accessed 18 May 2017.
176. "HAMA." The Middle East and Africa: International Dictionary of Historic Places. 2014. Accessed 18 May 2017.
177. Pritchard, 278-80.
178. "Tiglath-Pileser III 47." *ORACC.*
179. Luckenbill, 67, 102.
180. Pritchard, 284.
181. Edward Lipinski. *The Aramaeans: Their Ancient History, Culture, Religion*. Louvain: Peeters Publishers. 2000. p. 249. Accessed 18 May 2017.
182. Payne, *Iron Age Hieroglyphic Luwian Inscriptions*, 8.
183. Annick Payne. *Hieroglyphic Luwian: An Introduction with Original Texts*. 2nd ed. Wiesbaden: Harrassowitz Verlag. 2010. p. 53. Accessed 18 May 2017.
184. Payne, *Hieroglyphic Luwian: An Introduction with Original Texts*, 160.
185. Payne, *Hieroglyphic Luwian: An Introduction with Original Texts*, 49.
186. Payne, *Hieroglyphic Luwian: An Introduction with Original Texts*, 54-55.
187. Adrian Room. *Placenames of the World*. Jefferson: McFarland. 1997. p. 148. Accessed 18 May 2017.
188. C.E. Bonechi. *Art and History Syria*. Florence: Casa Editrice Bonechi. 2004. p. 38. Accessed 18 May 2017.
189. *The New Strong's Complete Dictionary of Bible Words*, "7497."
190. *The New Strong's Complete Dictionary of Bible Words* "6062."
191. *The New Strong's Complete Dictionary of Bible Words* "5303."
192. Pritchard, 328-29.
193. Clyde E. Billington. "Goliath and the Exodus Giants: How tall were they?." *Journal of the Evangelical Theological Society*. Sept. 2007. pp. 489-508. tccsa.tc/articles/goliath_and_giants.pdf. Accessed 2 June 2017.
194. James P. Allen. *The Context of Scripture: Archival Documents from the Biblical World*. Vol. 3. Ed. W. W. Hallo. Leiden: Brill. 2003. p. 13. Accessed 2 June 2017.
195. Wolfgang Röllig. "EINE NEUE PHOENIZISCHE INSCHRIFT AUS BYBLOS." *Neue Ephemeris für Semitische Epigraphik*. vol. 2. 1974. pp. 1-15. Accessed 2 June 2017.
196. Nicolas Wyatt. Thy Mythic Mind: Essays on cosmology and Religion in Ugaritic and Old Testament Literature. New York: Routledge. 2014. p. 212. Accessed 2 June 2017.

197. Wilfred G.E. Watson "He Unfurrowed His Brow and Laughed": Essays in Honour of Professor Nicolas Wyatt. Munster: Ugarit-Verlag. 2007. p. 327. Accessed 2 June 2017.
198. K. Lawson Younger, ed. *Ugarit at Seventy-Five*. Winona Lake: Eisenbrauns. 2007. p. 65. Accessed 2 June 2017.

Chapter 21

1. "8035." *The New Strong's Complete Dictionary of Bible Words*. 1996.
2. "Semite." *Online Etymology Dictionary*. 2017. Accessed 7 June 2017.
3. Flavius Josephus. "The Antiquities of the Jews". *The Works of Josephus Complete and Unabridged*. Peabody: Hendrickson Publishers. 1987. 1.6.143-147.
4. "The Book of Jubilees." *The Apocrypha and Pseudepigrapha of the Old Testament in English*. ed. R H. Charles. Oxford: Clarendon Press. 1913. 7.16.
5. *The Book of Jasher*. Salt Lake City: J. H. Parry & Company. 1887. http://www.sacred-texts.com/chr/apo/jasher/. Accessed 25 Jan. 2017. 7.15-18.
6. "The Book of Jubilees," 10.35.
7. "The Book of Jubilees," 8.12-30.
8. Isidore of Seville. *The Etymologies of Isidore of Seville*. trans. Stephen A. Barney, W J. Lewis, J A. Beach, and Oliver Berghof. Cambridge: Cambridge University Press. 2006. IX.ii.3-4.
9. William Camden. Dana F. Sutton, ed. Trans. Philemon Holland. *Britannia*. The Philological Museum. 2004. www.philological.bham.ac.uk/cambrit/. Accessed 27 Jan. 2017.
10. James Anderson. *Royal Genealogies: or, the Genealogical Tables of Emperors, Kings, and Princes from Adam to thefe Times; In Two Parts*. Vol. I. London: James Bettesworth, 1732. II parts. p. 3. Accessed 27 Jan. 2017.
11. Augustine. *The Fathers of the Church: Saint Augustine the City of God*. 1952. trans. Gerald G. Walsh and Grace Monahan, Washington D. C.: The Catholic University of America Press, Inc. 2008. p. 492. Accessed 7 June 2017.
12. Anderson, 2.
13. Sebastian C. Adams. *Adams' Syn Chronological Chart or Map of History*. Chart. 1871. Attic Books. 2013.
14. *The Book of Jasher*, 16.11-12.
15. A. Rosalie David. *The Pyramid Builders of Ancient Egypt*. London & New York: Routledge. 2002. Accessed 19 Apr 2017. 137.
16. James H. Breasted. *Ancient Records of Egypt: From the Earliest Time to the Persian Conquest*. Vol. II. Chicago: The University of Chicago Press. 1906. p. 292-93. Accessed 7 Jun 2017.
17. Breasted, 122.

Chapter 22

1. "5867." *The New Strong's Complete Dictionary of Bible Words*. 1996.
2. Roger D. Woodard. *The Ancient Languages of Mesopotamia, Egypt and Aksum*. Cambridge: Cambridge University Press. 2008. pp. 47-50. Accessed 9 June 2017.
3. Matthew W. Stolper and Elizabeth Carter. *Elam: Surveys of Political History and Archaeology*. Vol. 25. Berkley: University of California Press. 1984. pp. 3-4. Accessed 9 June 2017.
4. I.E.S. Edwards, C.J. Gadd, and N.G.L Hammond. *The Cambridge Ancient History*. Vol. 1. Cambridge: Cambridge University Press. 1971. p. 644. Accessed 9 June 2017.
5. *"The Epic of Gilgamesh"*. vol. 1. W. W. Norton & Company. 2nd ed. New York: W. W. Norton & Company. 2009. II.
6. Walther Hinz and Jennifer Barnes. *The Lost World of Elam*. London: Sidwick & Jackson. 1972. p. 22. Accessed 9 June 2017.
7. Arthur Mee, J.A. Hammerton, and A.D. Innes, eds. *Harmworth History of the World*. Vol. 3. London: Carmelite House. 1908. pp. 1699-1700. Accessed 9 June 2017.
8. Peter Heylyn. *Cosmographie in Four Books Containing the Chorographie and Historie of the Whole World*. 2nd ed. London: Henry Seile. 1657. pp. 815-16. Accessed 13 June 2017.
9. "The Book of Jubilees." *The Apocrypha and Pseudepigrapha of the Old Testament in English*. ed. R H. Charles. Oxford: Clarendon Press. 1913. 8.21.

10. *The Book of Jasher.* Salt Lake City: J. H. Parry & Company. 1887. http://www.sacred-texts.com/chr/apo/jasher/. Accessed 25 Jan. 2017. 7.15.
11. Isidore of Seville. *The Etymologies of Isidore of Seville.* Trans. Stephen A. Barney, W J. Lewis, J A. Beach, and Oliver Berghof. Cambridge: Cambridge University Press. 2006. IX.ii.3.
12. Flavius Josephus. "The Antiquities of the Jews". *The Works of Josephus Complete and Unabridged.* Peabody: Hendrickson Publishers. 1987. 1.6.143.
13. D.T. Potts. *The Archaeology of Elam.* Cambridge: Cambridge University Press. 2015. p. 5. Accessed 12 June 2017.
14. "Tiglath-Pileser III 47." *Open Richly Annotated Cuneiform Corpus.* Royal Inscriptions of the Neo-Assyrian Period (RINAP) Project. 2017.
15. "Sennacherib 001." *ORACC.*
16. James B. Pritchard, ed. *Ancient Near Eastern Texts Relating to the Old Testament.* 3rd ed. Princeton: Princeton University Press. 1969. pp. 267, 270. Accessed 26 Apr. 2017.
17. Morris Jastrow Junr. "The Fourteenth Chapter of Genesis and Recent Research." *The Jewish Quarterly Review.* vol. 13, no. 1. 1900. pp. 42–51. *JSTOR.* DOI: 10.2307/1450664.
18. Pritchard, 298, 300.
19. Pritchard, 301-03.
20. John Swinton, John Campbell, George Shelvocke, Archibald Bower, George Psalmanazar, and George Sale. *An Universal History from the Earliest Account of Time.* Vol. V. London: Printed for T. Osborne. 1747. pp. 160-70. Accessed 13 June 2017.
21. John F. Hansman. "Elymais." *Encyclopaedia Iranica.* VIII/4. pp. 373-76. 1998. Accessed 13 June 2017.
22. "Elymais." *A Classical Dictionary of Biography, Mythology and Geography.* 1891. Accessed 13 June 2017.
23. "Elymäis." *Harpers Dictionary of Classical Antiquities.* 1898. Accessed 13 June 2017.
24. Strabo. *Geography.* Trans. H C. Hamilton and W Falconer. London: George Bell & Sons. 1903. Accessed 13 June 2017. 11.13.
25. Strabo, 15.3
26. Strabo, 16.1.
27. Titus Livius. *The History of Rome.* Trans. Evan T. Sage. Cambridge: Harvard University Press. 1935. Accessed 13 June 2017. 35.48.
28. Titus Livius. *The History of Rome.* Trans. William A. McDevitte. Bunga: John Child and son. 1850. Accessed 13 June 2017. 37.40.
29. Plutarch. *Pompey.* Trans. Bernadotte Perrin, Cambridge, Harvard University Press. p. 36. Accessed 13 June 2017.
30. Polybius. *Histories.* Trans. Evelyn S. Shuckburgh. New York: Macmillan Company. 1962. Accessed 13 June 2017. 5.44.
31. Pliny. *The Natural History.* Trans. John Bostock and H T. Riley. London: Taylor and Francis. 1855. Accessed 13 June 2017. 16.28.
32. Cornelius Tacitus. *The Annals.* Trans. Alfred J. Church, William J. Brodribb, and Sara Bryant. New York: Random House, Inc. 1942. Accessed 13 June 2017. 6.44.
33. Ghorbani, Mansour. *The Economic Geology of Iran: Mineral Deposits and Natural Resources.* New York: Springer. 2013. p. 192. Accessed 9 June 2017.
34. A. David Napier. *Masks, Transformation, and Paradox.* Berkley: University of California Press. 1986. p. 131. Accessed 9 June 2017.
35. Joseph S. Exell, ed. "The Patriarchal Times." *The Monthly Interpreter.* vol. IV. no. XX. June 1886. p.475. Accessed 9 June 2017.
36. C.R. Lepsius. *Zeitschrift für ägyptische sprache und altertumskunde.* Leipzig: J.C. Hinrichs'sche Buchhandlung. 1868. p. 116. Accessed 9 June 2017.
37. Theophilus G. Pinches. "On Certain Inscriptions and Records Referring to Babylonia, Elam, and Their Rulers, and other Matters." *Journal of the Transactions of the Victoria Institute.* vol. XXIX. 1866. pp. 45-66. Accessed 9 June 2017.
38. R.W.R. "CHEDORLAOMER." *The Jewish Encyclopedia.* Isidore Singer, ed. Vol. 4. 1903. p. 7. Accessed 10 May 2018.
39. "CHEDORLAOMER." *Eerdmans Dictionary of the Bible.* 2000. p. 232. Accessed 10 May 2018.

40. Herman Vanstiphout. *Epics of Sumerian Kings: The Matter of Aratta*. Atlanta: Society of Biblical Literature. 2003. Writings from the Ancient World 20. p. 61. Accessed 12 June 2017.
41. Prudence O. Harper, Joan Aruz, and Francoise Tallon, eds. *The Royal City of Susa: Ancient Near Eastern Treasures in the Louvre*. New York: The Metropolitan Museum of Art. 1992. pp. 2,7,9,10,123,199,262. Accessed 12 June 2017.
42. Katrien de Graef, and Jan Tavernier, eds. *Susa and Elam. Archaeological, Philosophical, Historical and Geographical Perspectives*. Leiden: Brill. 2012. p. 286. Accessed 12 June 2017.
43. Pritchard, 268.

Chapter 23

1. "804." *The New Strong's Complete Dictionary of Bible Words*. 1996.
2. Flavius Josephus. "The Antiquities of the Jews". *The Works of Josephus Complete and Unabridged*. Peabody: Hendrickson Publishers. 1987. 1.6.143.
3. "The Book of Jubilees." *The Apocrypha and Pseudepigrapha of the Old Testament in English*. ed. R H. Charles. Oxford: Clarendon Press. 1913. 8.21.
4. *The Book of Jasher*. Salt Lake City: J. H. Parry & Company. 1887. http://www.sacred-texts.com/chr/apo/jasher/. Accessed 25 Jan. 2017. 7.16.
5. P. Kyle McCarter. "The Balaam Texts from Deir 'Allā: The First Combination." *Bulletin of the American Schools of Oriental Research*. no. 239. 1980. pp. 49-60. *JSTOR*. doi: 10.2307/1356759. Accessed 14 June 2017.
6. Edward Lipinski. *Studies in Aramaic Inscriptions and Onomastics*. Vol. 2. Leuven: Peeters Publishers. 1994. pp. 110-11. Accessed 14 June 2017.
7. Daniel D. Luckenbill. *Ancient Records of Assyria and Babylonia*. Vol. I. Chicago: University of Chicago Press. 1926. p. 202. Accessed 14 June 2017.
8. Abraham S. Anspacher. *Tiglath Pileser III*. Vol. 5, New York: Columbia University Press. 1912. pp. 5, 10, 16-17. Accessed 20 June 2017.
9. James B. Pritchard, ed. *Ancient Near Eastern Texts Relating to the Old Testament*. 3rd ed. Princeton: Princeton University Press. 1969. p. 272. Accessed 26 Apr. 2017.
10. Sebastian C Adams. *Adams' Syn Chronological Chart or Map of History*. Chart. 1871. Attic Books. 2013.
11. "1 Chronicles 5:26 (KJV) - And the God of Israel." Blue Letter Bible. 20 Jun. 2017.
12. Pritchard, 283-84, 287.
13. Pritchard, 274.
14. Luckenbill, *ARAB*. Vol. I, 287.
15. Luckenbill, *ARAB*. Vol. I, 274.
16. Pritchard, 272.
17. "SHALAMESER." 3. *The Encyclopaedia Britannica*. 11th ed., 1911. Accessed 21 June 2017.
18. "Tiglath-Pileser 46." *Open Richly Annotated Cuneiform Corpus*. Royal Inscriptions of the Neo-Assyrian Period (RINAP) Project. 2017.
19. *ORACC*, "Tiglath-Pileser 2001."
20. *ORACC*, "Shalmaneser V 1."
21. Sarah C. Melville. *The Campaigns of Sargon II, King of Assyria, 721-705 B.C.* Norman: University of Oklahoma Press. 2016. Accessed 21 June 2017.
22. Luckenbill, *ARAB*. Vol. I, 252, 260-61, 280.
23. Pritchard, 274-76.
24. Pritchard, 288.
25. Austen H. Layard. *Discoveries among the Ruins of Nineveh and Babylon*. New York: Harper & Brothers. 1853. pp. 127-29. Accessed 4 May 2018.
26. Pritchard, 290.
27. John Boederman, ed. *The Cambridge Ancient History*. 2nd ed., vol. III, Part 2. Cambridge: Cambridge University Press. 1991. p. 121. Accessed 21 June 2017.
28. Emmet J. Sweeney. *The Ramessides, Medes, and Persians*. New York: Algora Publishing. 2008. Accessed 21 June 2017.
29. Arthur Gibson. *Text and Tablet: Near Eastern Archaeology, the Old Testament and New Possibilities*. Burlington: Ashgate. 2000. p. 240. Accessed 21 June 2017.

30. Pritchard, 289.
31. Daniel D. Luckenbill. *Ancient Records of Assyria and Babylonia*. Vol. II. Chicago: University of Chicago Press. 1927. pp. 200-01, Accessed 14 June 2017.
32. Pritchard, 294.
33. Luckenbill, *ARAB*. Vol. II, 442.
34. *The Tell-El-Amarna Letters*. Trans. Hugo Winckler. London: Luzac & Co. 1896. p. 29. Accessed 6. Oct. 2017.
35. Pritchard, 305.
36. Luckenbill, *ARAB*. Vol. II, 417.
37. Herodotus. *The Histories*. Cambridge: Harvard University Press. 1920. Accessed 21 Apr. 2017. 2.159.
38. Josephus, 10.5.74-10.6.95.
39. Pritchard, 308.
40. Pritchard, 303-04.
41. Luckenbill, *ARAB*. Vol. I, 41.
42. Luckenbill, *ARAB*. Vol. III, 272, 439.
43. Jean-Jacques Glassner. *Mesopotamian Chronicles*. Translated by Benjamin R. Foster. Leiden: Brill. 2005. p. 137. Accessed 23 June 2017.
44. Eric Orlin. "Assur." *Routledge Encyclopedia of Ancient Mediterranean Religions*. 2015. p. 100. Accessed 23 June 2017.
45. Luckenbill, *ARAB*. Vol. I, 11.
46. Omur Harmansah. *Cities and the Shaping of Memory in the Ancient Near East*. Cambridge: Cambridge University Press. 2013. p. 72. Accessed 23 June 2017.
47. Christopher Johnson. "The Epistolary Literature of the Assyrians and Babylonians." *Journal of the American Oriental Society*. vol. 19. 1898. p. 86. Accessed 23 June 2017.
48. Margaret E. Harkness. *Assyrian Life and History*. London: Religious Tract Society. 1883. p. 12. Accessed 26 June 2017.
49. Luckenbill, *ARAB*. Vol. I, 282.
50. Luckenbill, *ARAB*. Vol. II, 283, 285, 301.
51. Luidi L. Cavalli-Sforza, Paolo Menozzi, and Alberto Piazza. *The History and Geography of Human Genes*. Princeton: Princeton University Press. 1994. p. 243. Accessed 27 June 2017.
52. Carl Skutsch. "Assyrians." *Encyclopedia of the World's Minorities Vol. 1 A-F*. Ed. Martin Ryle. 2005. Accessed 27 June 2017.
53. Joel J. Elias. "The Genetics of Modern Assyrians and their Relationship to Other People of the Middle East." *Atour: Assyrian Information Management*. Atour. 20 July 2000. Accessed 27 June 2017.
54. Robert Rollinger. "The Terms 'Assyria' and 'Syria' Again." *Journal of Near Eastern Studies*. vol. 65, no. 4. 2006. pp. 283–287. *JSTOR*. DOI: 10.1086/511103.
55. Pritchard, 265.
56. Luckenbill, *ARAB*. Vol. I, 55, 257.

Chapter 24

1. "775." *The New Strong's Complete Dictionary of Bible Words*. 1996.
2. "The Book of Jubilees." *The Apocrypha and Pseudepigrapha of the Old Testament in English*. ed. R H. Charles. Oxford: Clarendon Press. 1913. 7.16
3. *The New Strong's Complete Dictionary of Bible Words*, "7973."
4. *The New Strong's Complete Dictionary of Bible Words*, "7974."
5. Peter Edwell. *Between Rome and Persia: the Middle Euphrates, Mesopotamia and Palmyra Under Roman Control*. New York: Routledge. 2007. pp. 74-75. Accessed 28 May 2018.
6. John Bright. *A History of Israel*. Louisville: Westminster John Knox Press. 4th ed. 2000. pp. 77-78. Accessed 28 May 2018.
7. Flavius Josephus. "The Antiquities of the Jews". *The Works of Josephus Complete and Unabridged*. Peabody: Hendrickson Publishers. 1987. 1.6.144.
8. *The Book of Jasher*. Salt Lake City: J. H. Parry & Company. 1887. http://www.sacred-texts.com/chr/apo/jasher/. Accessed 25 Jan. 2017. 7.16

9. "The Book of Jubilees," 8.1-7.
10. "The Book of Jubilees," 8.1.
11. "The Book of Jubilees," 8.8-10.
12. "The Book of Jubilees," 8.2-6, 10.35.
13. "The Book of Jubilees," 11.1-3.
14. "The Book of Jubilees," 9.4-5.
15. *The New Strong's Complete Dictionary of Bible Words*, "3777."
16. *The New Strong's Complete Dictionary of Bible Words*, "3778."
17. *The New Strong's Complete Dictionary of Bible Words*, "3779."
18. Josephus, 1.7.158-160, 1.8.166-168.
19. Biblical References from *The Holy Bible, New International Version:* 2Ki. 25:1-5, 10, 13, & 24-26, 2Ch. 36:17, Jer. 21:4 & 9, 22:25, 24:5, 32:4-43, 33:5, 35:11, 37:5-14, 38:2-23, 39:5-840:9-10).
20. *The New Strong's Complete Dictionary of Bible Words*, "3679."
21. "Tiglath-Pileser III 24." *Open Richly Annotated Cuneiform Corpus*. Royal Inscriptions of the Neo-Assyrian Period (RINAP) Project. 2017.
22. *ORACC*, "Tiglath-Pileser III 47."
23. Robert D. Wilson. *Studies in the Book of Daniel*. New York: G. P Putnam's Sons. 1917. p. 338. Accessed 11 July 2017.
24. *ORACC*, "Tiglath-Pileser 39."
25. A.K. Grayson. *Assyrian and Babylonian Chronicles*. Winona Lake: Eisenbrauns. 2000. pp. 91, 260. Accessed 11 July 2017.
26. Trevor Bryce. *The Routledge Handbook of the People and Places of Ancient Western Asia*. New York: Routledge. 2009. p. 67. Accessed 11 July 2017.
27. Martha A. Morrison, Ernest R. Lacheman, and David I. Owen. *Studies on the Civilizations and Culture of Nuzi and the Hurrians*. Vol. 2. Winona Lake: Eisenbrauns. 1987. p. 226. Accessed 11 July 2017.
28. Martha A. Morrison, Ernest R. Lacheman, and David I. Owen. *Studies on the Civilizations and Culture of Nuzi and the Hurrians*. Vol. 4. Winona Lake: Eisenbrauns. 1993. p. 141. Accessed 11 July 2017.
29. James B. Pritchard, ed. *Ancient Near Eastern Texts Relating to the Old Testament*. 3rd ed. Princeton: Princeton University Press. 1969. p. 309. Accessed 26 Apr. 2017.
30. *ORACC*, "Tiglath-Pileser 2006."
31. H.F. Talbot. *Assyrian Texts Translated*. Vol. 1. Tulsa: Harrison. 1856. p. 5. Accessed 11 July 2017.
32. Samuel Bochart. *Geophraphia Sacra*. Frankfurt Am Main: Johann David Zunner. 1681. p. 83. Accessed 11 July 2017.
33. Peter Heylyn. *Cosmography in Four Books Containing the Chorography and History of the World*. London: P. Chetwind. 1677. p. 8. Accessed 11 July 2017.
34. "ARRHAPACHITIS." *A Dictionary of Greek and Roman geography by Various Writers*. 1872. Accessed 11 July 2017.
35. Isidore of Seville. *The Etymologies of Isidore of Seville*. Trans. Stephen A. Barney, W.J. Lewis, J.A. Beach, and Oliver Berghof. Cambridge: Cambridge University Press. 2006. IX.ii.3.
36. M.E.L. Mallowan and J. Cruikshank Rose. *Prehistoric Assyria the Excavations at Tall Arpachiyah*. Vol. II. London: Oxford University Press. 1935. p. 3. Accessed 13 July 2017.
37. Campbell, Stuart. "The Burnt House at Arpachiyah: A Reexamination." *Bulletin of the American Schools of Oriental Research*. no. 318. May 2000. doi:10.2307/1357725. Accessed 13 July 2017.
38. Isidore Singer. "CHALDEA." 1 & 2. *The Jewish Encyclopedia*. 1901. Accessed 13 July 2017.
39. Dina Katz. *Gilgamesh and Akka*. Leiden: Brill. 1993. p. 18. Accessed 14 July 2017.
40. W. W. Norton & Company. *The Epic of Gilgamesh*. vol. 1. W. W. Norton & Company. 2nd ed. New York: W. W. Norton & Company. 2009. I, XI.
41. H.L. Herman and L.J. Vanstiphout. *Epics of Sumerian Kings: The Matter of Aratta*. Leiden: Brill. 2004. p. 65. Accessed 10 Apr. 2017.
42. Leonard Wooley. *Excavations at Ur*. London: Kegan Paul. 2006. p. 127-8. Accessed 14 July 2017.

43. "Sanliurfa." *International Dictionary of Historic Places: Volume 3 Southern Europe.* 1995. Accessed 21 July 2017.
44. *The Book of Jasher,* 8.1-36.
45. Edward Lipinski. Studies in Aramaic Inscriptions and Onomastics. Vol. 2. Leuven: Peeters Publishers. 1975. p. 172. Accessed 21 July 2017.
46. Anne Habermehl. "Where in the World Is the Tower of Babel?" *Answers Research Journal.* vol. 24. 2011. pp. 25-36. Accessed 18 Sept. 2018.

Chapter 25

1. "5676." *The New Strong's Complete Dictionary of Bible Words.* 1996.
2. *The New Strong's Complete Dictionary of Bible Words,* "5677."
3. *The New Strong's Complete Dictionary of Bible Words,* "5680."
4. Flavius Josephus. "The Antiquities of the Jews". *The Works of Josephus Complete and Unabridged.* Peabody: Hendrickson Publishers. 1987. 1.6.146.
5. Isidore of Seville. *The Etymologies of Isidore of Seville.* Trans. Stephen A. Barney, W J. Lewis, J A. Beach, and Oliver Berghof. Cambridge: Cambridge University Press. 2006. IX.ii.5.
6. Giovanni Pettinato. "The Royal Archives of Tell Mardikh-Ebla." *The Biblical Archaeologist.* vol. 39, no. 2. May 1976. pp. 44-52. doi:10.2307/3209352. Accessed 17 July 2017.
7. K.A. Kitchen. *The Bible in Its World: The Bible and Archaeology Today.* Eugene: Wipf and Stock Publishers. 2004. pp. 42-44. Accessed 17 July 2017.
8. *The New Strong's Complete Dictionary of Bible Words,* "6389."
9. *The New Strong's Complete Dictionary of Bible Words,* "6385."
10. *The Book of Jasher.* Salt Lake City: J. H. Parry & Company. 1887. http://www.sacred-texts.com/chr/apo/jasher/. Accessed 25 Jan. 2017.7.19.
11. "The Book of Jubilees." *The Apocrypha and Pseudepigrapha of the Old Testament in English.* ed. R H. Charles. Oxford: Clarendon Press. 1913. 8.6-8.
12. "The Book of Jubilees," 8.9-11, 10.18-27.
13. Peter Edwell. *Between Rome and Persia: the Middle Euphrates, Mesopotamia and Palmyra Under Roman Control.* New York: Routledge. 2007. pp. 74-75. Accessed 28 May 2018.
14. John Bright. *A History of Israel.* Louisville: Westminster John Knox Press. 4th ed. 2000. pp. 77-78. Accessed 28 May 2018
15. *The New Strong's Complete Dictionary of Bible Words,* "3355."
16. Robert D. Burrowes. *Historical Dictionary of Yemen.* 2nd ed. Plymouth: Rowman & Littlefield. 2010. p. 319. Accessed 4 Apr. 2017.
17. Augustus. *The Deeds of Divine Augustus.* Trans. Thomas Bushnell. The Internet Classics Archive. 1998. p. 26. Accessed 4 Apr. 2017.
18. Kenneth A Kitchen. *On the Reliability of the Old Testament.* Grand Rapids: William B. Eerdmans Publishing Company. 2003. p. 437. Accessed 4 Apr. 2017.
19. Josephus, 1.6.147.
20. Edward Lipinski. *Semitic Languages: Outline of a Comparative Grammar.* 2nd ed., Leuven: Peeters Publishers. 2001. p. 87. Accessed 23 July 2017.
21. *The Book of Jasher,* 7.21.
22. Charles Forster. *The Historical Geography of Arabia.* Vol. 1. London: Duncan and Malcolm. 1844. p. 107. Accessed 31 July 2017.
23. Forster, *HGA* Vol. 1, 126.
24. William Drummond and Thomas J. Matthias. *Origines; or, Remarks on the Origin of Several Empires, States, and Cities.* Vol. III. London: Baldwin and Co. 1826. p. 358. Accessed 3 Aug. 2017.
25. George W. Bury. *Arabia Infelix: or, the Turks in Yamen.* London: Macmillan Company. 1915. pp. 3-4. Accessed 3 Aug. 2017.
26. Johann L. Burckhardt. *Notes on the Bedouins and Wahabys, Collected During His Travels in the East.* Vol. II. London: H. Colburn and R. Bentley. 1831. pp. 46, 296, 325. Accessed 3 Aug. 2017.

27. De Lacy O'Leary. *Arabia Before Muhammad.* 1927. London: Routledge. 2000. p. 18. Accessed 3 Aug. 2017.
28. Josiah C. Nott and George R. Gliddon. *Types of Mankind: Or, Ethnological Researches, Based Upon the Ancient Monuments, Paintings, Sculptures, and Crania of Races, and Upon Their Natural, Geographical, Philological and Biblical History.* Philadelphia: Lippincott, Grambo & Company. 1855. p. 549. Accessed 3 Aug. 2017.
29. "MACORABA." *Dictionary of Greek and Roman Geography.* 1854. Accessed 3 Aug. 2017.
30. Syed Ahmed Khan Bahador. *A Series of Essays on the Life of Mohammed.* Vol. I. London: Trubner & Co., 1870. Accessed 3 Aug. 2017. 30.
31. William R. Cooper. London: Samuel Bagster and Sons. 1876. p. 622. Accessed 3 Aug. 2017.
32. Charles Forster. *The Historical Geography of Arabia.* Vol. 2. London: Duncan and Malcolm. 1844. pp. 255-56. Accessed 9 Aug 2017.
33. "אֲבִימָאֵל." *Gesenius Hebrew Chaldee Lexicon of the Old Testament Scriptures.* 1857. Accessed 9 Aug. 2017.
34. Strabo. *Geography.* Trans. H C. Hamilton and W Falconer. London: George Bell & Sons. 1903. Accessed 9 Aug. 2017. 16.4.
35. Samuel Bochart. *Geophraphia Sacra.* Cadomi: Petri Cardoneli. 1651. pp. 137-38. Accessed 9 Aug. 2017.
36. Pliny. *The Natural History.* Trans. John Bostock and H T. Riley. London: Taylor and Francis. 1855. Accessed 9 Aug. 2017. 6.32.
37. *The New Strong's Complete Dictionary of Bible Words*, "2699."
38. Pliny, 12.30.
39. "CHATRAMOTITAE." *Dictionary of Greek and Roman Geography.* 1854. Accessed 9 Aug 2017.
40. *The New Strong's Complete Dictionary of Bible Words*, "1913."
41. Gesenius, "הֲדוֹרָם."
42. James B. Pritchard, ed. *Ancient Near Eastern Texts Relating to the Old Testament.* 3rd ed. Princeton: Princeton University Press. 1969. p. 299. Accessed 23 July 2017.
43. "hdrmt – Word list occurrences. *CSAI: Corpus of South Arabian Inscriptions.* Accessed 9 Aug 2017.
44. Jan Retso. *The Arabs in Antiquity: Their History from the Assyrians to the Umayyads.* London & New York: Routledge. 2013. p. 537. Accessed 9 Aug. 2017.
45. Josephus, 8.6.163-64.
46. Diodorus. *The Historical Library of Diodorus the Sicilian.* Trans. G. Booth. vol. I. London: W. McDowell. 1814. pp. 141, 158. Accessed 11 Aug. 2017.
47. W.M. Muller. "Egyptological Researches: Results of a Journey in 1906." *Carnegie Institution of Washington.* vol. II. no. 53. 1910. p. 86. Accessed 11 Aug. 2017.
48. Serge Cleuziou, Maurizio Tousi, and Juris Zarins. *Essays on the Late Prehistory of the Arabian Peninsula.* Rome: Istituto Italiano per l'Africa e l'Oriente. 2002. p. 385. Accessed 11 Aug. 2017.
49. *The Book of Adam and Eve.* Trans. S.C. Malan. London: Williams and Norgate. 1882. pp. 174, 189. Accessed 13 Aug. 2017.
50. *The Book of the Cave of Treasures.* Trans. E.A. Wallis Budge. London: The Religious Tract Society. 1927. p. 136. Accessed 13 Aug. 2017.
51. Ted Kaizer. 'Eupolemos(723)'. Brill's New Jacoby.Ed.Ian Worthington (University of Missouri) et al. Brill Reference Online. Accessed 13 Aug. 2017. 8.
52. Gesenius, "אוּזָל."
53. Robert A Wahab. "SANA." *Encyclopaedia Britannica.* Ed. High Chisholm, 11th ed., 1911. Accessed 9 Aug. 2017.
54. Al-Hasan ibn Ahmad al-Hamdani, Nabih A. Faris, and Anistas al-Karmali. *The antiquities of south Arabia, being a translation from the Arabic with linguistic, geographic and historic notes.* Oxford: Oxford University Press. 1938. pp. 8-9, 16, 19. Accessed 9 Aug. 2017.
55. "Al-Salif." *Encyclopedia Britannica.* Accessed 9 Aug. 2017.
56. Sayyid A. Kahn. *The Life of Muhammad and subjects subsidiary thereto.* Lahore: Sang-e-Meel. 2008. p. 47. Accessed 9 Aug. 2017.
57. Bahador, 28.
58. Forster, *HGA* Vol. 1, 110.

59. "DIKLAH." *The Proper Names of the Old Testament Scriptures*. 1856. Accessed 9 Aug. 2017.
60. Gesenius, "דִּקְלָה."
61. *The New Strong's Complete Dictionary of Bible Words*, "5745."
62. *The New Strong's Complete Dictionary of Bible Words*, "5858."
63. Josephus, 1.6.151.
64. *The New Strong's Complete Dictionary of Bible Words*, "2039."
65. *The New Strong's Complete Dictionary of Bible Words*, "2022."
66. *The New Strong's Complete Dictionary of Bible Words*, "2042."
67. *The New Strong's Complete Dictionary of Bible Words*, "2771."
68. *The New Strong's Complete Dictionary of Bible Words*, "2787."
69. "Sanliurfa." *International Dictionary of Historic Places: Volume 3 Southern Europe*. 1995. Accessed 21 July 2017.
70. Edward Lipinski. *Studies in Aramaic Inscriptions and Onomastics*. Vol. 2. Leuven: Peeters Publishers. 1975. p. 172. Accessed 21 July 2017.
71. S.W. Holloway. *Assur is King! Assur is King!: Religion in the Exercise of Power in the Neo-Assyrian Empire*. Leiden: Brill.2002. p. 391. Accessed 21 July 2017.
72. Pritchard, 206, 311-12.
73. *The New Strong's Complete Dictionary of Bible Words* "5152."
74. *The New Strong's Complete Dictionary of Bible Words* "5170."
75. Wilbur L. Cross, ed. *Yale Review*. Vol. II. New Haven: Yale Publishing. 1913. p. 127. Accessed 23 July 2017.
76. Edward Lipinski. *The Arameans: Their Ancient History, Culture, Religion*. Leuven: Peeters Publishers. 2000. p. 65. Accessed 23 July 2017.
77. Wolfgang Heimpel. *Letters to the King of Mari: A New Translation, with Historical Introduction, Notes, and Commentary*. Winona Lake: Eisenbrauns. 2003. pp. xxii-xxiii, 261-62, 310-11. Accessed 23 July 2017.
78. Roland de Vaux. *The Early History of Israel*. Vol. 2. London: Darton, Longman and Todd. 1978. pp. 195-96. Accessed 29 May 2018.
79. *The New Strong's Complete Dictionary of Bible Words*, "763."
80. Pritchard, 29, 234-35, 339-41, 245-47.
81. *The Tell-El-Amarna Letters*. Trans. Hugo Winckler. London: Luzac & Co. 1896. pp. 310-11. Accessed 6. Oct. 2017.
82. *The New Strong's Complete Dictionary of Bible Words*, "6307."
83. Lipinski, *The Arameans*, 73.
84. "The Book of Jubilees," 11.14-15.
85. "The Book of Jubilees," 11.1-10, 12.15-16.
86. *The New Strong's Complete Dictionary of Bible Words*, "3478."
87. Austen Henry Layard. *Discoveries among the ruins of Nineveh and Babylon*. New York: Harper & Brothers. 1853. pp. 128-29. Accessed 4 Jun. 2018.
88. Pritchard, 321-22.
89. *The First and Second Books of the Maccabees*. Trans. J R. Bartlett. Cambridge: Cambridge University Press. 1973. pp. 2-5. Accessed 13 Sept. 2017.
90. Cornelius Tacitus. *The Complete Works of Tacitus*. "The History." 1873. Trans. Alfred J. Church, William J. Brodribb, and Sara Bryant. New York: Random House. Inc. 1942. Accessed 30 Sept. 2017. V.
91. Michael Avi-Yonah, ed. *A History of Israel and the Holy Land*. New York: Continuum. 2003. pp. 278-79, 323-32. Accessed 30 Sept. 2017.
92. A. Edwards Park, and Samuel H. Taylor, eds. *The Bibliotheca Sacra*. Vol. 27. Andover: Warren F. Draper. 1870. p. 629. Accessed 21 Sept. 2017.
93. Anson F Rainey. "Syntax, Hermeneutics and History." *Israel Exploration Journal*. vol. 48, no. 3/4. 1998. pp. 239-51. Accessed 26 Sept. 2017.
94. Avraham Biran and Joseph Naveh. "An Aramaic Stele Fragment from Tel Dan." *Israel Exploration Journal*. vol. 43, no. 2/3. 1993. pp. 81-98. Accessed 26 Sept. 2017.
95. Pritchard, 279.
96. Pritchard, 280-81.
97. Pritchard, 282-84.
98. Pritchard, 287.
99. Pritchard, 288-90.

100. Pritchard, 284, 294.
101. Pritchard, 308.
102. *Ancient Egyptian Literature*. Trans. Miriam Lichtheim. vol. II. Berkley: University of California Press. 1976. Accessed 20 Apr. 2017.
103. Mitchell, Elizabeth. "Doesn't Egyptian Chronology Prove That the Bible is Unreliable?". *The New Answers Book 2*. Ed. Ken Ham. Green Forest: Master Books. 2010. p. 261.
104. Pritchard, 297-300.
105. *The New Strong's Complete Dictionary of Bible Words*. "5032."
106. "SHI'SHAK." *Smith's Dictionary of the Bible*. 1878. Accessed 18 Sept. 2017.
107. Israel Eph'al. *The Ancient Arabs: Nomads on the Borders of the Fertile Crescent 9th-5th Centuries B.C.* Leiden: Brill. 1982. pp.183-84,219,221. Accessed 18 Sept. 2017.
108. Frederick V. Winnett and William L. Reed. *Ancient Records from North Arabia*. Toronto: University of Toronto Press. 1970. pp.31, 99-100. Accessed 18 Sept. 2017.
109. "NEBA'IOTH." *Dr. William Smith's Dictionary of the Bible*. 1888. pp. 2080-82. Accessed 18 Sept. 2017.
110. Gosta W. Ahlstrom. *The History of Ancient Palestine*. Minneapolis: Fortress Press. 1993. p. 905. Accessed 18 Sept. 2017.
111. *The New Strong's Complete Dictionary of Bible Words*, "6938."
112. Pritchard, 19-21.
113. Grant Frame. *Babylonia 689-627: A Political History*. 1992. Istanbul: Nederlands Historisch-Archaeologische Instituut. 2007. pp. 151-52. Accessed 19 Sept. 2017.
114. Oded Lipschitz, Gary N. Knoppers, and Rainer Albertz, eds. *Judah and the Judeans in the Fourth Century B. C. E.* Winona Lake: Eisenbrauns. 2007. pp. 148-49. Accessed 19 Sept. 2017.
115. Pliny, 5.12.
116. Charles B Elliott. *Travels in the Three Great Empires of Austria, Russia, and Turkey.* Vol. II. London: Richard Bentley. 1838. p. 321. Accessed 19 Sept. 2017.
117. Daniel D. Luckenbill. *Ancient Records of Assyria and Babylonia*. Vol. II. Chicago: University of Chicago Press. 1927. pp. 129-30. Accessed 29 Aug 2017.
118. Herodotus. *The Histories*. Trans. A D. Godley. London: Harvard University Press. 1920. Accessed 19 Sept. 2017. 2.8, 2.141.
119. Pritchard, 291.
120. John Boardman, I. E. S. Edwards, N. G. L. Hammond, E Sollberger, and C. B. F. Walker, eds. *The Cambridge Ancient History: The Assyrian and Babylonian Empires and Other States of the Near East, from the Eighth to Sixth Centuries B. C.* 2nd ed., vol. III, part 2. Cambridge: Cambridge University Press. 1992. p. 112. Accessed 19 Sept. 2017.
121. Daniel D. Luckenbill. *Ancient Records of Assyria and Babylonia*. Vol. I. Chicago: University of Chicago Press. 1926. p. 223. Accessed 29 Aug 2017.
122. Pritchard, 279.
123. "Tiglath-Pileser III 35." *Open Richly Annotated Cuneiform Corpus*. Royal Inscriptions of the Neo-Assyrian Period (RINAP) Project. 2017.
124. *ORACC*, "Tiglath-Pileser III 20."
125. Luckenbill, *ARAB* Vol. II, 158, 214.
126. Eph'al, 225.
127. Pritchard, 298.
128. Kenneth A. Kitchen. *Documentation for Ancient Arabia*. Liverpool: Liverpool University Press. 1994. p. 741. Accessed 19 Sept. 2017.
129. Pritchard, 306.
130. "KEDAR, KINGDOM OF." *Routledge Encyclopedia of Ancient Mediterranean Religions*. 507. 2016. Accessed 19 Sept. 2017.
131. Oystein S. LaBianca and Sandra A. Scham, eds. *Connectivity in Antiquity: Globalization as Long-Term Historical Process*. London: Routledge. 2010. p. 81. Accessed 19 Sept. 2017.
132. B. Harris Cowper, ed. *The Journal of Sacred Literature and Biblical Record*. London: Williams and Norgate. 1862. p. 108. Vol. 1. Accessed 19 Sept. 2017.
133. *ORACC*, "Sennacherib 018."
134. *ORACC*, "Tiglath-Pileser III 42."
135. Pritchard, 300, 313.

136. Raymond P. Dougherty. "A Babylonian City in Arabia." *American Journal of Archaeology.* vol. 34, no. 3. Jul.-Sept. 1930. pp. 296-312. doi:10.2307/497985. Accessed 21 Sept. 2017.
137. "Na'phish." *Cyclopaedia of Biblical, Theological, and Ecclesiastical Literature, Vol. VI.* 840. 1894. Accessed 20 Sept. 2017.
138. Strabo, 16.
139. "ITURAEA." *Dictionary of Greek and Roman Geography.* 1854. Accessed 9 Aug 2017.
140. Vergil. *Bucolics, Aeneid, and Georgics of Vergil.* Trans. J B. Greenough. Boston: Ginn & Co. 1900. Accessed 20 Sept. 2017. 2.448.
141. "LEMUEL AND AGUR." *Dictionary of the Old Testament: Wisdom, Poetry & Writings.* 2010. Accessed 18 Sept. 2017.
142. Sarah I. Johnston, ed. *Religions of the Ancient World: A Guide.* Cambridge: Harvard University Press. 2004. pp. 173, 178, 356, 400. Accessed 20 Sept. 2017.
143. Forster, *HGA* Vol. 1, 286-89.
144. Eph'al, 215-16.
145. Edward Curtis and Albert Madsen. *A Critical and Exegetical Commentary on the Books of Chronicles.* Edinburgh: T & T Clark. 1994. p. 72. Accessed 18 Sept. 2017.
146. *The New Strong's Complete Dictionary of Bible Words,* "6924."
147. *The New Strong's Complete Dictionary of Bible Words,* "6929."
148. *The New Strong's Complete Dictionary of Bible Words,* "6932."
149. Josephus, 1.15.238-41.
150. *The Book of Jasher,* 25.6-7.
151. "The Book of Jubilees," 20.12-13.
152. "ZAARAM." *A Classical Dictionary Containing a Copious Account of All the Proper Names Mentioned in Antient Authors.* 1839. Accessed 25 Aug. 2017.
153. Arrowsmith, Aron. *A Compendium of Ancient and Modern Geography.* London: E. Williams. 1831. p. 576. Accessed 25 Aug. 2017.
154. *Gesenius,* "זִמְרָן."
155. S.R. Driver. *The Book of Genesis with Introduction and Notes.* 2nd ed. London: Methuen & Co. 1904. p. 240. Accessed 26 Aug. 2017.
156. Robert G. Hoyland. *Arabia and the Arabs: From the Bronze Age to The Coming of Islam.* London & New York: Routledge. 2001. pp. 66-67. Accessed 25 Aug. 2017.
157. Pritchard, 304.
158. Pritchard, 277-78.
159. Luckenbill, *ARAB* Vol. I, 216-17.
160. Pritchard, 275.
161. George Rawlinson. *The Five Great Monarchies of the Ancient Eastern World.* New York: Dodd, Mead, and Company. 1881. p. 87. Accessed 29 Aug. 2017.
162. Hope W. Hogg. "ANAH." *The Encyclopaedia Britannica.* Ed. Hugh Chisholm, 11th ed. 1911. Accessed 29 Aug. 2017.
163. Luckenbill, *ARAB* Vol. I, 417, 419.
164. *The Book of Jasher,* 62.1-22.
165. "MADYAN SHU'AIB." *E. J. Brill's First Encyclopaedia of Islam, 1913-1936, Vol. V.* 1993. Accessed 28 Aug. 2017.
166. John F. A. Sawyer and David J. A. Clines, eds. *Midian Moab and Edom: The History and Archaeology of Late Bronze and Iron Age Jordan and North-West Arabia.* Sheffield: JSOT Press. 1983. p. 39. Accessed 28 Aug. 2017.
167. James K. Hoffmeier. *Ancient Israel in Sinai.* Oxford: Oxford University Press. 2005. p. 242. Accessed 21 Aug. 2017.
168. Eveline J. Van Der Steen. *Tribes and Territories in Translation.* Leuven: Peeters Publishers. 2004. p. 20. Accessed 21 Aug. 2017.
169. James H. Breasted. *Ancient Records of Egypt.* Chicago: The University of Chicago. 1906. pp. 51, 70-71, 211. Accessed 19 Aug. 2017.
170. Pritchard, 254.
171. Biblical References from *The Holy Bible, New International Version:* Isa. 11:14, 21:11, 34:5-6, 63:1, Jer. 9:26, 25:21, 27:3, 49:7-22, Lam 4:21-22, Ezk. 32:29, 35:1-15, 36:5, Joe. 3:19, Oba. 1:1-21, Mal. 1:2-4.
172. George L. Robinson. "The True Mount Hor." *The Biblical World.* vol. 31, no. 2. Feb. 1908. pp. 86-100. Accessed 19 Aug. 2017.

173. Samuel H. Isaacs. *The True Boundaries of the Holy Land.* 1917. p. 32. Accessed 19 Aug. 2017.
174. Palestine Exploration Fund. *Quarterly Statement.* London: Office of the Fund. 1907. p. 287. Accessed 19 Aug. 2017.
175. Gary D. Pratico and Robert A. DiVito. *Nelson Glueck's 1938-1940 excavations at Tell el-Kheleifeh.* Scholars Press. 1993. pp. 17-20. Accessed 19 Aug. 2017.
176. "Aqaba/Eilat." *Cities of the Middle East and North Africa.* 2007. pp. 41-42. Accessed 19 Aug. 2017.
177. Breasted, 306.
178. *ORACC,* "Tiglath-Pileser III 47."
179. *ORACC,* "Sennacherib 004."
180. *ORACC,* "Esarhaddon 001."
181. *ORACC,* "Udumayu [OF EDOM]."
182. Josephus, 2.1.1-3.
183. Appian. *Mithridatic Wars.* Trans. Horace White. New York: The Macmillan Company. 1899. p. 16. Accessed 21 Aug. 2017.
184. Haggai Mizgav. "Two Notes on the Ostraca from Horvat 'Uza." *Israel Exploration Journal.* vol. 40, no. 2/3. 1990. pp. 215-17. Accessed 21 Aug. 2017.
185. Kyle C. Dunham. *The Pious Sage in Job.* Eugene: Wipf and Stock Publishers. 2016. p. 130. Accessed 24 Aug. 2017.
186. Josephus, 2.1.4-6.
187. *Gesenius,* "תֵּימָנִי."
188. Luckenbill, *ARAB* Vol. I, 111-14.
189. *The New Strong's Complete Dictionary of Bible Words,* "6002."
190. *The New Strong's Complete Dictionary of Bible Words,* "6003."
191. Biblical References from The Holy Bible, New International Version: Ex. 17:8-16, Num. 13:29, 14:25-45, Deut. 25:17-18, Jdg. 5:14, 12:15.
192. B. Routledge. *Moab in the Iron Age: Hegemony, Polity, Archaeology.* Philadelphia: University of Pennsylvania Press. 2004. pp. 44-45. Accessed 2 Sep. 2017.
193. Trevor Bryce. "Iron Age Palestine and Transjordan: main regions". In *Atlas of the Ancient Near East.* New York: Routledge. 2016. p. 177. Accessed 2 Sep. 2017.
194. William L. Reed and Fred V. Winnett. "A Fragment of an Early Moabite Inscription from Kerak." *Bulletin of the American Schools of Oriental Research.* no. 172. Dec. 1963. pp. 1-9, doi:10.2307/1355710. Accessed 3 Sept. 2017.
195. Douglas R. Clark, Larry G. Herr, Oystein S. LaBianca, and Randall W. Younker, eds. *The Madaba Plains Project.* New York: Routledge. 2011. pp. 71, 159-60. Accessed 3 Sep. 2017.
196. Claude R. Conder. *The Survey of Eastern Palestine.* Vol. 1. London: Committee of the Palestine Exploration Fund. 1889. pp. 16, 104, 156, 176, 221, 228, 237, 253. Accessed 3 Sept. 2017.
197. Roland E. Murphy and O. Carm. "A Fragment of an Early Moabite Inscription from Dibon." *Bulletin of the American Schools of Oriental Research.* no. 125. Feb. 1952. pp. 20-23. doi:10.2307/1355936. Accessed 3 Sept. 2017.
198. "Jazer." *Zondervan Illustrated Bible Dictionary.* 2011. Accessed 3 Sept. 2017.
199. *Zondervan Illustrated Bible Dictionary,* "Beth Gamul."
200. Deirdre Dempsey. "An Ostracon from Tell Nimrin." *Bulletin of the American Schools of Oriental Research.* no. 289, Feb. 1993. pp. 55-58. doi:10.2307/1357363. Accessed 3 Sept. 2017.
201. Crystal M. Bennett. "Excavations at Buseirah, Southern Jordan 1972: Preliminary Report." *The Journal of the Council for British Research in the Levant.* vol. 6, no. 1. 1974. pp. 1-24. doi:10.1179. Accessed 3 Sept. 2017.
202. George Armstrong. *Names and Places in the Old and New Testament Apocrypha.* 2nd ed. London: Committee of the Palestine Exploration Fund. 1895. pp. 90, 112. Accessed 4 Sept. 2017.
203. Luckenbill, *ARAB* Vol. I, 282.
204. Luckenbill, *ARAB* Vol. I, 301.
205. Luckenbill, *ARAB* Vol. I, 287, 291.
206. Carolyn R. Higginbotham. *Egyptianization and Elite Emulation in Ramesside Palestine.* Leiden: Brill. 2000. p. 31. Accessed 5 Sept. 2017.
207. "Amman." *Cities of the Middle East and North Africa.* 2007. Accessed 7 Sept. 2017.

208. Pliny, 5.16.
209. Conder, 19.
210. Alan H. Simmons, Ilse Köhler-Rollefson, Gary O. Rollefson, Rolfe Mandel, and Zeidan Kafafi. "'Ain Ghazal: A Major Neolithic Settlement in Central Jordan." *Science.* vol. 240, no. 4848. 1 Apr. 1988. pp. 35-39. Accessed 7 Sept. 2017.
211. Abdulla Al-Shorman and Ali Khwaileh. "Burial Practices in Jordan from the Natufians to the Persians." *Estonian Journal of Archaeology.* vol. 15, no. 2. 2011. pp. 88-108. doi:10.3176/arch.2011.2.02. Accessed 9 Sept. 2017.
212. Shanks, Hershel. "First Person: Human Sacrifice to an Ammonite God?" *Biblical Archaeology Review.* 23 Sept. 2014. https://www.biblicalarchaeology.org/daily/ancient-cultures/daily-life-and-practice/first-person-human-sacrifice-to-an-ammonite-god/. Accessed 9 Sept. 2017.
213. Josephus, 4.5.96-99.
214. *Gesenius*, "יַבֹּק."
215. *The New Strong's Complete Dictionary of Bible Words.* "1151."
216. Frank M. Cross. "Ammonite Ostraca from Heshbon: Heshbon Ostraca IV-VIII." *Andrews University:* Harvard University. 1 Jan. 1975. p. 6, 11. https://www.andrews.edu/library/car/cardigital/Periodicals/AUSS/1975-1/1975-1-01.pdf. Accessed 11 Sept. 2017.
217. Daniel Block. "Bny 'mwn: THE SONS OF AMMON." *Andrews University Seminary Studies.* vol. 22, no. 2. 1984. pp. 197-212. Accessed 11 Sept. 2017.
218. Pritchard, 301.
219. *The First and Second Books of the Maccabees*, 68-69.
220. Burton MacDonald and Randall W. Younker, eds. *Ancient Ammon.* Leiden: Brill. 1999. pp. 233-34. Accessed 13 Sept. 2017.
221. Oded Lipschitz. *Ammon in Transition from Vassal Kingdom to Babylonian Province.* Tel Aviv: Tel Aviv University. 2003. pp. 38-39. Accessed 13 Sept. 2017.
222. Josephus, 13.13.374-75.
223. B Maisler. "Two Hebrew Ostraca from Tell Qasile." *Journal of Near Eastern Studies.* vol. 10, no. 4. Oct. 1951. pp. 265-67. JSTOR. Accessed 13 Aug. 2017.
224. Craig W. Tyson *The Ammonites: Elites, Empires, and Sociopolitical Change (1000-500 BCE).* New York: Bloomsbury. 2015. pp. 92-94. Accessed 5 Mar. 2019

Chapter 26

1. "3685." *The New Strong's Complete Dictionary of Bible Words.* 1996.
2. Flavius Josephus. "The Antiquities of the Jews". *The Works of Josephus Complete and Unabridged.* Peabody, Hendrickson Publishers. 1987. 1.6.144.
3. *The Book of Jasher.* Salt Lake City: J. H. Parry & Company. 1887. http://www.sacred-texts.com/chr/apo/jasher/. Accessed 25 Jan. 2017. 7.17.
4. Daniel D. Luckenbill. *Ancient Records of Assyria and Babylonia.* Vol. I. Chicago: University of Chicago Press. p. 202. 1926. Accessed 14 June 2017.
5. "The Book of Jubilees." *The Apocrypha and Pseudepigrapha of the Old Testament in English.* ed. R H. Charles. Oxford: Clarendon Press. 1913. 9.6-8.
6. Isidore of Seville. *The Etymologies of Isidore of Seville.* Trans. Stephen A. Barney, W J. Lewis, J A. Beach, and Oliver Berghof. Cambridge: Cambridge University Press. 2006. IX.ii.3.
7. George M. A. Hanfmann. *Sardis from prehistoric Roman Times.* Cambridge: Harvard University Press. 1983. p. 89. Accessed 15 July 2017.
8. Georges Perrot and Charles Chipiez. *History of Art in Phrygia, Lydia, Caria, and Lycia.* London: Chapman and Hall. p. 235. 1892. Accessed 15 July 2017.
9. Herodotus. *The Histories.* trans. A D. Godley. Cambridge: Harvard University Press. 1920. Accessed 15 July 2017. 7.74.
10. Strabo. *The Geography of Strabo.* Translated by H C. Hamilton and W Falconer. London: George Bell & Sons. 1903. Accessed 15 July 2017. 13.
11. D. G. Lyon. *Beginner's Assyrian.* New York: Hippocrene Books. 1998. p. 22. Accessed 15 July 2017.
12. Albert K. Grayson. *Assyrian and Babylonian Chronicles.* Winona Lake: Eisenbrauns. 2000. p. 104. Accessed 15 July 2017.

13. James B. Pritchard, ed. *Ancient Near Eastern Texts Relating to the Old Testament.* 3rd ed. Princeton: Princeton University Press. 1969. pp. 206, 308. Accessed 15 Jul. 2017.
14. Pliny. *The Natural History.* trans. John Bostock and H T. Riley. London: Taylor and Francis. 1855. Accessed 15 July 2017. 5.30.
15. Strabo, 14.1.
16. "Lydia." *Harpers Dictionary of Classical Antiquities.* 1898. Accessed 15 July 2017.
17. Stephanus of Byzantium. *Stephanus de Urbibus. Que Primus Thomas de Pinedo.* Amsterdam: Rod & Gerh Wetstenios. 1725. p. 417. Accessed 15 July 2017.

Chapter 27

1. "758." *The New Strong's Complete Dictionary of Bible Words.* 1996.
2. *The New Strong's Complete Dictionary of Bible Words,* "761."
3. *The New Strong's Complete Dictionary of Bible Words,* "763."
4. *The New Strong's Complete Dictionary of Bible Words,* "6307."
5. James B. Pritchard, ed. *Ancient Near Eastern Texts Relating to the Old Testament.* 3rd ed. Princeton: Princeton University Press. 1969. pp.29, 234-35, 339-41,245-47. Accessed 23 July 2017.
6. *The Tell-El-Amarna Letters.* Trans. Hugo Winckler. London: Luzac & Co. 1896. pp. 310-11. Accessed 6. Oct. 2017.
7. *The Book of Jasher.* Salt Lake City: J.H. Parry & Company. 1887. http://www.sacred-texts.com/chr/apo/jasher/.Accessed 25 Jan. 2017.7.17,10.31-34.
8. "The Book of Jubilees." *The Apocrypha and Pseudepigrapha of the Old Testament in English.* ed. R H. Charles. Oxford: Clarendon Press. 1913.9.5.
9. Flavius Josephus. "The Antiquities of the Jews". *The Works of Josephus Complete and Unabridged.* Peabody: Hendrickson Publishers. 1987. 1.6.143-45.
10. Cyrus H. Gordon and Gary Rendsburg. *Eblaitica.* Vol. 4. Winona Lake: Eisenbrauns, 2002. p. 66. Accessed 1 Oct. 2017.
11. Edward Lipinski. *The Arameans: Their Ancient History, Culture, Religion.* Leuven: Peeters Publishers. 2000. p. 26. Accessed 1 Oct. 2017.
12. Lipinski, 32.
13. Lipinski, 27.
14. Lloyd E. Cotsen. *Urkesh and the Hurrians.* Malibu: Undena Publications. 1998. p. 93. Accessed 1 Oct. 2017.
15. Pritchard, 268.
16. Albrecht Goetze. "An Inscription of Simbar-šīḫu." *Journal of Cuneiform Studies.* vol. 19, no. 4. 1965. pp. 121-35, doi:10.2307/1359115. Accessed 10 Oct. 2017.
17. *The Tell-El-Amarna Letters,* 260,262.
18. K. Lawson Younger Jr. *A Political History of the Arameans: Their Origins to the End of Their Politics.* Atalanta: SBL Press. 2016. pp. 35-37. Accessed 11 Oct. 2017.
19. "Tiglath-Pileser III 35." *Open Richly Annotated Cuneiform Corpus.* Royal Inscriptions of the Neo-Assyrian Period (RINAP) Project. 2017.
20. *ORACC,* "Tiglath-Pileser III 39."
21. Daniel D. Luckenbill. *Ancient Records of Assyria and Babylonia.* Vol. I. Chicago: University of Chicago Press. 1926. p. 278. Accessed 29 Aug 2017.
22. Lipinski, 249.
23. *ORACC,* "Tiglath-Pileser III 14."
24. Lipinski, 400.
25. Luckenbill *ARAB* Vol. I, 40.
26. Luckenbill *ARAB* Vol. I, 83, 99.
27. Pritchard, 275.
28. H. Tadmor. "The Southern Border of Aram." *Israel Exploration Journal.* vol. 12, no. 2. 1962. pp. 114-22. Accessed 6 Oct. 2017.
29. Luckenbill *ARAB* Vol. I, 111-12.
30. Luckenbill *ARAB* Vol. I, 181-82.
31. Luckenbill *ARAB* Vol. I, 203-04, 223.
32. Pritchard, 278-79.
33. Luckenbill *ARAB* Vol. I, 202.

34. John Boardman, I. E. S. Edwards, N. G. L. Hammond, and E Sollberger, eds. *The Cambridge Ancient History: The Prehistory of the Balkans; The Middle East and the Aegean World, Tenth to Eighth Centuries B.C.* 2nd ed., vol. III. Cambridge: Cambridge University Press. 1982. p. 335. Accessed 6 Oct. 2017.
35. Emil G. H. Kraeling. *Aram and Israel: The Aramaeans in Syria and Mesopotamia.* Eugene: Wipf and Stock Publishers. 2008. p. 46. Accessed 1 Oct. 2017.
36. Robinson, E. "Robinson's Journey in Palestine." *The Journal of Sacred Literature.* vol. 5, no. IX. Oct. 1853. p. 46-47. Accessed 1 Oct. 2017.
37. Luckenbill *ARAB* Vol. I, 205-06.
38. Avraham Biran and Joseph Naveh. "An Aramaic Stele Fragment from Tel Dan." *Israel Exploration Journal.* vol. 43, no. 2/3. 1993. pp. 81-98. Accessed 26 Sept. 2017.
39. Luckenbill *ARAB* Vol. I, 261, 263.
40. *ORACC,* "Tiglath-Pileser III 32."
41. Pritchard, 283.
42. Luckenbill *ARAB* Vol. I, 280.
43. Luckenbill *ARAB* Vol. I, 269.
44. *ORACC,* "Tiglath-Pileser III 20."
45. Luckenbill *ARAB* Vol. I, 279.
46. Daniel D Luckenbill. *Ancient Records of Assyria and Babylonia.* Vol. II. Chicago: University of Chicago Press. 1927. p. 36. Accessed 29 Aug 2017.
47. Luckenbill *ARAB* Vol. II, 41.
48. Josephus, 18.1.1.
49. Strabo. *Geography.* Trans. H C. Hamilton and W Falconer. London: George Bell & Sons. 1903. Accessed 10 Oct. 2017. 12.6.
50. Philip Schaff. *Theological Propaedeutic: A General Introduction to the Study of Theology.* Eugene: Wipf and Stock Publishers. 2007. p. 108. Accessed 10 Oct. 2017.
51. Bezalel Porten. *The Elephantine Papyri in English: Three Millennia of Cross-Cultural Continuity and Change.* Leiden: Brill. 1996. Accessed 10 Oct. 2017. pp. 74-276.
52. George V. Yana. *Ancient and Modern Assyrians: A Scientific Analysis.* Xlibris Corporation. 2008. p.87. Accessed 10 Oct. 2017.
53. Herodotus. *The Histories.* Trans. A D. Godley. Cambridge: Harvard University Press. 1920. Accessed 10 Oct. 2017. 7.63.
54. "Syria." *The Online Etymology Dictionary.* 2017. Accessed 10 Oct. 2017.
55. Klaus Beyer. *The Aramaic Language, Its Distribution and Subdivisions.* Trans. John F. Healey. Gottingen: Vandenhoeck & Ruprecht. 1986. pp.53-54. Accessed 10 Oct. 2017.
56. Anthony O'Mahony and Emma Loosley, editors. *Eastern Christianity in the Modern Middle East.* London: Routledge. 2009. p. 13. Accessed 10 Oct. 2017.
57. "Israeli Christians Officially Recognized as Arameans, Not Arabs." *Israel Today.* 18 Sept. 2014. Accessed 10 Oct. 2017.

Chapter 28
1. "5780." *The New Strong's Complete Dictionary of Bible Words.* 1996.
2. *The Book of Jasher.* Salt Lake City: J. H. Parry & Company. 1887. http://www.sacred-texts.com/chr/apo/jasher/. Accessed 25 Jan. 2017. 7.17, 10.33.
3. Flavius Josephus. "The Antiquities of the Jews". *The Works of Josephus Complete and Unabridged.* Peabody: Hendrickson Publishers. 1987. 1.6.145.
4. Geza Vermes. *The Dead Sea Scrolls in English.* 4th ed., Sheffield: Sheffield Academic Press. 1995. p. 127. Accessed 12 Oct. 2017.
5. Charles Forster. *The Historical Geography of Arabia.* Vol. 2. London: Duncan and Malcolm. 1844. p. 60. Accessed 16 Oct 2017.
6. *The Tell-El-Amarna Letters.* Trans. Hugo Winckler. London: Luzac & Co. 1896. pp. 260, 262. Accessed 6. Oct. 2017.
7. Edward Lipinski. *The Arameans: Their Ancient History, Culture, Religion.* Leuven: Peeters Publishers. 2000. p. 249. Accessed 1 Oct. 2017.
8. "Tiglath-Pileser III 14." *Open Richly Annotated Cuneiform Corpus.* Royal Inscriptions of the Neo-Assyrian Period (RINAP) Project. 2017.
9. Josias L. Porter. *The Giant Cities of Bashan: And Syria's Holy Places.* New York: T. Nelson and Sons. 1867. pp. 15, 24, 93. Accessed 12 Oct. 2017.

10. *The New Strong's Complete Dictionary of Bible Words*, "709."
11. *The New Strong's Complete Dictionary of Bible Words*, "5139."
12. Strabo. *Geography*. Trans. H C. Hamilton and W Falconer. London: George Bell & Sons. 1903. Accessed 12 Oct. 2017. 16.2.16, 20.
13. Isidore of Seville. *The Etymologies of Isidore of Seville*. Trans. Stephen A. Barney, W J. Lewis, J A. Beach, and Oliver Berghof. Cambridge: Cambridge University Press. 2006. IX.ii.4.
14. H.A.R. Gibb. "Ladja." *The Encyclopaedia of Islam*. Ed. C.E. Bosworth. 1954. p. 593. Accessed 12 Oct. 2017.
15. *The New Strong's Complete Dictionary of Bible Words*, "347."
16. *The New Strong's Complete Dictionary of Bible Words*, "3103."
17. *The New Strong's Complete Dictionary of Bible Words*, "2343."
18. "The Book of Jubilees." *The Apocrypha and Pseudepigrapha of the Old Testament in English*. ed. R H. Charles. Oxford: Clarendon Press. 1913. 9.5-6.
19. James Anderson. *Royal Genealogies: or, the Genealogical Tables of Emperors, Kings, and Princes from Adam to thefe Times; In Two Parts*. Vol. I. London: James Bettesworth. 1732. pp. 3-4. II parts. Accessed 27 Jan. 2017.
20. Movses Khorenatsi. *History of Armenia*. Trans. G. Sargsyan. Hayastan. 1990. www.vehi.net/istoriya/armenia/khorenaci/index.html. Accessed 16 Oct. 2017. 1.5.
21. Symon. *A Commentary upon the First Book of Moses, called Genesis*. London: R. Chiswell. 1695. p.207. Accessed 16 Oct. 2017.
22. Edward Wells. *Sacred Geography of A Companion to the Holy Bible*. Charlestown: Samuel Ethridge. 1817. p. 26. Accessed 16 Oct. 2017.
23. Thomas T. Smiley. *Scripture Geography*. Philadelphia: John C. Clark. 1835. p. 22. Accessed 16 Oct. 2017.
24. Mavor, William F. *Universal History Ancient and Modern from the Earliest Records of Time to the General Peace of 1801*. Vol. I. London: Richard Philips. 1802. p. 135. XXV vols. Accessed 16 Oct. 2017.
25. *The New Strong's Complete Dictionary of Bible Words*, "1666."
26. Anson F. Rainey. *Canaanite in the Amarna Tablets: A Linguistic Dialect Used by Scribes from Canaan*. Vol. 2. Leiden: Brill. 1996. p. 128. Accessed 16 Oct. 2017.
27. Rami Arav and Richard A. Freund. *Bethsaida: A City by the North Shore of the Sea of Galilee*. Vol. 3. Kirksville: Truman State University Press. 2004. pp. 3-4. Accessed 16 Oct. 2017.
28. K. Lawson Younger Jr. *A Political History of the Arameans: Their Origins to the End of Their Politics*. Atlanta: SBL Press. 2016. pp. 212-13. Accessed 16 Oct. 2017.
29. Nadav Na'aman. "The Kingdom of Geshur in History and Memory." *Scandinavian Journal of the Old Testament*. vol.26, no.1. 2012. pp.88-101. Accessed 16 Oct.2017.
30. Arav and Freund, 12-13.
31. Yigal Kipnis. *The Golan Heights: Political History, Settlement and geography since 1949*. London: Routledge. 2013. pp. 136, 145. Accessed 16 Oct. 2017.
32. *The New Strong's Complete Dictionary of Bible Words*, "4851."
33. Luckenbill, Daniel D. *Ancient Records of Assyria and Babylonia*. Vol. I. Chicago: University of Chicago Press. 1926. p. 130. Accessed 18 Oct 2017.
34. Strabo, 11.
35. "גשם." *A Hebrew Lexicon to the Books of the Old Testament: Including the Geographical Names and Chaldaic Words in Daniel, Ezra, &c*. 1828. Accessed 18 Oct. 2017.
36. Parkin, William. *A Genealogical, Chronological, Historical and Topographical Exposition of the Tenth Chapter of Genesis*. Vol. I. Sheffield: Saxton & Chaloner. 1837. p. 189. II vols. Accessed 18 Oct. 2017.
37. *The Epic of Gilgamesh: The Babylonian Epic Poem and Other Texts in Akkadian and Sumerian*. Translated by Andrew George. London: Penguin Books. 1999. p. 71. Accessed 18 Oct. 2017.
38. Sémhur. *Carte physique vierge du Proche-Orient*. 17 Aug 2008. Accessed 5 May 2018.

Chapter 29

1. "The Book of Jubilees." *The Apocrypha and Pseudepigrapha of the Old Testament in English*. ed. R H. Charles. Oxford: Clarendon Press. 1913. 10.18-27.

2. *The Book of Jasher*. Salt Lake City: J. H. Parry & Company. 1887. http://www.sacred-texts.com/chr/apo/jasher/. Accessed 25 Jan. 2017. 9.20-10.4.
3. Flavius Josephus. "The Antiquities of the Jews". *The Works of Josephus Complete and Unabridged*. Peabody: Hendrickson Publishers. 1987. 1.4.109-117.
4. Josephus, 1.4.118.
5. Samuel N. Kramer. "The "Babel of Tongues": A Sumerian Version." *Journal of the American Oriental Society*. vol. 88, no. 1, Jan.-Mar. 1968. pp. 108-11. Accessed 9 Nov. 2017.
6. "Etemenaki." *Routledge Encyclopedia of Ancient Mediterranean Religions*. 2016. Accessed 11 Nov. 2017.
7. Henry C. Rawlinson. "On the Birs Nimrud, or the Great Temple of Borsippa." *Journal of the Royal Asiatic Society of Great Britain and Ireland*. vol. 18. 1861. pp. 27-31. Accessed 25 June 2018.
8. Benjamin R. Foster. *Before the Muses: An Anthology of Akkadian Literature*. Vol. 1, 2nd Ed. Bethsaida: CDL Press. 1996. pp. 384-85.
9. Jacob Klein. *Three Sugli Hymns: Sumerian Royal Hymns Glorifying King Sugli of Ur*. Ramat Gan: Bar-Ilan University Press. 1981. pp. 128, 162, 239. Accessed 11 Nov. 2017.
10. George Smith. *Assyrian Discoveries: An Account of Explorations and Discoveries on the Site of Nineveh, During 1873 and 1874*. New York: Scribner. Armstrong & Co., 1875. p. 59. Accessed 4 Jan. 2018.
11. George Smith. "Assyria Discoveries." *The London Quarterly Review*. vol. 49. Jan. 1878. pp. 275-76. Accessed 11 Jan. 2018.
12. *The Book of Adam and Eve*. Translated by Solomon C. Malan. London: Williams and Norgate. 1882. pp. 177-78. Accessed 11 Nov. 2017.
13. Juansher Juansheriani. *Concise History of the Georgians* or *The Kingdom of Abkhazia*. Trans. Robert Bedrosian. 1991. www.conflicts.rem33.com/images/ Georgia /KArtlis%20Tskhovreba.htm. Accessed 27 Jan. 2017. 1.1-5.
14. Kevork Bardakjian, and Sergio La Porta. *The Armenian Apocalyptic Tradition: A Comparative Perspective*. Leiden: Brill. 2014. p. 193. Accessed 11 Nov. 2017.
15. *Apollodorus' Library and Hyginus' Fabulae: Two Handbooks of Greek Mythology*. Trans. R. Scott Smith and Stephen M. Trzaskoma. Indianapolis: Hackett Publishing Company, Inc. 2007. p. 147. Accessed 11 Nov. 2017.
16. Deborah L. Gera. *Ancient Greek Ideas on Speech, Language and Civilization*. Oxford: Oxford University Press. 2003. p. 118. Accessed 11 Nov. 2017.
17. Herodotus. *The History of Herodotus*. Trans. George Rawlinson vol. 1. London: J. Murray. 1862. 4 vols. 254-55.
18. William Camden. *Britannia*. Dana F. Sutton, ed. Trans. Philemon Holland. The Philological Museum. 2004. www.philological.bham.ac.uk/cambrit/. Accessed 27 Jan. 2017. 17.
19. *Lebor Gabala Erenn: The Book of the Taking of Ireland*. Trans. R. A. Stewart Macalister. Dublin: Irish Texts Society. 1938. pp. 35-39. Accessed 13 Nov. 2017.
20. *Auraicept Na n-Eces: The Scholars' Primer*. Trans. George Calder. Edinburgh: John Grant. 1917. pp. 2-13. Accessed 13 Nov. 2017.
21. Alexandra J. Cutcher. *Displacement, Identity and Belonging: An Arts-Based, Auto/Biographical Portrayal of Ethnicity and Experience*. Rotterdam: Sense Publishers. 2015. pp. xviii-xxii. Accessed 15 Nov. 2017.
22. Henry Tyrrell and Henry A. Haukeil. *The History of Russia from the foundation of the empire to the war with Turkey in 1877-'78*. Vol. II. London: The London Printing and Publishing Company. 1879. pp. 338-39. Accessed 15 Nov. 2017.
23. Kristin Kuutma. *Studies in Estonian Folkloristics and Ethnology: A Reader and Reflexive History*. ed. Tiiu Jaago. Tartu: Tartu University Press: 2005. pp. 230-31. Accessed 9 Jan. 2018.
24. Snorri Sturluson. *The Prose Edda*. Translated by Arthur G. Brodeur. New York: The American-Scandinavian Foundation. 1916. p. 21. Accessed 21 Dec. 2017.
25. Kathleen N. Daly. "Humans." *Norse Mythology A to Z*. Ed. Marian Rengel. 3rd ed., 2010. p. 52. Accessed 21 Dec. 2017.
26. A.L. Kroeber. "Indian Myths of South Central California." *University of California Publications American Archaeology and Ethnology*. vol. 4, no. 4. May 1907. pp. 173. Accessed 4 Jan. 2018.

27. Kroeber, 184-85.
28. F.A. Golder. "Tlingit Myths." *The Journal of American Folklore*. vol. 20, no. 79, Oct.-Dec. 1907. pp. 290-95. doi:10.2307/534478. JSTOR. Accessed 5 Jan. 2018.
29. Marian K. Gould, James A. Tiet, Livingston Farrand, and Herbert J. Spinden. *Folk-Tales of Salishan and Sahaptin Tribes*. New York: The American Folk-Lore Society. 1917. pp. 111-12. Accessed 5 Jan. 2018.
30. Clark Wissler and D.C. Devall. "Mythology of the Blackfoot Indians." *Anthropological Papers of the American Museum of Natural History*. vol.II,pt.I.New York: Order of the Trustees.1909. pp.19-21.Accessed 21 June 2018.
31. Elias Johnson. *Legends, Traditions and Laws, of the Iroquois, or Six Nations, and History of the Tuscarora Indians*. Lockport: Union Printing and Publishing. 1881. pp. 40-43. Accessed 5 Jan. 2018.
32. David I. Bushnell. "Myths of the Louisiana Choctaw." *American Anthropologist*. vol. 12, no. 4, Oct.-Dec. 1910. pp. 526-35. *JSTOR*. Accessed 8 Jan. 2018.
33. Richard Erdoes and Alfonso Ortiz, eds. *American Indian Myths and Legends*. New York: Pantheon Books. 2013. pp. 487-89. Accessed 8 Jan. 2018
34. John T. Short. *The North Americans of Antiquity*. 2nd ed. New York: Harper & Brothers. 1880. p. 214-15. Accessed 8 Jan. 2018.
35. Louis E. Hills. *Historical Data from Ancient Records and Ruins of Mexico and Central America*. Independence: Louis. E. Hills. 1919. p. 7. Accessed 8 Jan. 2018.
36. Albert B. Reagan. *The Sun God, Moccasin Tales: Some flood myths of the Indians*. M. H. Graham printing Company. 1936. p. 32. Accessed 15 Nov. 2017.
37. Susan Hale. *The Story of Mexico*. New York: G. P. Putnam's Sons. 1888. p. 23. Accessed 15 Nov. 2017.
38. James A. Teit. "Kaska Tales." *Journal of America Folklore*. vol. 30, no. 118, Oct.-Dec. 1917. 10.2307/534495. JSTOR. Accessed 15 Nov. 2017.
39. F. Mason. "On the dwellings, works of Art, Laws, &c. of the Karens." *Journal of the Asiatic Society of Bengal*. vol. 37, pt. 2. 1868. pp. 125-71. Accessed 9 Jan. 2018.
40. James G Frazer. *Folk-lore in the Old Testament: Studies in Comparative Religion, legend and Law*. Vol. 1. London: Macmillan and Co. 1919. 3 vols. p. 383. Accessed 11 Nov. 2017.
41. H. Beverley. *Report on the Census of Bengal*. Calcutta: The Bengal Secretariat Press. 1872. p. 160. Accessed 9 Jan. 2018.
42. Edward Stack. ed. Charles Lyall. *The Mikirs: From the Papers of the Late Edward Stack*. London: David Nutt. 1908. pp. 70-72. Accessed 9 Jan. 2018.
43. Andrew D. White. "New Chapters in the Warfare of Science. XI. From Babel to Comparative Philology." *The Popular Science Monthly*. vol. 38, Jan. 1891. p. 292. Accessed 25 June 2018.
44. Frazer, 384-85.
45. David Livingstone. *Missionary Travels and Researches in South Africa*. London: John Murray. 1857. p. 526. Accessed 11 Jan. 2018.
46. Emil Torday. *Camp and Tramp in African Wilds*. London: Seeley, Service & Co., 1913. pp. 242-43. Accessed 11 Jan. 2018.
47. Frazer, 377-78.
48. E.H. Man. "On the Aboriginal Inhabitants of the Andaman Islands (Part II.)." *The Journal of the Anthropological Institute of Great Britain and Ireland*. vol. 12. 1883. pp. 117-75. doi:10.2307/2841953. Accessed 11 Jan. 2018.
49. George Taplin and A. Meyer. *The Native Tribes of South Australia*. Adelaide: E. S. Wigg & Son. 1879, pp. 60, 204-05. Accessed 25 June 2018.
50. Robert W Williamson. *Religious and Cosmis Beliefs of Central Polynesia*. Vol. 1. Cambridge: University of Cambridge Press. 1933. p. 94. 2 vols. Accessed 11 Jan. 2018.

Chapter 30

1. John 3:16-17. *Holy Bible, New King James Version*. Nashville: Thomas Nelson Publishing. 1982. p. 458.

Index

Abimael, 174, 175
Abraham, 7, 83, 84, 98, 106, 114, 115, 123, 125, 127, 128, 130, 131, 132, 146, 147, 150, 165, 166, 167, 168, 169, 171, 172, 173, 177, 178, 179, 180, 181, 183, 189, 197, 203, 207, 244, 245, 255
Adam, xii, 2, 6, 9, 10, 19, 48, 63, 114, 163, 236, 239, 243, 244, 247, 248, 255
Admah, 115, 119
Africa, 74, 75, 76, 104, 110, 114, 139, 169, 176, 237, 238, 255
Ahasuerus, 151
Akkad, 88, 90, 124, 172
Akkadian, 88, 91, 92, 116, 117, 126, 129, 137, 150, 161, 208, 255
Alexander, 49, 56, 122, 151, 255
Almodad, 174
Amalekites, 82, 195, 196
Amel-Marduk, 89, 255
Ammon, 127, 146, 181, 189, 197, 198, 199, 200, 201, 212, 255
Ammonites, 128, 141, 167, 180, 199, 201, 209, 255
Amorites, 74, 89, 113, 123, 125, 126, 127, 128, 129, 137, 140, 162, 191, 209
Anak, 141, 142
Anakites, 123, 141, 142
Anamites, 74, 95
Anatolia, 24, 32, 36, 37, 50, 53, 54, 58, 63, 66, 107, 108, 124, 147, 204
Arabs, 78, 134, 185, 186, 187, 188, 189, 255
Aram, 55, 146, 147, 162, 165, 178, 179, 182, 207, 208, 209, 210, 211, 212, 213, 214, 217, 218, 220, 221, 222, 255
Aram Naharaim, 179, 207, 209
Aramaic, 9, 185, 199, 201, 207, 212, 214, 224, 255
Aramean, 207, 208, 209, 210
Arameans, 9, 124, 167, 195, 207, 208, 209, 210, 211, 214, 217, 220, 255
Ark, 4, 29, 113, 138, 145, 165, 169, 243
Arkites, 74, 113, 132, 136, 137
Armenia, 29, 30, 31, 34, 36, 66, 67, 220, 255
Arphaxad, 9, 89, 145, 146, 147, 149, 161, 162, 165, 166, 167, 168, 169, 171, 180, 197, 245
Artaxerxes, 47, 150, 151
Arvadites, 74, 113, 135
Ashdod, 107, 141, 158, 246
Ashkenaz, 16, 23, 29, 30, 40, 62, 67, 245
Ashurnasirpal, 124, 136, 190
Asia, 5, 7, 17, 30, 35, 37, 40, 67, 72, 79, 114, 134, 135, 236, 238, 255
Asshur, 46, 56, 74, 92, 146, 147, 149, 150, 155, 156, 161, 162, 165, 204, 220, 226, 245
Assyria, 18, 32, 46, 54, 66, 88, 91, 92, 96, 101, 106, 109, 125, 128, 129, 136, 139, 151, 155, 156, 157, 158, 159, 160, 161, 162, 167, 173, 182, 183, 184, 185, 188, 190, 194, 195, 198, 201, 209, 210, 213, 214, 218, 221, 222, 255
Assyrian, 29, 32, 33, 50, 62, 91, 92, 104, 126, 132, 150, 151, 152, 153, 156, 157, 159, 161, 162, 163, 184, 185, 186, 188, 190, 201, 214, 224, 255
Atrahasis, 90
Australia, 8, 135, 238, 255
Babel, xi, 2, 7, 8, 10, 16, 17, 19, 22, 29, 32, 33, 39, 42, 46, 67, 69, 78, 88, 90, 91, 92, 94, 97, 98, 124, 131, 132, 133, 147, 149, 150, 156, 161, 163, 165, 168, 169, 173, 180, 217, 223, 224, 226, 227, 228, 229, 230, 231, 233, 237, 239, 245, 247, 251, 255
Babylon, 7, 9, 46, 78, 87, 88, 89, 90, 91, 93, 94, 101, 102, 110, 129, 139, 150, 151, 155, 156, 158, 161, 162, 167, 169, 173, 185, 186, 187, 188, 189, 204, 208, 213, 228, 229, 231, 236, 255
Babylonian, 46, 89, 91, 110, 126, 139, 150, 156, 160, 167, 168, 194, 201, 208, 213, 255
Belshazzar, 89, 150, 167, 255
Ben-Ammi, 197, 199, 200
Ben-Hadad, 188, 210, 211, 212
Bible, ii, 16, 19, 255
Calah, 92, 93
Camden, 18, 22, 24, 25, 147, 231, 255
Canaan, 9, 73, 74, 75, 77, 106, 107, 113, 114, 115, 116, 117, 119, 121, 122, 123, 124,

125, 126, 127, 128, 130, 131, 132, 133, 134, 135, 136, 138, 140, 141, 146, 148, 150, 181, 183, 192, 209, 213, 255
Cappadocia, 66
Carthage, 255
Casluhites, 74, 95, 106, 107
Celtic, 22, 23, 255
Celts, 22, 23, 24, 25, 26, 54, 63, 71, 72, 255
Chaldea, 147, 166, 167, 168, 169, 218
Chaldeans, 50, 89, 98, 166, 167, 169, 218, 219
China, 9, 134, 135, 255
Christ, iii, xi, xii, xiii, 2, 11, 92, 145, 146, 148, 165, 173, 180, 197, 214, 244, 246, 247, 248
Chul, 208, 220
Crete, 108, 175
Cush, 9, 73, 77, 78, 79, 81, 82, 83, 84, 85, 87, 90, 95, 96, 103, 106, 109, 110, 160, 174, 187, 246
Cushan-Rishathaim, 209
Cushite, 78, 83, 84
Cyrus, 47, 150, 151, 181, 255
Damascus, 91, 137, 138, 157, 188, 198, 207, 208, 209, 210, 211, 212, 213, 214, 217, 218, 219, 221
Daniel, 46, 78, 89, 91, 150, 153, 167, 214, 219, 255
Darius, 46, 47, 150, 151, 255
David, 78, 116, 120, 124, 126, 131, 132, 138, 141, 176, 182, 183, 184, 193, 196, 197, 199, 200, 209, 221, 237, 255
Dead Sea Scrolls, 57, 218, 255
Dedan, 74, 77, 82, 83, 84, 184, 186, 187, 189, 192, 255
Deluge, 58, 78

Diklah, 174, 177
Dodanim, 49, 57, 58, 59
East, 5, 7, 17, 22, 40, 46, 76, 145, 147, 169, 177, 183, 184, 185, 189, 191, 194, 200, 214, 217, 218, 219, 238, 247, 255
Eber, 56, 145, 156, 165, 171, 172, 173
Edom, 84, 93, 120, 171, 181, 190, 191, 192, 193, 194, 195, 217, 218, 219, 255
Edomites, 131, 132, 146, 171, 191, 193, 194, 195, 212, 218
Eglon, 196, 197
Egypt, 7, 9, 55, 61, 74, 75, 76, 78, 79, 82, 91, 92, 95, 96, 97, 98, 99, 100, 101, 102, 103, 104, 105, 106, 107, 109, 110, 115, 116, 121, 124, 125, 126, 129, 130, 133, 136, 137, 139, 142, 148, 158, 159, 160, 162, 166, 167, 180, 183, 184, 185, 189, 190, 191, 193, 194, 195, 196, 199, 203, 208, 236, 255
Egyptians, 7, 58, 71, 75, 95, 96, 97, 99, 100, 102, 104, 106, 107, 110, 114, 116, 117, 124, 134, 137, 139, 148, 160, 176, 179, 208, 209
Elam, 9, 45, 46, 47, 74, 146, 147, 149, 150, 151, 152, 153, 161, 165, 166, 245, 255
Elamite, 150, 153, 224
Elamites, 47, 147, 149, 150, 151, 153, 160
Elishah, 16, 49, 53, 54, 55
Emites, 141
England, 8, 42
Enmerkar, 76, 90, 94, 153, 168, 229
Erech, 90, 168
Esarhaddon, 54, 79, 92, 106, 121, 136, 160, 161, 183, 186, 194, 199, 255

Esau, 115, 123, 130, 131, 146, 178, 179, 180, 181, 183, 184, 192, 193, 195
Esther, 151, 153, 196
Ethiopia, 9, 75, 77, 79, 84, 96, 106
Etruscans, 58, 70, 71, 255
Euphrates, 32, 91, 101, 123, 129, 156, 165, 166, 168, 169, 181, 190, 204, 209, 210, 218, 222, 255
Europe, 5, 7, 9, 16, 17, 21, 22, 23, 24, 25, 26, 30, 31, 32, 35, 39, 40, 41, 46, 63, 65, 66, 67, 70, 71, 152, 169, 238, 255
Eve, 10
Exile, 45, 186
Exodus, 98, 99, 100, 106, 148, 191, 193, 196, 255
Ezekiel, xi, 33, 36, 39, 53, 61, 65, 83, 84, 109, 120, 134, 203, 255
Fertile Crescent, 255
Flood, 3, 4, 5, 29, 67, 79, 88, 91, 146, 224, 227, 229, 255
France, 22, 23
Gath, 107, 141, 212
Gaul, 22, 23, 26, 55, 255
Gaza, 74, 95, 106, 107, 115, 119, 141, 246
Genesis, xi, xii, 1, 2, 3, 10, 15, 18, 22, 49, 58, 87, 88, 90, 91, 95, 96, 98, 102, 115, 132, 152, 179, 193, 219, 226, 232, 248, 255
Georgia, 24, 31, 36, 255
Germanic, 40, 41, 42, 71, 72, 255
Germany, 23, 255
Gether, 41, 207, 208, 220
Giant, 255
Gilgamesh, 90, 153, 168, 222, 255
Girgashites, 74, 113, 129, 130
Gog, xi, 32, 39, 42, 61, 65, 109
Gomer, 9, 15, 16, 17, 21, 22, 23, 24, 25, 26, 29, 31, 32, 33, 35, 36, 39,

42, 45, 55, 63, 218, 220, 226, 230, 245
Gomorrah, 115, 119, 150
Greece, 47, 49, 54, 55, 58, 185, 255
Greek, 16, 18, 33, 39, 45, 48, 50, 56, 57, 58, 71, 79, 102, 104, 121, 122, 135, 176, 213, 255
Hadad, 96, 100, 182, 183, 185, 188, 190, 193, 210, 211, 212
Hadoram, 174, 175
Hagar, 95, 183
Ham, 15, 16, 17, 46, 53, 62, 73, 74, 75, 76, 77, 79, 81, 88, 95, 96, 97, 109, 113, 114, 115, 141, 145, 146, 163, 174, 189, 223, 226, 246, 255
Hamath, 91, 125, 136, 137, 138, 139, 158, 209, 212
Hamathites, 74, 113, 137, 138, 139, 140, 210
Hammurabi, 129, 151, 255
Haran, 166, 177, 178, 180, 197
Harran, 169, 177, 178, 179
Hatshepsut, 100
Havilah, 73, 77, 82, 174, 176, 184
Hayk, 33, 34, 220, 230
Hazarmaveth, 174, 175
Hebrew, 7, 9, 15, 21, 29, 31, 32, 39, 45, 49, 53, 54, 56, 57, 61, 65, 69, 78, 81, 82, 83, 85, 87, 88, 91, 95, 99, 103, 104, 105, 106, 107, 109, 113, 121, 122, 125, 127, 130, 132, 133, 135, 136, 137, 138, 145, 149, 150, 155, 157, 159, 165, 167, 172, 173, 178, 180, 185, 194, 203, 207, 217, 219, 220, 222, 224, 228, 255
Herodotus, 30, 40, 46, 55, 66, 70, 101, 160, 204, 231, 255
Heth, 113, 122, 124

Hezion, 210
Hiram, 120, 176
Hittites, 32, 55, 62, 74, 92, 113, 116, 122, 123, 124, 129, 138, 178, 192, 193, 209, 255
Hivites, 74, 113, 130, 131, 132, 138, 193
Horites, 131, 132, 193
Hul, 207, 218, 220
Iber, 63
Iberia, 23, 55, 62, 63, 66
Iberians, 23, 54, 62, 63
Ice Age, 5, 7, 8, 67, 91, 255
India, 46, 176, 236, 255
Ion, 51
Iran, 35, 46, 47, 152, 153, 255
Iraq, 89, 162, 168, 169
Isaac, 115, 123, 178, 180, 181, 189, 192, 255
Ishbak, 180, 189, 190
Ishmael, 82, 95, 146, 171, 180, 183, 184, 187, 188, 189, 192, 193
Ishmaelites, 95, 98, 171, 181, 183, 184, 186, 188, 189, 190
Israel, xii, 8, 45, 46, 54, 74, 77, 78, 91, 96, 101, 106, 107, 114, 115, 116, 120, 121, 123, 124, 125, 126, 127, 128, 130, 133, 134, 138, 140, 146, 147, 148, 151, 155, 156, 157, 158, 159, 165, 176, 177, 179, 180, 181, 182, 184, 185, 186, 188, 189, 190, 191, 192,194, 196, 197, 198, 199, 200, 201, 208, 209, 210, 211, 212, 213, 214, 221, 226, 244, 246, 255
Israelites, 8, 74, 82, 83, 89, 96, 98, 99, 100, 101, 106, 116, 117, 120, 122, 123, 124, 125, 127, 129, 130, 131, 134, 138, 139, 140, 142, 155, 158, 162, 173, 181, 191,

192, 193, 195, 196, 197, 200, 255
Italy, 57, 58, 59, 62, 70, 71, 122, 255
Jacob, 8, 74, 115, 119, 123, 146, 178, 179, 180, 181, 192, 208, 255
Japheth, 15, 16, 17, 18, 19, 21, 22, 23, 24, 26, 33, 39, 46, 48, 50, 61, 62, 67, 69, 71, 73, 74, 81, 88, 108, 109, 110, 114, 124, 125, 145, 146, 163, 203, 204, 220, 223, 231, 246
Jasher, 16, 29, 31, 32, 34, 35, 36, 39, 50, 62, 75, 93, 105, 115, 130, 132, 133, 135, 136, 139, 146, 153, 156, 173, 174, 177, 189, 204, 208, 217, 220, 227, 228, 255
Javan, 15, 16, 18, 48, 49, 50, 51, 53, 54, 55, 56, 57, 58, 59, 61, 63, 65, 69, 110, 231, 245
Jebus, 125, 126
Jebusites, 74, 113, 123, 125, 126, 131
Jerah, 174, 175
Jerusalem, 2, 47, 101, 125, 126, 127, 131, 150, 151, 212, 214, 245, 246, 255
Jesus, 102, 117, 121, 194, 213, 247, 255
Job, 2, 77, 83, 84, 116, 167, 176, 178, 187, 190, 195, 217, 218, 219, 255
Jobab, 174, 175, 219
Jokshan, 84, 85, 180, 189
Joktan, 73, 82, 83, 146, 165, 171, 172, 173, 174, 190
Jordan, 127, 128, 130, 131, 191, 194, 197, 198, 199, 200, 201, 211, 219, 255
Josephus, 15, 16, 18, 22, 29, 31, 32, 33, 40, 46, 50, 53, 54, 62, 66, 69, 75, 79, 82, 85, 89, 95, 98, 101, 104, 105, 106, 109, 114, 121,

122, 130, 131, 132, 133, 135, 136, 139, 146, 147, 150, 155, 160, 166, 173, 174, 175, 176, 177, 184, 189, 194, 195, 203, 208, 217, 218, 220, 222, 228, 255
Jubilees, 16, 17, 21, 31, 39, 46, 50, 62, 66, 69, 73, 75, 77, 114, 119, 145, 146, 147, 150, 153, 156, 166, 173, 180, 189, 204, 208, 220, 222, 227, 228, 255
Judea, 75, 95, 114, 121, 171
Kasdim, 166, 168
Kedorlaomer, 91, 131
Keturah, 180, 189, 218
King, 78, 83, 89, 90, 91, 101, 120, 121, 125, 129, 133, 138, 140, 151, 157, 160, 176, 182, 186, 196, 198, 232, 247, 255
Kittim, 16, 49, 55, 56, 57, 156
Language, 7, 42, 134, 239, 255
Lasha, 115, 119
Legends, 255
Lehabites, 74, 95
Lot, 146, 148, 150, 166, 171, 172, 177, 180, 181, 197, 199
Lower Egypt, 96, 105
Lud, 50, 103, 146, 147, 203, 204, 245
Ludites, 74, 95
Lydia, 42, 78, 203, 204, 255
Maccabees, 56, 201, 255
Madai, 9, 15, 35, 45, 46, 47, 48, 49, 90, 147, 150, 151, 152, 166, 185, 245
Magog, xi, 15, 25, 39, 40, 41, 42, 62, 63, 65, 70, 109
Mankind, 2, 3, 4, 10, 88, 233, 238, 243, 244, 255
Medan, 180, 189, 190
Medes, 30, 45, 46, 47, 48, 89, 147, 149, 150, 152, 158, 255

Media, 45, 46, 47, 101, 150, 151, 152
Mediterranean, 26, 50, 53, 54, 55, 56, 57, 58, 108, 122, 133, 147, 181, 203, 255
Medo-Persia, 46
Melchizedek, 147
Mesha, 146, 182, 198, 218
Meshech, 15, 39, 61, 62, 63, 65, 66, 67, 185, 222
Mesopotamia, 74, 79, 88, 91, 93, 94, 116, 117, 123, 125, 127, 129, 132, 133, 140, 141, 149, 155, 165, 169, 171, 172, 179, 196, 197, 207, 208, 219, 222, 255
Mexico, 235, 255
Midian, 78, 180, 189, 190, 191, 255
Moab, 120, 127, 128, 146, 156, 181, 182, 189, 190, 191, 194, 196, 197, 198, 199, 255
Moabite, 197, 198, 255
Moabites, 128, 141, 167, 180, 191, 197
Moses, 78, 82, 96, 99, 172, 190, 191, 196, 198, 255
Myths, 18, 255
Nahor, 166, 177, 178, 179, 180, 195, 217
Names, i, 8, 9, 255
Naphtuhites, 74, 95
Nations, i, xii, 6, 7, 8, 66, 226, 243, 255
Native, 255
Nebuchadnezzar, 89, 101, 102, 110, 160, 167, 168, 183, 204, 229, 255
Necho, 101
Neco, 96, 101, 139, 160
Neferbity, 100
Neferhotep, 100
Neriglissar, 89
Nimrod, 9, 74, 75, 77, 78, 81, 87, 88, 89, 90, 91, 92, 93, 94, 155, 161, 167, 168, 228, 230, 231, 232, 236, 255

Nineveh, 92, 93, 109, 155, 160, 161, 168, 186, 255
Noah, xi, 5, 6, 8, 9, 10, 15, 17, 18, 19, 21, 33, 42, 48, 49, 50, 58, 63, 65, 72, 73, 75, 113, 114, 145, 161, 163, 173, 219, 220, 223, 224, 226, 230, 231, 232, 236, 239, 243, 244, 247, 248, 255
North, 67, 74, 234, 236, 247, 255
North America, 67, 234, 236, 255
Norway, 41, 42
Obal, 174, 177
Og, 128, 140, 141, 142, 219, 221
Ophir, 174, 176
Paddan Aram, 179, 207
Parthia, 47, 152
Parthians, 47, 149, 152
Pathrusites, 74, 95
Paul, 2, 22, 57, 121, 205, 214, 246, 255
Peleg, 82, 165, 166, 172, 173, 227, 236
Pentecost, xi, 2, 24, 31, 32, 45, 57, 66, 74, 79, 81, 88, 95, 102, 104, 108, 111, 149, 155, 171, 205, 245
Persia, 45, 46, 47, 49, 65, 91, 110, 114, 150, 151, 152, 255
Persians, 46, 47, 89, 110, 122, 147, 150, 151, 214, 255
pharaoh, 95, 97, 98, 99, 100, 101
Pharaoh, 98, 99, 100, 101, 116, 121, 133, 137, 193, 255
Philista, 106
Philistia, 106, 107, 120, 141, 158
Philistines, 74, 78, 95, 106, 107, 108, 221, 255
Phoenicia, 116, 117, 121, 122, 131, 135, 136, 213, 246, 255
Phoenicians, 55, 113, 116, 117, 119, 120, 121, 122, 131, 133,

134, 135, 136, 137, 138, 255
Phrygia, 32, 255
Pliny, 30, 62, 66, 84, 104, 110, 134, 136, 137, 139, 152, 175, 185, 187, 255
Plutarch, 58, 152, 255
Polybius, 152, 255
Polynesia, 255
Pontus, 30, 255
Portugal, 54
Pul, 156
Put, 73, 78, 103, 104, 105, 109, 110, 114, 245
Queen, 186, 255
Raamah, 73, 77, 81, 83, 84
Rabbah, 200
Rehoboth Ir, 92, 93, 155
Rephaites, 140, 141, 142, 219
Resen, 92, 93, 155
Rezin, 209, 212
Rezon, 210
Riphath, 16, 31, 32
Rodanim, 16, 49, 57
Romans, 18, 23, 41, 54, 57, 58, 70, 83, 132, 151, 182, 194, 246
Rome, 152, 213, 255
Russia, 30, 32, 34, 41, 43, 66, 67, 232, 255
Sabtah, 73, 77, 82, 85
Sabteca, 73, 77, 85
Salem, 148
Salvation, xii, 245, 248
Sanliurfa, 169, 255
Sargon, 32, 66, 89, 92, 107, 125, 136, 137, 139, 151, 158, 159, 160, 182, 199, 213, 255
Saudi Arabia, 78, 184, 189, 191
Saxons, 42
Scandinavia, 41, 42, 67
Scripture, xii, 1, 3, 9, 10, 15, 16, 17, 19, 32, 42, 45, 46, 47, 49, 50, 53, 54, 56, 57, 58, 61, 62, 65, 69, 72, 73, 74, 75, 76, 77, 79, 81, 82, 83, 84, 85, 87, 88, 89, 90, 91, 92, 93, 95, 96, 97, 98, 99, 100, 101, 103, 105, 106, 107, 113, 114, 115, 116, 119, 120, 121, 123, 124, 126, 127, 128, 130, 131, 133, 134, 135, 136, 137, 138, 140, 142, 145, 146, 148, 149, 150, 152, 155, 156, 158, 159, 160, 161, 163, 165, 166, 167, 168, 172, 173, 174, 175, 176, 177, 178, 179, 183, 184, 185, 186, 187, 188, 189, 190, 192, 193, 195, 196, 198, 199, 200, 203, 204, 207, 208, 209, 210, 213, 214, 217, 219, 221, 222, 224, 226, 227, 228, 229, 230, 231, 233, 239, 243, 244, 255
Seba, 73, 77, 81, 82, 83, 84, 174, 176
Seboiim, 115
Seir, 131, 192, 193, 194, 196, 217, 219
Semarites, 74
Sennacherib, 32, 62, 92, 107, 121, 129, 135, 158, 159, 160, 168, 183, 186, 187, 194, 199, 255
Seth, 76, 255
Shalmaneser, 96, 101, 125, 132, 136, 139, 156, 157, 158, 159, 161, 182, 190, 209, 210, 212, 221, 255
Sheba, 74, 77, 81, 82, 83, 84, 174, 176, 187, 189, 255
Shelah, 165, 166, 171, 172
Sheleph, 174, 177
Shem, 17, 46, 53, 69, 73, 74, 75, 76, 77, 79, 81, 83, 88, 92, 103, 109, 114, 119, 125, 145, 146, 147, 148, 155, 163, 165, 166, 167, 172, 177, 180, 203, 204, 207, 208, 220, 223, 224, 245
Shinar, 6, 46, 74, 76, 88, 91, 93, 94, 146, 149, 169, 228, 232
Shishak, 78, 96, 100
Shuah, 180, 189, 190
Siberia, 5, 40, 62, 255
Sidon, 74, 108, 113, 115, 116, 117, 119, 120, 121, 122, 131, 132, 136, 138
Sihon, 127, 128
Sinai, 133, 134, 184, 191, 196, 255
Sinites, 74, 113, 133, 134
Sobekneferu, 99
Sodom, 115, 119, 197
Solomon, 84, 100, 101, 120, 123, 126, 131, 132, 139, 176, 187, 193, 198, 200, 210, 219, 255
South, 146, 236, 238, 247, 255
South America, 236, 238
Spain, 8, 18, 23, 54, 55, 62, 63, 114, 147, 255
Strabo, 23, 30, 34, 53, 55, 66, 70, 83, 84, 121, 122, 133, 134, 151, 152, 175, 219, 255
Sumerian, 76, 78, 88, 90, 92, 128, 153, 162, 168, 229, 255
Suppiluliumas, 32, 124
Sweden, 42
Syria, 124, 128, 138, 139, 162, 172, 188, 207, 213, 214, 219, 220, 255
Table of Nations, xi, 7, 15, 16, 21, 73, 88, 106, 113, 146, 173, 223, 226, 248, 255
Tabrimmon, 210
Taphenes, 96, 100
Tarshish, 16, 49, 50, 54, 55, 84, 255
Tell, 79, 93, 99, 126, 133, 137, 160, 168, 172, 176, 186, 194, 199, 200, 221, 255
Tema, 84, 183, 184, 186, 187, 188
Terah, 166, 173, 177, 180
Text, 32, 255
Thor, 40, 72
Thracians, 69, 70, 71, 72
Thutmose, 100, 124, 132, 133, 136, 137, 139, 148

Tiglath-Pileser, 62, 66, 121, 129, 133, 136, 137, 139, 156, 157, 158, 167, 182, 186, 187, 188, 189, 199, 209, 213, 214, 255
Tigris, 161, 169, 213, 222
Tiras, 15, 42, 69, 70, 71, 72, 233
Togarmah, 16, 32, 33, 34, 35, 36, 41, 65, 67
Tongue, 255
Tower, 4, 6, 10, 16, 18, 88, 91, 169, 173, 223, 226, 228, 229, 230, 231, 237, 251, 255
Tubal, 15, 23, 32, 39, 54, 61, 62, 63, 65, 66, 67
Turkey, 22, 24, 30, 32, 33, 36, 50, 58, 62, 115, 124, 162, 169, 178, 204, 210, 220, 222, 255
Tyr, 69, 72, 255
Tyre, 32, 53, 54, 55, 56, 61, 65, 83, 108, 113, 117, 119, 120, 121, 122, 129, 131, 135, 136, 138, 176, 203, 209, 255
Ugaritic, 96, 107, 121, 130, 142, 201, 255
Upper Egypt, 77, 97, 105
Ur, 98, 115, 127, 146, 166, 168, 169, 171, 172, 177, 178, 180, 229, 255
Urartu, 29, 66, 169, 208
Urfa, 168, 169, 178
Urkesh, 255
Uruk, 90, 94, 168
Utnapishtim, 90
Uz, 178, 207, 208, 217, 218, 219
Uzal, 174, 176
West, 35, 123, 128, 188, 247, 255
Xerxes, 47, 151
Ziggurat, 229
Zimran, 180, 189
Zuzites, 141

www.ingramcontent.com/pod-product-compliance
Lightning Source LLC
Chambersburg PA
CBHW071220080526
44587CB00013BA/1438